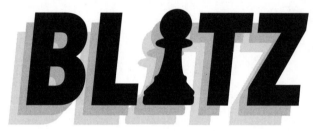

Volume 2

Original creation: **Cédric BISCAY**
Illustrator: **Daitaro NISHIHARA**
Written by **Cédric BISCAY** & **Tsukasa MORI**

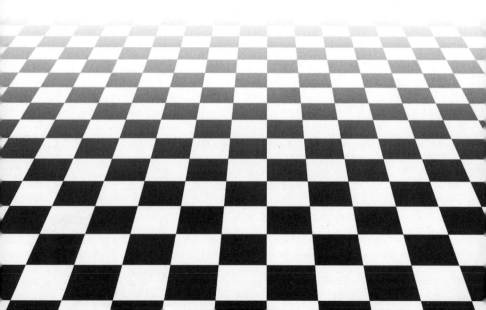

SUMMARY

Tom is a middle-school student and a bit of a troublemaker, who can't help but feel bored out of his mind at the International School of Shibuya. He is in love with Harmony, but the girl is completely enamored with chess. And so, Tom decides to join the chess club to get closer to her. However, the club president, Laurent, does not accept that and challenges Tom to a public match! With the help of his friend Jean-Marc, Tom learns to play chess in only two months.

Despite his efforts, the little troublemaker ends up losing against Laurent. The heartbroken young boy runs out of school with Harmony's good-luck knight in hand. After an unfortunate encounter and a fight, Tom loses the chess piece in a canal.

In his efforts to find a present that could get Harmony to forgive him, he makes it to a strange shop. He then leaves with a mysterious VR set in hand, the Caïssa.

This VR set allows its wearer to gain access to a ton of data about chess. While watching one of Garry Kasparov's games, the amazed teenager is suddenly struck by lightning before losing consciousness. After waking up in the hospital, Tom has only one thing in mind: playing chess.

Unbeknownst to him, he ends up playing online against Karl, the junior chess champion who was also staying in the hospital at the same time.
During a special press conference, Tom and other amateur chess players around the world find out that Garry Kasparov is holding an international chess championship aimed at younger players: "Project T". After finally joining the school chess club, Tom is ready to fight to secure a spot in the tournament.

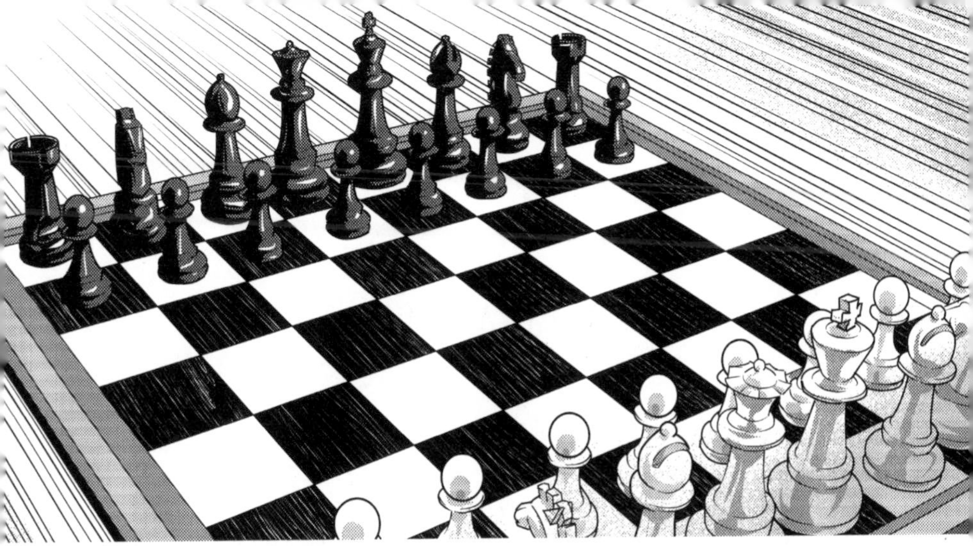

CHARACTERS

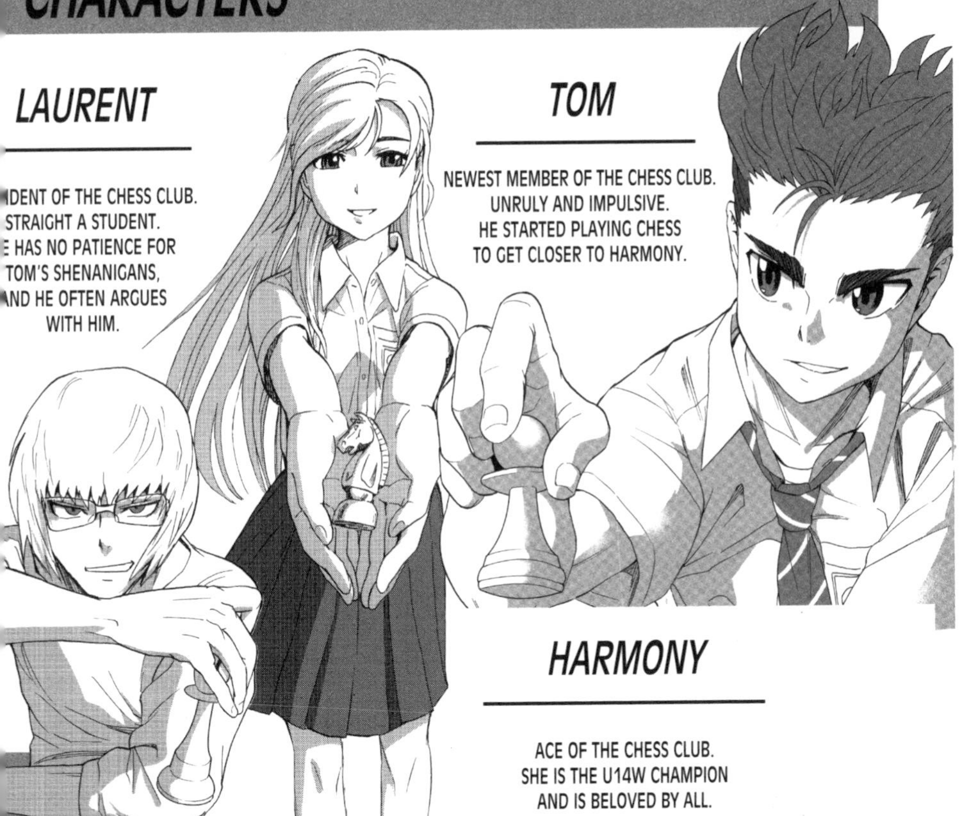

LAURENT

IDENT OF THE CHESS CLUB.
STRAIGHT A STUDENT.
E HAS NO PATIENCE FOR
TOM'S SHENANIGANS,
ND HE OFTEN ARGUES
WITH HIM.

TOM

NEWEST MEMBER OF THE CHESS CLUB.
UNRULY AND IMPULSIVE.
HE STARTED PLAYING CHESS
TO GET CLOSER TO HARMONY.

HARMONY

ACE OF THE CHESS CLUB.
SHE IS THE U14W CHAMPION
AND IS BELOVED BY ALL.

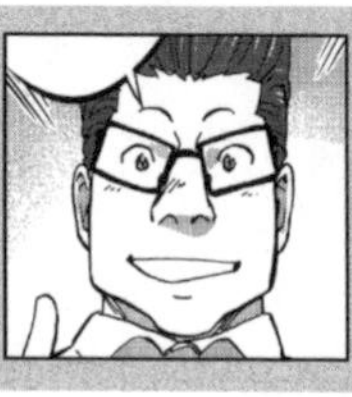

MISTER DOYLE

CHESS CLUB COUNSELOR.
FRIEND OF JEAN-MARC.
CHEMISTRY PROFESSOR AND
TOM'S HOMEROOM TEACHER.

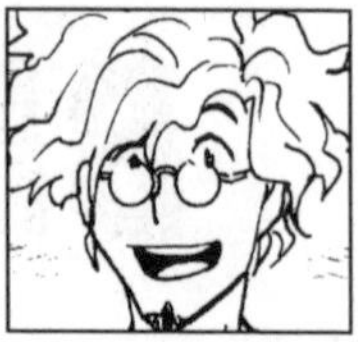

MISTER SOUMILLO

ASSISTANT COUNSELOR
THE CHESS CLUB. COMPU
SCIENCE TEACHER.

KARL

14-YEAR OLD JUNIOR CHESS
CHAMPION. HIS COMPOSED
PLAYSTYLE EARNED HIM THE
NICKNAME OF AICE (ACE + ICE).

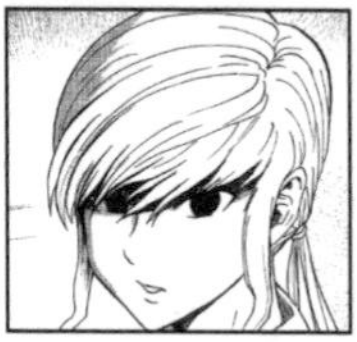

GARRY KASPAROV

FAMOUS CHESS CHAMPION.
HE LAUNCHED "PROJECT T"
FOR THE FUTURE OF CHESS.

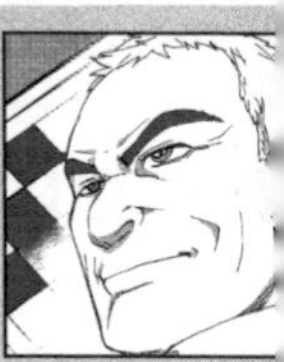

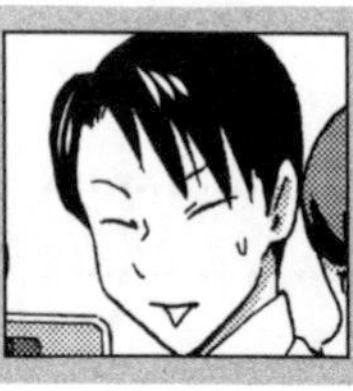

ZHANG

CHESS CLUB MEMBER.
VERY GOOD AT GETTING
INFORMATION.

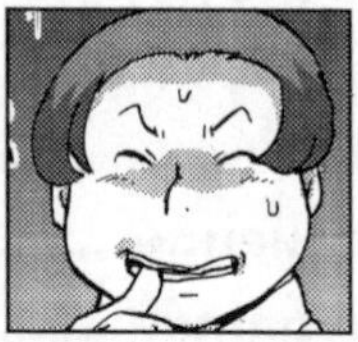

MARIUS

CHESS CLUB MEMBE
EXPERT IN SWEETS.

OWNER OF YORUZUDO

OWNER OF AN ANTIQUE SHOP.
HE LENT CAÏSSA TO TOM.

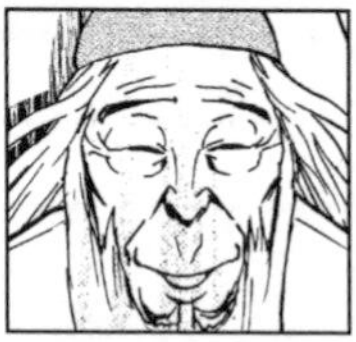

JEAN-MARC

OWNER OF A PANCAKE SHOP.
TOM'S BEST FRIEND.
HE HAS ALWAYS BEEN
INTERESTED IN CHESS.

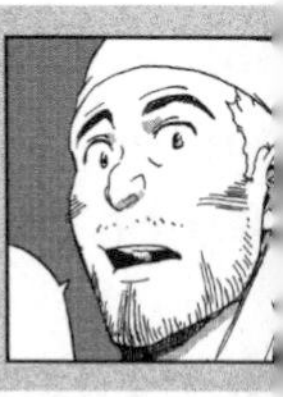

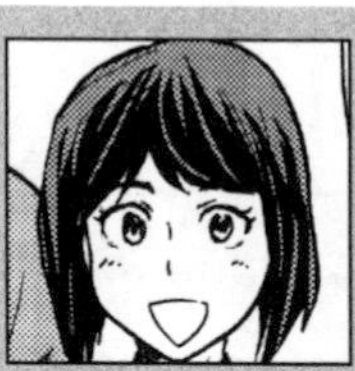

SAORI

NEW MEMBER OF THE CHESS CLUB.
SHE HAS RECENTLY STARTED
PLAYING CHESS.

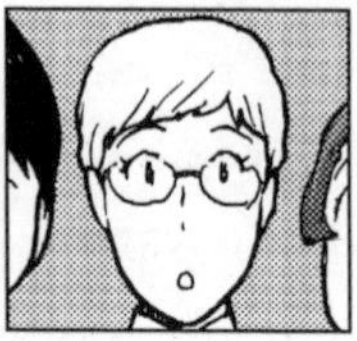

ANNE

CHESS CLUB MEMBE
SHE USES A COIN AS
A GOOD-LUCK CHAR

BLITZ

ABLE OF CONTENTS

ɔNUS PAGES

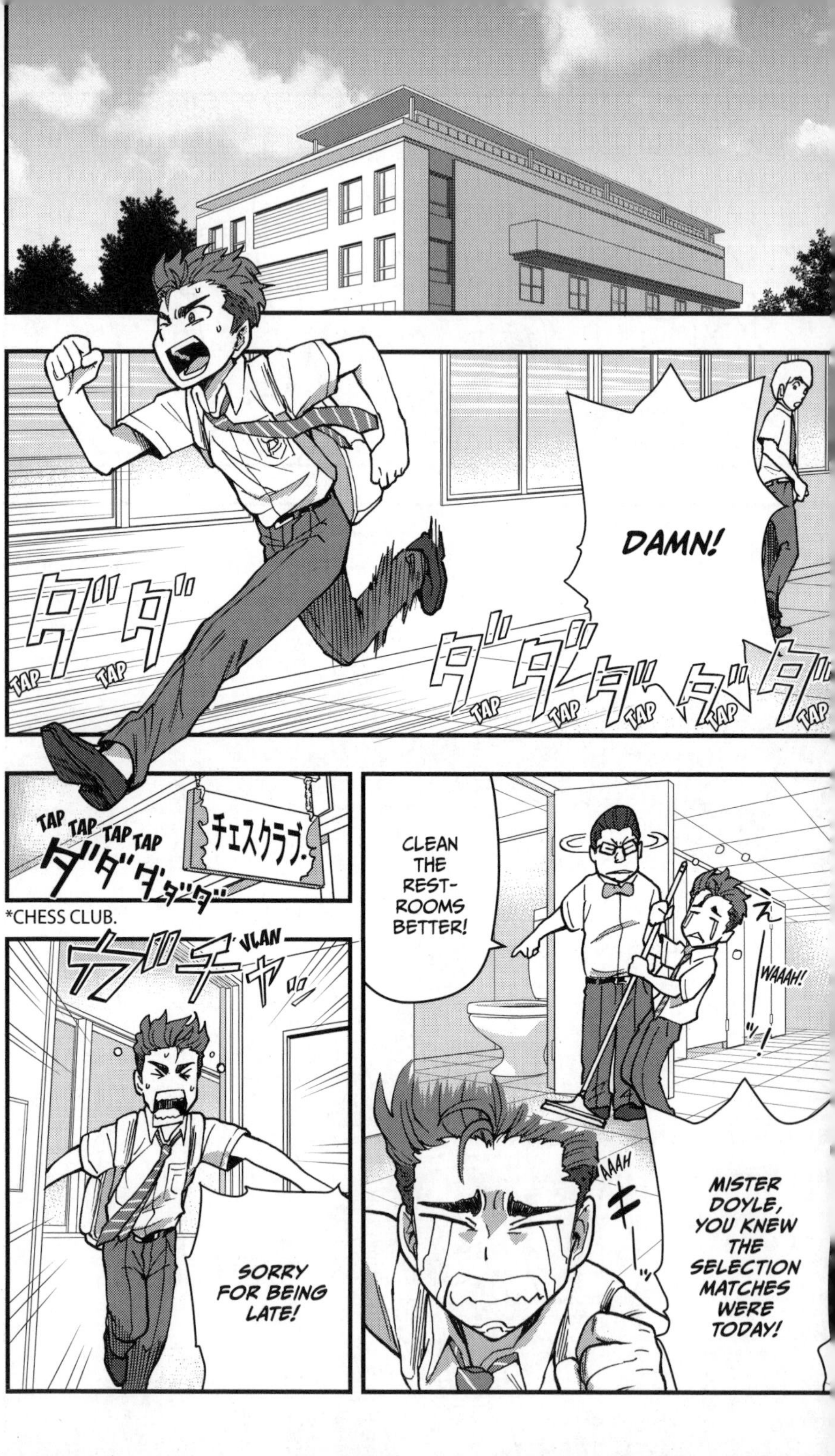
DAMN!
TAP TAP TAP TAP TAP TAP TAP
CLEAN THE REST-ROOMS BETTER!
WAAAH!
AAAH
MISTER DOYLE, YOU KNEW THE SELECTION MATCHES WERE TODAY!
チェスクラブ
TAP TAP TAP TAP
*CHESS CLUB.
VLAN
SORRY FOR BEING LATE!

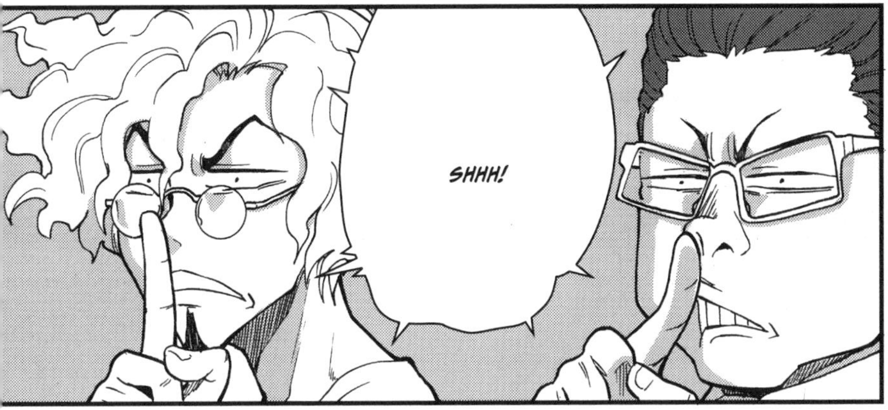
SHHH!
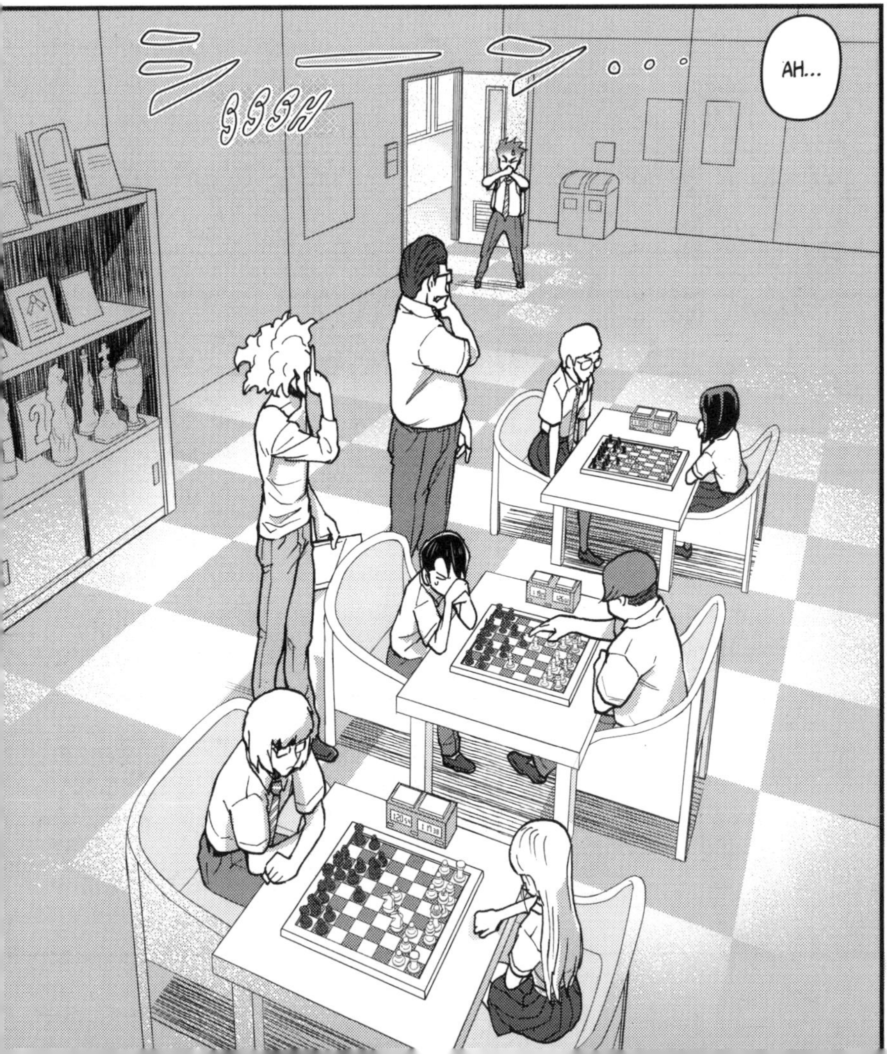
AH...
SSSH

Chapter 10: Who is the key piece?

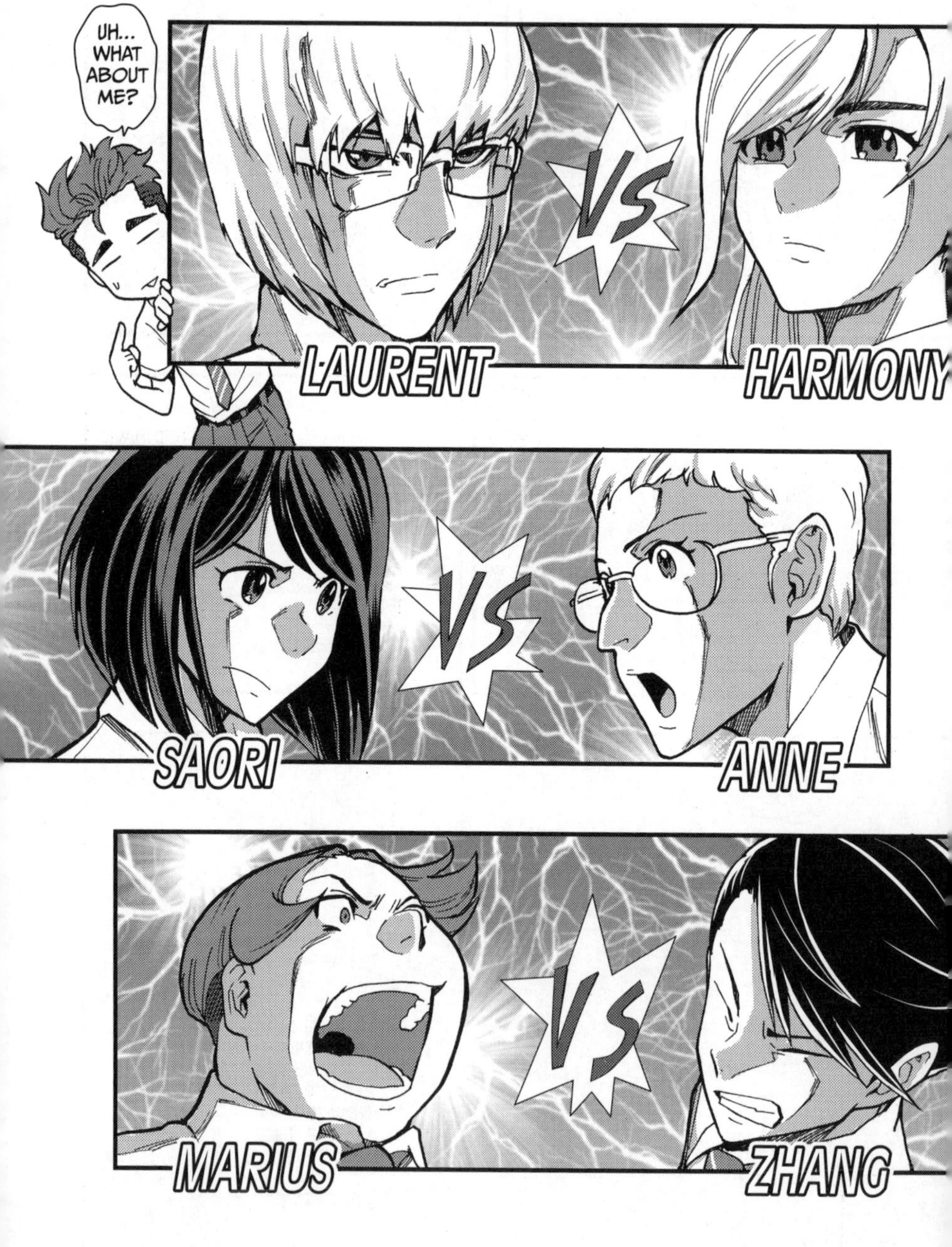
HARMONY
VS
LAURENT
UH... WHAT ABOUT ME?
ANNE
VS
SAORI
ZHANG
VS
MARIUS

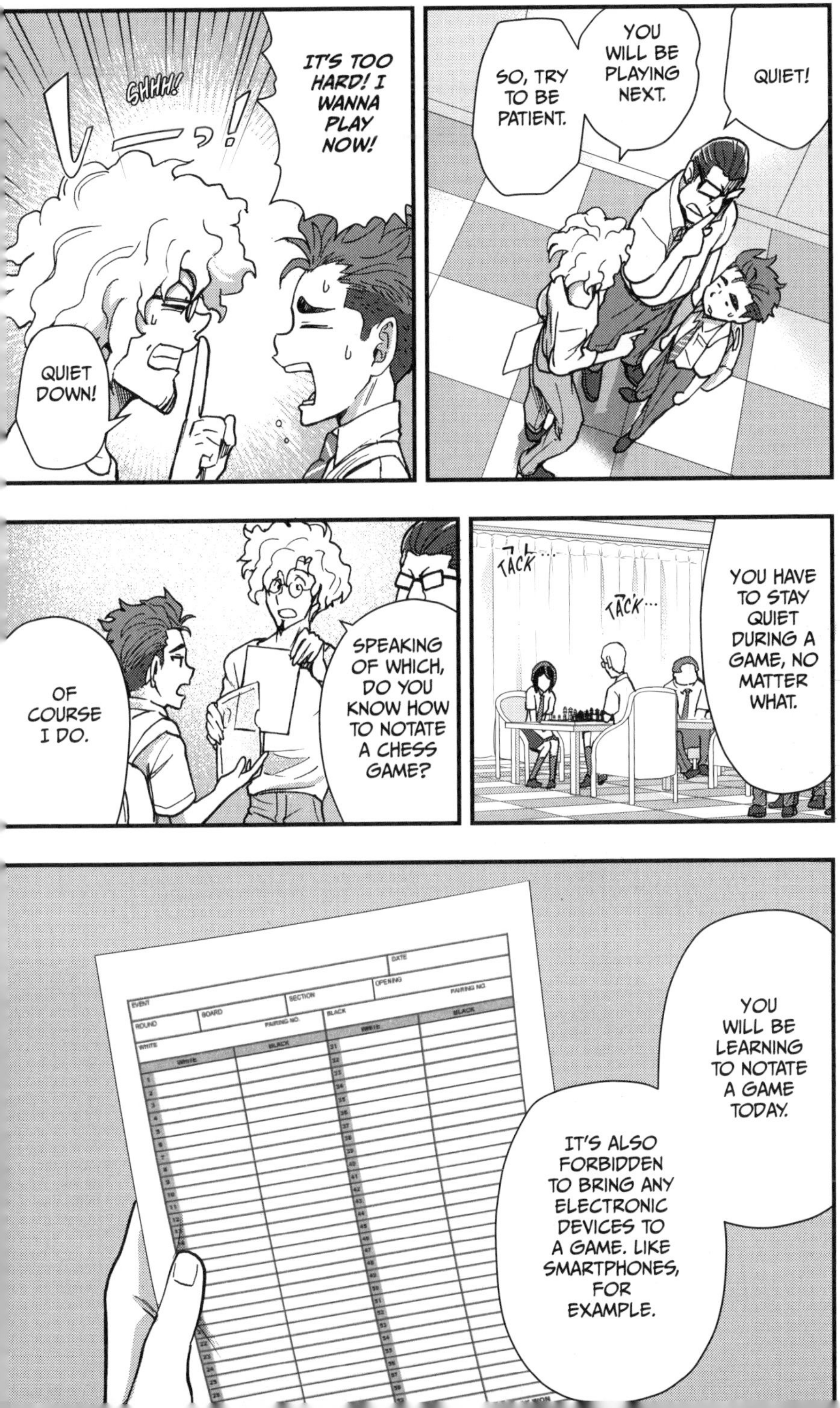
QUIET!
YOU WILL BE PLAYING NEXT.
SO, TRY TO BE PATIENT.
IT'S TOO HARD! I WANNA PLAY NOW!
SHHH!
QUIET DOWN!
YOU HAVE TO STAY QUIET DURING A GAME, NO MATTER WHAT.
TACK...
TACK...
SPEAKING OF WHICH, DO YOU KNOW HOW TO NOTATE A CHESS GAME?
OF COURSE I DO.
YOU WILL BE LEARNING TO NOTATE A GAME TODAY.
IT'S ALSO FORBIDDEN TO BRING ANY ELECTRONIC DEVICES TO A GAME. LIKE SMARTPHONES, FOR EXAMPLE.

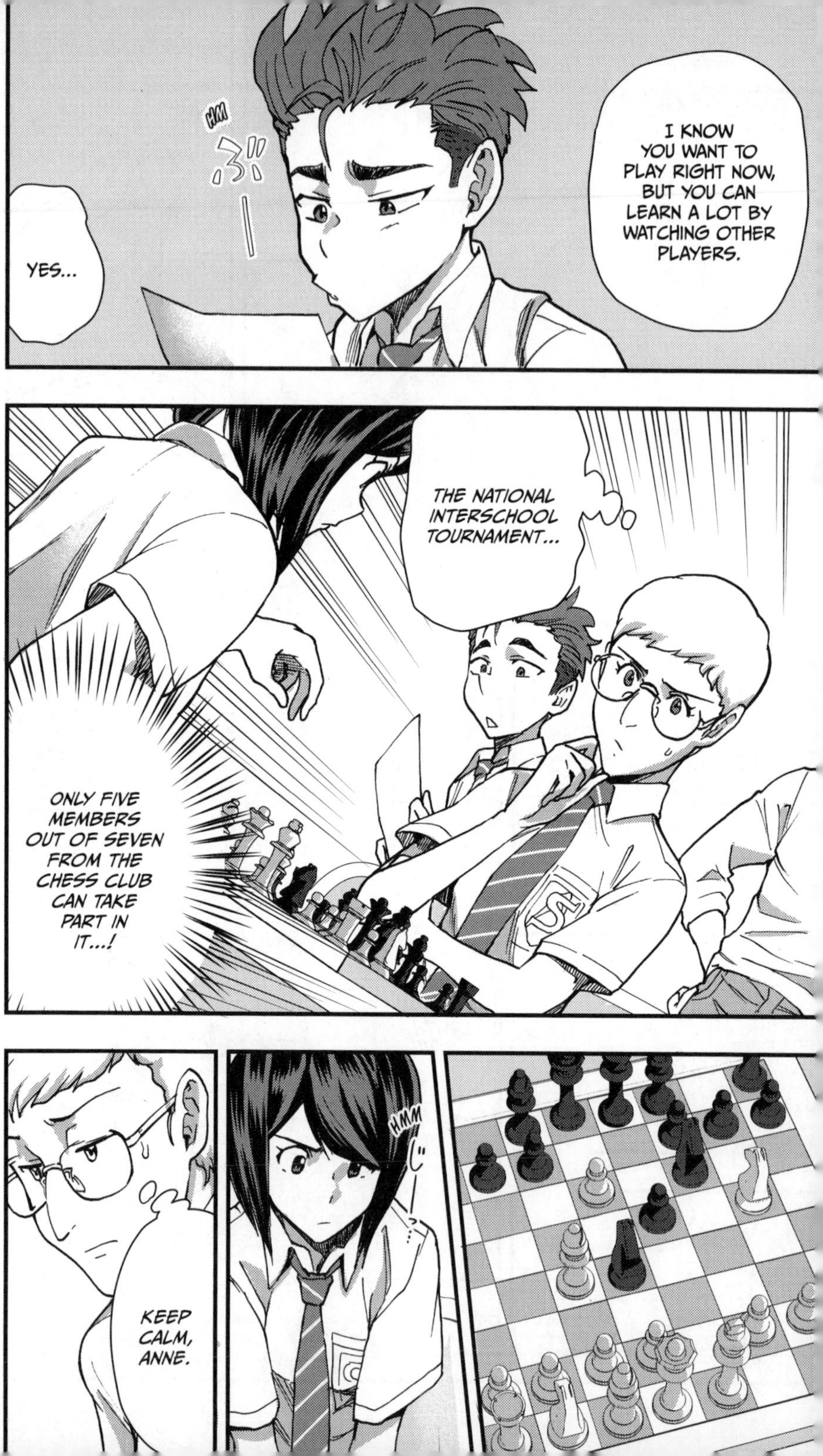
I KNOW YOU WANT TO PLAY RIGHT NOW, BUT YOU CAN LEARN A LOT BY WATCHING OTHER PLAYERS.
HM
YES...
THE NATIONAL INTERSCHOOL TOURNAMENT...
ONLY FIVE MEMBERS OUT OF SEVEN FROM THE CHESS CLUB CAN TAKE PART IN IT...!
HMM
KEEP CALM, ANNE.

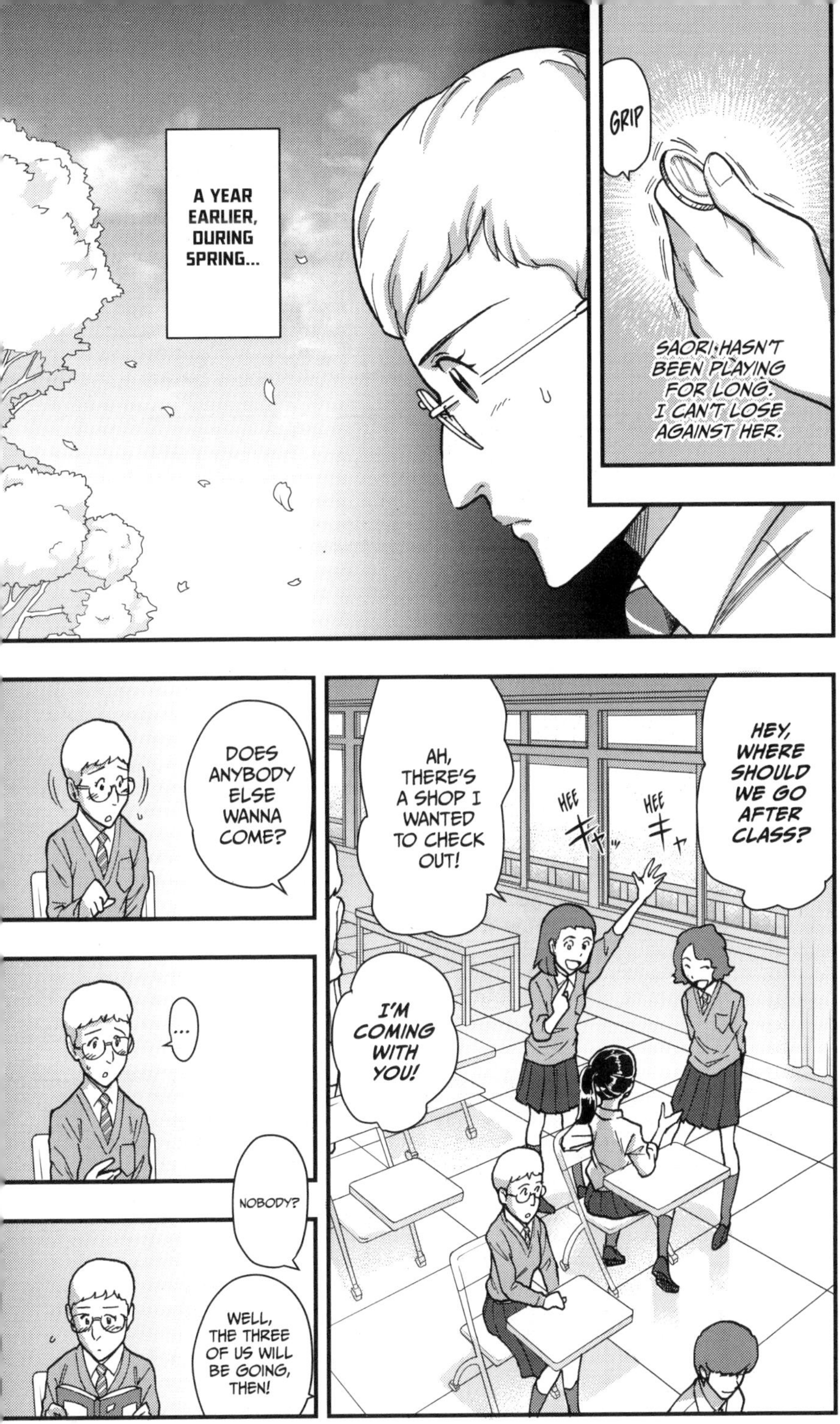
GRIP
SAORI HASN'T BEEN PLAYING FOR LONG. I CAN'T LOSE AGAINST HER.
A YEAR EARLIER, DURING SPRING...
HEY, WHERE SHOULD WE GO AFTER CLASS?
HEE
HEE
AH, THERE'S A SHOP I WANTED TO CHECK OUT!
I'M COMING WITH YOU!
DOES ANYBODY ELSE WANNA COME?
...
NOBODY?
WELL, THE THREE OF US WILL BE GOING, THEN!

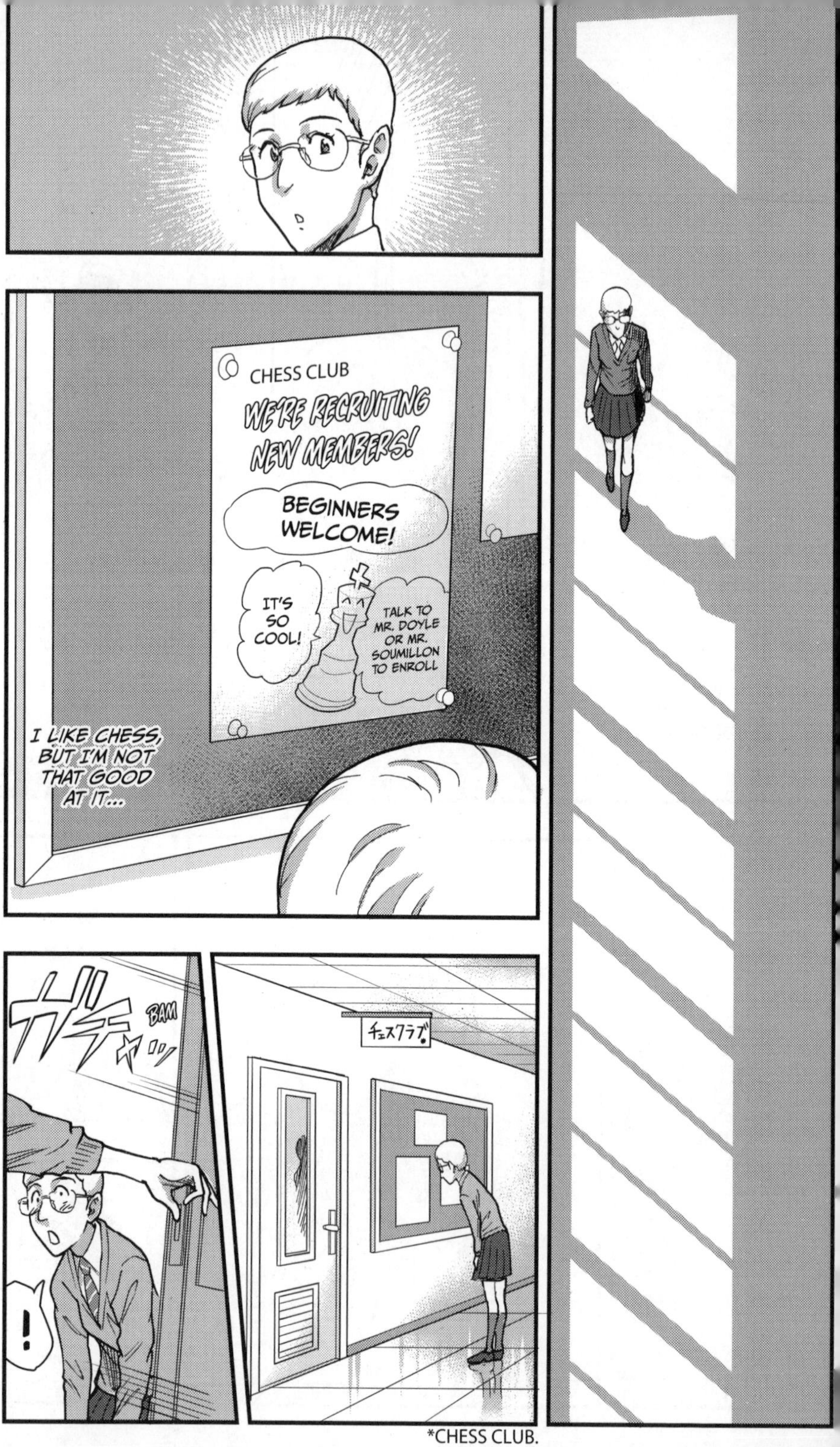
CHESS CLUB
WE'RE RECRUITING NEW MEMBERS!
BEGINNERS WELCOME!
IT'S SO COOL!
TALK TO MR. DOYLE OR MR. SOUMILLON TO ENROLL
I LIKE CHESS, BUT I'M NOT THAT GOOD AT IT...
チェスクラブ*
ガチャッ
BAM
!

*CHESS CLUB.

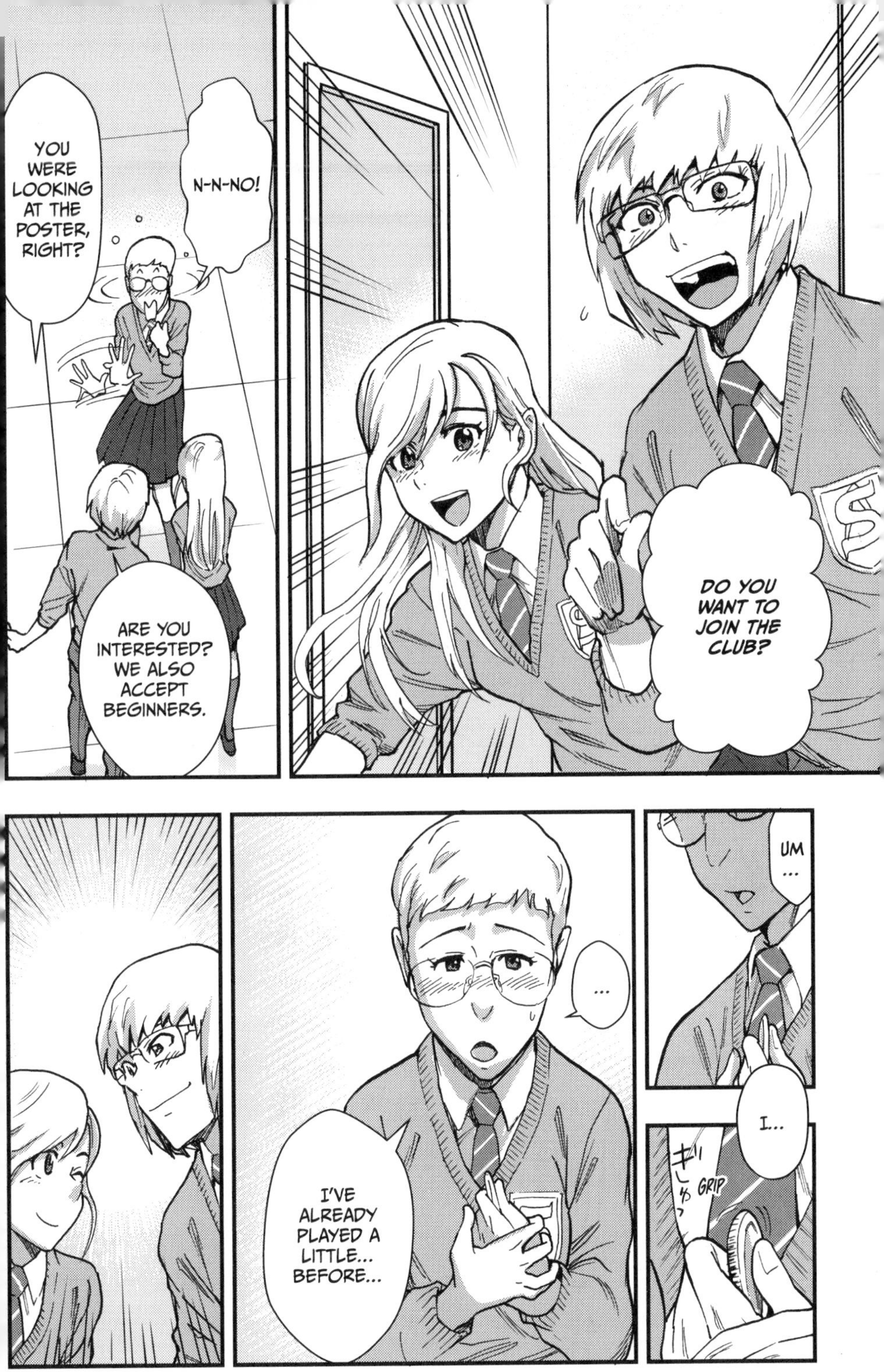
DO YOU WANT TO JOIN THE CLUB?
YOU WERE LOOKING AT THE POSTER, RIGHT?
N-N-NO!
ARE YOU INTERESTED? WE ALSO ACCEPT BEGINNERS.
UM ...
I...
GRIP
...
I'VE ALREADY PLAYED A LITTLE... BEFORE...

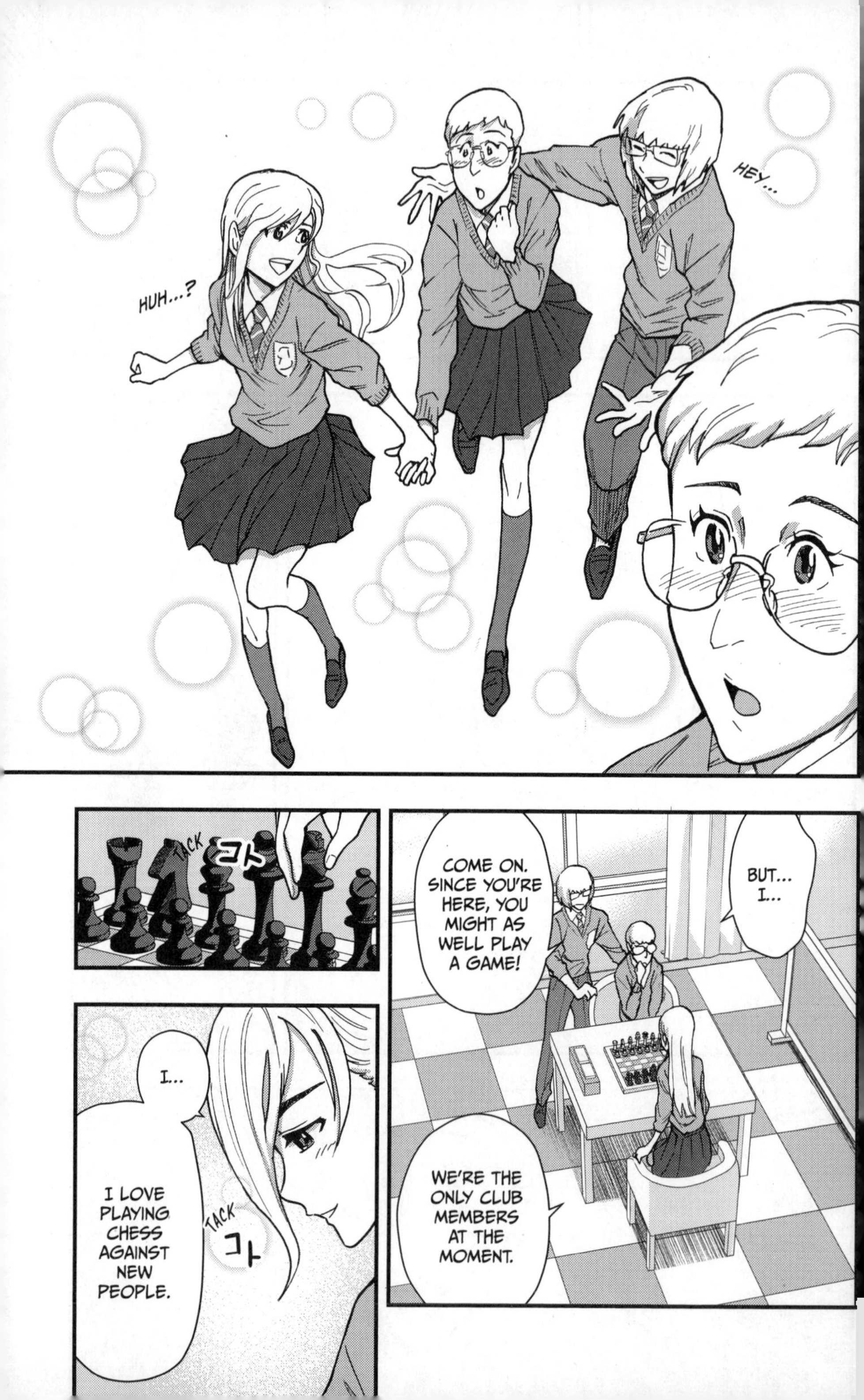
HEY...
HUH...?
BUT... I...
COME ON. SINCE YOU'RE HERE, YOU MIGHT AS WELL PLAY A GAME!
WE'RE THE ONLY CLUB MEMBERS AT THE MOMENT.
TACK
コト
I...
TACK
コト
I LOVE PLAYING CHESS AGAINST NEW PEOPLE.

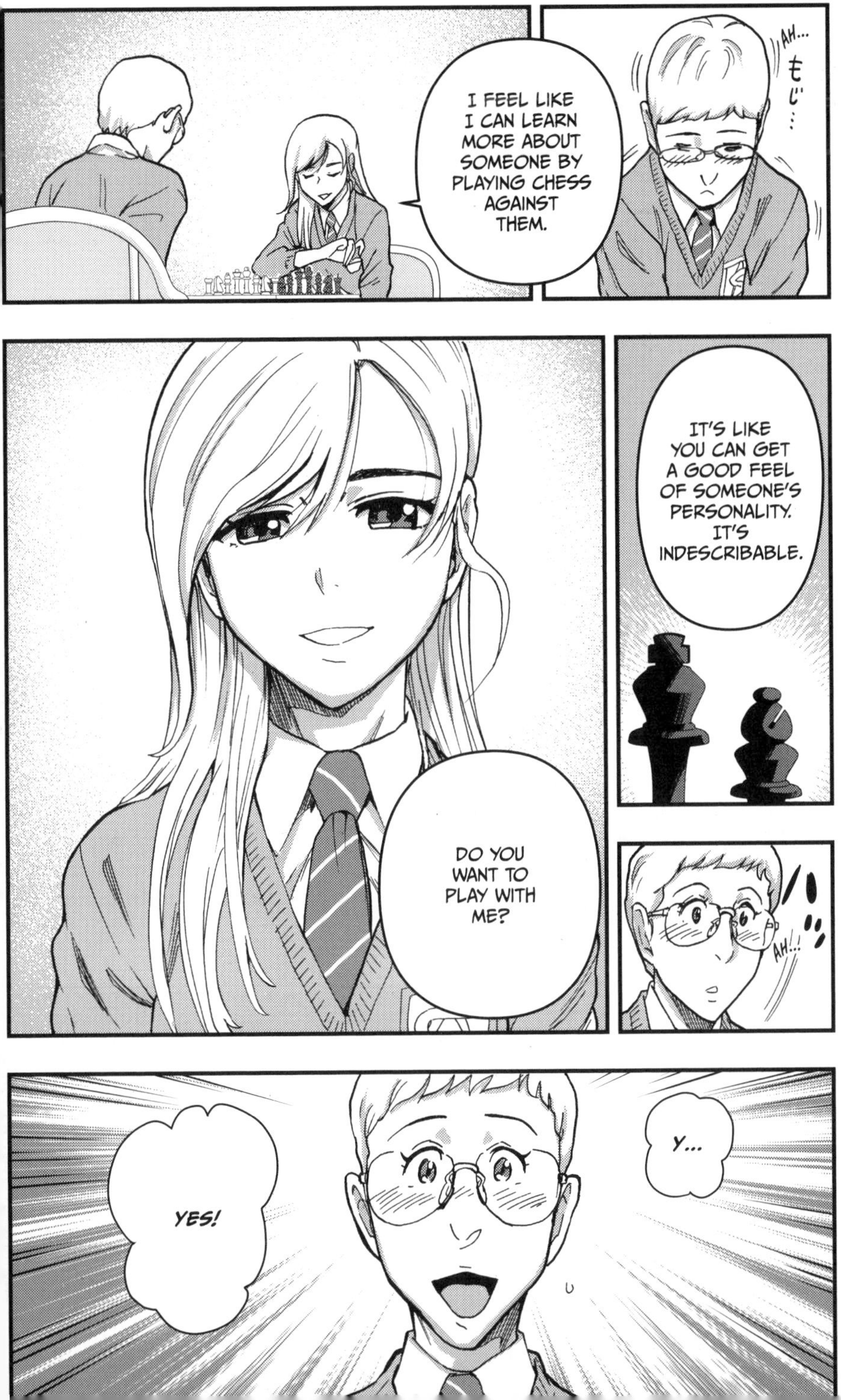

I FEEL LIKE I CAN LEARN MORE ABOUT SOMEONE BY PLAYING CHESS AGAINST THEM.
AH...
もじ…
IT'S LIKE YOU CAN GET A GOOD FEEL OF SOMEONE'S PERSONALITY. IT'S INDESCRIBABLE.
DO YOU WANT TO PLAY WITH ME?
AH!!
Y...
YES!

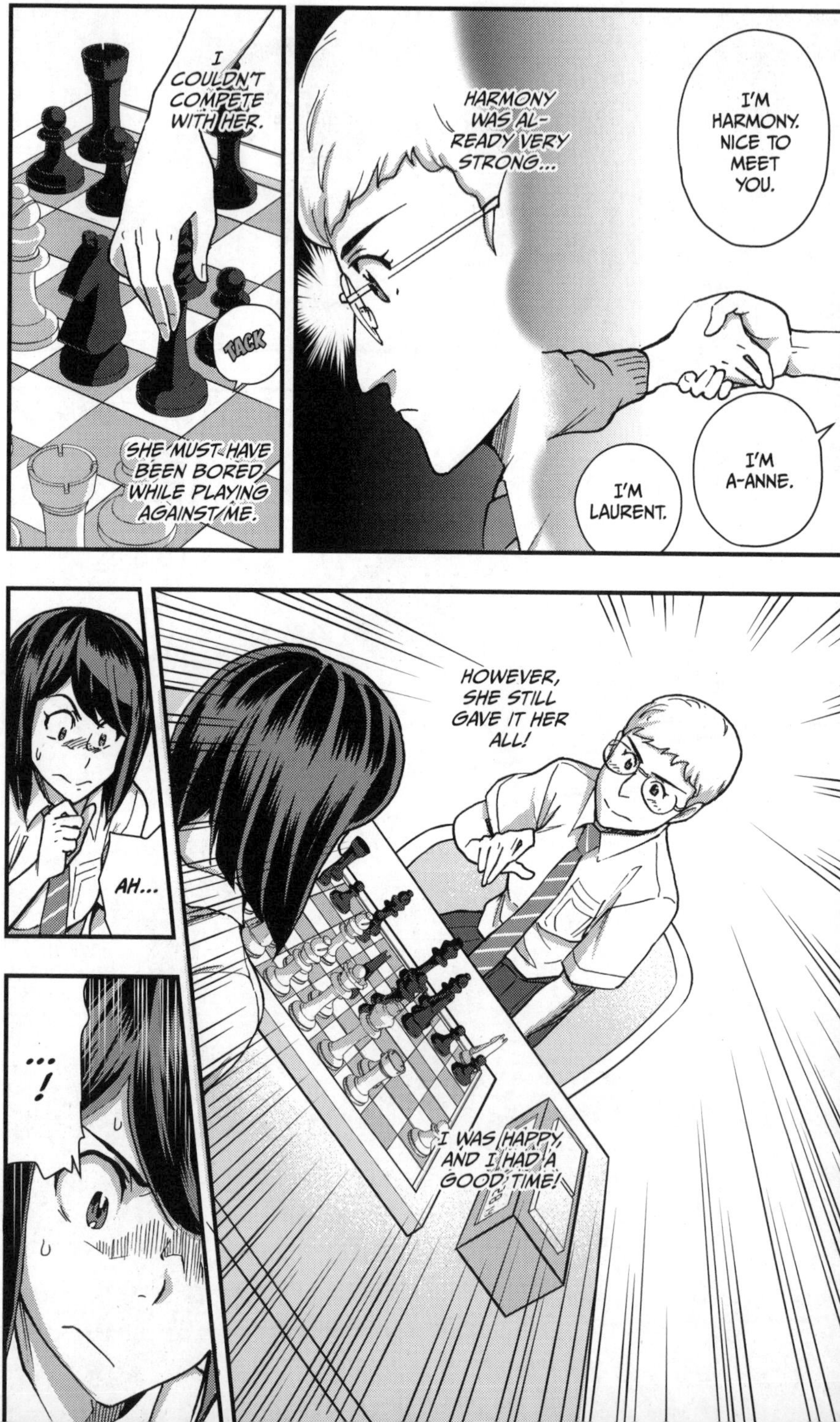
I'M HARMONY. NICE TO MEET YOU.
HARMONY WAS AL-READY VERY STRONG...
I'M A-ANNE.
I'M LAURENT.
I COULDN'T COMPETE WITH HER.
TACK
SHE MUST HAVE BEEN BORED WHILE PLAYING AGAINST ME.
HOWEVER, SHE STILL GAVE IT HER ALL!
I WAS HAPPY, AND I HAD A GOOD TIME!
AH...
...!

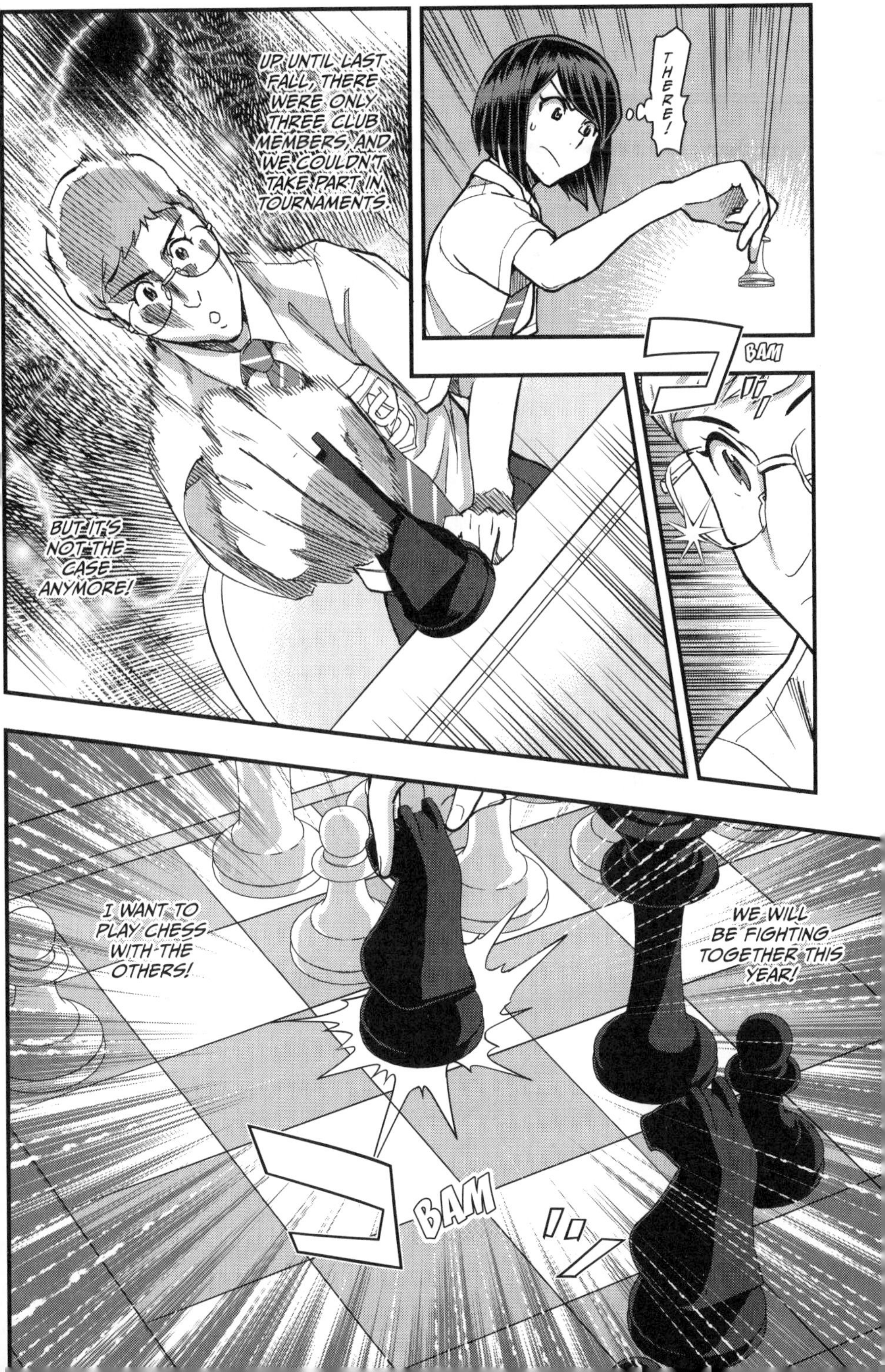
THERE!
BAM
UP UNTIL LAST FALL, THERE WERE ONLY THREE CLUB MEMBERS, AND WE COULDN'T TAKE PART IN TOURNAMENTS.
BUT IT'S NOT THE CASE ANYMORE!
WE WILL BE FIGHTING TOGETHER THIS YEAR!
I WANT TO PLAY CHESS WITH THE OTHERS!
BAM

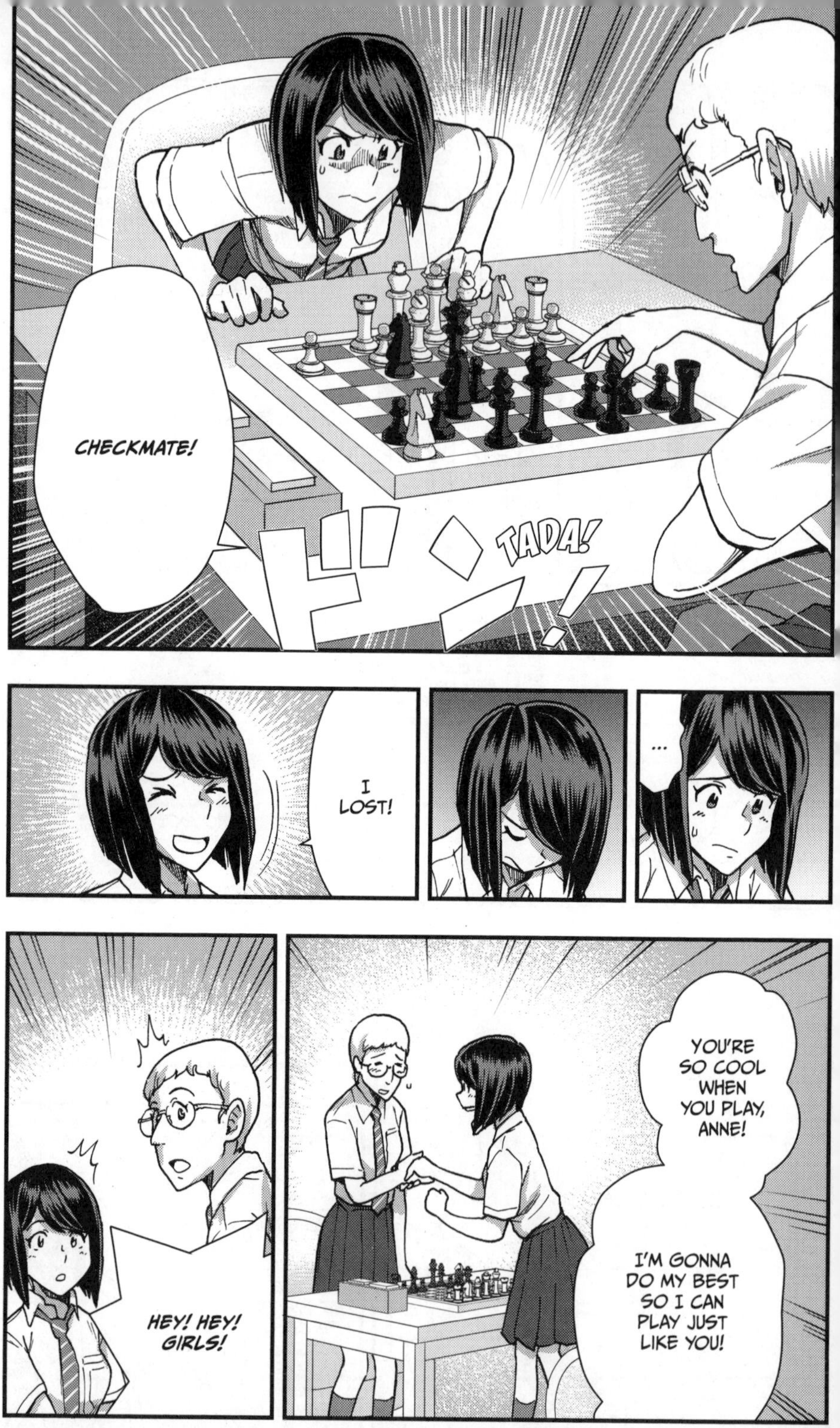
CHECKMATE!
ドン!
TADA!
...
I LOST!
YOU'RE SO COOL WHEN YOU PLAY, ANNE!
I'M GONNA DO MY BEST SO I CAN PLAY JUST LIKE YOU!
HEY! HEY! GIRLS!

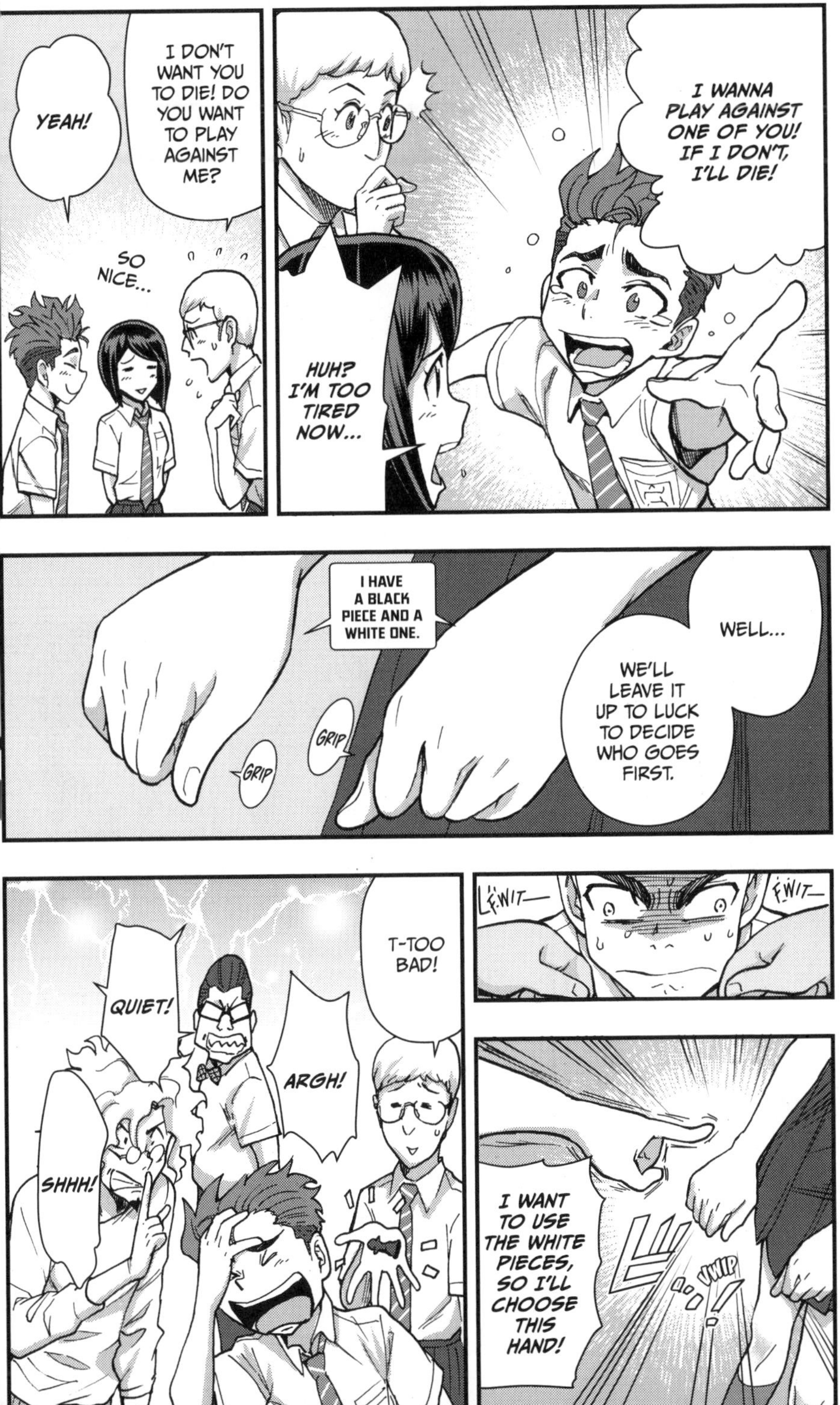
I WANNA PLAY AGAINST ONE OF YOU! IF I DON'T, I'LL DIE!
HUH? I'M TOO TIRED NOW...
I DON'T WANT YOU TO DIE! DO YOU WANT TO PLAY AGAINST ME?
YEAH!
SO NICE...
WELL...
WE'LL LEAVE IT UP TO LUCK TO DECIDE WHO GOES FIRST.
I HAVE A BLACK PIECE AND A WHITE ONE.
GRIP
GRIP
F.WIT—
F.WIT—
I WANT TO USE THE WHITE PIECES, SO I'LL CHOOSE THIS HAND!
VWIP
T-TOO BAD!
ARGH!
QUIET!
SHHH!

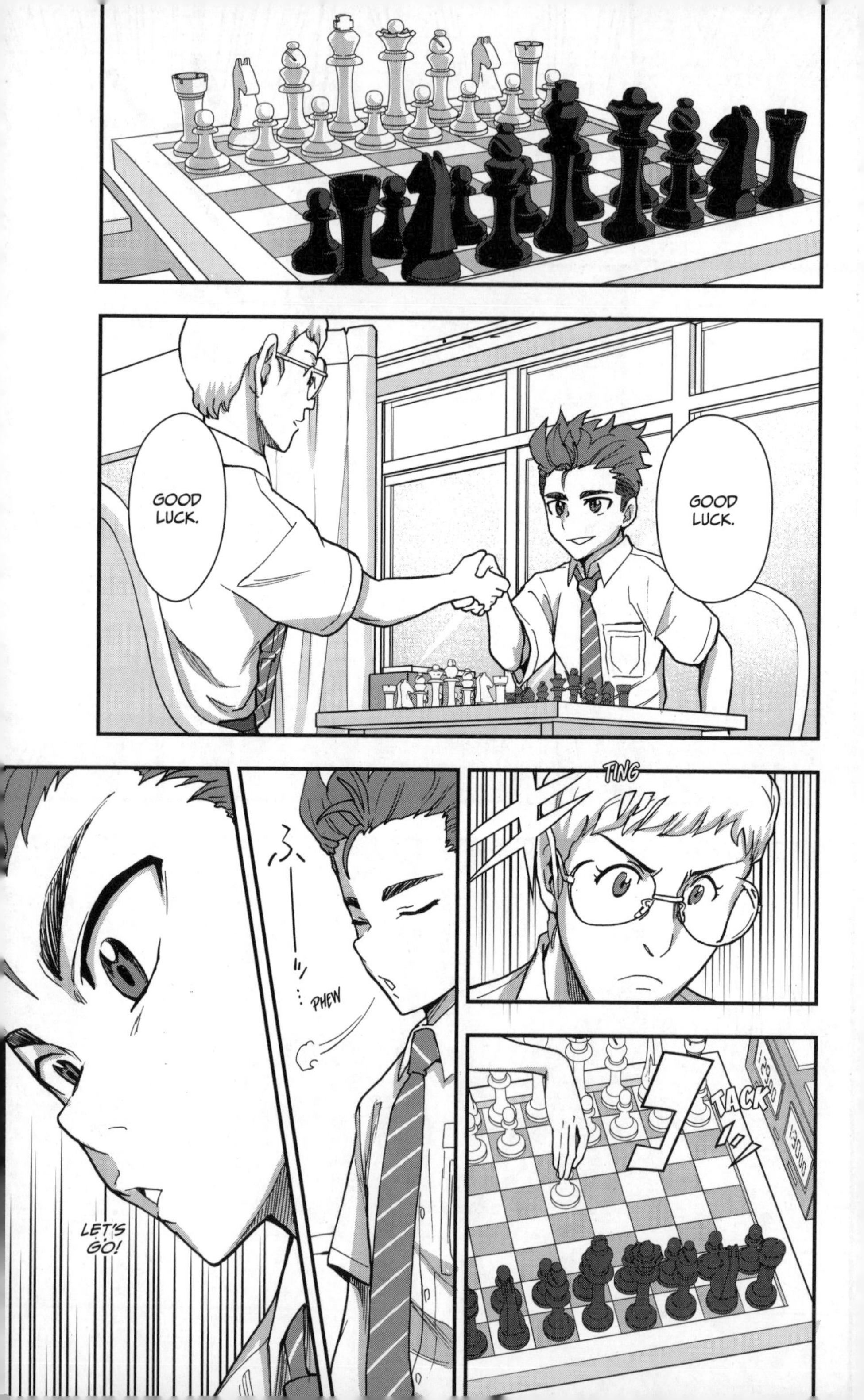
GOOD LUCK.
GOOD LUCK.
TING
TACK
ふ
PHEW
LET'S GO!

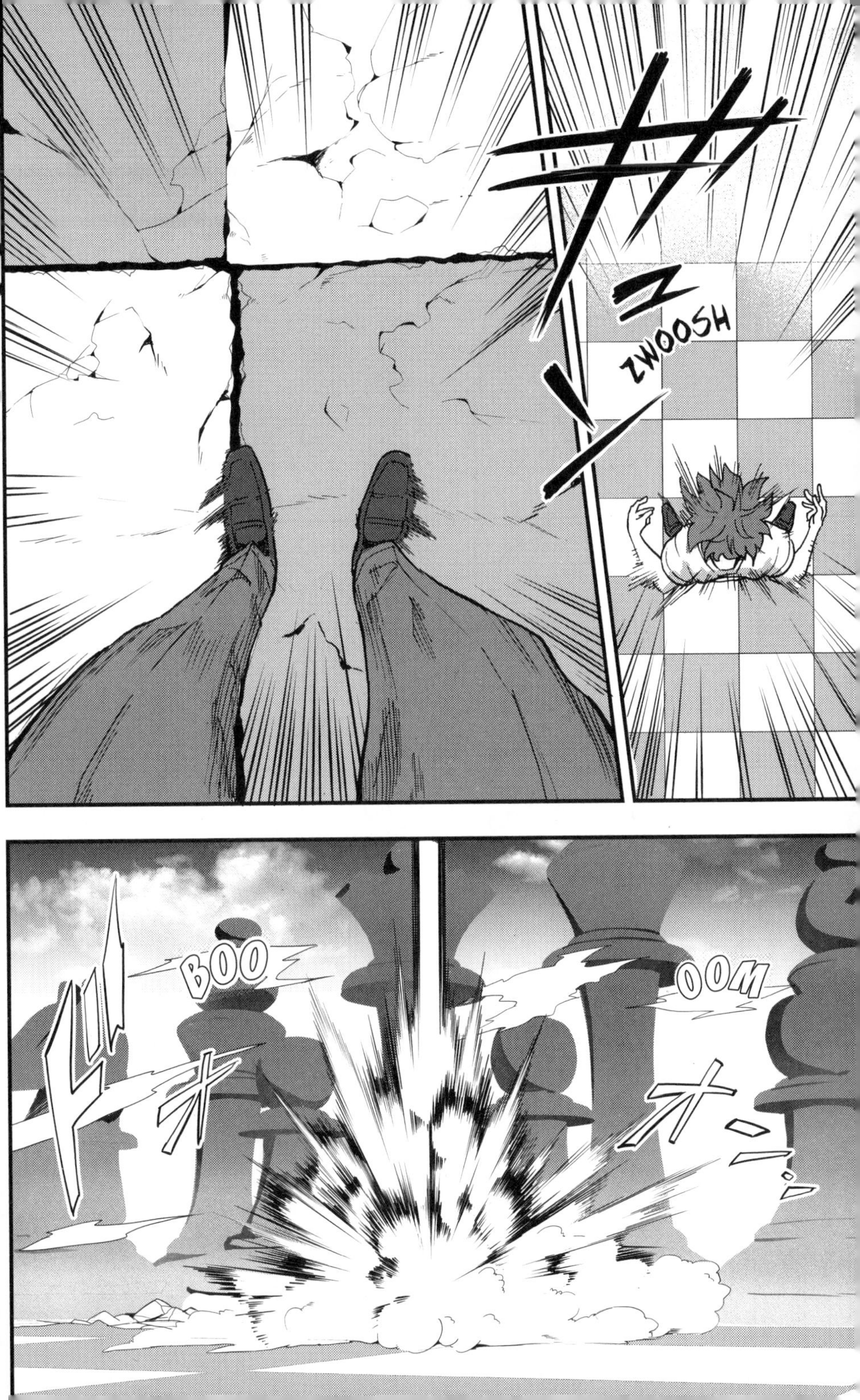
ZWOOSH
BOO
OOM

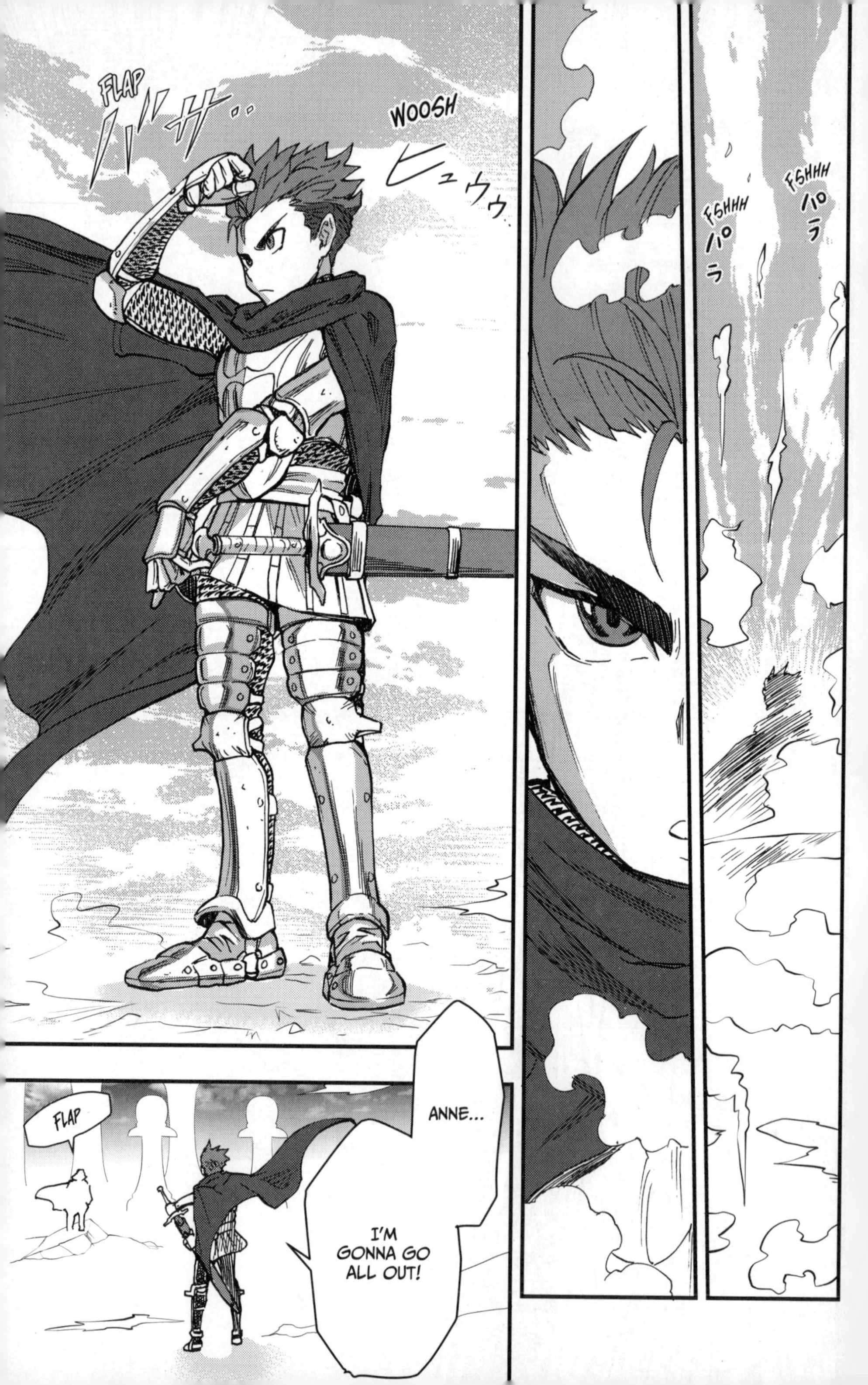

FSHHH
パラ
FSHHH
パラ
FLAP
WOOSH
ヒュウウ
FLAP
ANNE...
I'M GONNA GO ALL OUT!

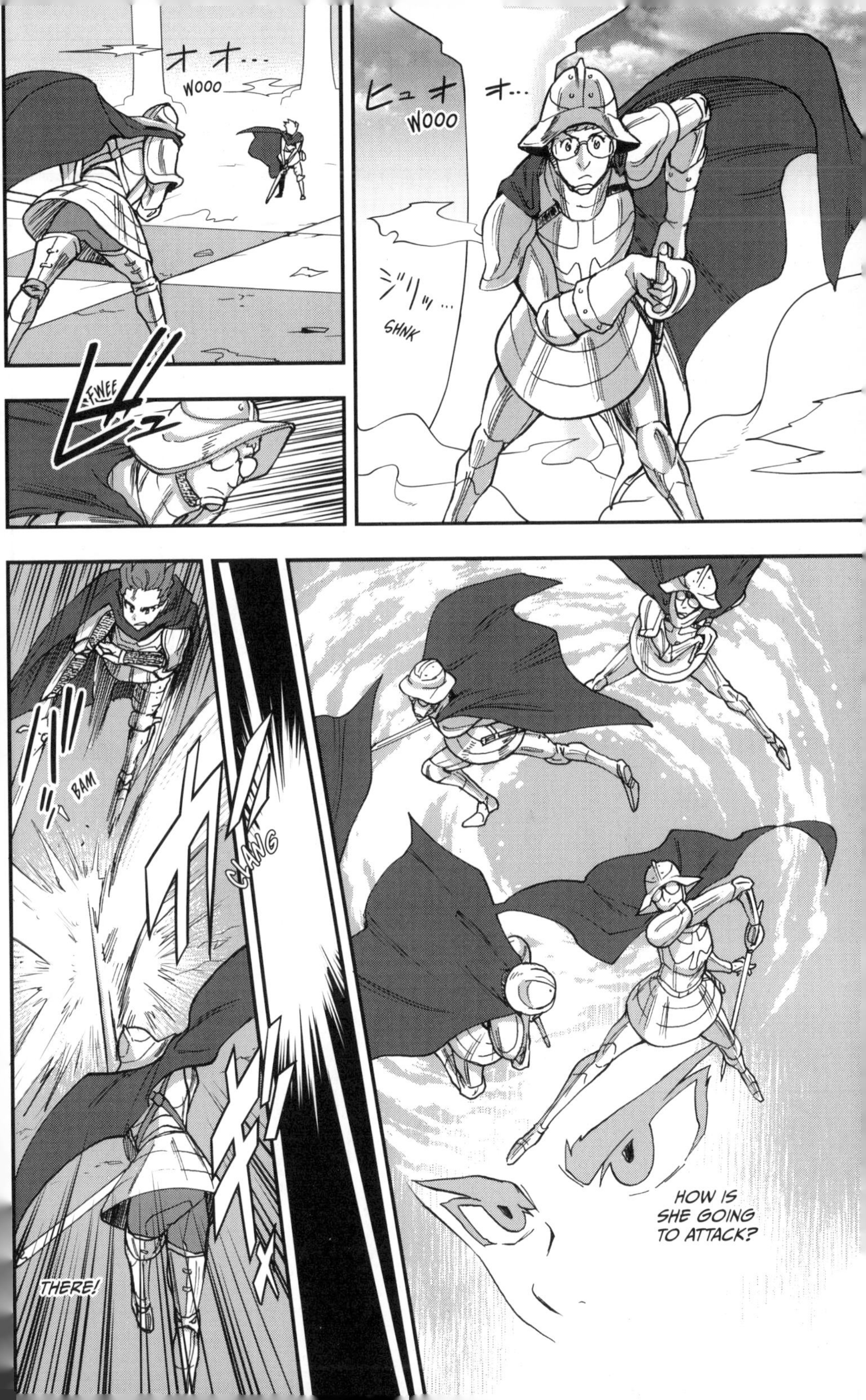
ヒュオ オ…
WOOO
ジリッ…
SHNK
オオ…
WOOO
ヒュ
FWEE
HOW IS
SHE GOING
TO ATTACK?
CLANG
BAM
THERE!

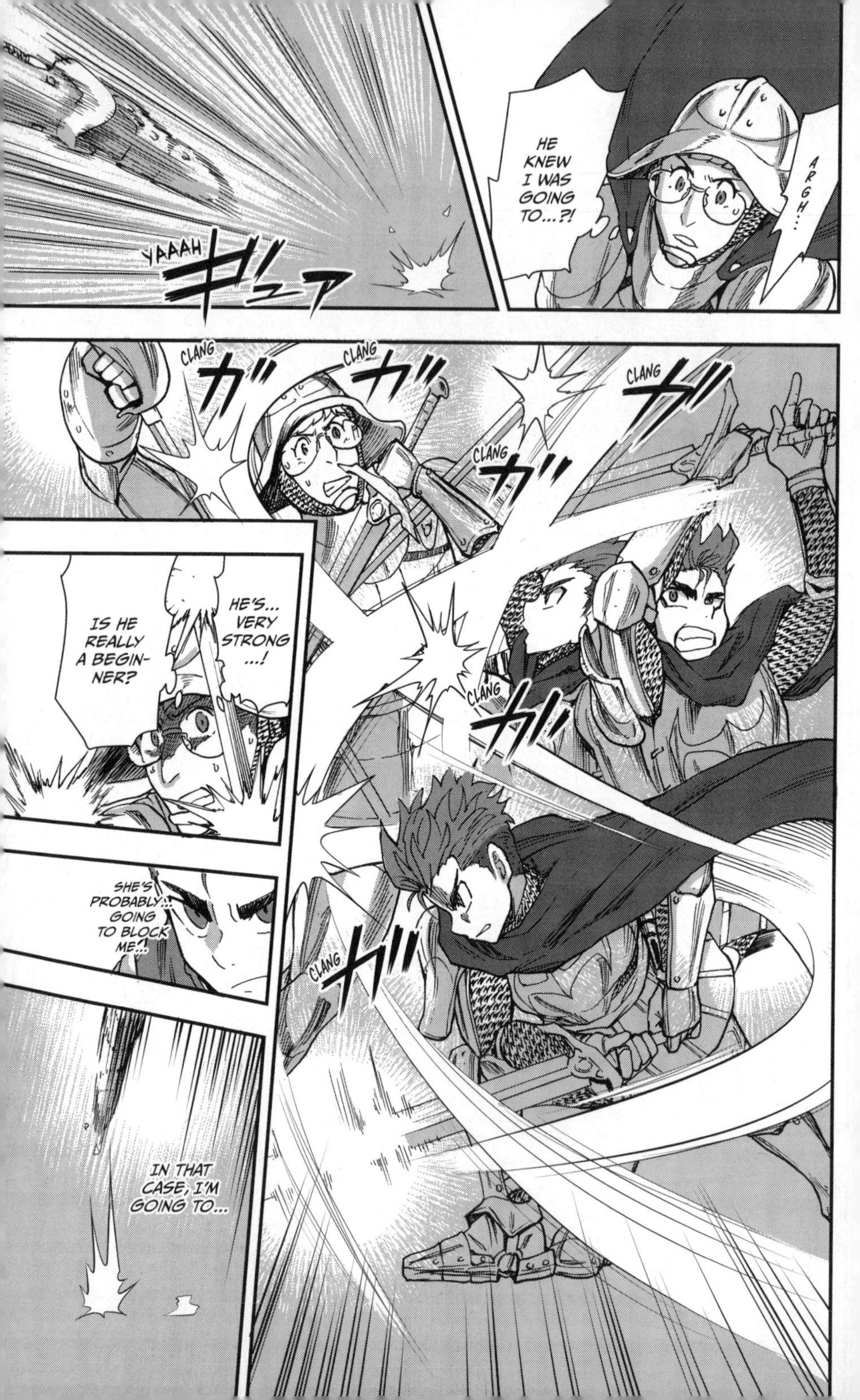
HE KNEW I WAS GOING TO...?!
ARGH...
YAAAH ギュア
CLANG ガ
CLANG ガ
CLANG ガ
CLANG ガ
HE'S... VERY STRONG ...!
IS HE REALLY A BEGIN-NER?
CLANG ガ
SHE'S PROBABLY... GOING TO BLOCK ME...!
CLANG ガ
IN THAT CASE, I'M GOING TO...

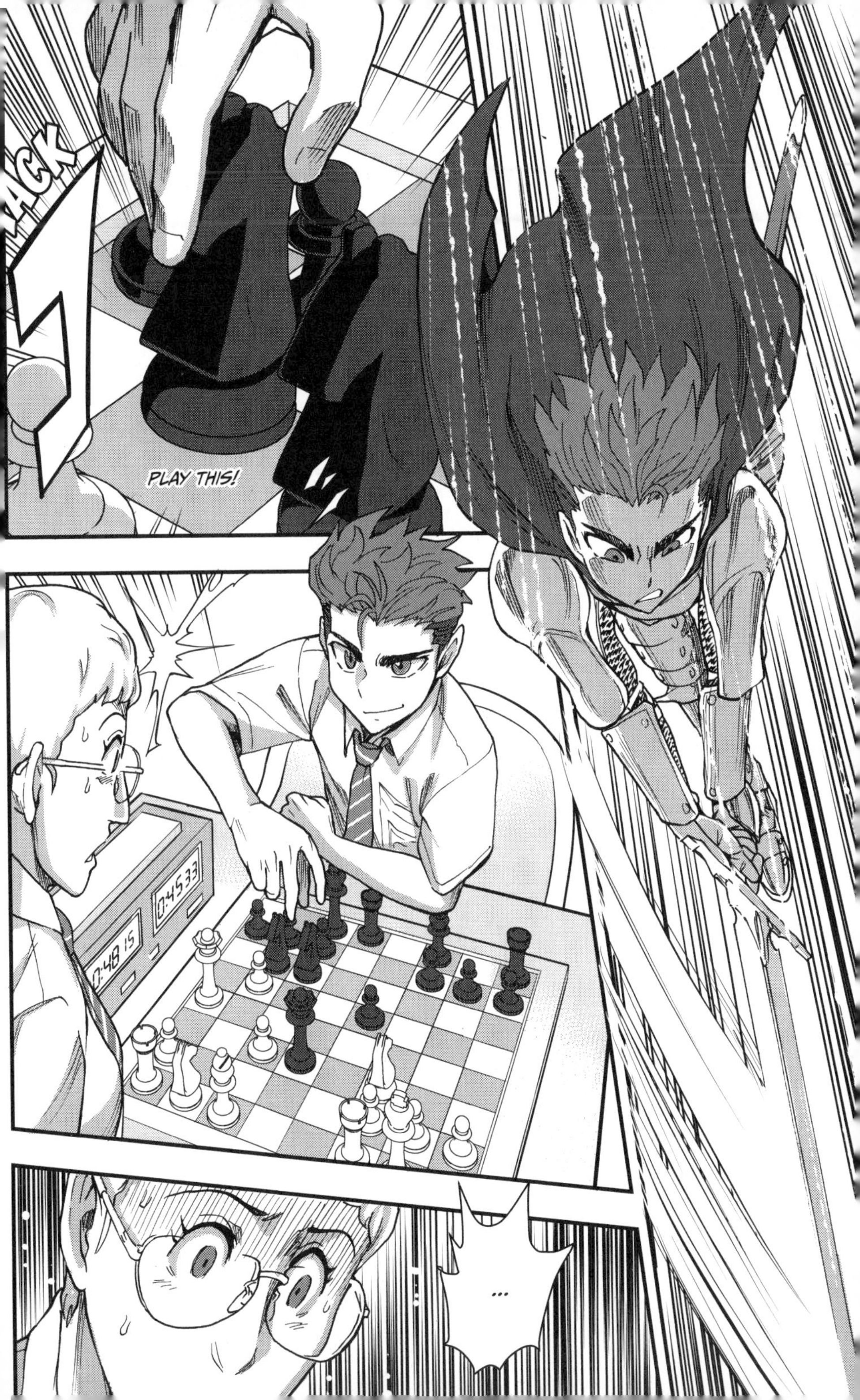
ACK
PLAY THIS!
0:48 15
0:45 33
...

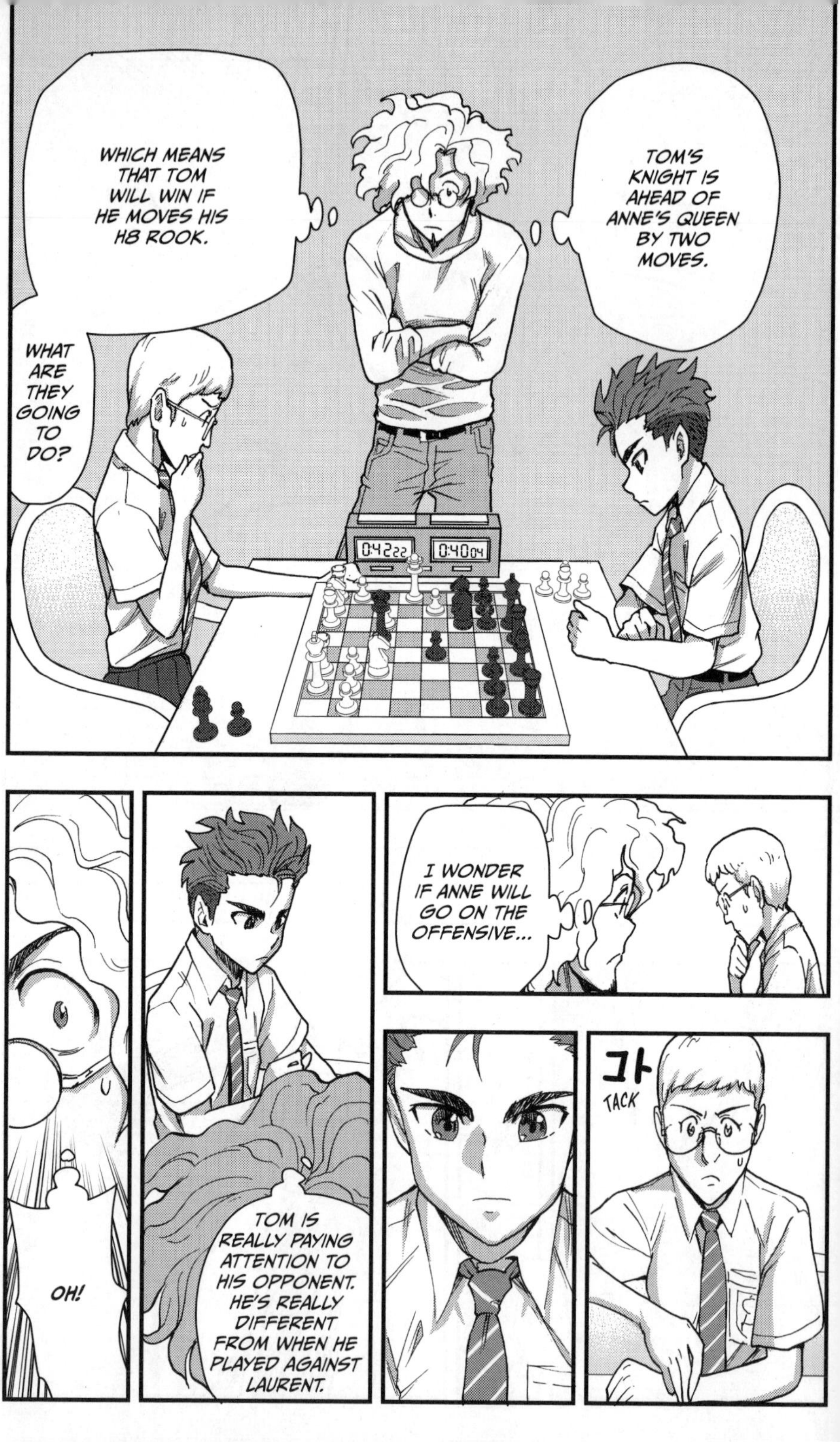
TOM'S KNIGHT IS AHEAD OF ANNE'S QUEEN BY TWO MOVES.
WHICH MEANS THAT TOM WILL WIN IF HE MOVES HIS H8 ROOK.
WHAT ARE THEY GOING TO DO?
0:42 22
0:40 04
I WONDER IF ANNE WILL GO ON THE OFFENSIVE...
コト
TACK
TOM IS REALLY PAYING ATTENTION TO HIS OPPONENT. HE'S REALLY DIFFERENT FROM WHEN HE PLAYED AGAINST LAURENT.
OH!

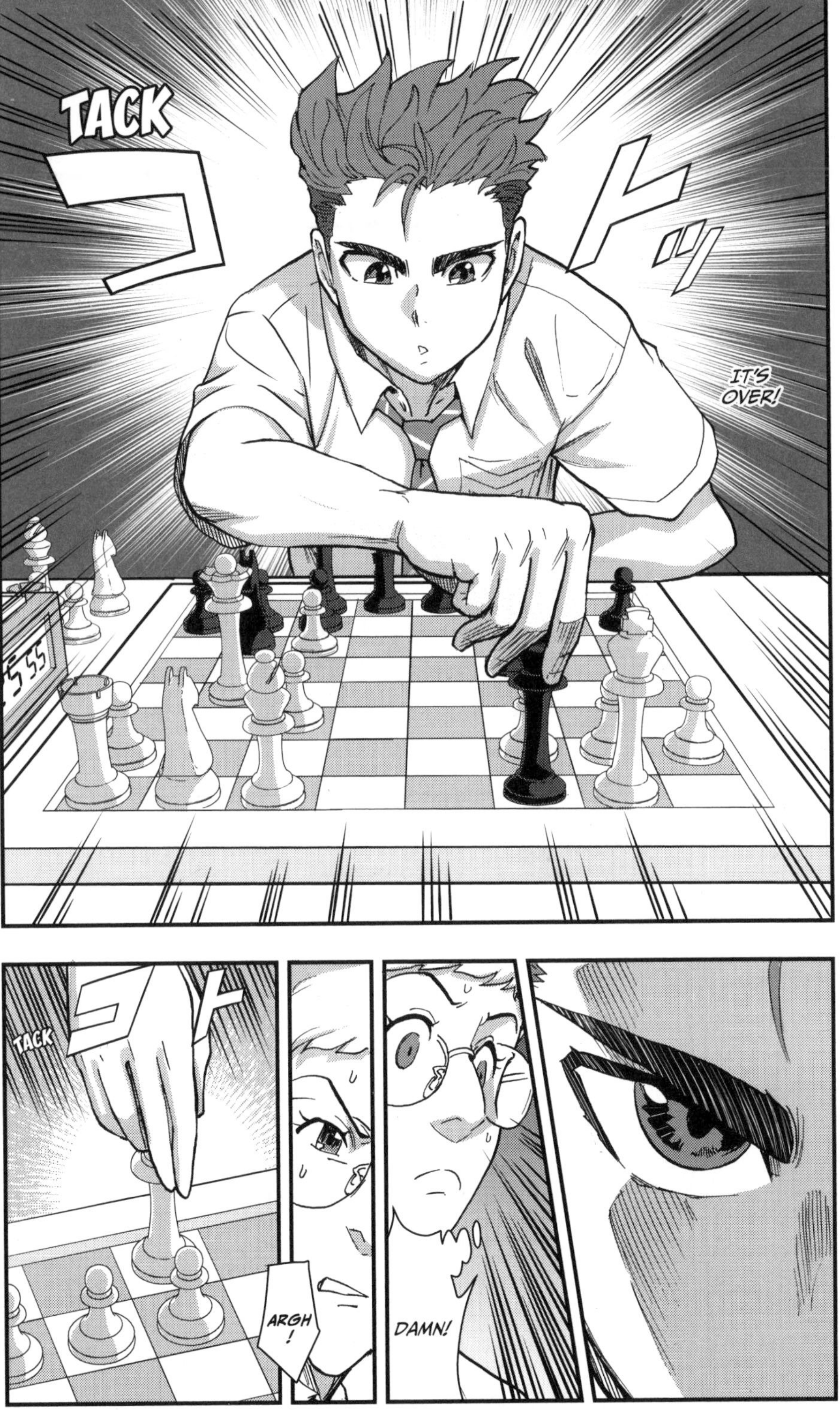
TACK
コトッ
IT'S OVER!
DAMN!
ARGH!
TACK

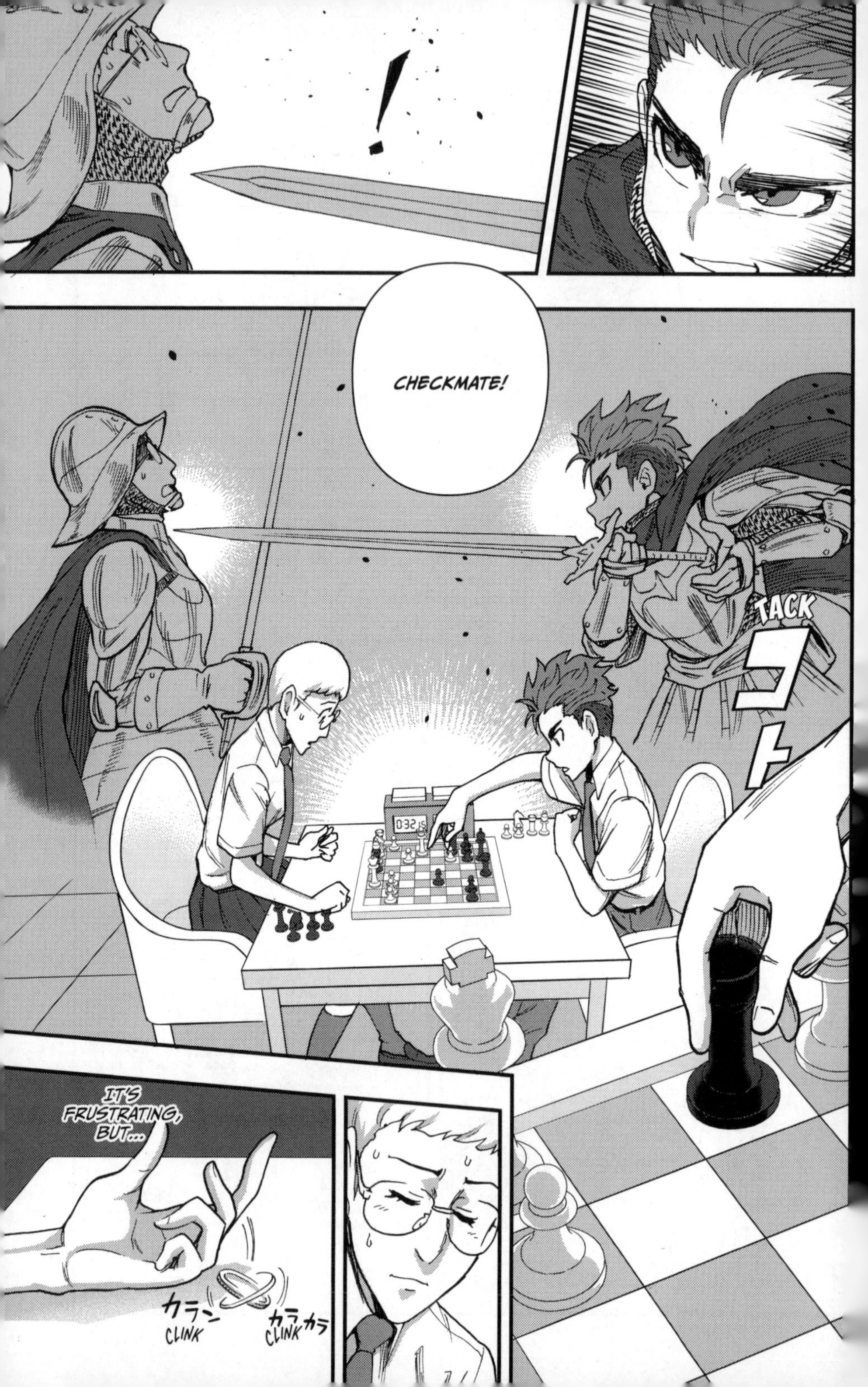
!
CHECKMATE!
TACK
コト
IT'S FRUSTRATING, BUT...
カラン
CLINK
カラカラ
CLINK

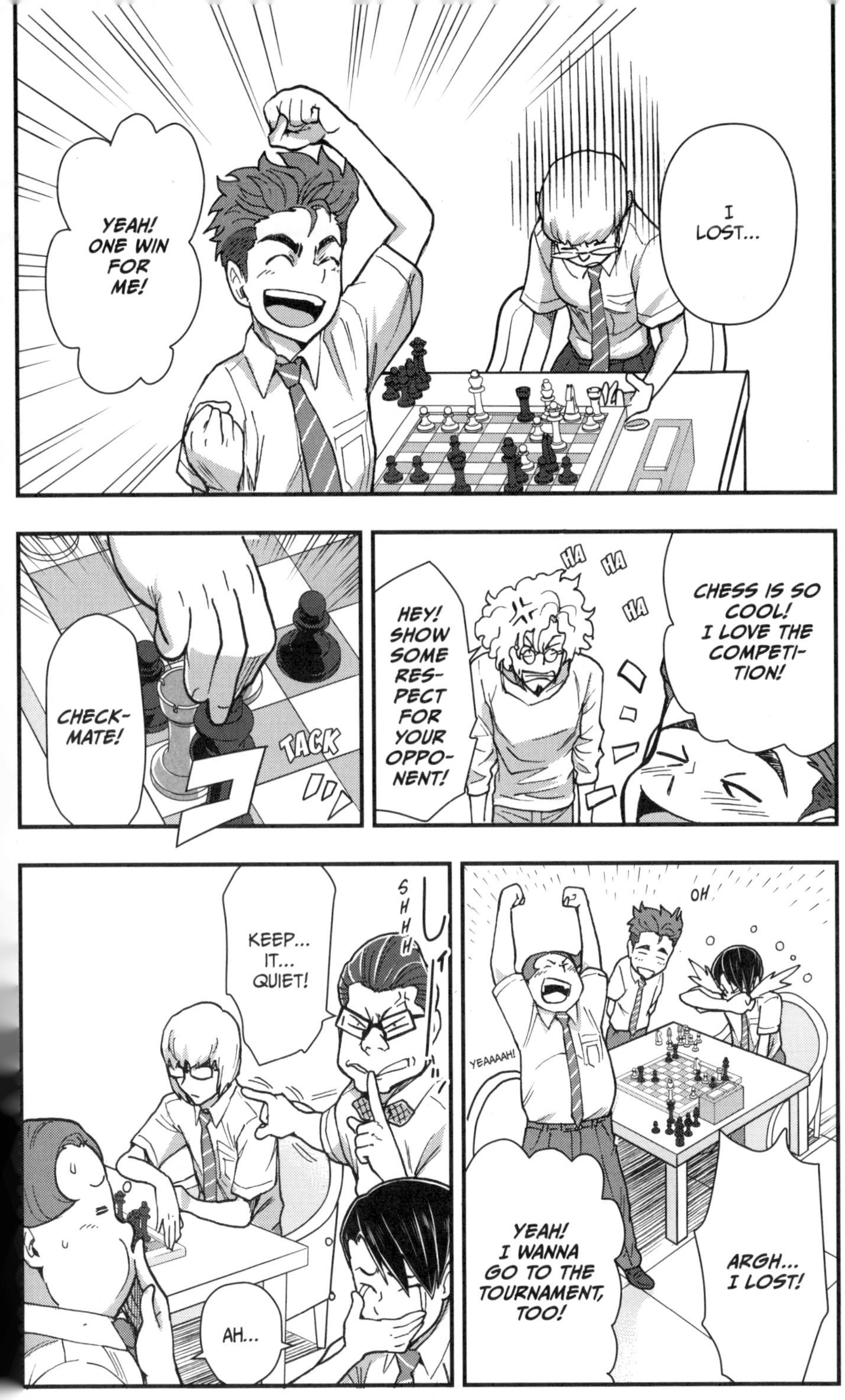
YEAH! ONE WIN FOR ME!
I LOST...
CHESS IS SO COOL! I LOVE THE COMPETI-TION!
HA HA HA
HEY! SHOW SOME RES-PECT FOR YOUR OPPO-NENT!
CHECK-MATE!
TACK
OH
YEAAAAH!
ARGH... I LOST!
YEAH! I WANNA GO TO THE TOURNAMENT, TOO!
SHHHH
KEEP... IT... QUIET!
AH...

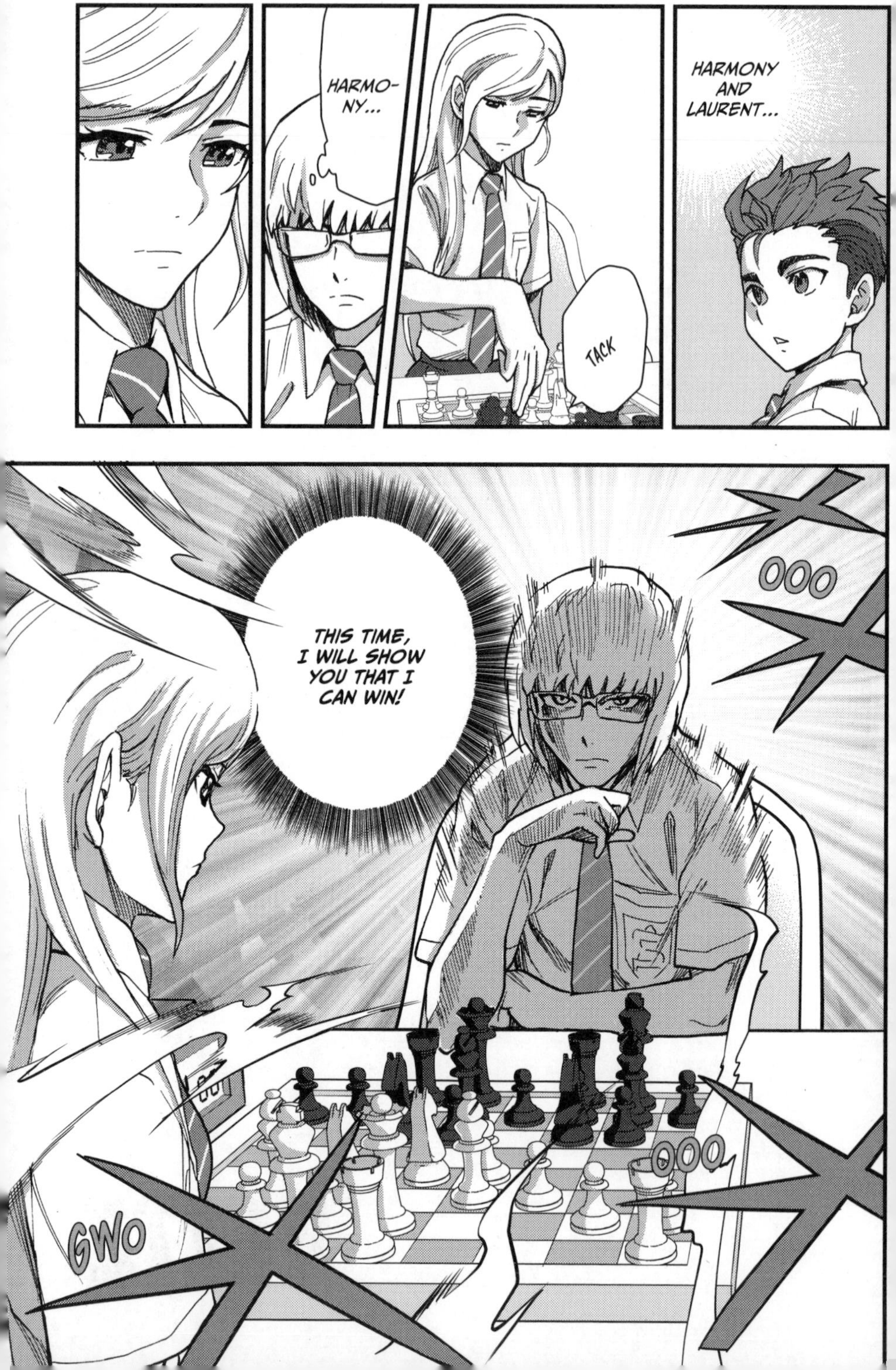
HARMONY AND LAURENT...
TACK
HARMO-NY...
OOO
THIS TIME, I WILL SHOW YOU THAT I CAN WIN!
OOO
GWO

BLiTZ

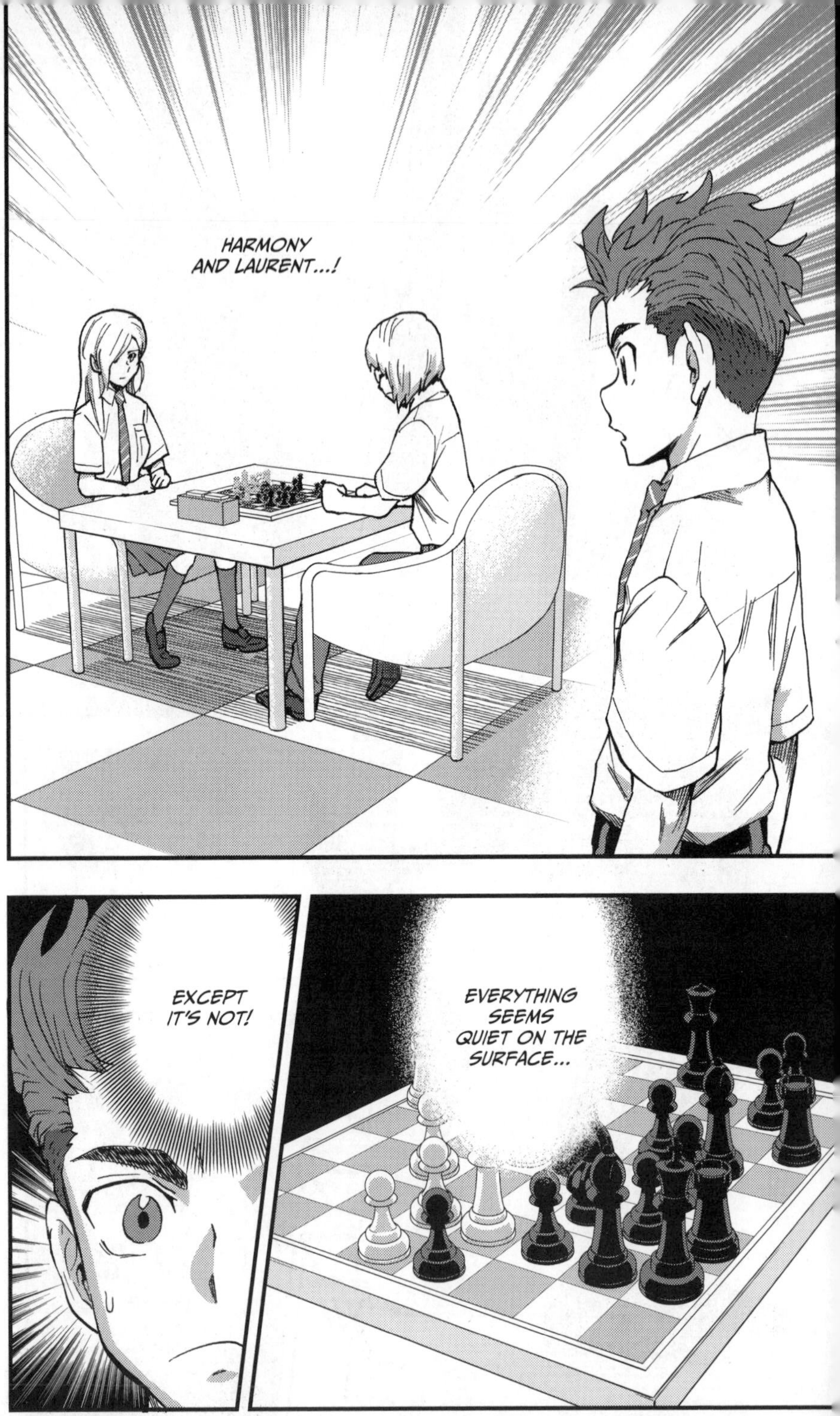
HARMONY AND LAURENT...!
EVERYTHING SEEMS QUIET ON THE SURFACE...
EXCEPT IT'S NOT!

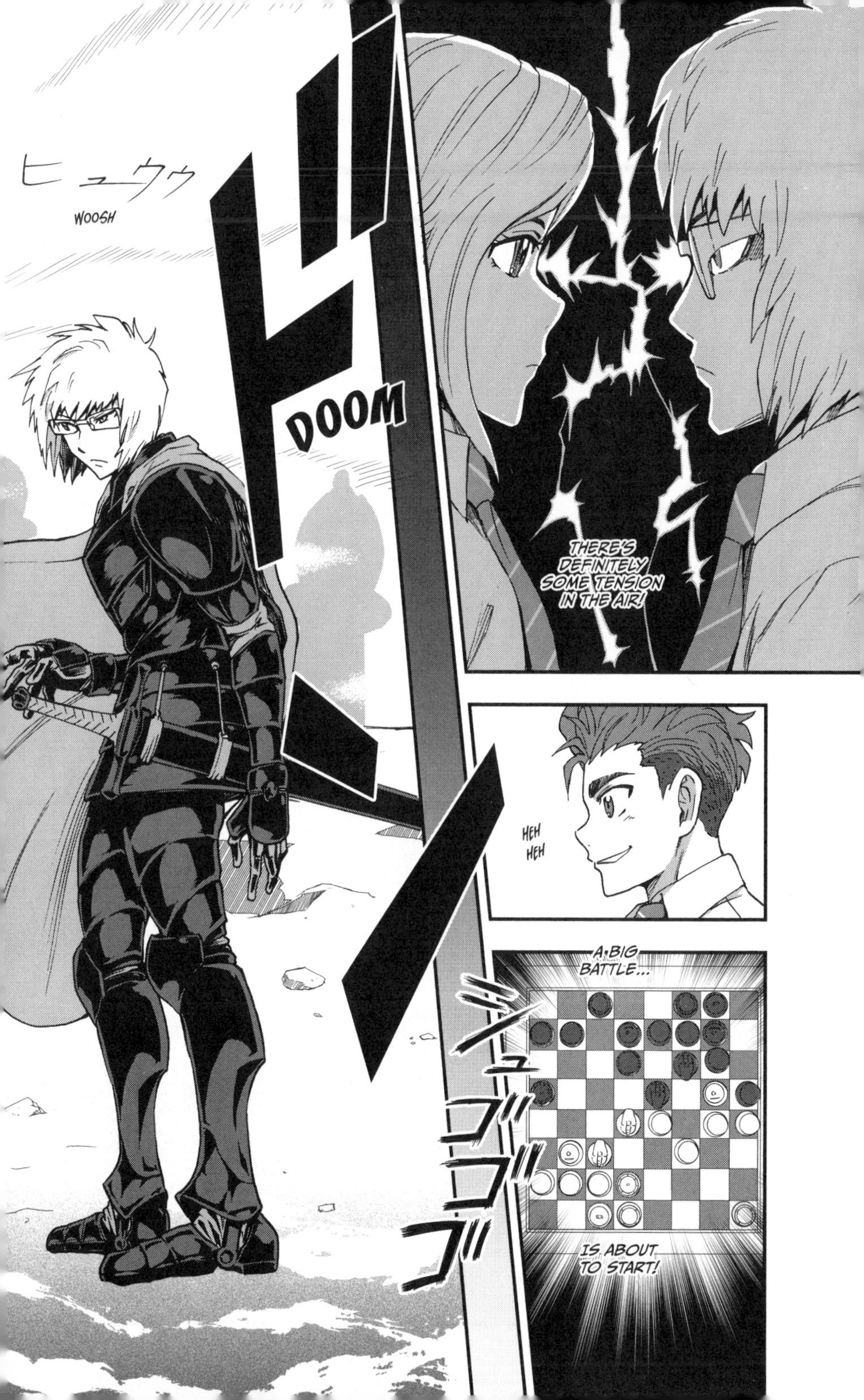
THERE'S DEFINITELY SOME TENSION IN THE AIR!
HEH HEH
A BIG BATTLE...
IS ABOUT TO START!
ヒュウウ
WOOSH
DOOM

Chapter 11: Tom's POV

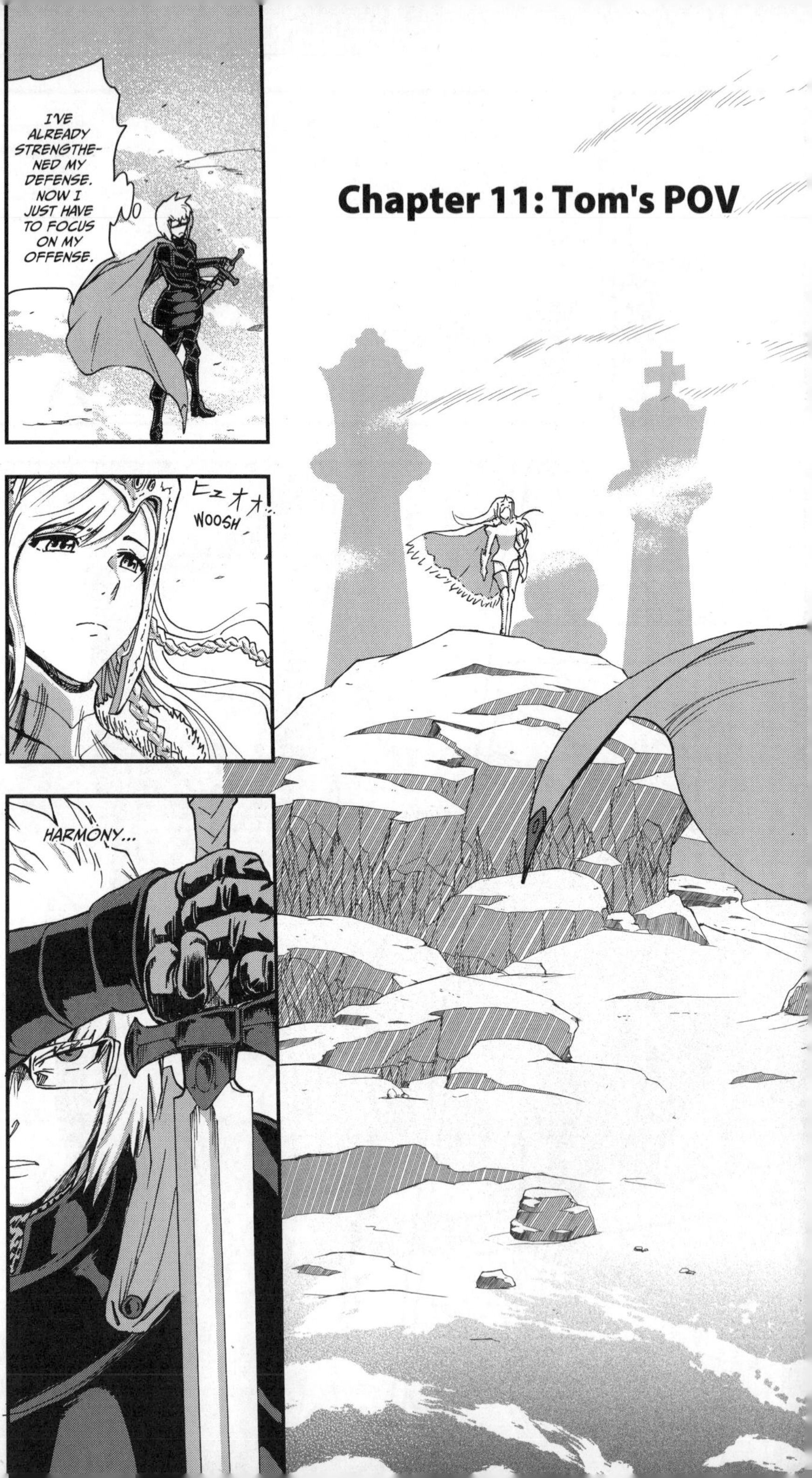
I'VE ALREADY STRENGTHENED MY DEFENSE. NOW I JUST HAVE TO FOCUS ON MY OFFENSE.
ヒュオオ…
WOOSH
HARMONY...

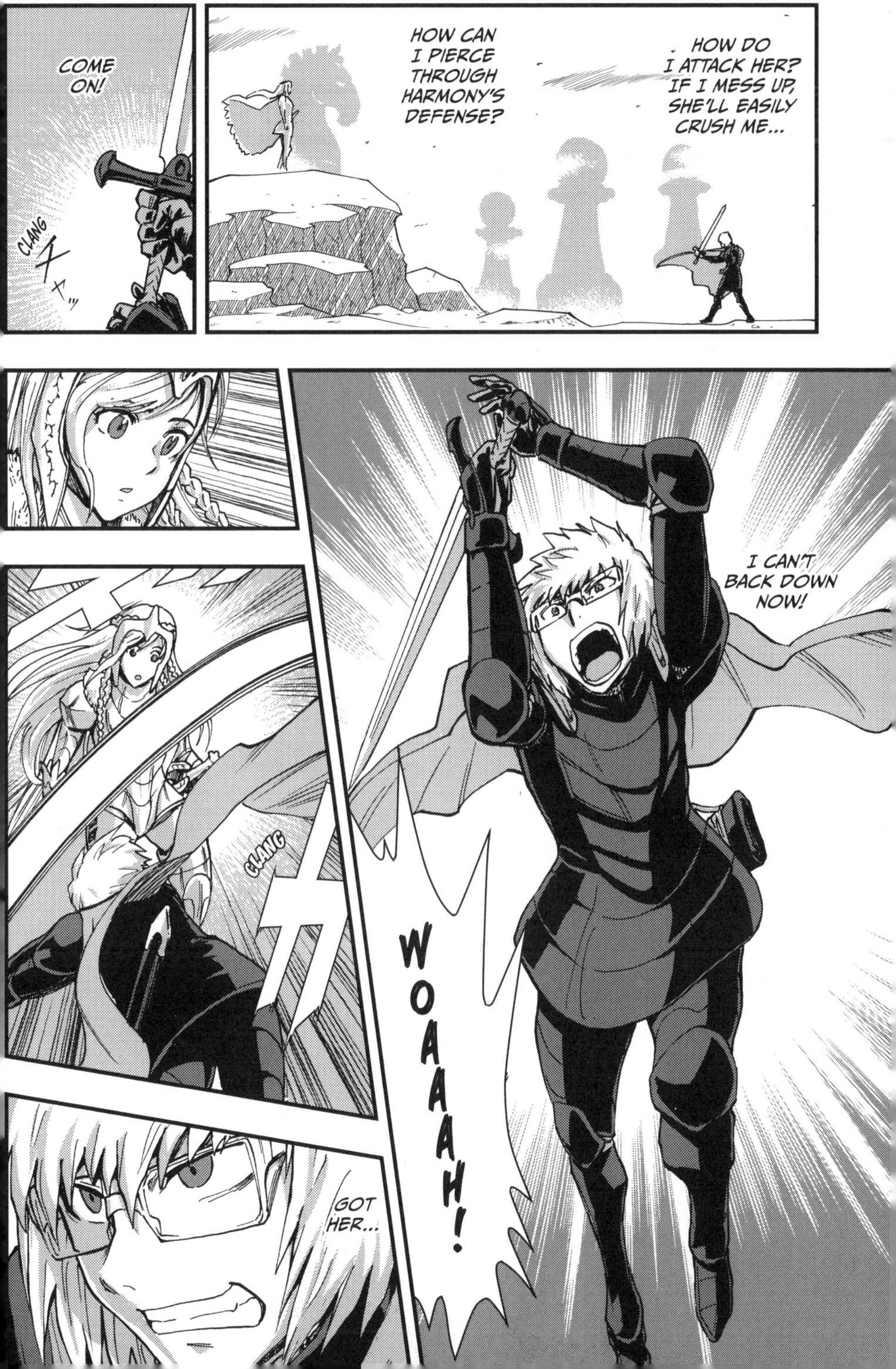
HOW DO I ATTACK HER? IF I MESS UP, SHE'LL EASILY CRUSH ME...
HOW CAN I PIERCE THROUGH HARMONY'S DEFENSE?
COME ON!
CLANG
I CAN'T BACK DOWN NOW!
WOAAAAH!
CLANG
GOT HER...

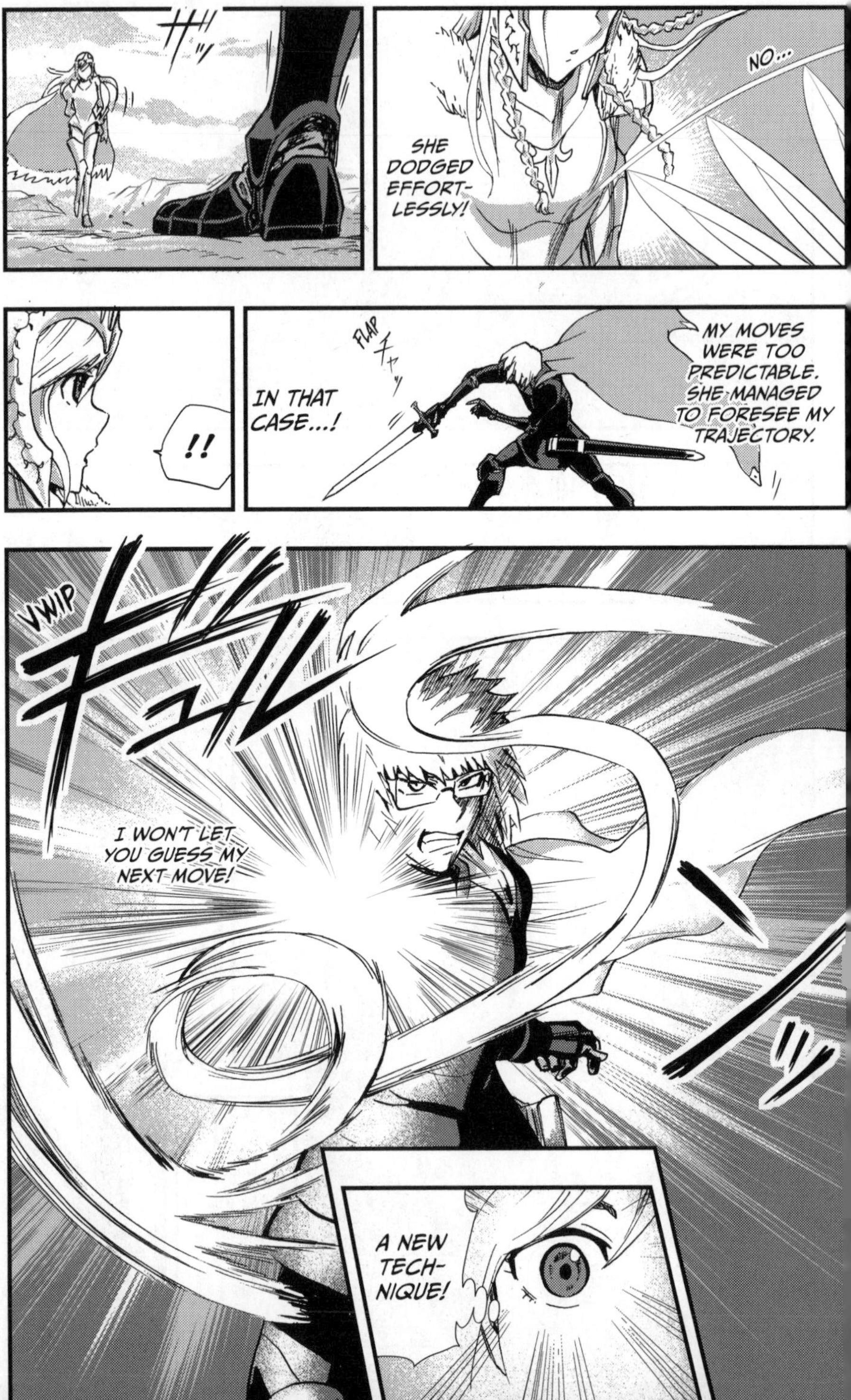
NO...
SHE DODGED EFFORT-LESSLY!
TAP
MY MOVES WERE TOO PREDICTABLE. SHE MANAGED TO FORESEE MY TRAJECTORY.
FLAP
IN THAT CASE...!
!!
VWIP
I WON'T LET YOU GUESS MY NEXT MOVE!
A NEW TECH-NIQUE!

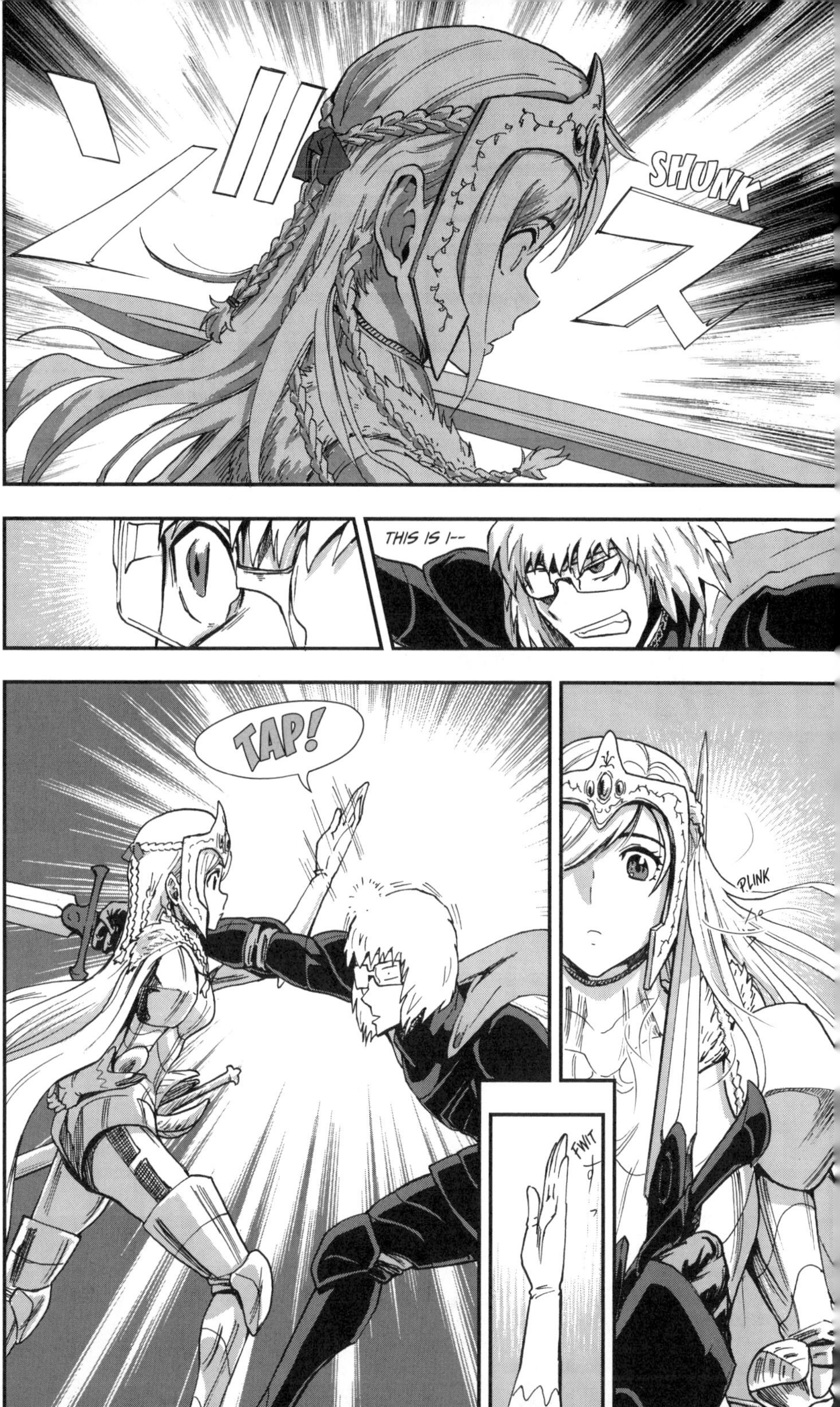
SHUNK
THIS IS I--
P.LINK
FWIT
TAP!

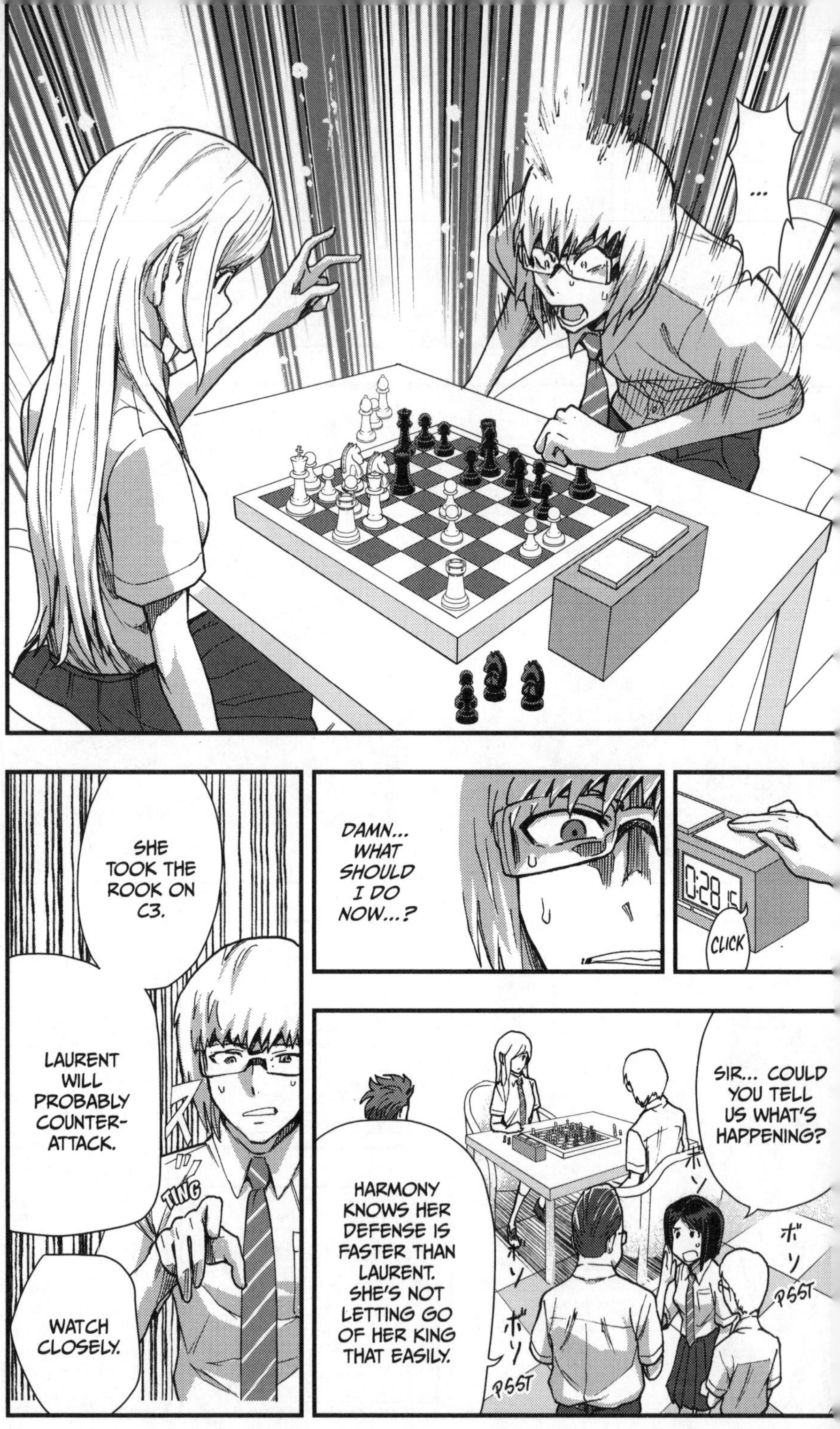
...
CLICK
DAMN... WHAT SHOULD I DO NOW...?
SIR... COULD YOU TELL US WHAT'S HAPPENING?
HARMONY KNOWS HER DEFENSE IS FASTER THAN LAURENT. SHE'S NOT LETTING GO OF HER KING THAT EASILY.
PSST
PSST
SHE TOOK THE ROOK ON C3.
LAURENT WILL PROBABLY COUNTER-ATTACK.
TING
WATCH CLOSELY.

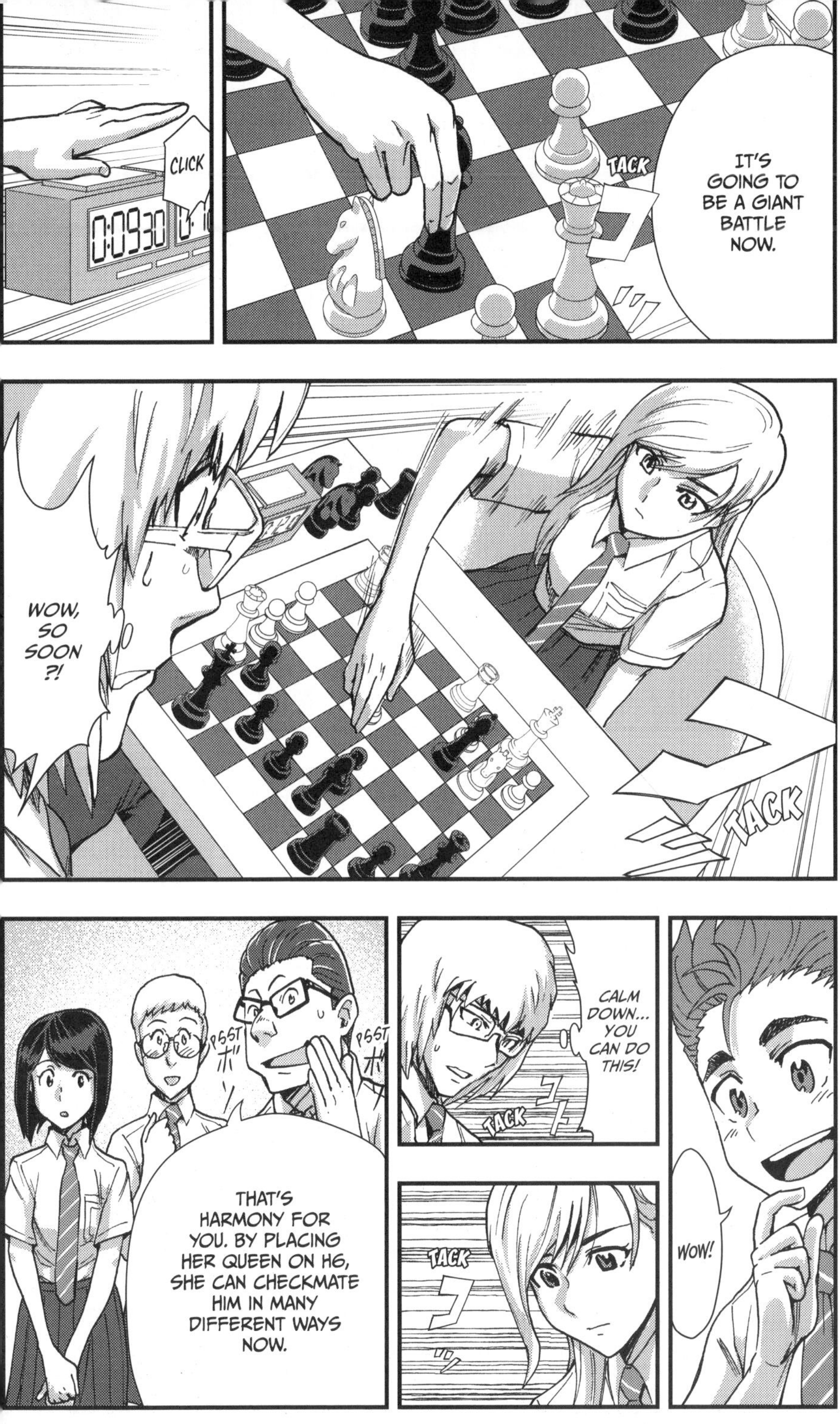
TACK
IT'S GOING TO BE A GIANT BATTLE NOW.
CLICK
0:09 30
WOW, SO SOON?!
TACK
WOW!
CALM DOWN... YOU CAN DO THIS!
TACK
TACK
PSST
PSST
THAT'S HARMONY FOR YOU. BY PLACING HER QUEEN ON H6, SHE CAN CHECKMATE HIM IN MANY DIFFERENT WAYS NOW.

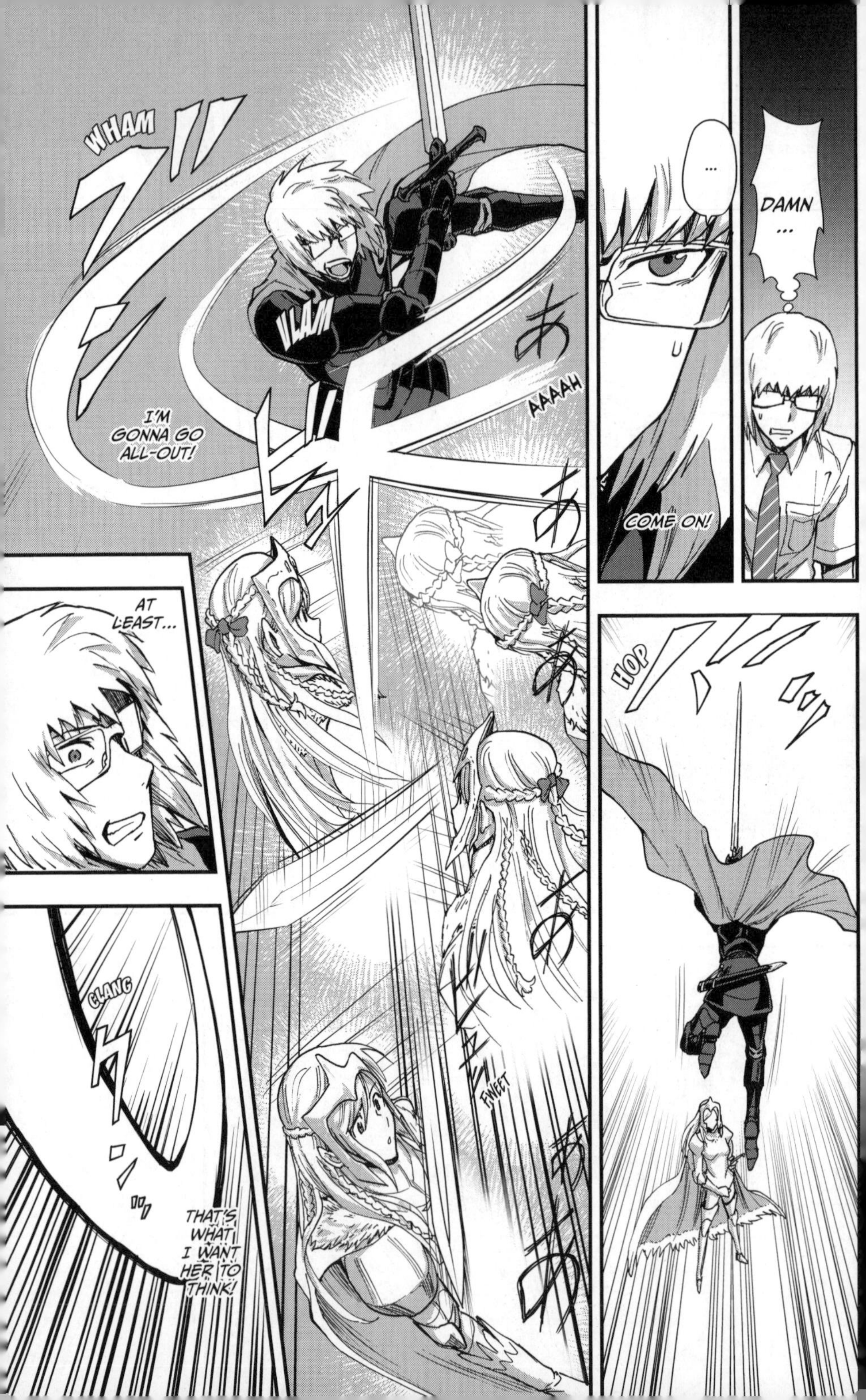
DAMN ...
...
COME ON!
WHAM
VLAM
AAAAH
I'M GONNA GO ALL-OUT!
HOP
FWEET
AT LEAST...
CLANG
THAT'S WHAT I WANT HER TO THINK!

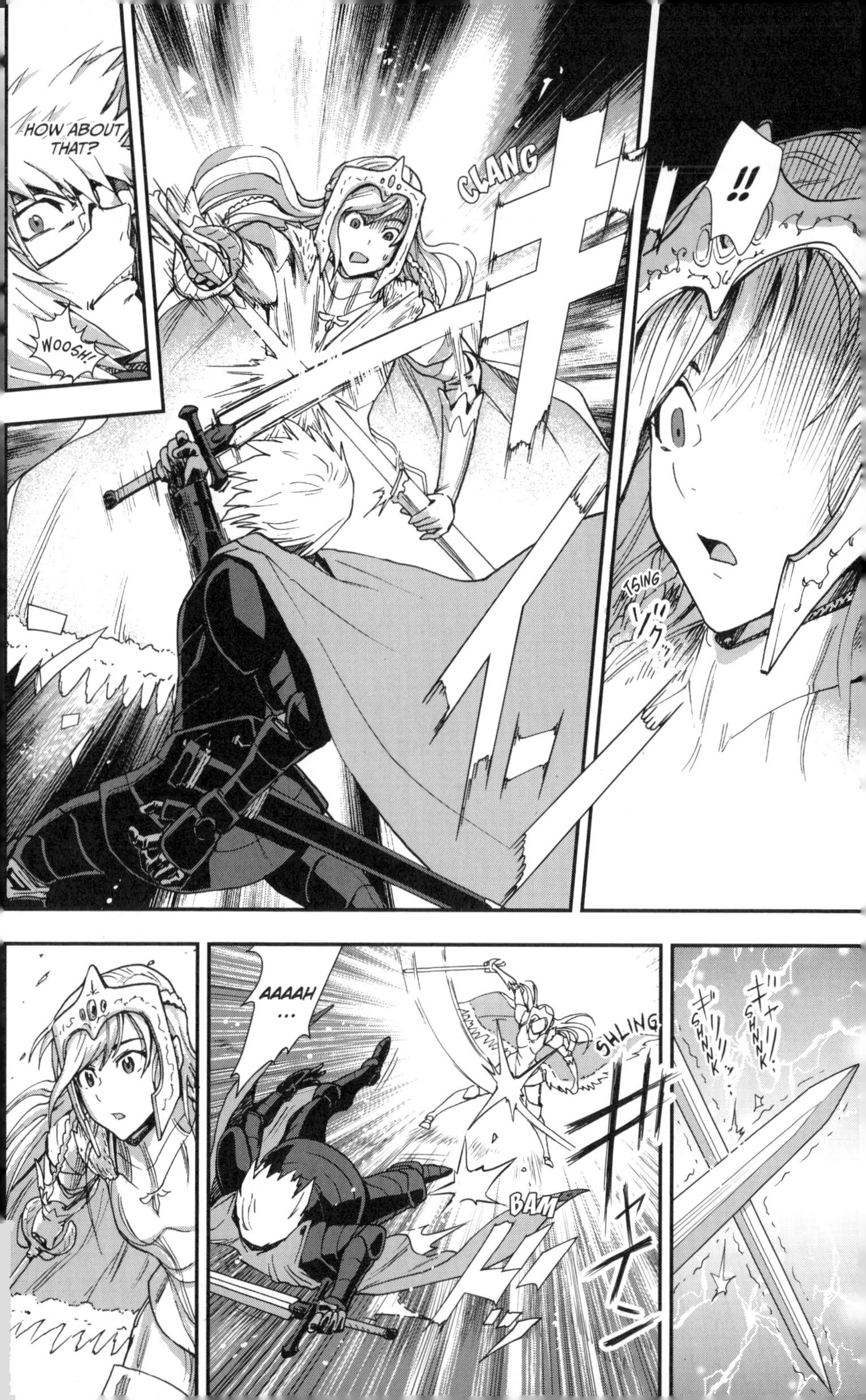
!!
TSING
CLANG
HOW ABOUT THAT?
WOOSH!
SHNNK!
SHNNK...
SHLING
AAAAH ...
BAM

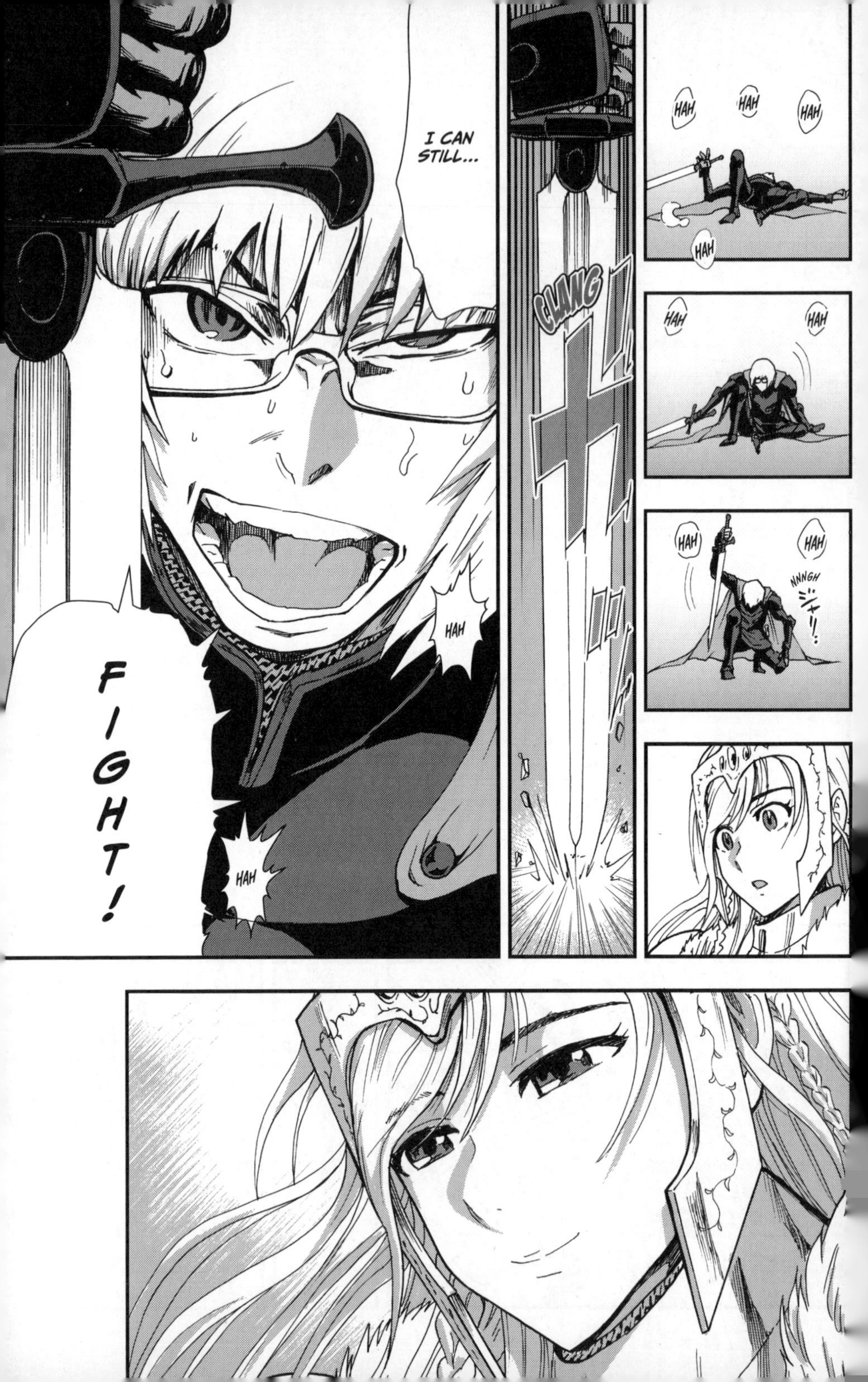
HAH
HAH
HAH
HAH
HAH
HAH
HAH
HAH
NNNGH
CLANG
I CAN STILL...
HAH
HAH
FIGHT!

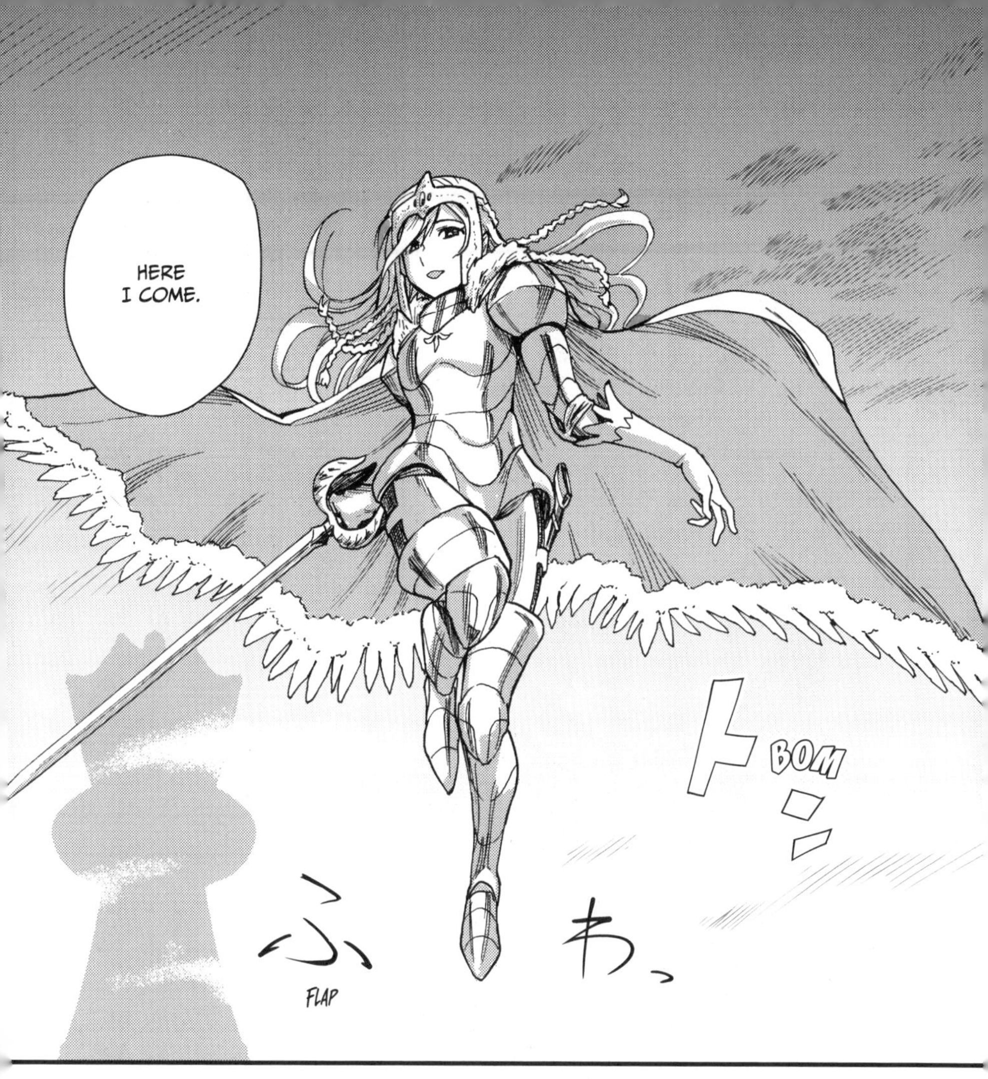
HERE I COME.
BOM
ふわっ
FLAP
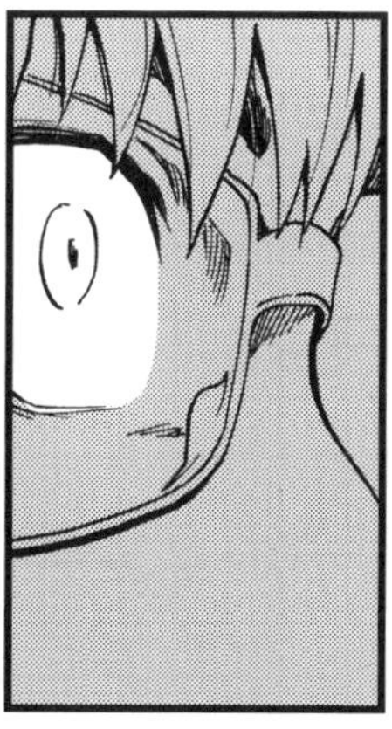
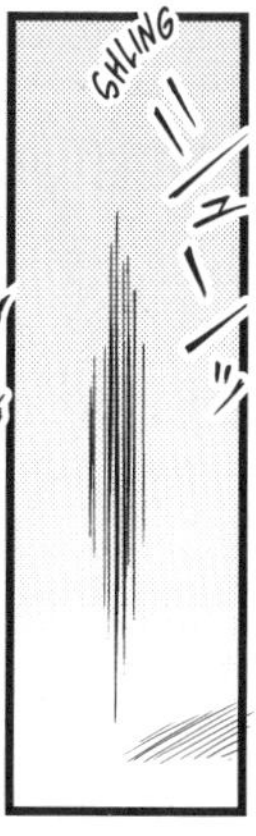
SHLING
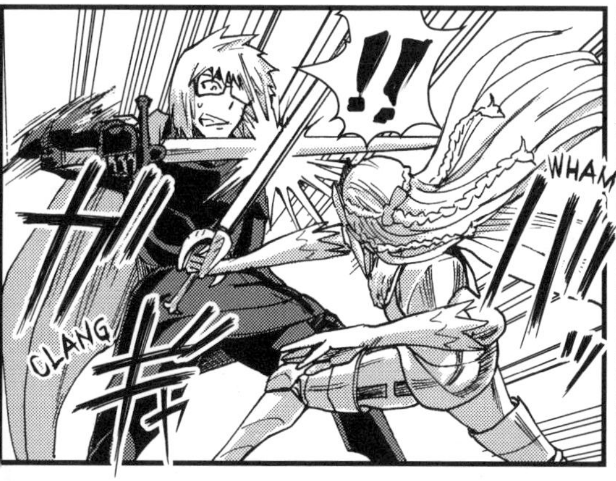
!!
WHAM
CLANG

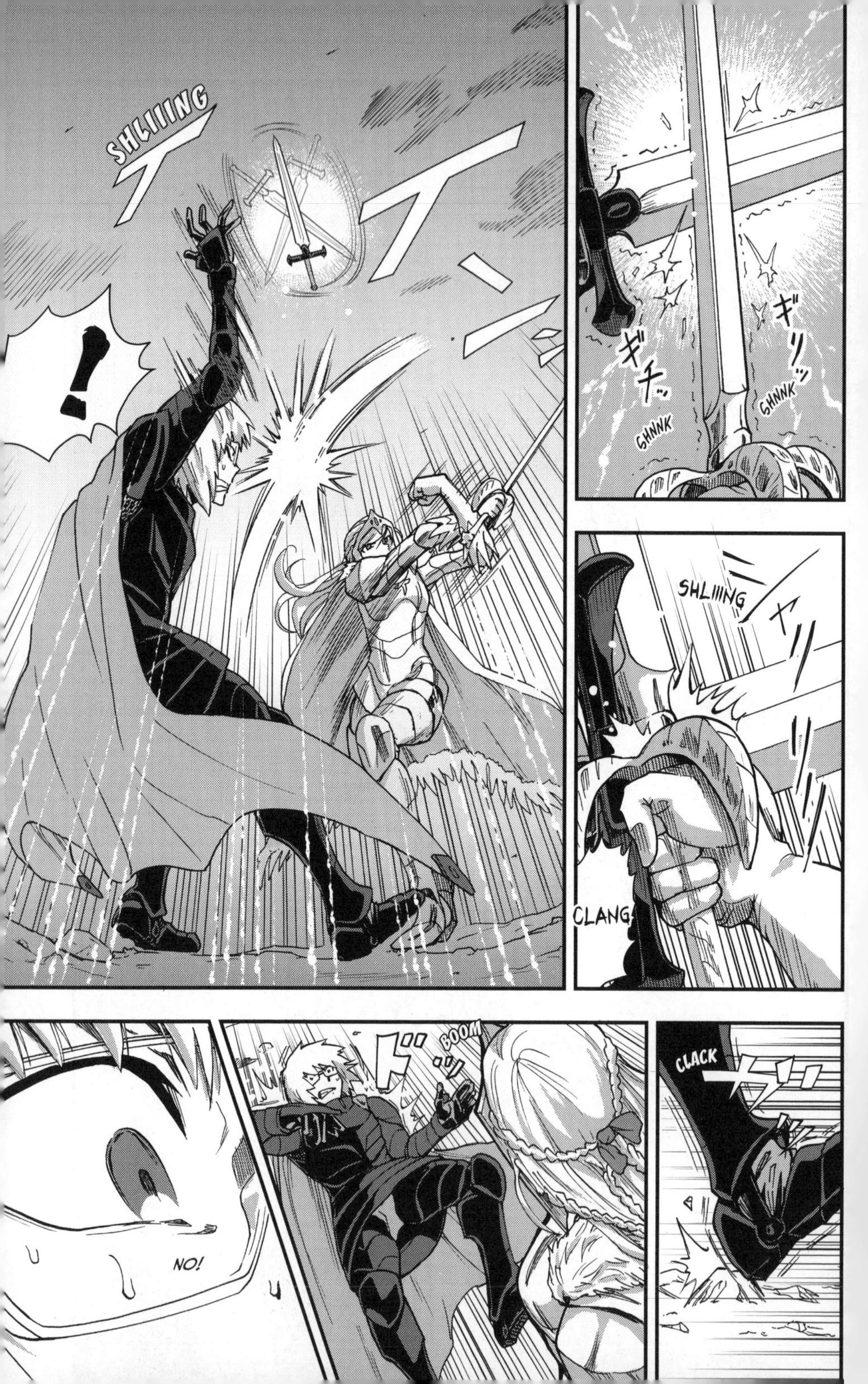

GHNNK
GHNNK
SHLIIING
CLANG
SHLIIING
!
CLACK
BOOM
NO!

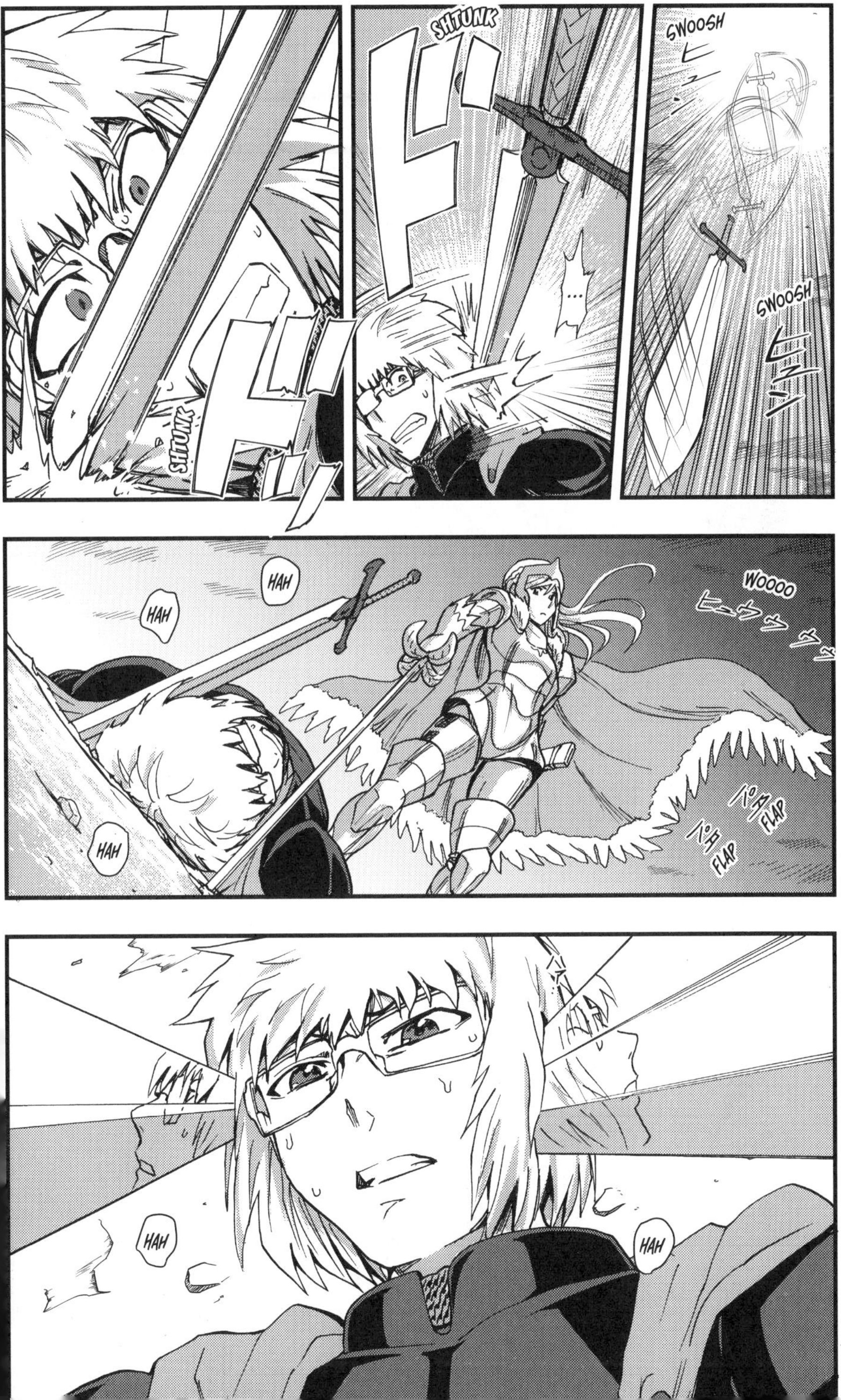
SWOOSH
SWOOSH
SHTUNK
...
SHTUNK
WOOOO
HAH
HAH
FLAP
FLAP
HAH
HAH
HAH

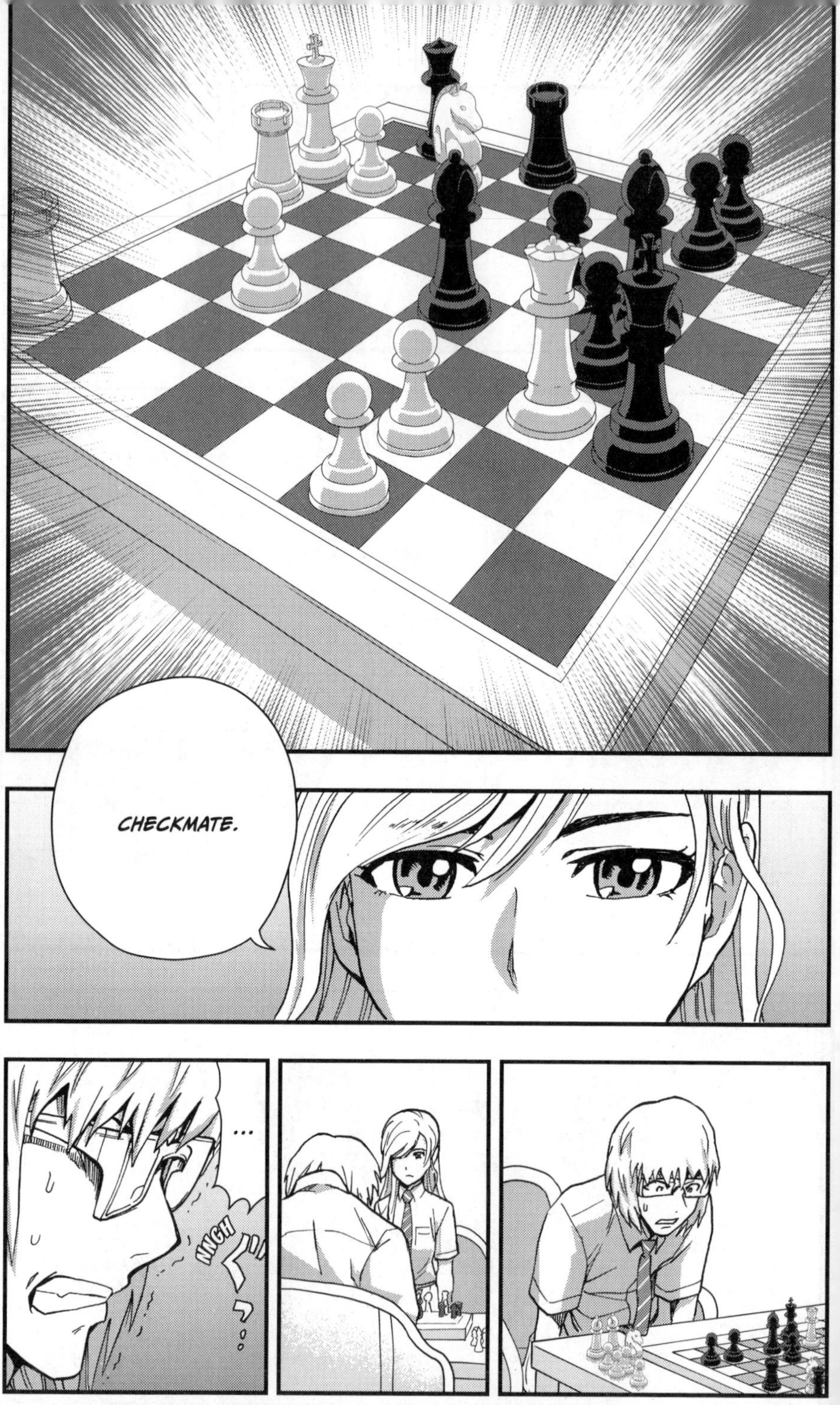
CHECKMATE.
...
NNGH

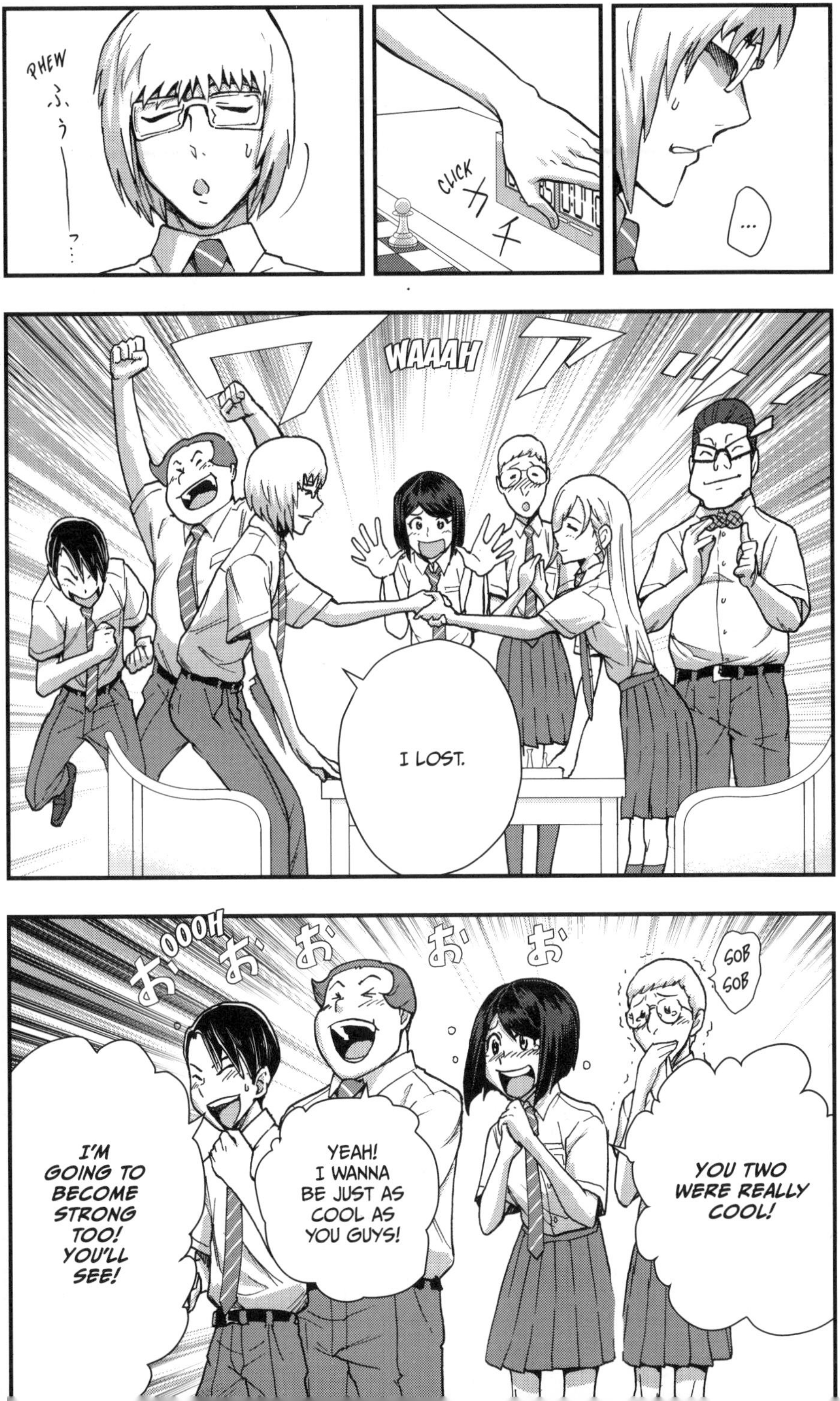
...
CLICK
カチ
PHEW
ふうーっ…
WAAAH
I LOST.
OOOH
おおおおお
SOB SOB
YOU TWO WERE REALLY COOL!
YEAH! I WANNA BE JUST AS COOL AS YOU GUYS!
I'M GOING TO BECOME STRONG TOO! YOU'LL SEE!

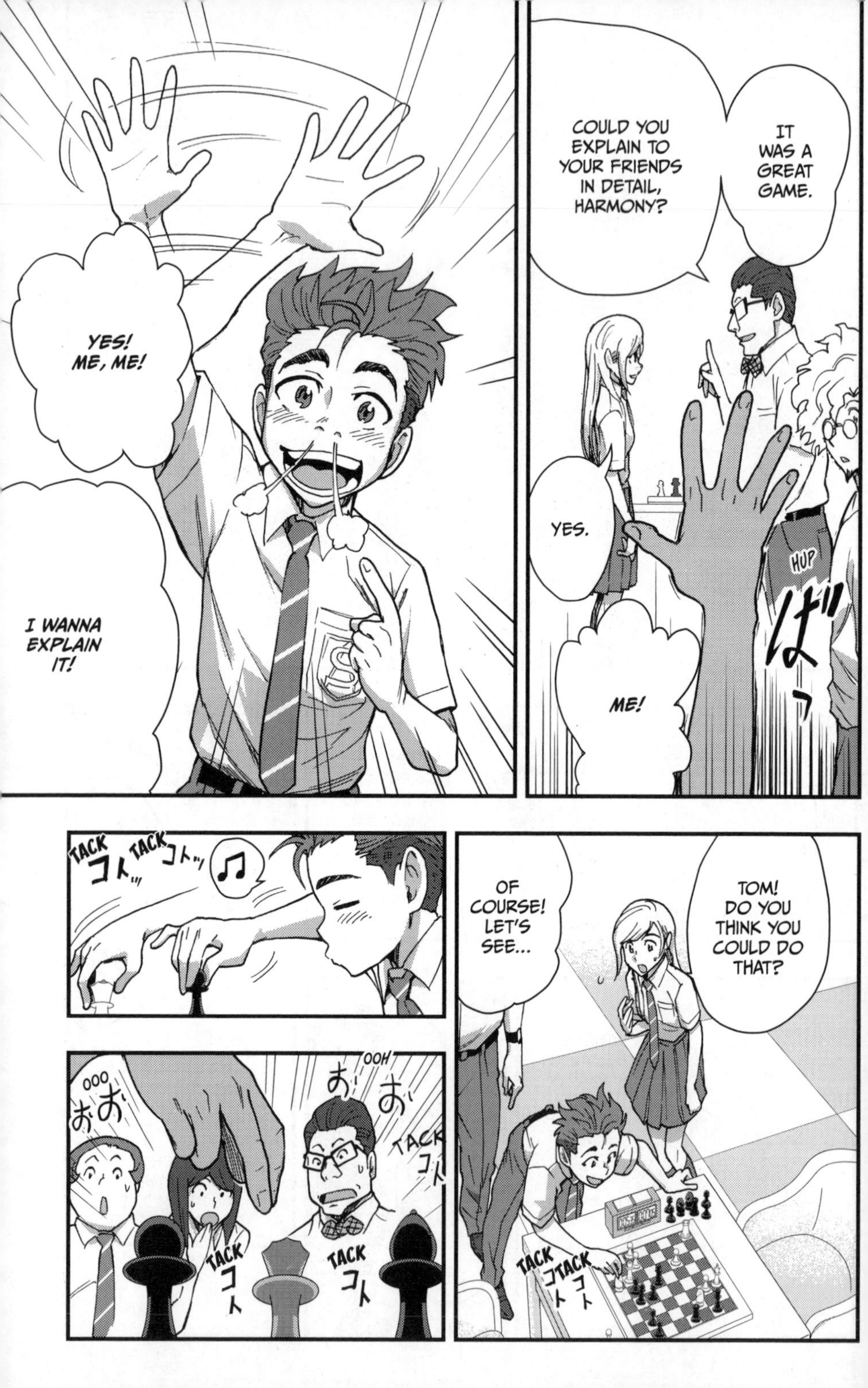
IT WAS A GREAT GAME.
COULD YOU EXPLAIN TO YOUR FRIENDS IN DETAIL, HARMONY?
YES.
HUP
ばっ
ME!
YES! ME, ME!
I WANNA EXPLAIN IT!
TOM! DO YOU THINK YOU COULD DO THAT?
OF COURSE! LET'S SEE...
TACK
コト
TACK
コト
TACK
コトッ
TACK
コトッ
♫
OOH
おぉ
OOO
おお
TACK
コト
TACK
コト
TACK
コト

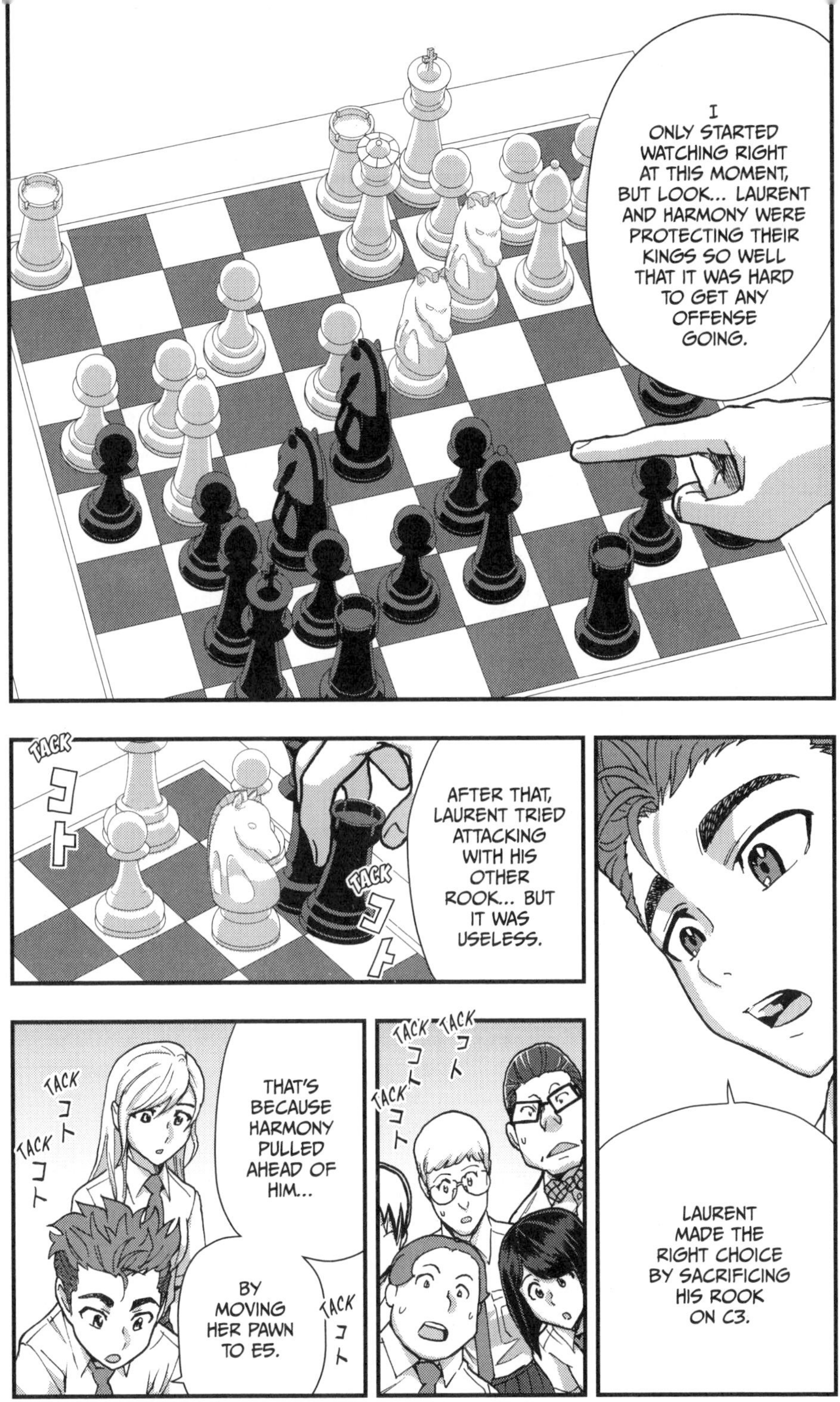
I ONLY STARTED WATCHING RIGHT AT THIS MOMENT, BUT LOOK... LAURENT AND HARMONY WERE PROTECTING THEIR KINGS SO WELL THAT IT WAS HARD TO GET ANY OFFENSE GOING.
TACK
コト
TACK
コト
AFTER THAT, LAURENT TRIED ATTACKING WITH HIS OTHER ROOK... BUT IT WAS USELESS.
TACK
コト
TACK
コト
TACK
コト
TACK
コト
TACK
コト
TACK
コト
THAT'S BECAUSE HARMONY PULLED AHEAD OF HIM...
BY MOVING HER PAWN TO E5.
LAURENT MADE THE RIGHT CHOICE BY SACRIFICING HIS ROOK ON C3.

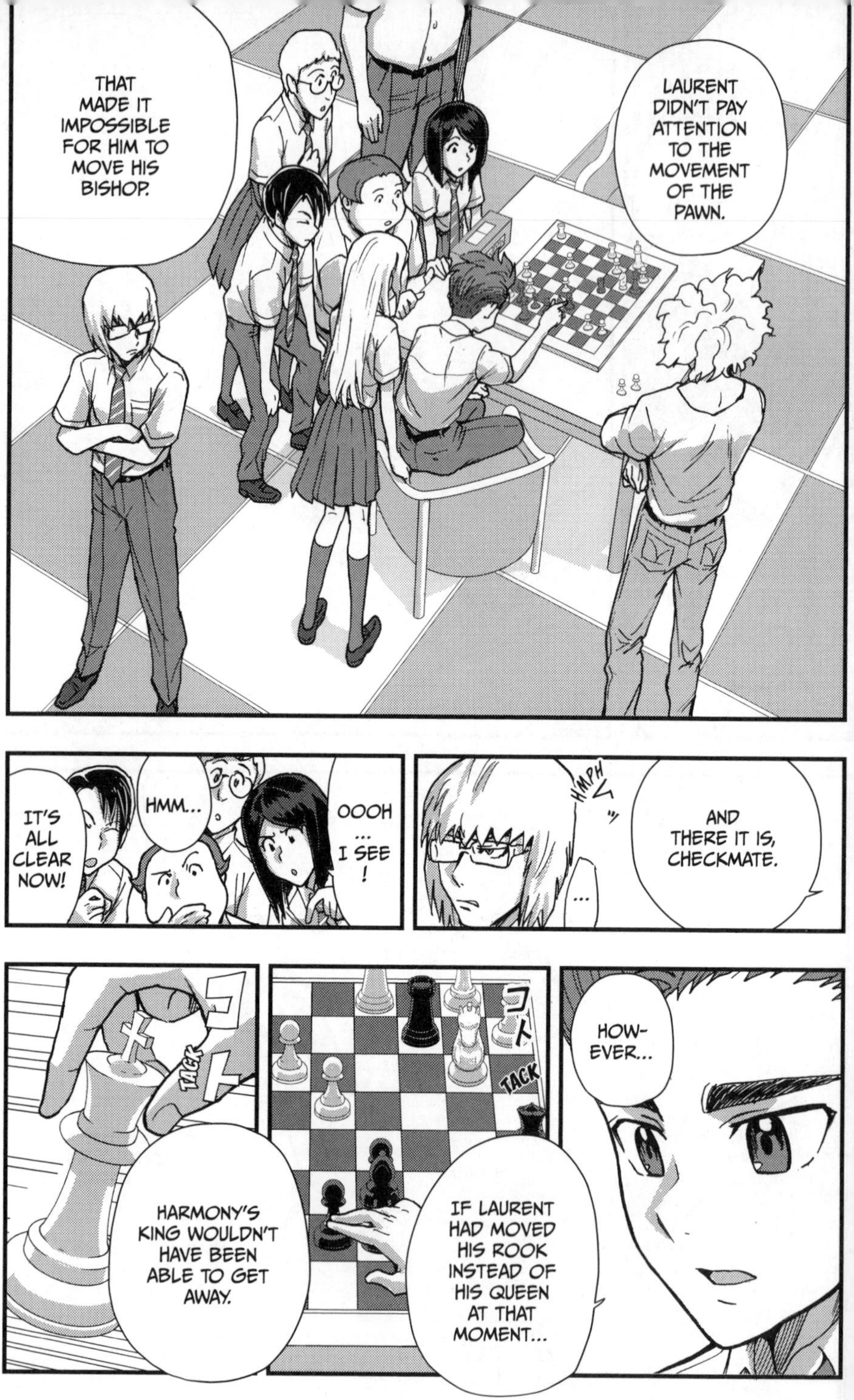
LAURENT DIDN'T PAY ATTENTION TO THE MOVEMENT OF THE PAWN.
THAT MADE IT IMPOSSIBLE FOR HIM TO MOVE HIS BISHOP.
AND THERE IT IS, CHECKMATE.
HMPH
...
OOOH ... I SEE !
HMM...
IT'S ALL CLEAR NOW!
HOW-EVER...
IF LAURENT HAD MOVED HIS ROOK INSTEAD OF HIS QUEEN AT THAT MOMENT...
コト
TACK
HARMONY'S KING WOULDN'T HAVE BEEN ABLE TO GET AWAY.
コト
TACK

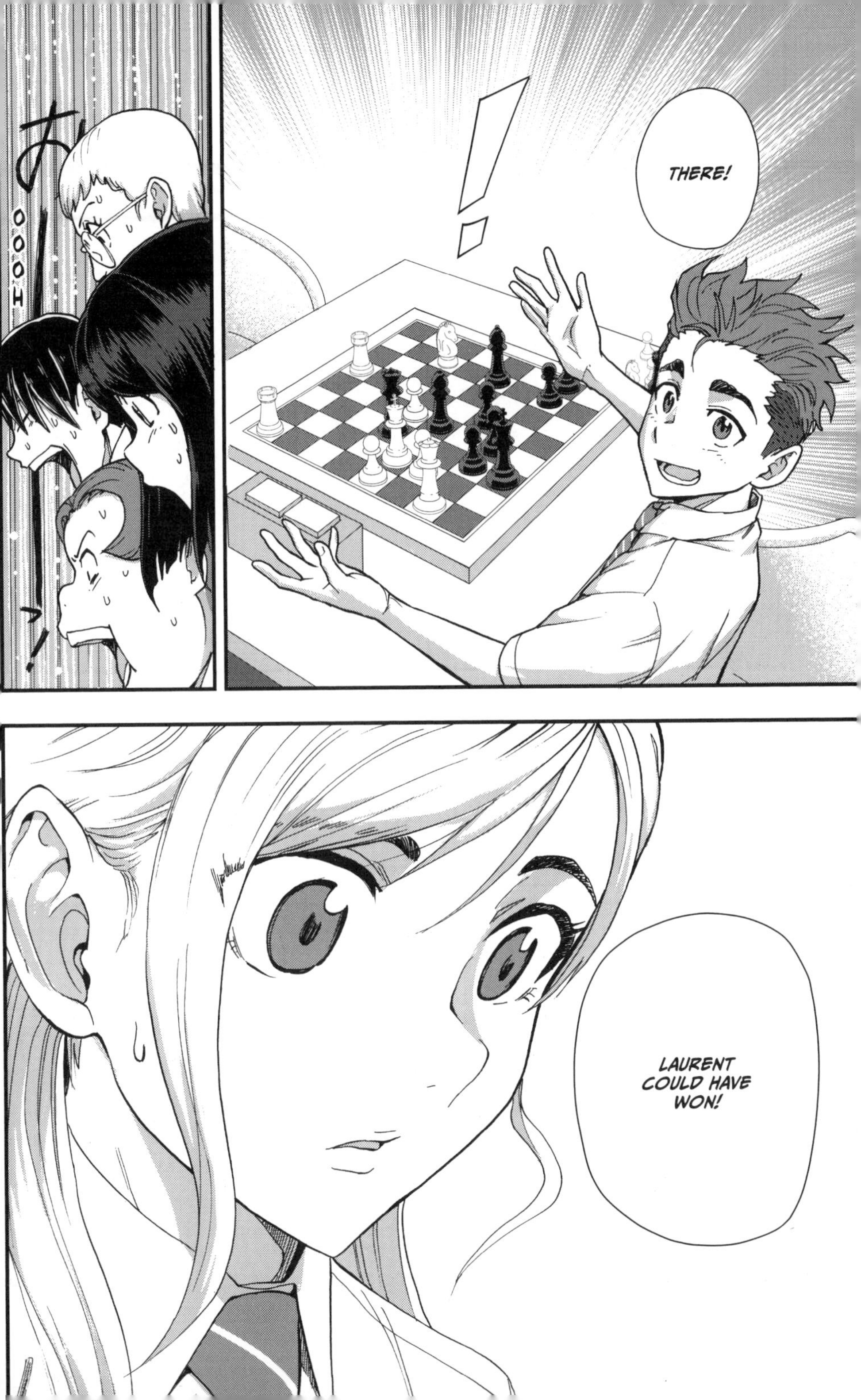
THERE!
OOOH
LAURENT COULD HAVE WON!

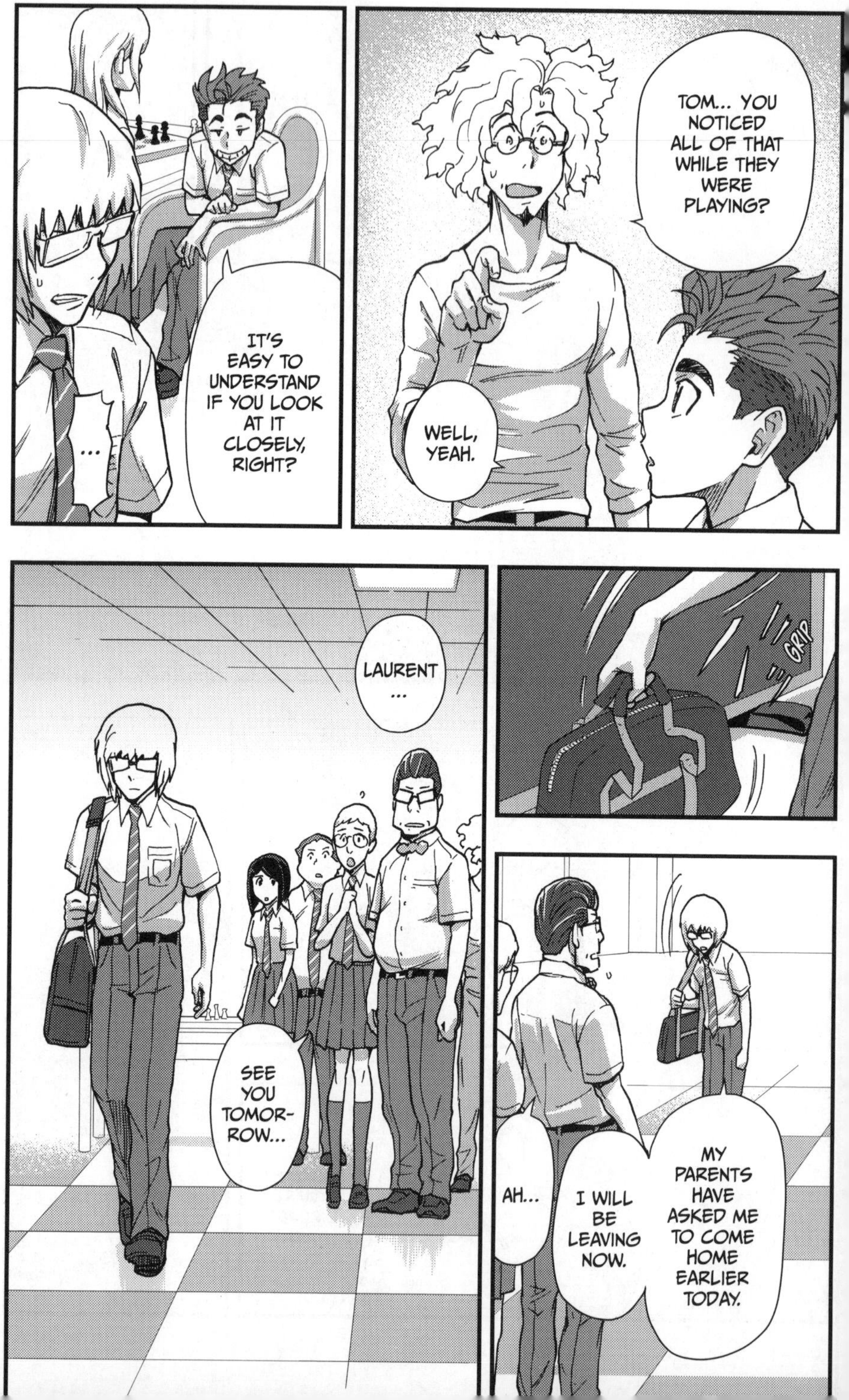
TOM... YOU NOTICED ALL OF THAT WHILE THEY WERE PLAYING?
WELL, YEAH.
IT'S EASY TO UNDERSTAND IF YOU LOOK AT IT CLOSELY, RIGHT?
...
GRIP
MY PARENTS HAVE ASKED ME TO COME HOME EARLIER TODAY.
I WILL BE LEAVING NOW.
AH...
LAURENT ...
SEE YOU TOMORROW...

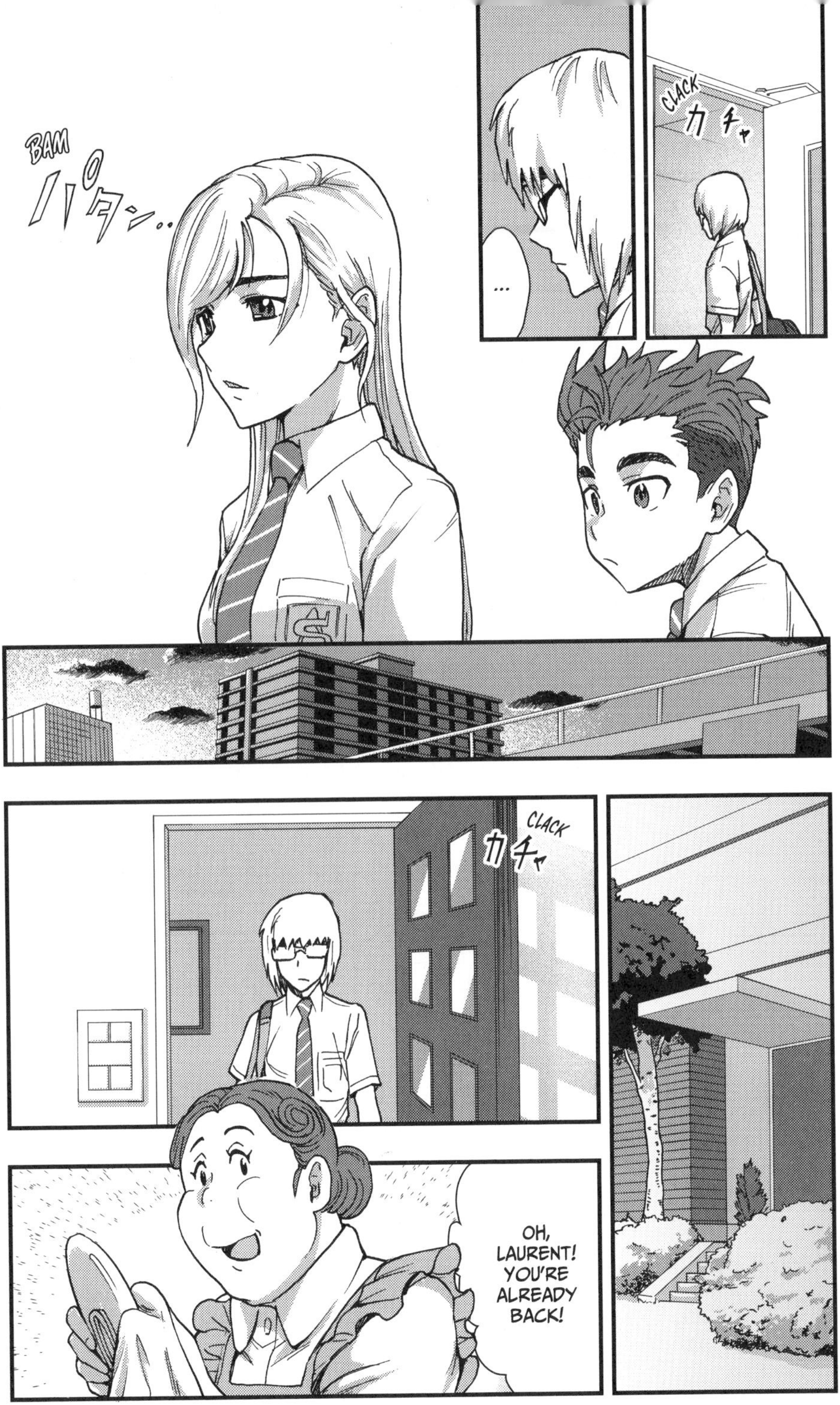
CLACK
カチャ
...
BAM
パタン‥
CLACK
カチャ
OH, LAURENT! YOU'RE ALREADY BACK!

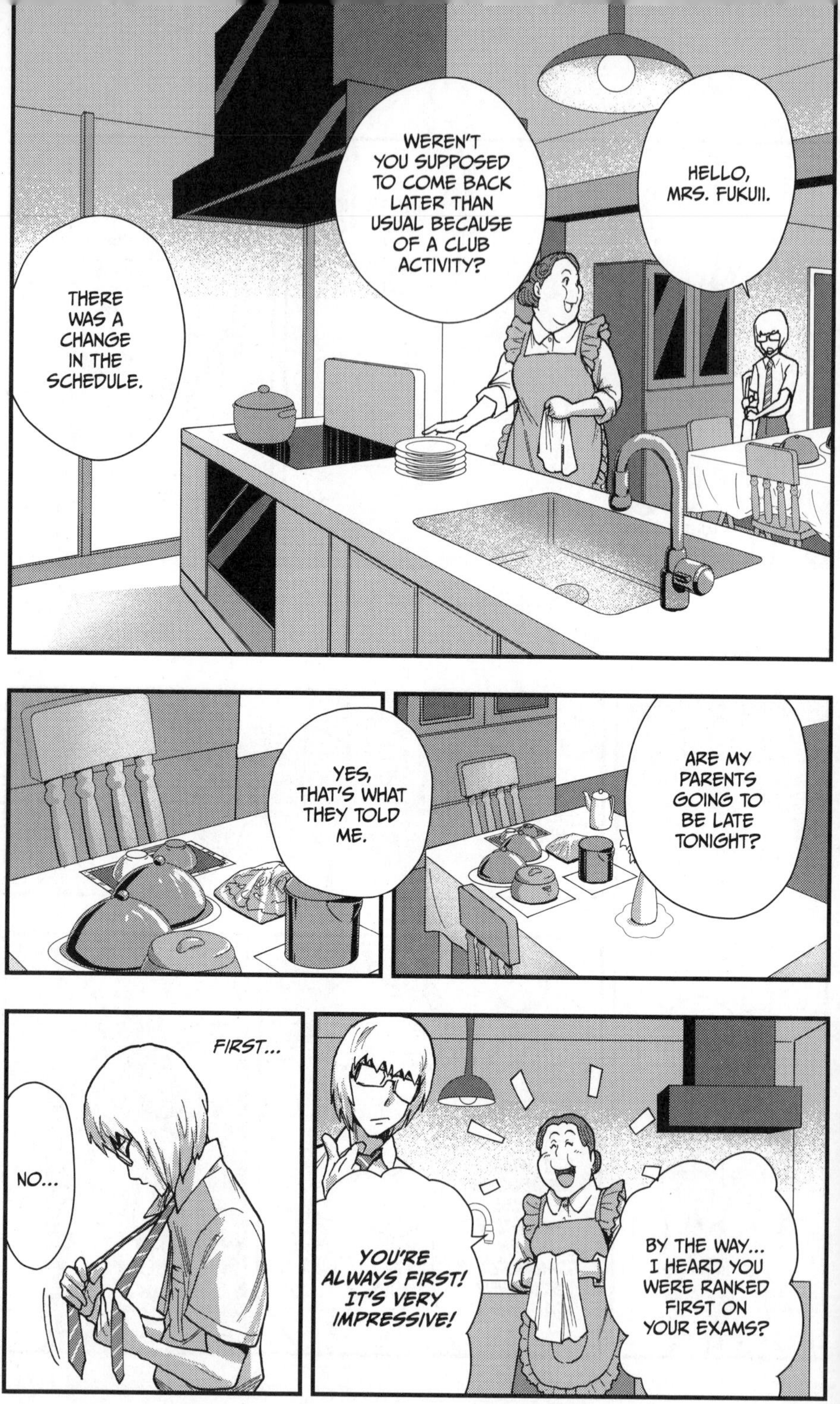
HELLO, MRS. FUKUII.
WEREN'T YOU SUPPOSED TO COME BACK LATER THAN USUAL BECAUSE OF A CLUB ACTIVITY?
THERE WAS A CHANGE IN THE SCHEDULE.
ARE MY PARENTS GOING TO BE LATE TONIGHT?
YES, THAT'S WHAT THEY TOLD ME.
BY THE WAY... I HEARD YOU WERE RANKED FIRST ON YOUR EXAMS?
YOU'RE ALWAYS FIRST! IT'S VERY IMPRESSIVE!
NO...
FIRST...

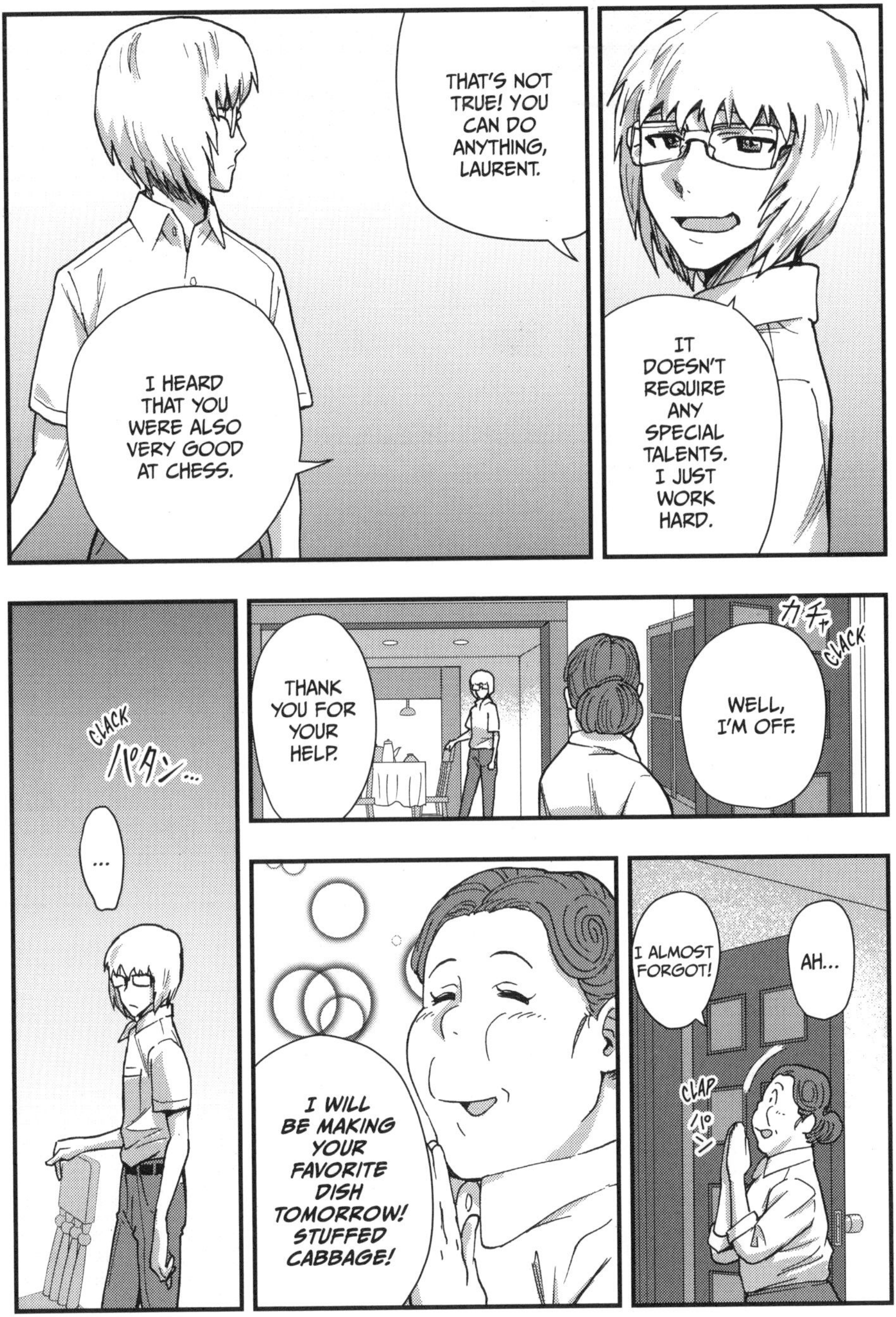
IT DOESN'T REQUIRE ANY SPECIAL TALENTS. I JUST WORK HARD.
THAT'S NOT TRUE! YOU CAN DO ANYTHING, LAURENT.
I HEARD THAT YOU WERE ALSO VERY GOOD AT CHESS.
カチャ
CLACK
WELL, I'M OFF.
THANK YOU FOR YOUR HELP.
AH...
I ALMOST FORGOT!
CLAP
パン
I WILL BE MAKING YOUR FAVORITE DISH TOMORROW! STUFFED CABBAGE!
CLACK
パタン...
...

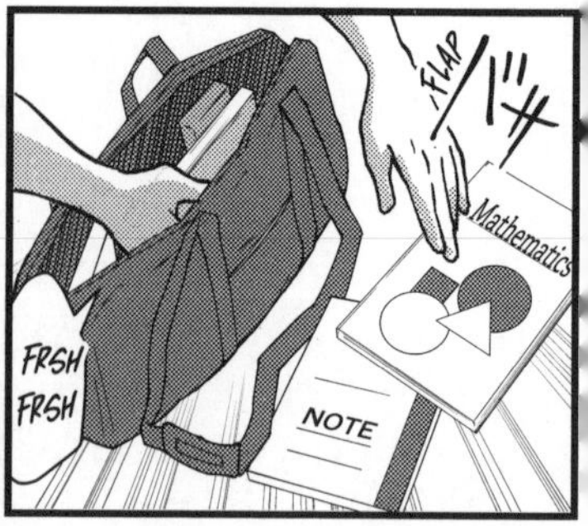
FLAP
バサ
Mathematics
FRSH
FRSH
NOTE

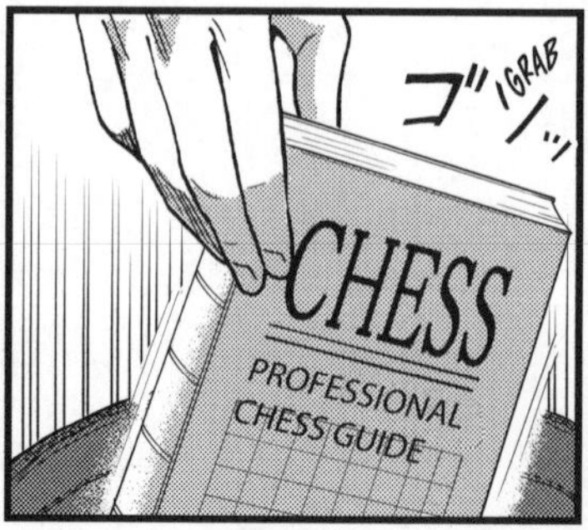
GRAB
ゴソッ
CHESS
PROFESSIONAL
CHESS GUIDE

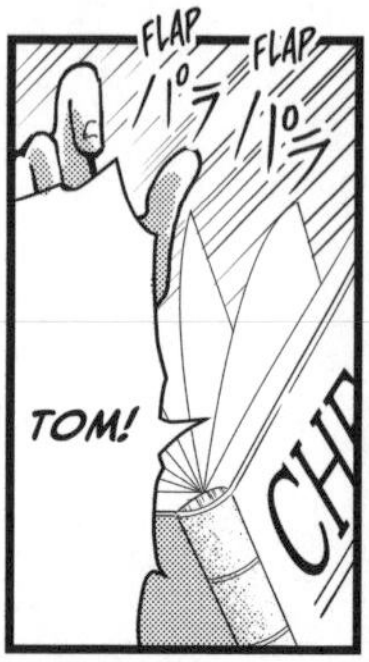
FLAP
パラ
FLAP
パラ
TOM!

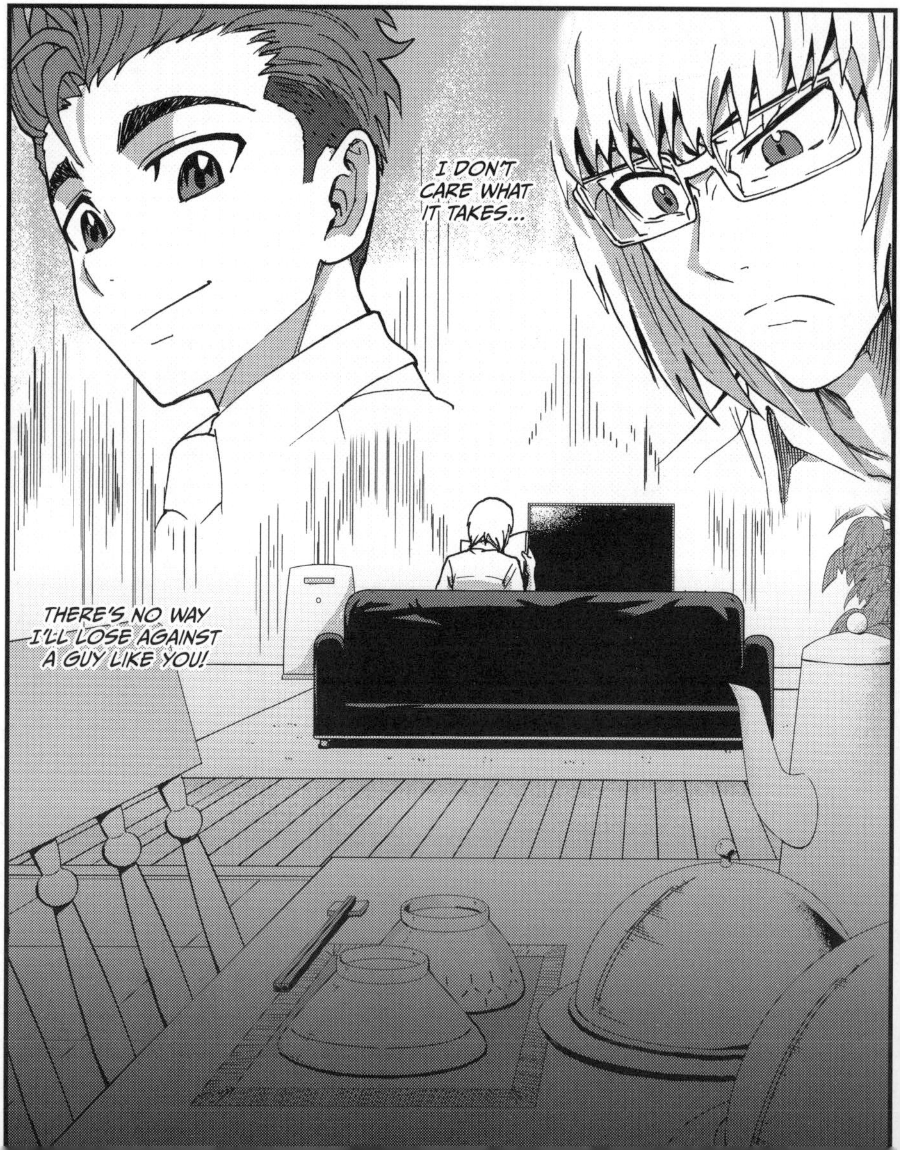
I DON'T CARE WHAT IT TAKES...
THERE'S NO WAY I'LL LOSE AGAINST A GUY LIKE YOU!

BLITZ

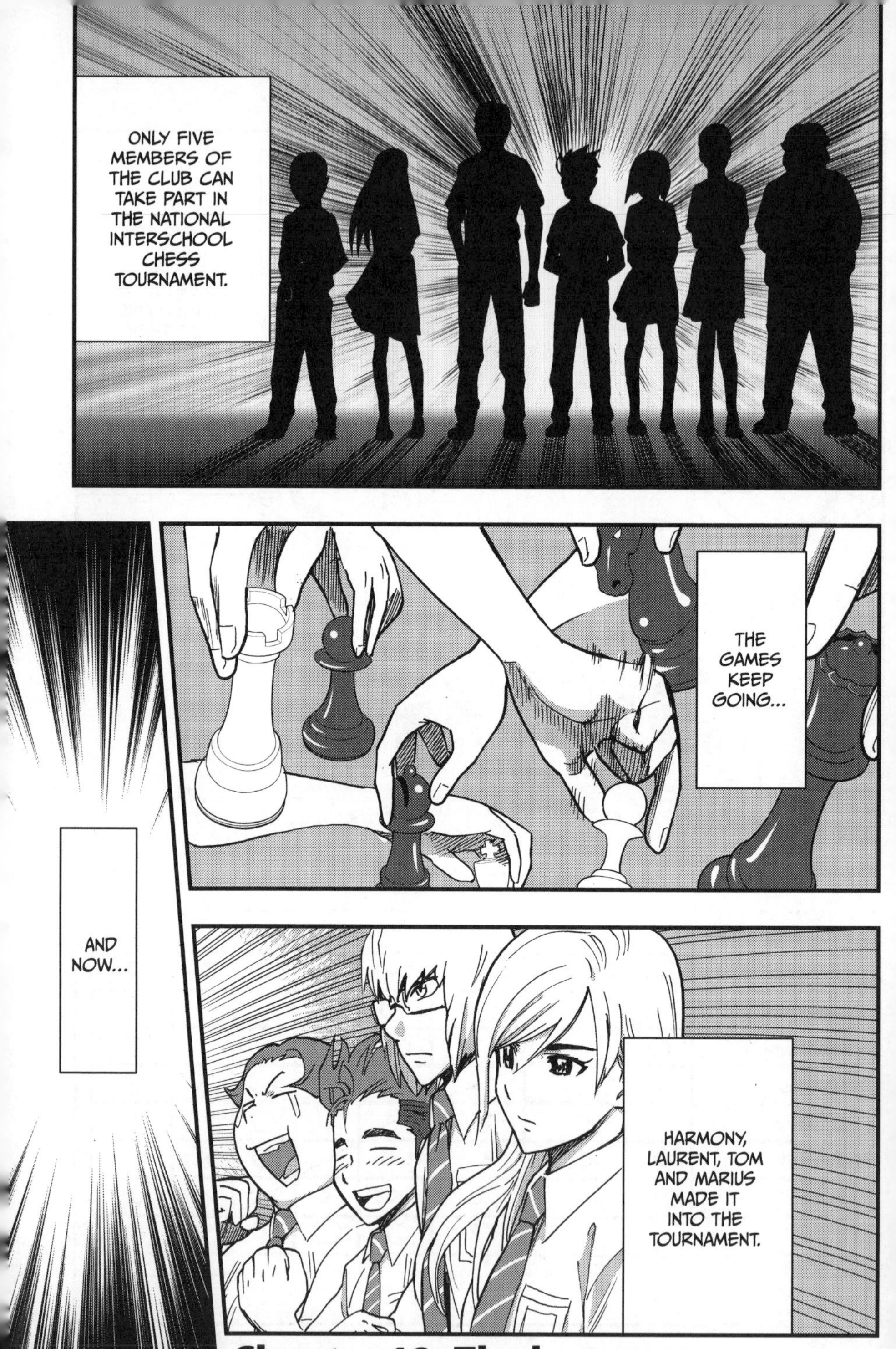
ONLY FIVE MEMBERS OF THE CLUB CAN TAKE PART IN THE NATIONAL INTERSCHOOL CHESS TOURNAMENT.
THE GAMES KEEP GOING...
AND NOW...
HARMONY, LAURENT, TOM AND MARIUS MADE IT INTO THE TOURNAMENT.

Chapter 12: The last spot

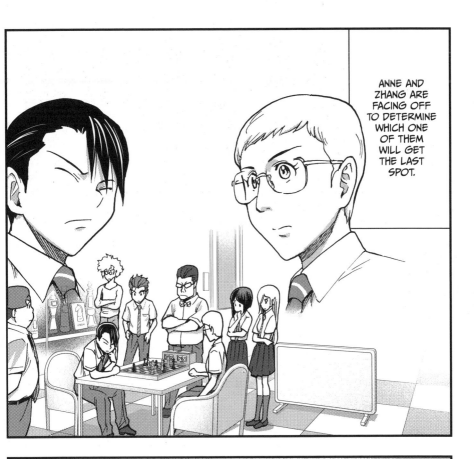

ANNE AND ZHANG ARE FACING OFF TO DETERMINE WHICH ONE OF THEM WILL GET THE LAST SPOT.

	Laurent	Harmony	Marius	Zhang	Anne	Saori	Tom	WINS
Laurent		X	O	O	O	O		4
Harmony	O		O	O	O	O		5
Marius	X	X		O	O	O	X	3
Zhang	X	X	X			O	X	1
Anne	X	X	X			O	X	1
Saori	X	X	X	X	X		X	0
Tom			O	O	O	O		4

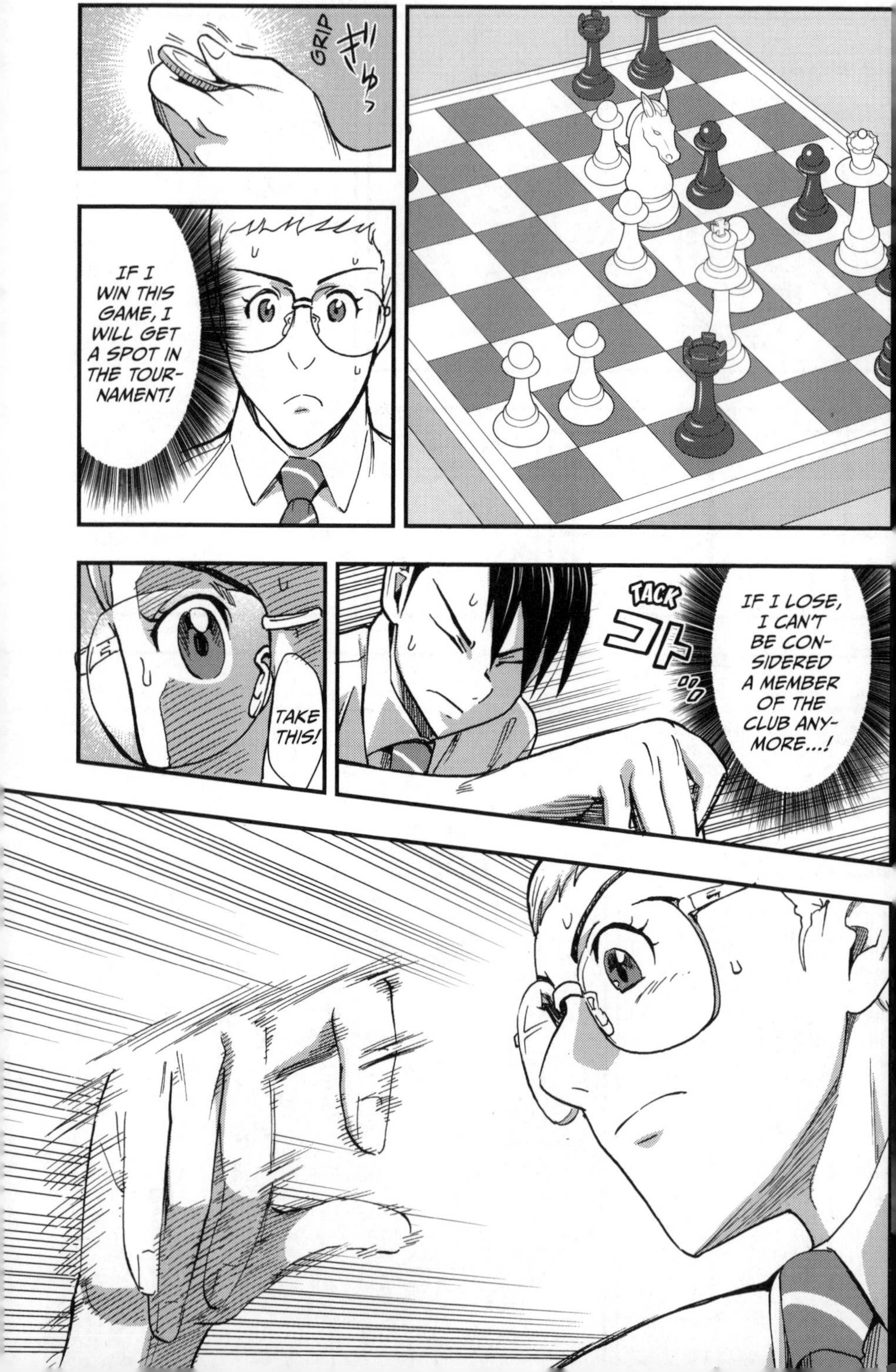
GRIP
ぎゅっ
IF I WIN THIS GAME, I WILL GET A SPOT IN THE TOURNAMENT!
IF I LOSE, I CAN'T BE CONSIDERED A MEMBER OF THE CLUB ANYMORE...!
TACK
コト
TAKE THIS!

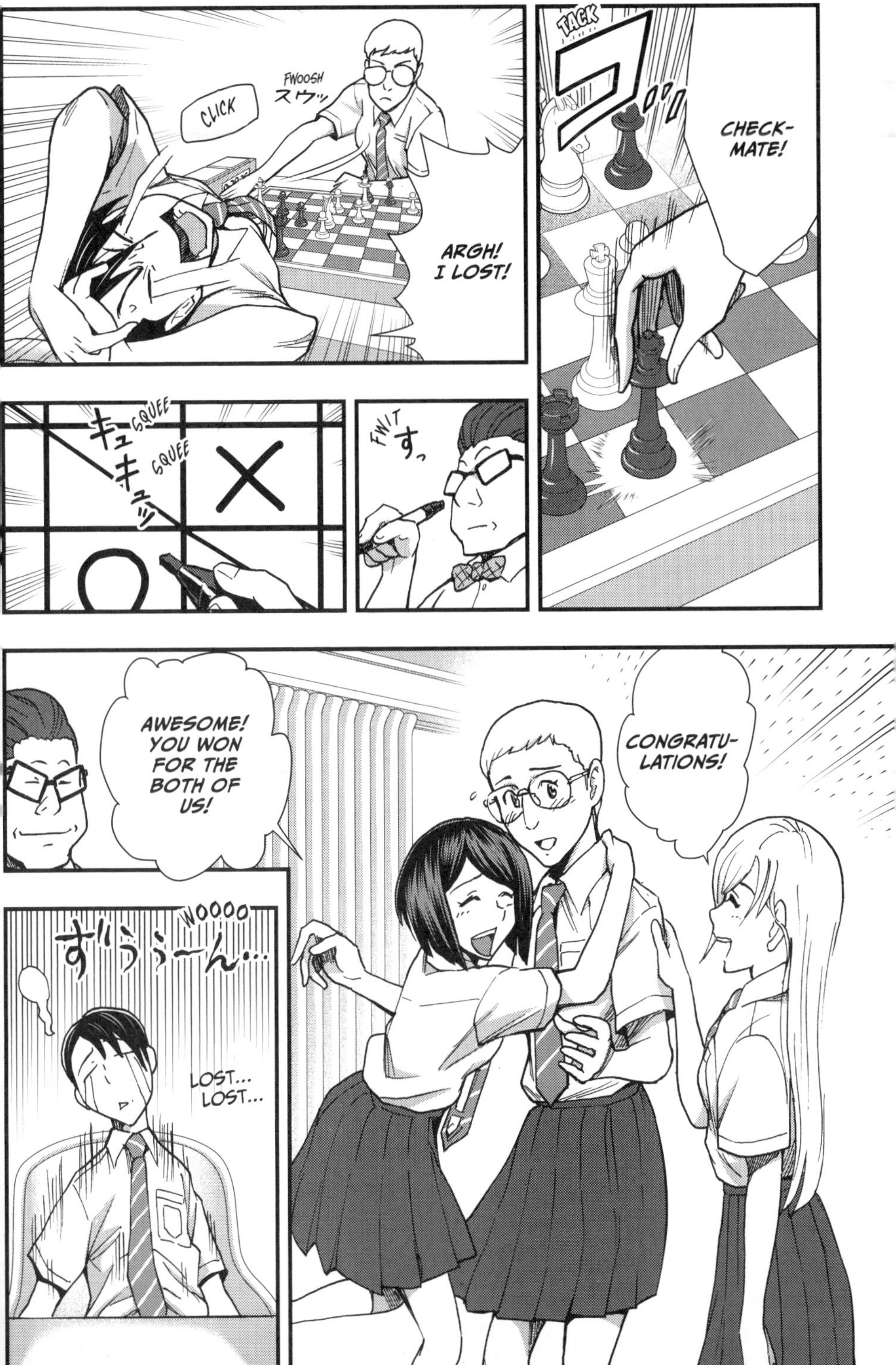
FWOOSH
スウッ
CLICK
ARGH! I LOST!
FWIT
すっ
キュ SQUEE
キュッ SQUEE
TACK
コッ
CHECK-MATE!
CONGRATU-LATIONS!
AWESOME! YOU WON FOR THE BOTH OF US!
WOOOO
ずぅぅ〜ん...
LOST... LOST...

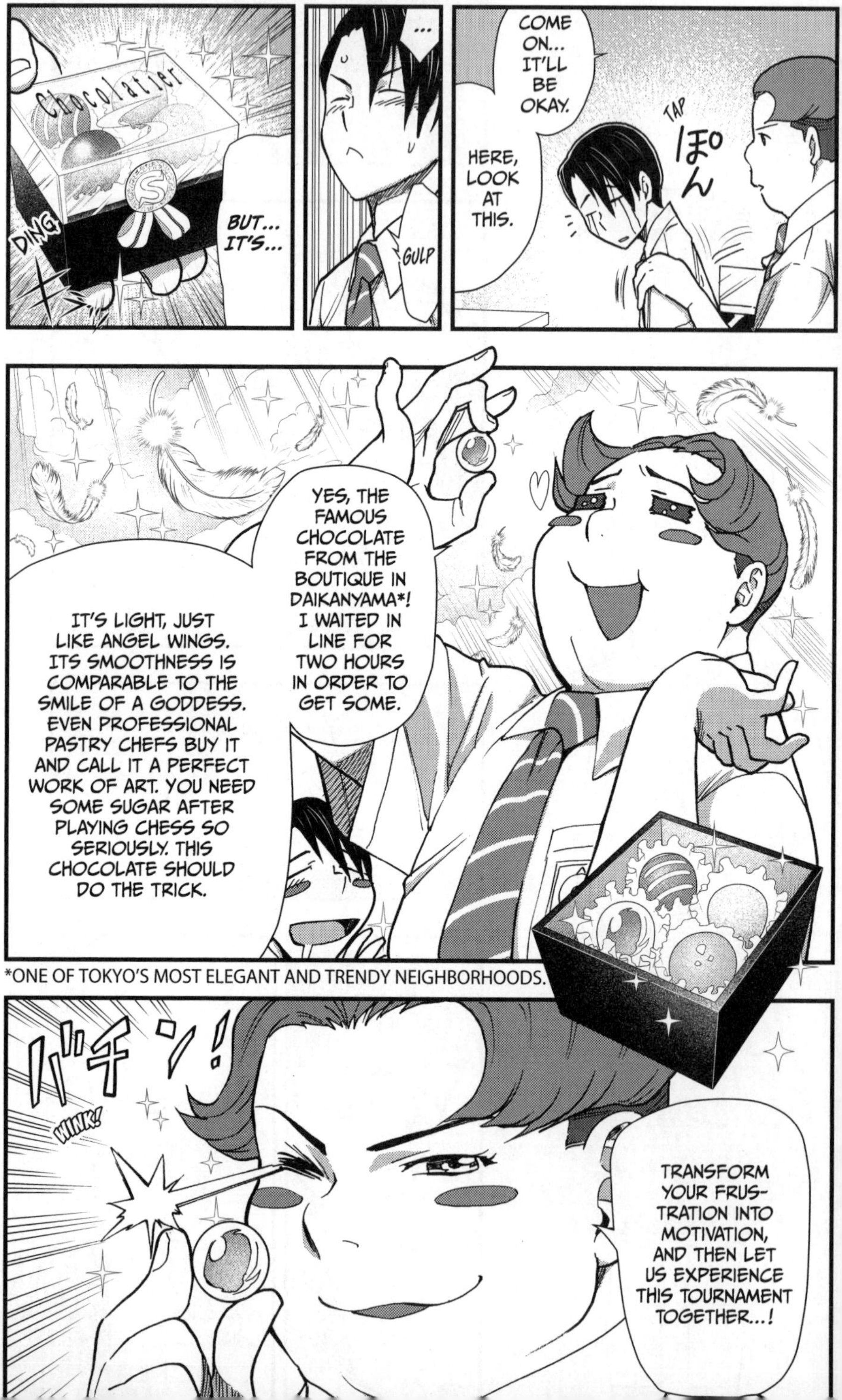
COME ON... IT'LL BE OKAY.
HERE, LOOK AT THIS.
TAP
ぽん
...
GULP
Chocolatier
BUT... IT'S...
DING
YES, THE FAMOUS CHOCOLATE FROM THE BOUTIQUE IN DAIKANYAMA*! I WAITED IN LINE FOR TWO HOURS IN ORDER TO GET SOME.
IT'S LIGHT, JUST LIKE ANGEL WINGS. ITS SMOOTHNESS IS COMPARABLE TO THE SMILE OF A GODDESS. EVEN PROFESSIONAL PASTRY CHEFS BUY IT AND CALL IT A PERFECT WORK OF ART. YOU NEED SOME SUGAR AFTER PLAYING CHESS SO SERIOUSLY. THIS CHOCOLATE SHOULD DO THE TRICK.
バチン!
WINK!
TRANSFORM YOUR FRUS-TRATION INTO MOTIVATION, AND THEN LET US EXPERIENCE THIS TOURNAMENT TOGETHER...!

*ONE OF TOKYO'S MOST ELEGANT AND TRENDY NEIGHBORHOODS.

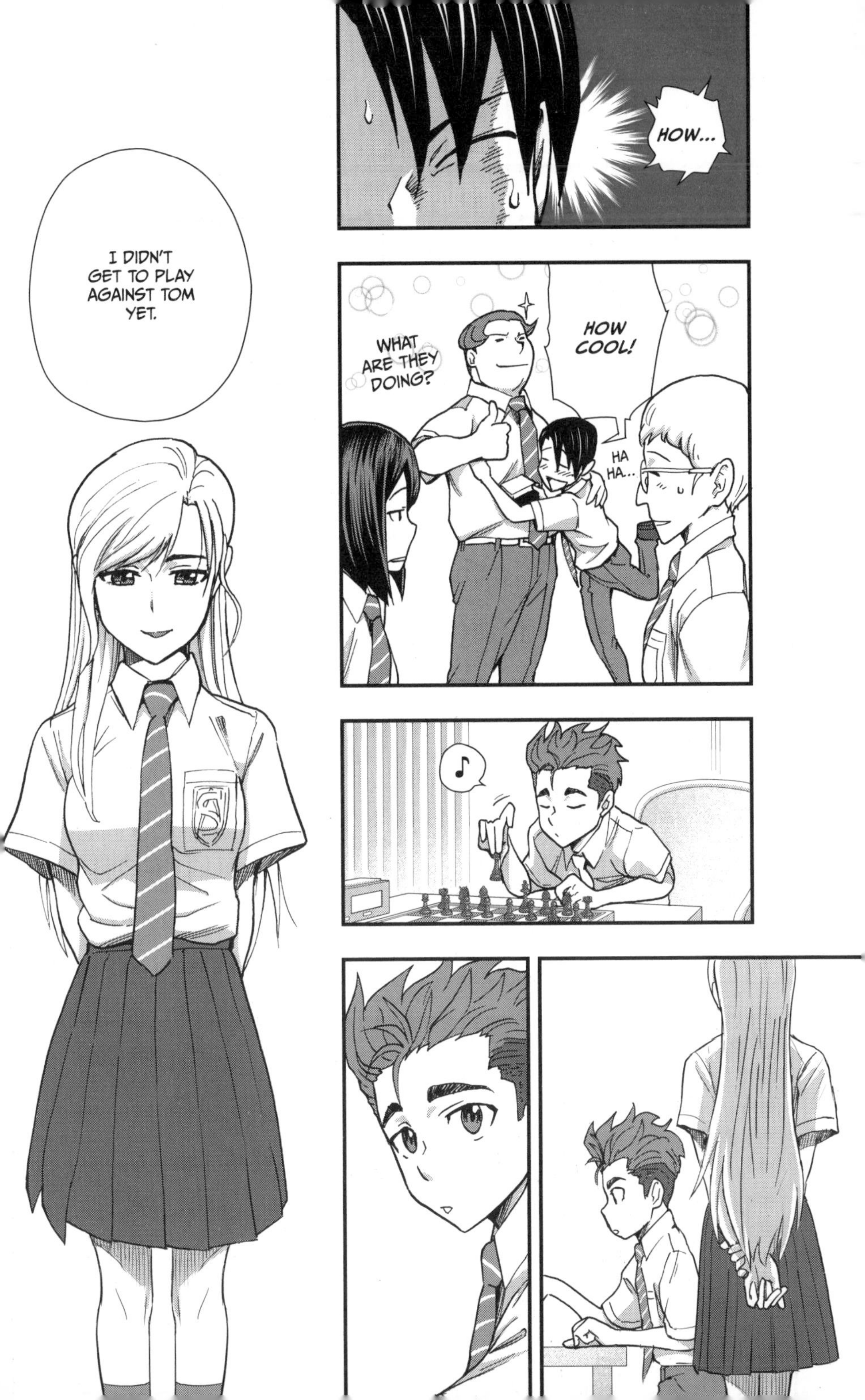
HOW...
HOW COOL!
WHAT ARE THEY DOING?
HA HA...
♪
I DIDN'T GET TO PLAY AGAINST TOM YET.

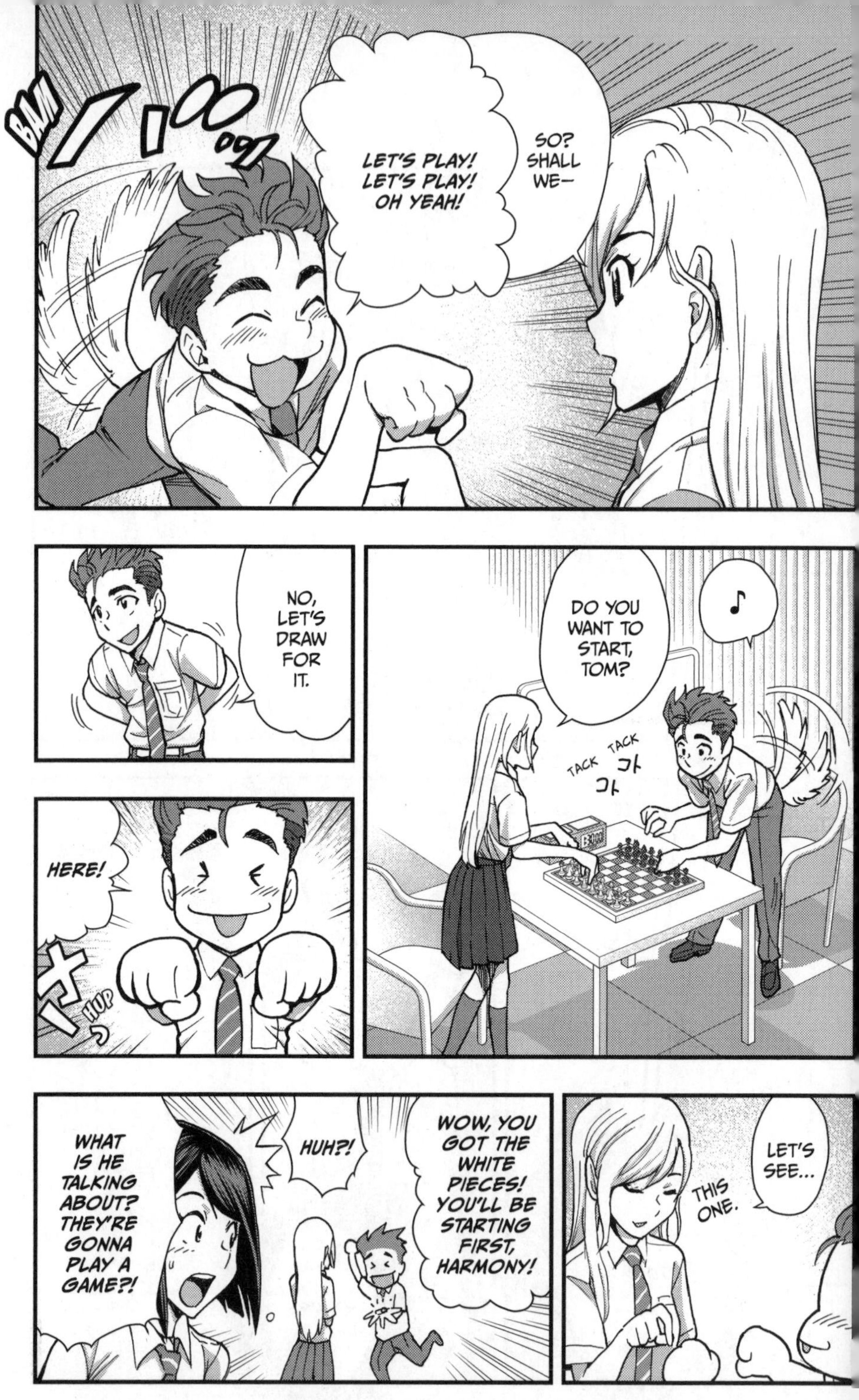
SO? SHALL WE—
LET'S PLAY! LET'S PLAY! OH YEAH!
BAM
DO YOU WANT TO START, TOM?
♪
TACK TACK
NO, LET'S DRAW FOR IT.
HERE!
HUP
LET'S SEE...
THIS ONE.
WOW, YOU GOT THE WHITE PIECES! YOU'LL BE STARTING FIRST, HARMONY!
HUH?!
WHAT IS HE TALKING ABOUT? THEY'RE GONNA PLAY A GAME?!

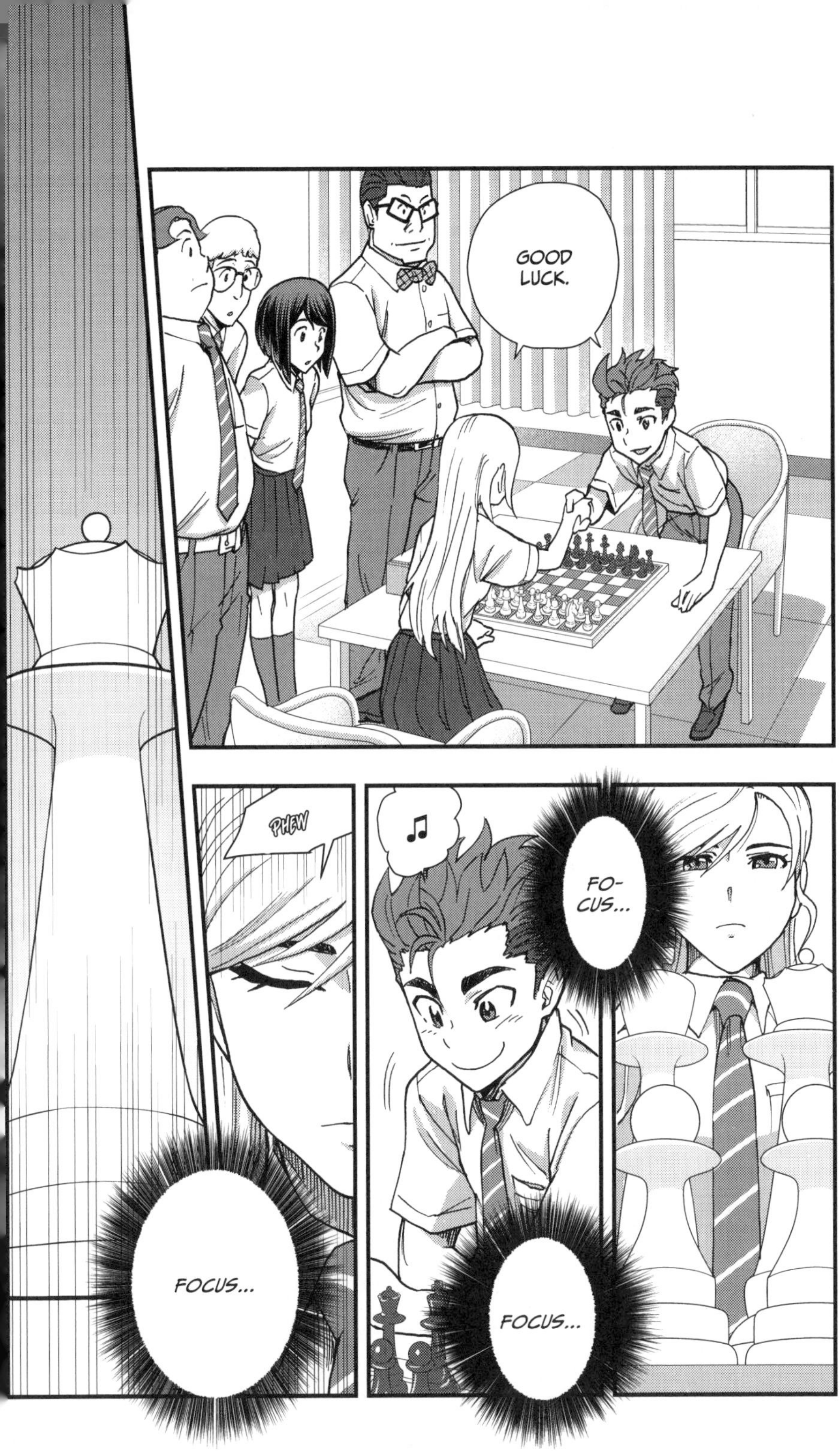
GOOD LUCK.
FO-CUS...
♪
FOCUS...
PHEW
FOCUS...

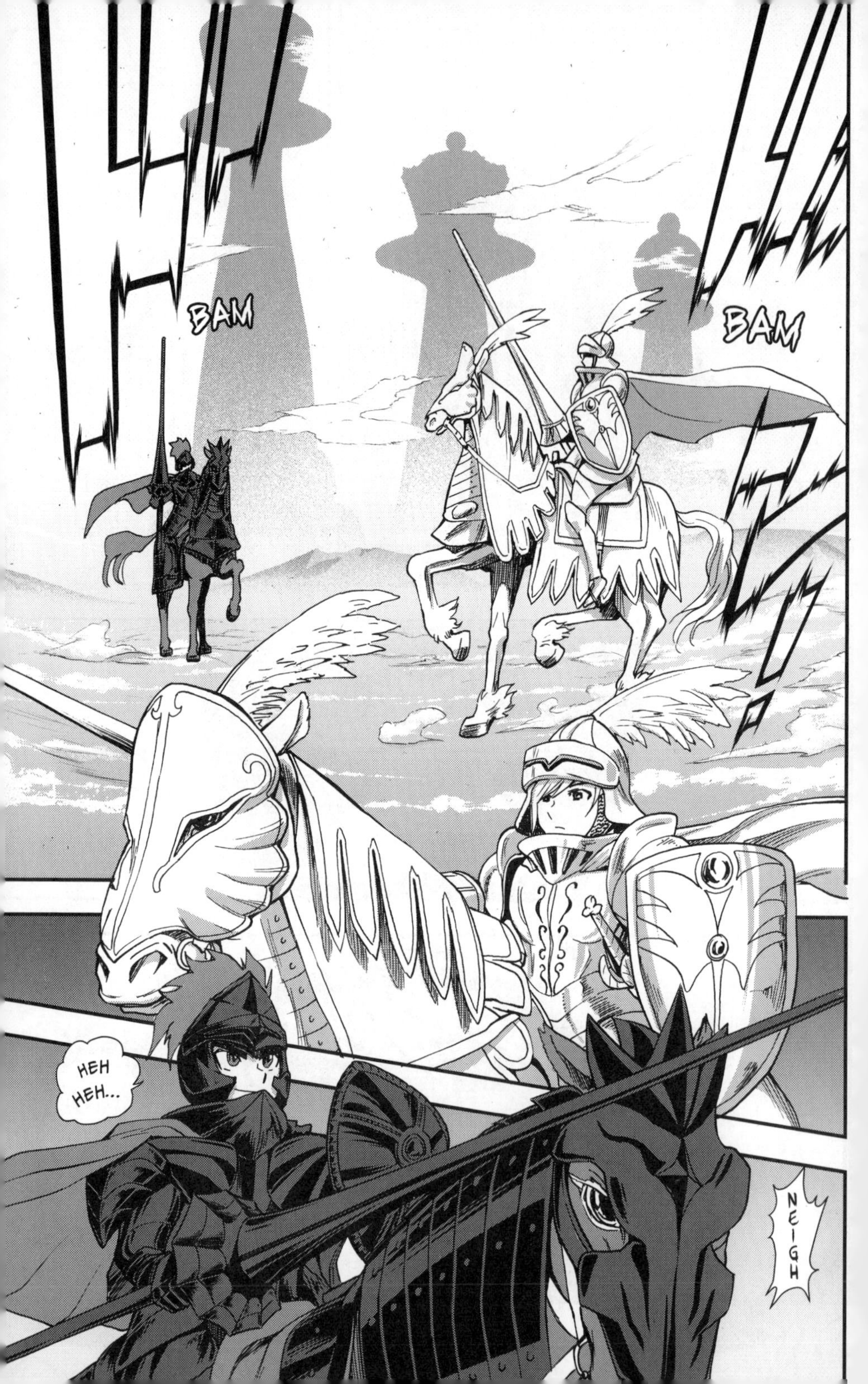
BAM
BAM
HEH HEH...
NEIGH

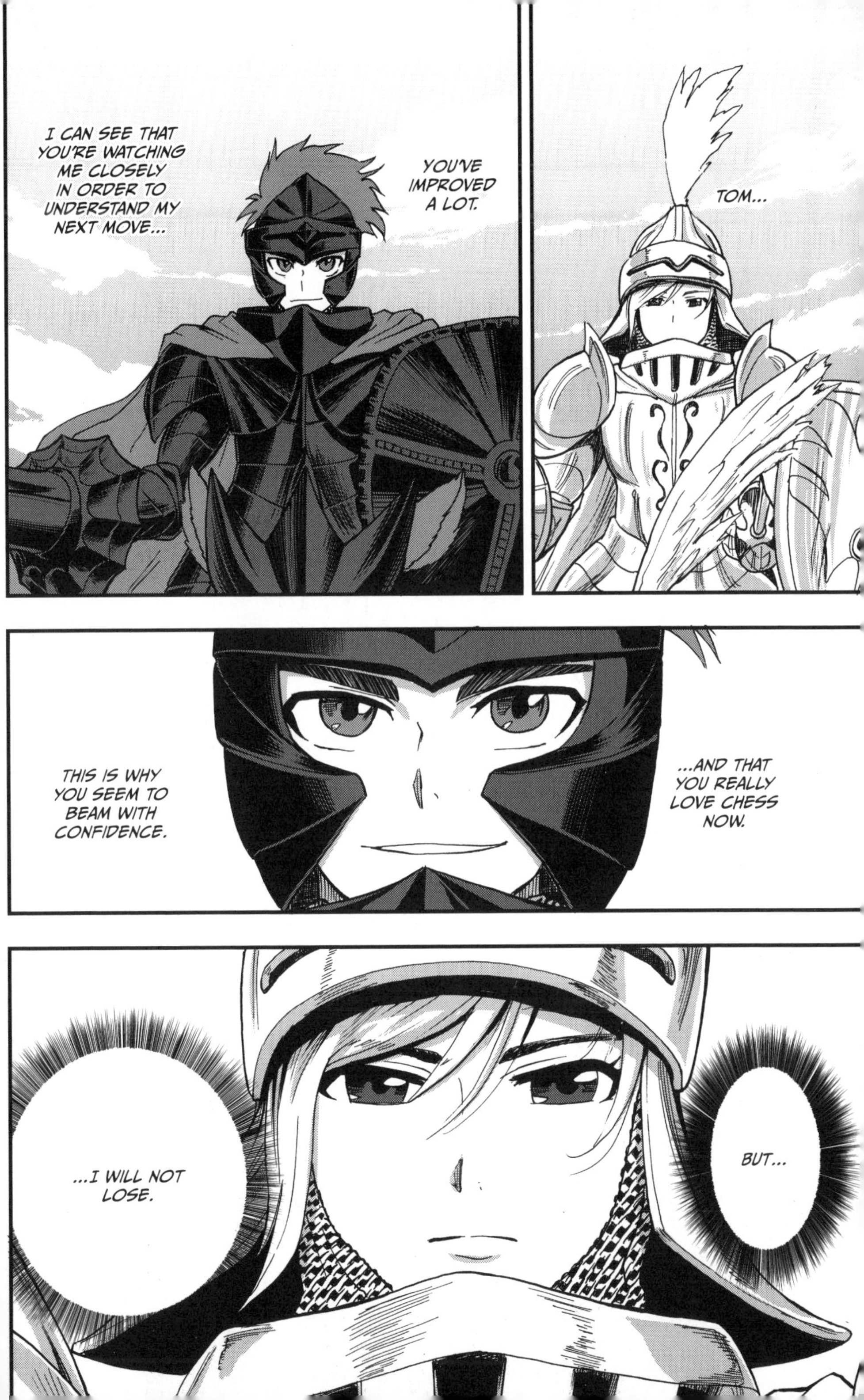
TOM...
YOU'VE IMPROVED A LOT.
I CAN SEE THAT YOU'RE WATCHING ME CLOSELY IN ORDER TO UNDERSTAND MY NEXT MOVE...
...AND THAT YOU REALLY LOVE CHESS NOW.
THIS IS WHY YOU SEEM TO BEAM WITH CONFIDENCE.
BUT...
...I WILL NOT LOSE.

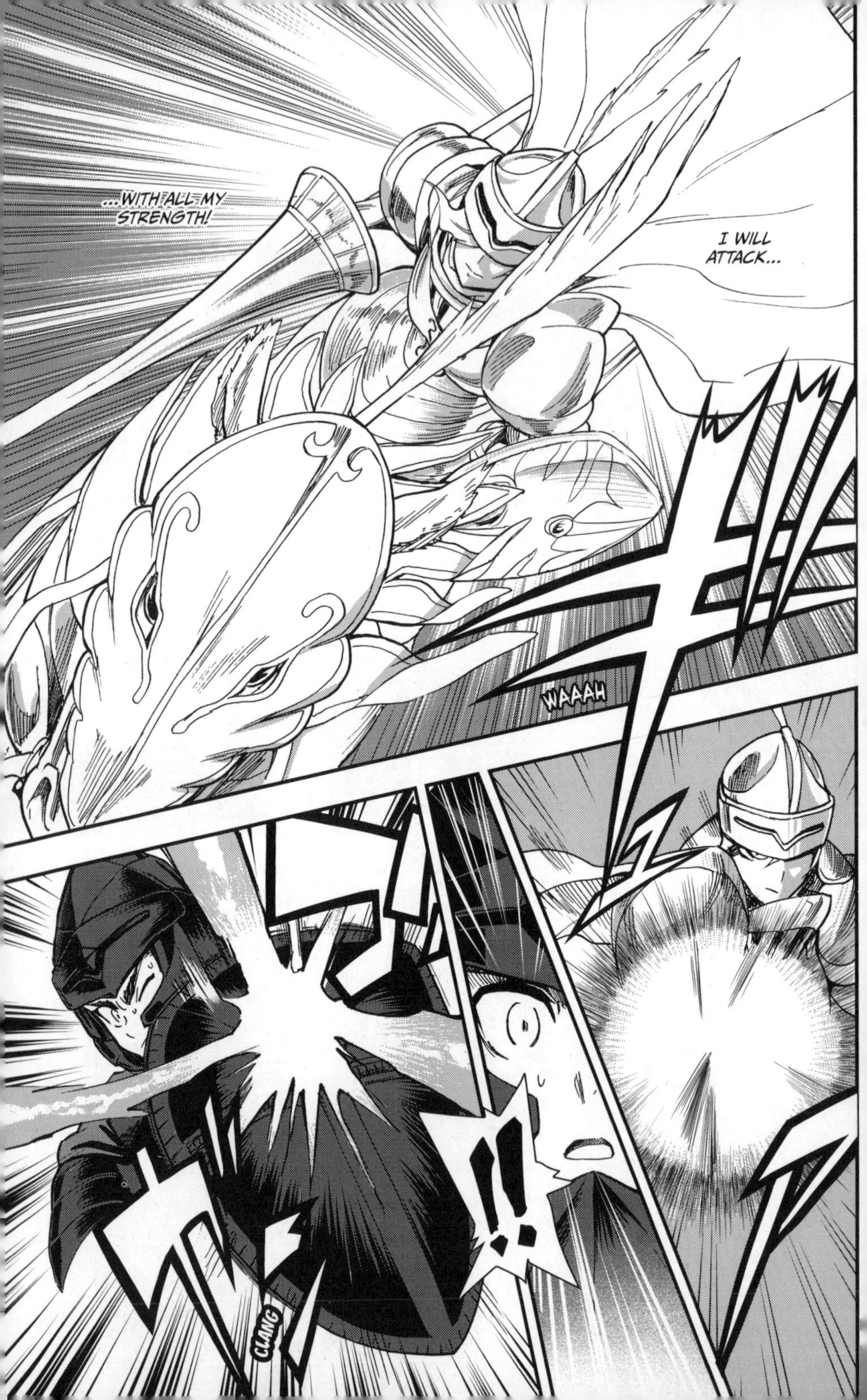
I WILL ATTACK...
...WITH ALL MY STRENGTH!
WAAAH
!!
CLANG

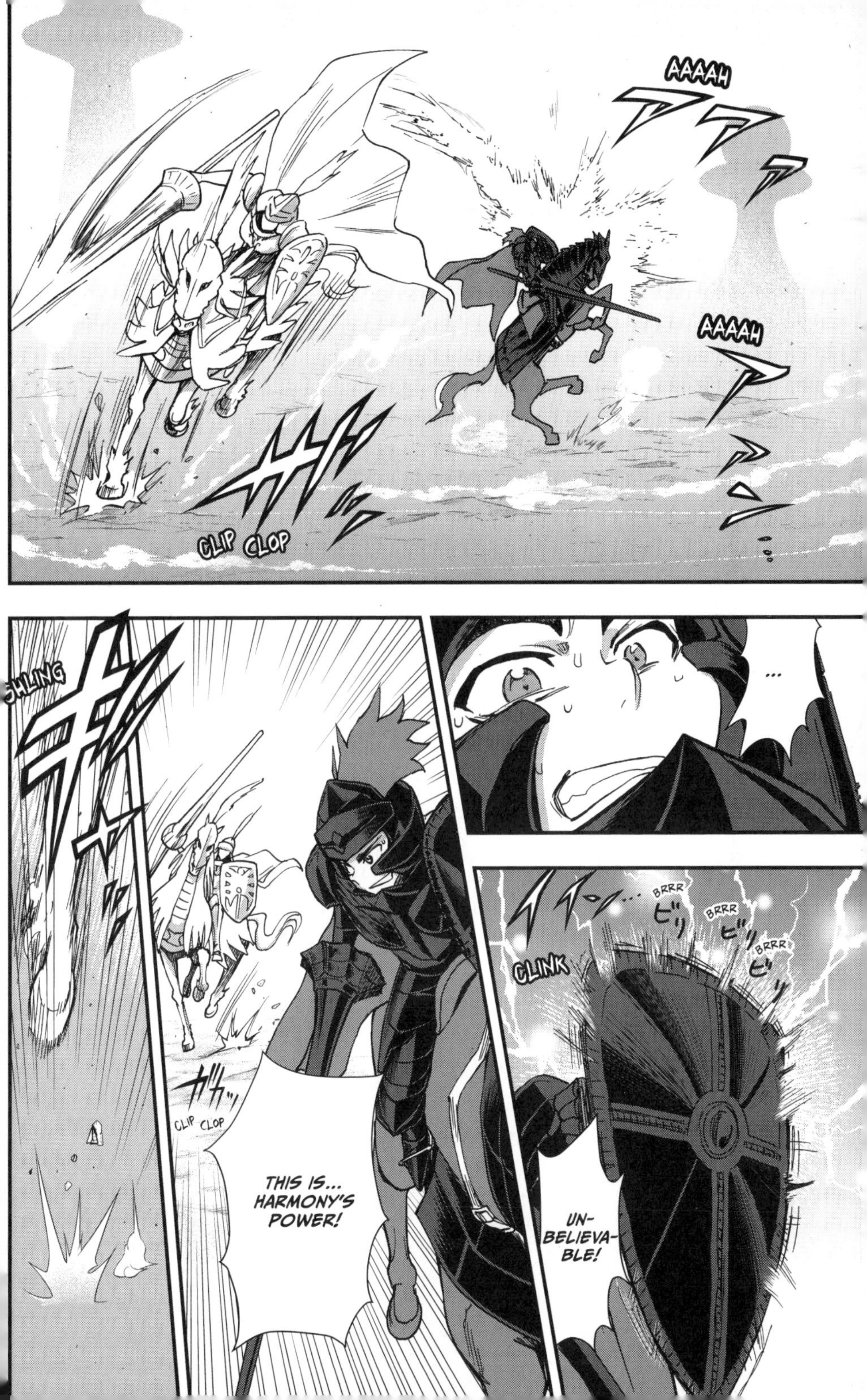
AAAAH
AAAAH
CLIP CLOP
...
CLINK
BRRR
BRRR
BRRR
UN-BELIEVA-BLE!
SHLING
CLIP CLOP
THIS IS... HARMONY'S POWER!

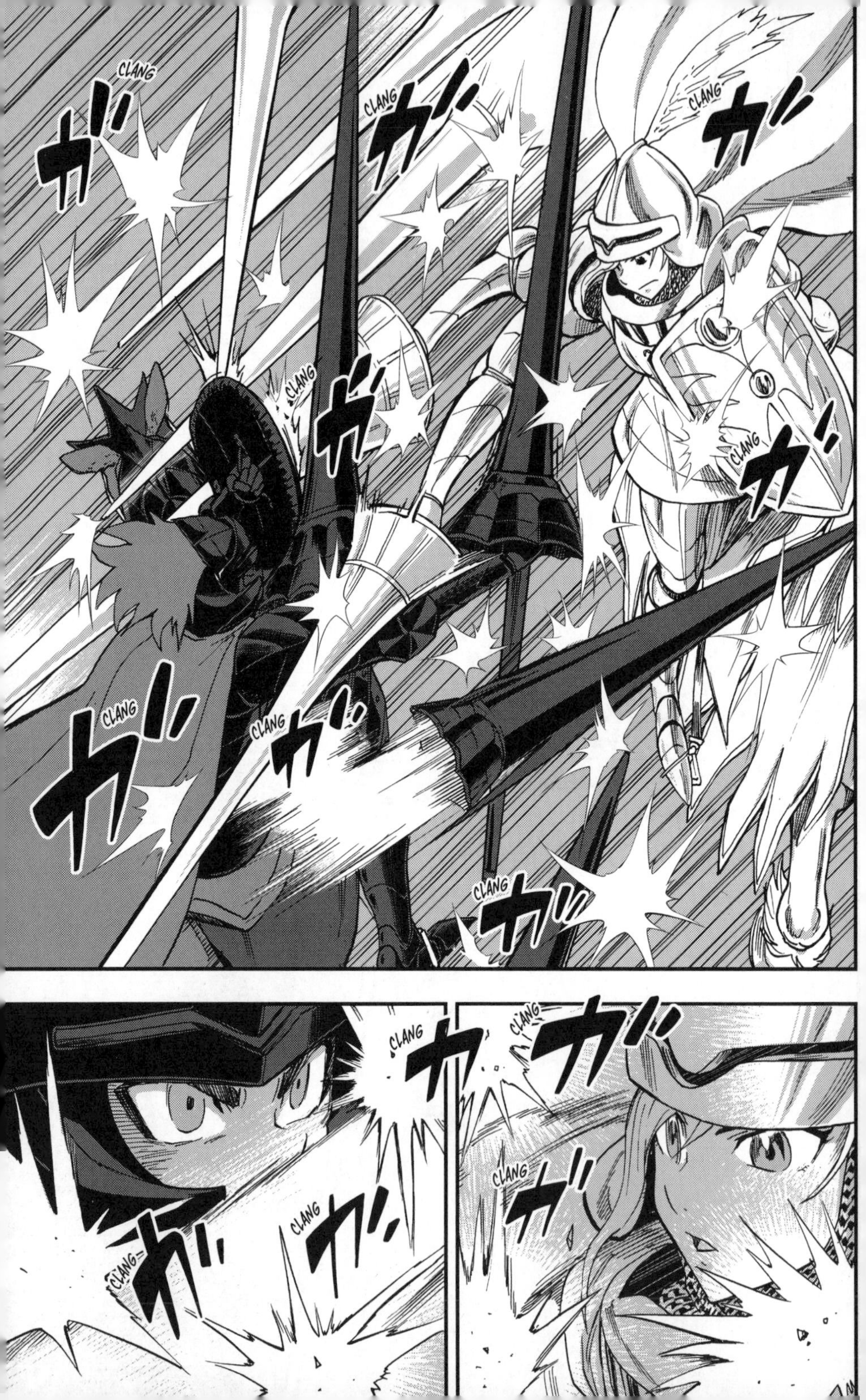
CLANG
CLANG
CLANG
CLANG
CLANG
CLANG
CLANG
CLANG
CLANG
CLANG
CLANG
CLANG
CLANG

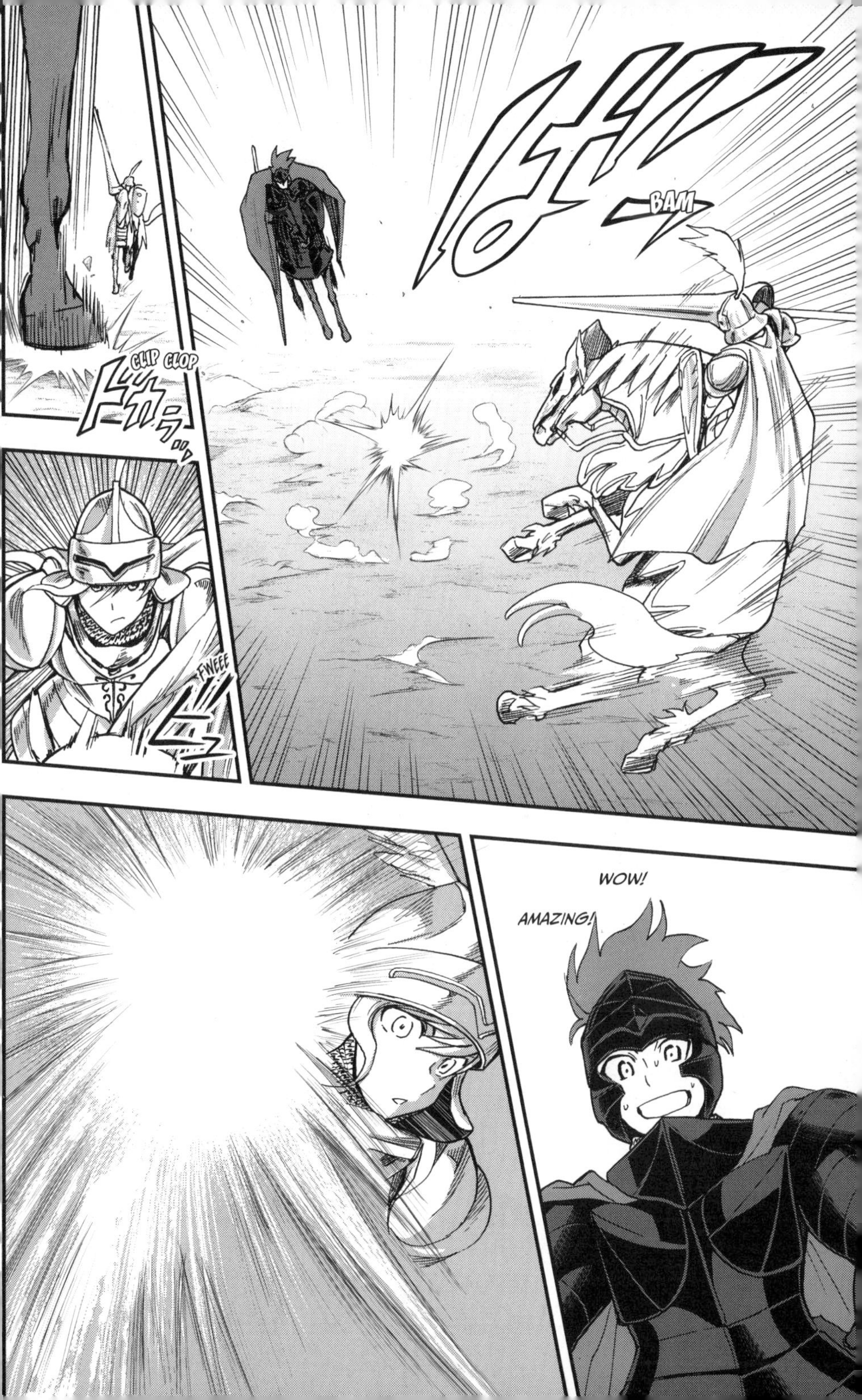
BAM
CLIP CLOP
FWEEE
WOW!
AMAZING!

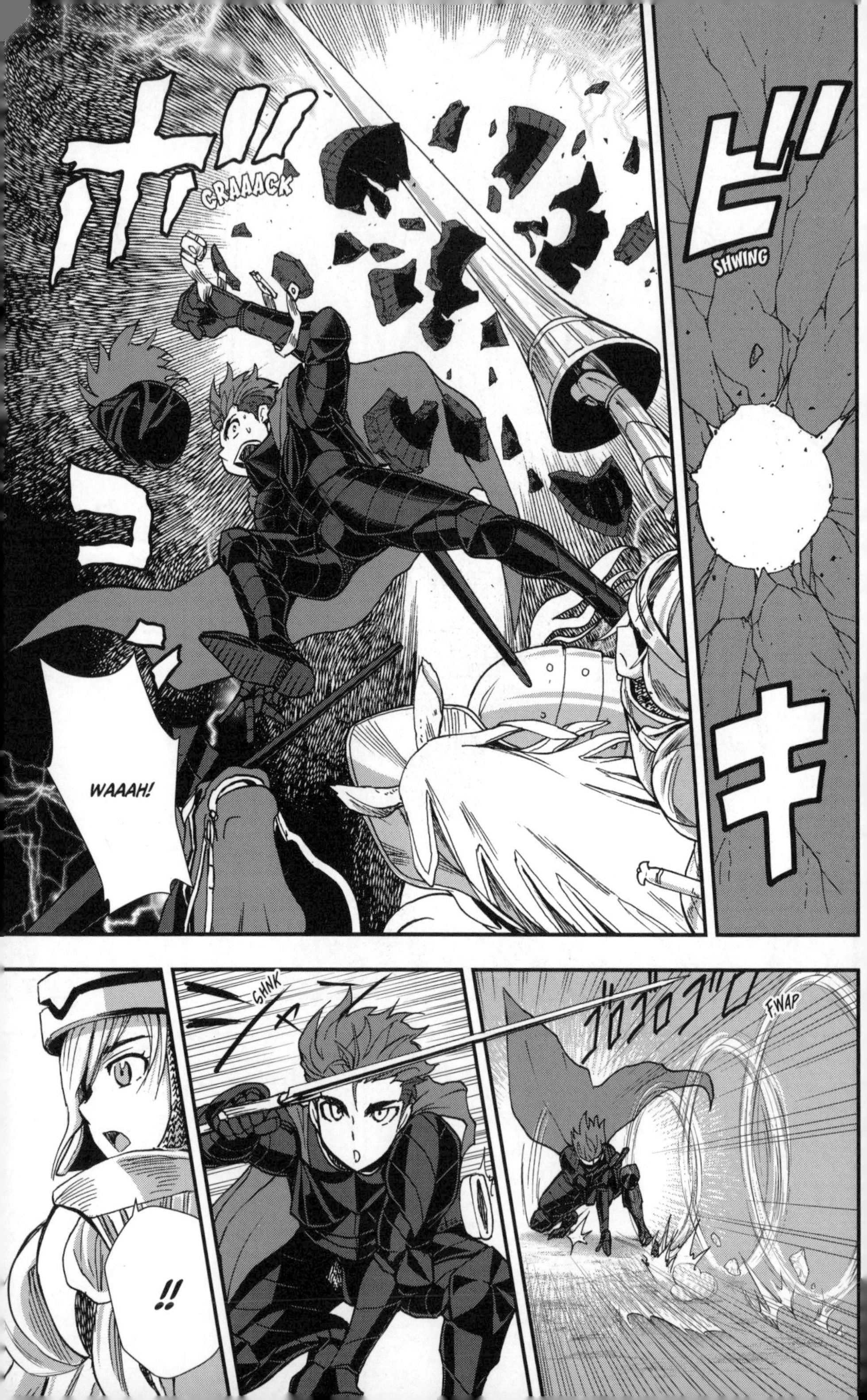
SHWING
CRAAACK
WAAAH!
FWAP
SHNK
!!

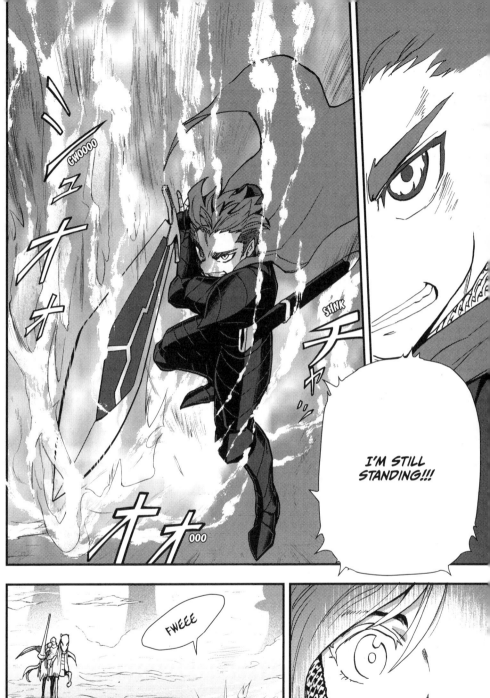

GWOOOO

SHNK

I'M STILL STANDING!!!

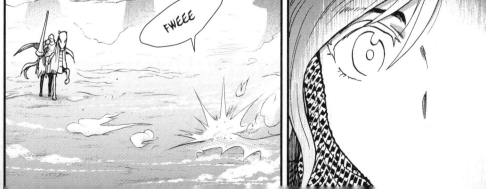

FWEEE

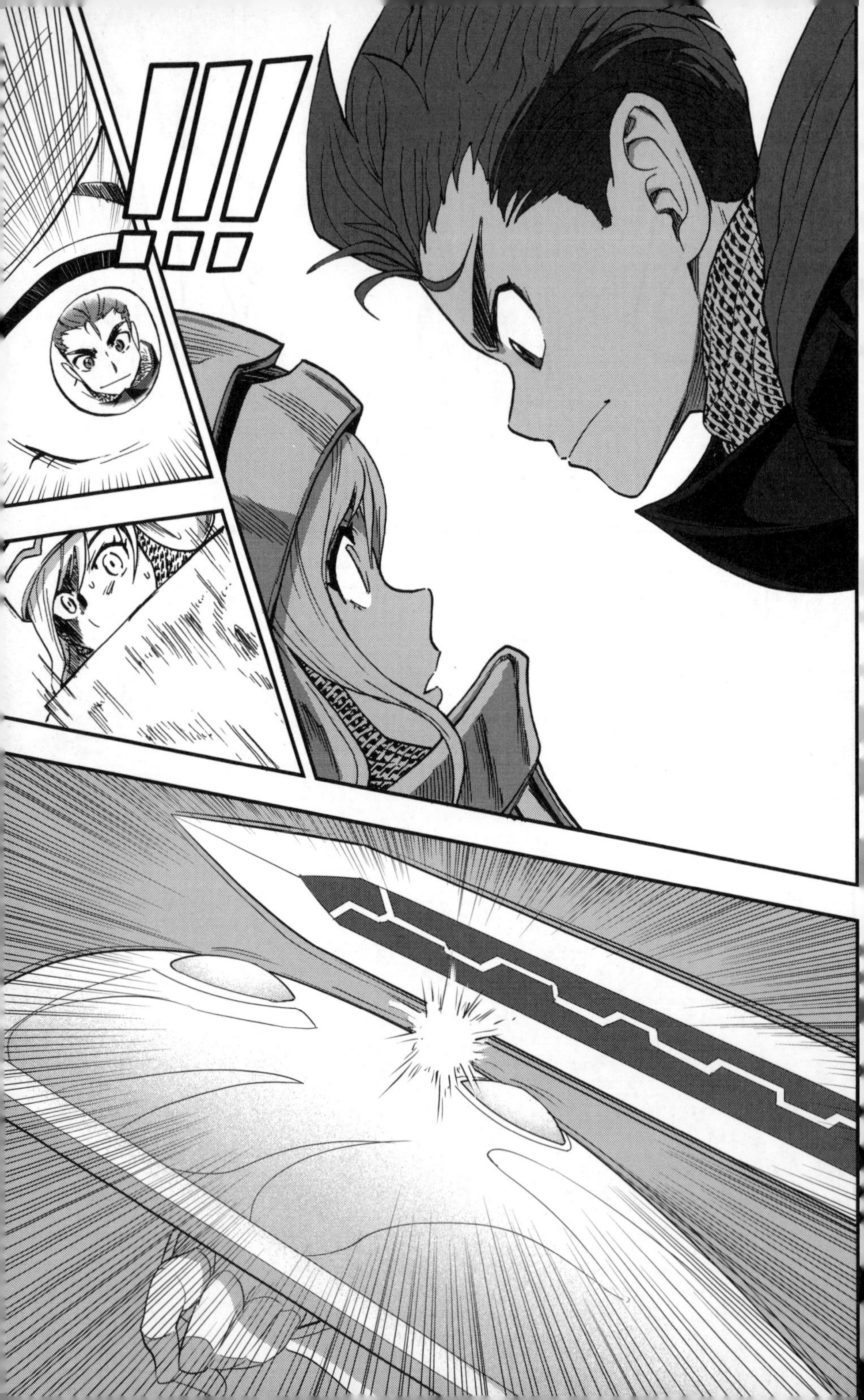
!!!

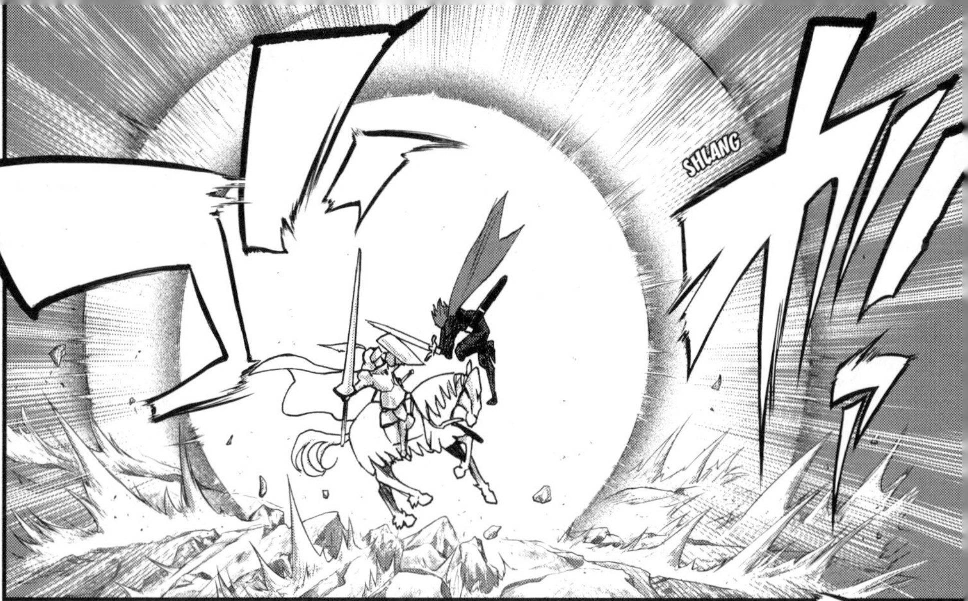
SHLANG
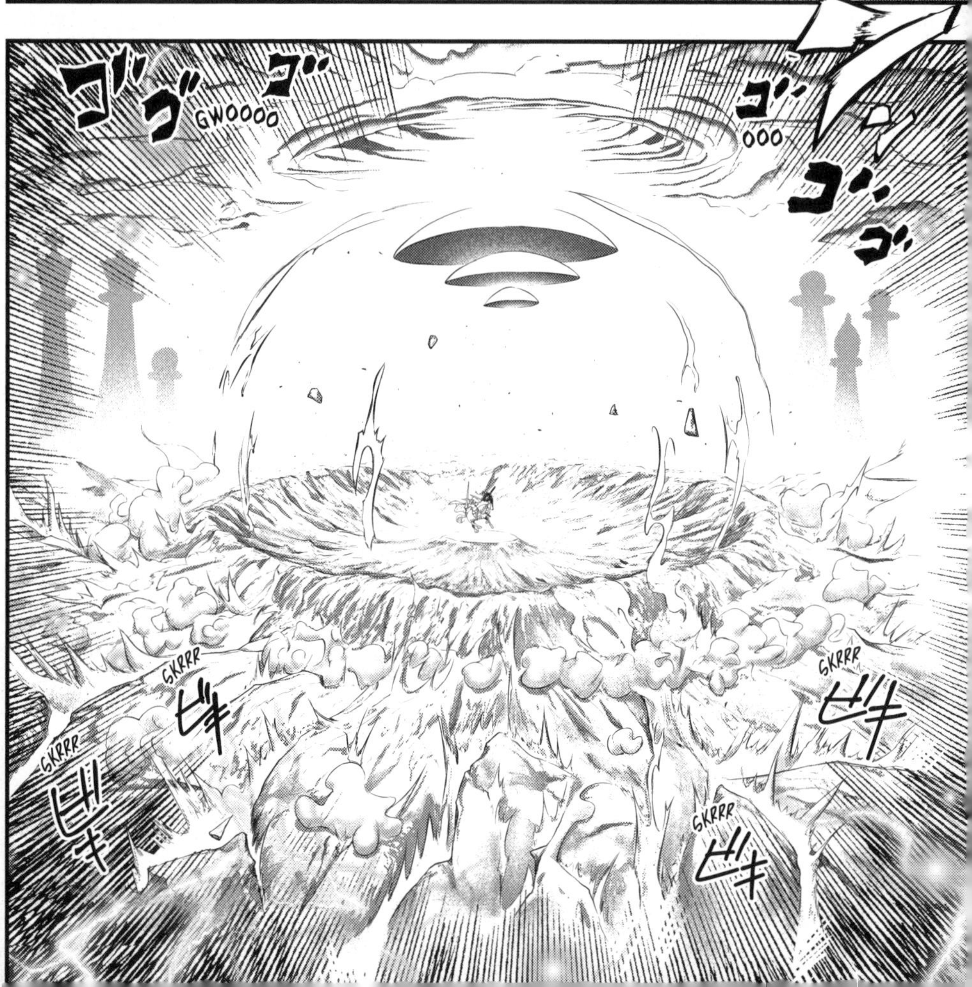
OOO
GWOOOO
SKRRR
SKRRR
SKRRR
SKRRR

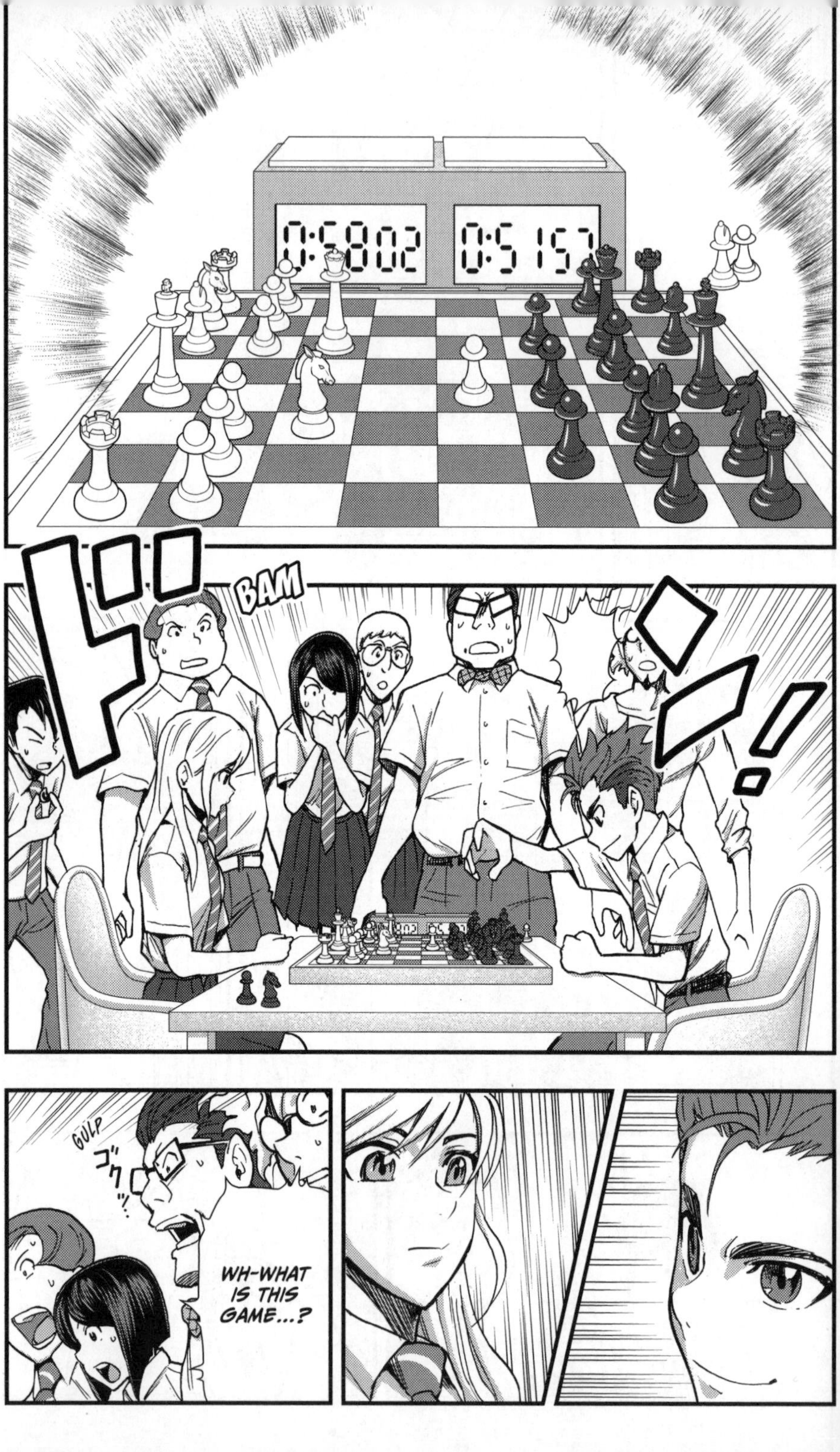
BAM
GULP
ゴクッ!
WH-WHAT IS THIS GAME...?

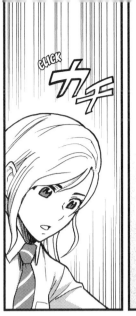

CLICK
カチ

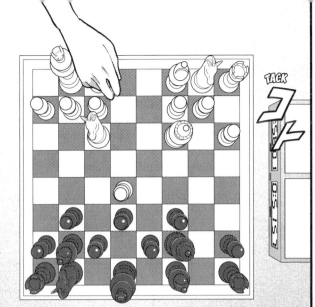

TACK
コト

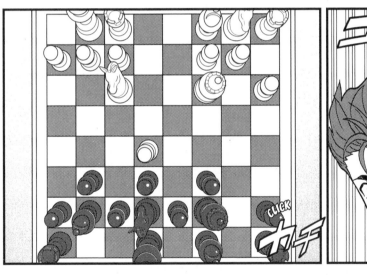

CLICK
カチ

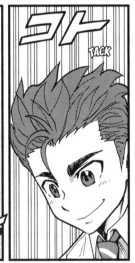

コト
TACK

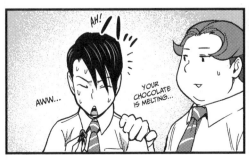

AH!

AWW...

YOUR
CHOCOLATE
IS MELTING...

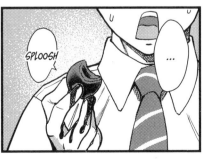

SPLOOSH

...

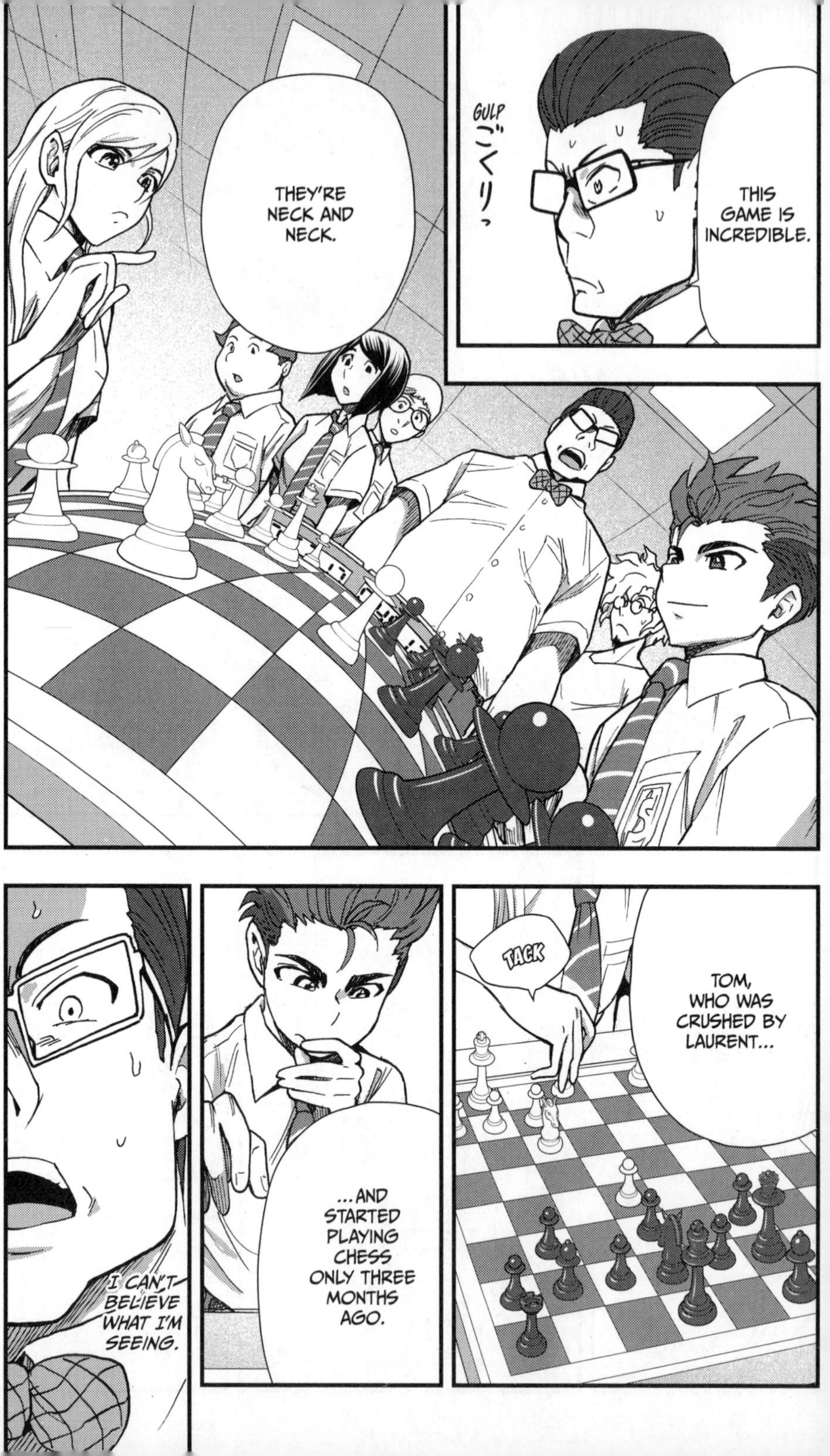
GULP
ごくりっ
THIS GAME IS INCREDIBLE.
THEY'RE NECK AND NECK.
TACK
TOM, WHO WAS CRUSHED BY LAURENT...
...AND STARTED PLAYING CHESS ONLY THREE MONTHS AGO.
I CAN'T BELIEVE WHAT I'M SEEING.

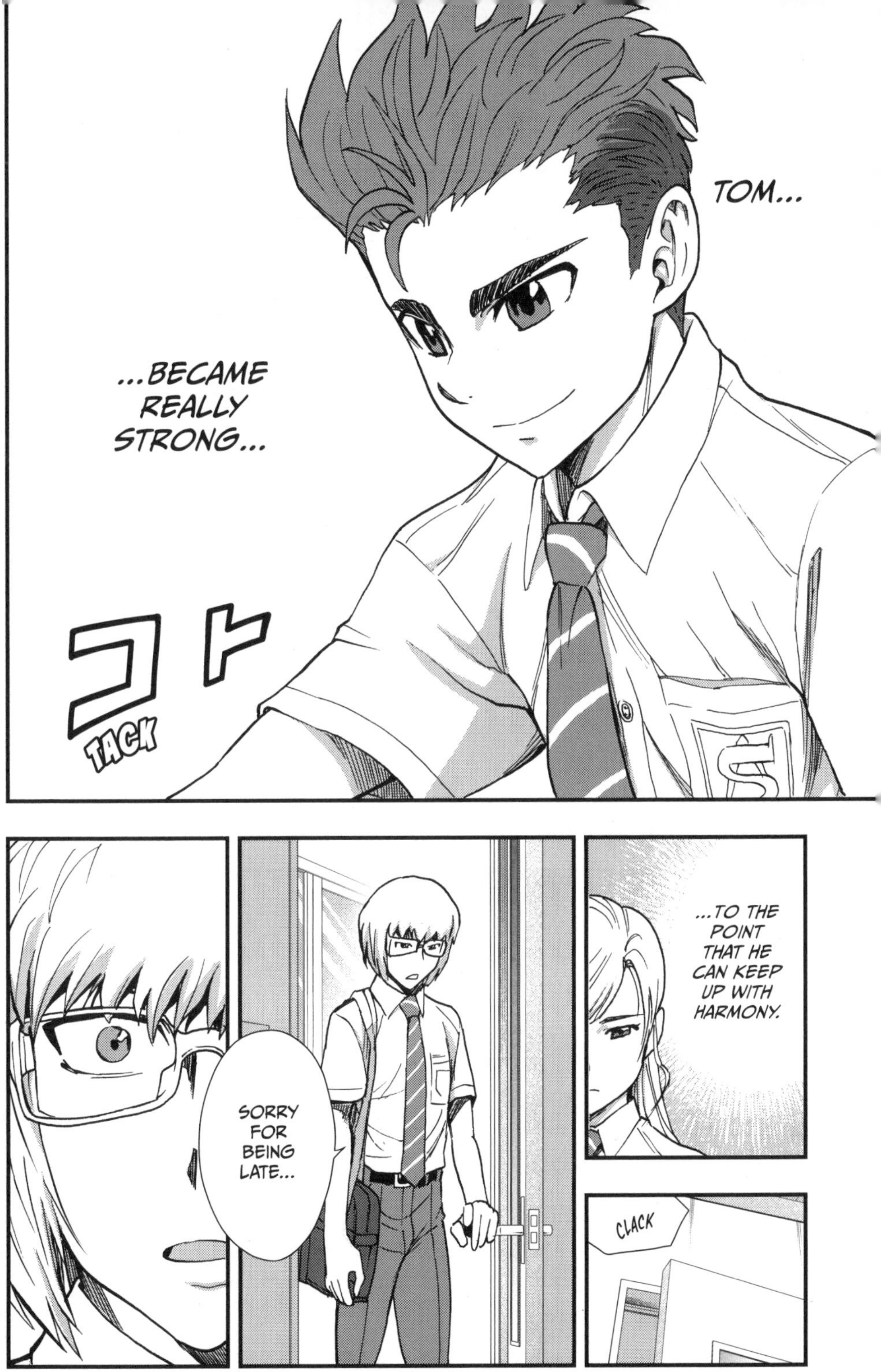
TOM...
...BECAME REALLY STRONG...
コト
TACK
...TO THE POINT THAT HE CAN KEEP UP WITH HARMONY.
CLACK
SORRY FOR BEING LATE...

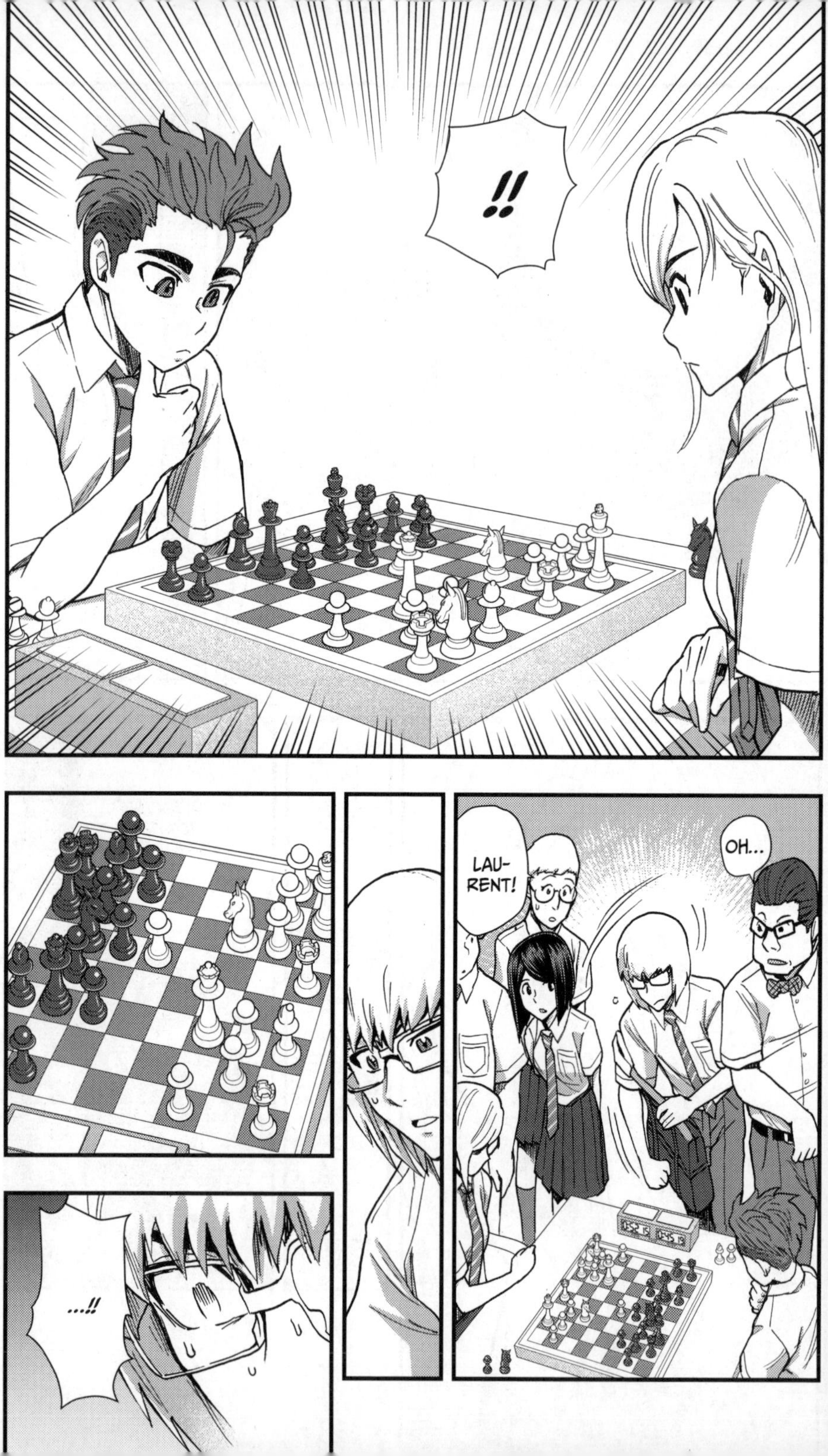
!!
OH...
LAU-RENT!
...!!

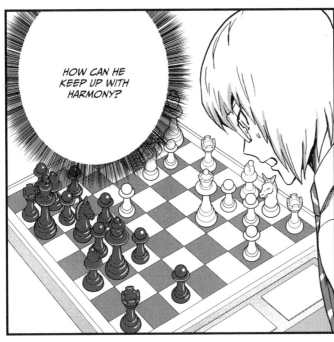

HOW CAN HE KEEP UP WITH HARMONY?

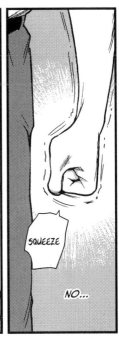

SQUEEZE

NO...

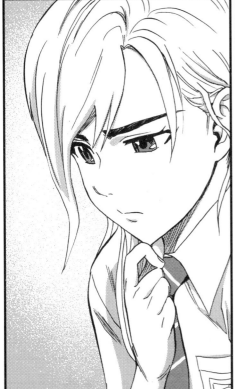

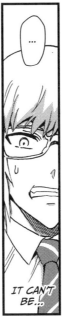

...

IT CAN'T BE...

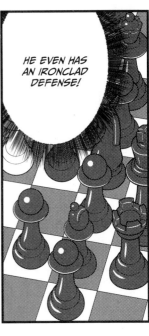

HE EVEN HAS AN IRONCLAD DEFENSE!

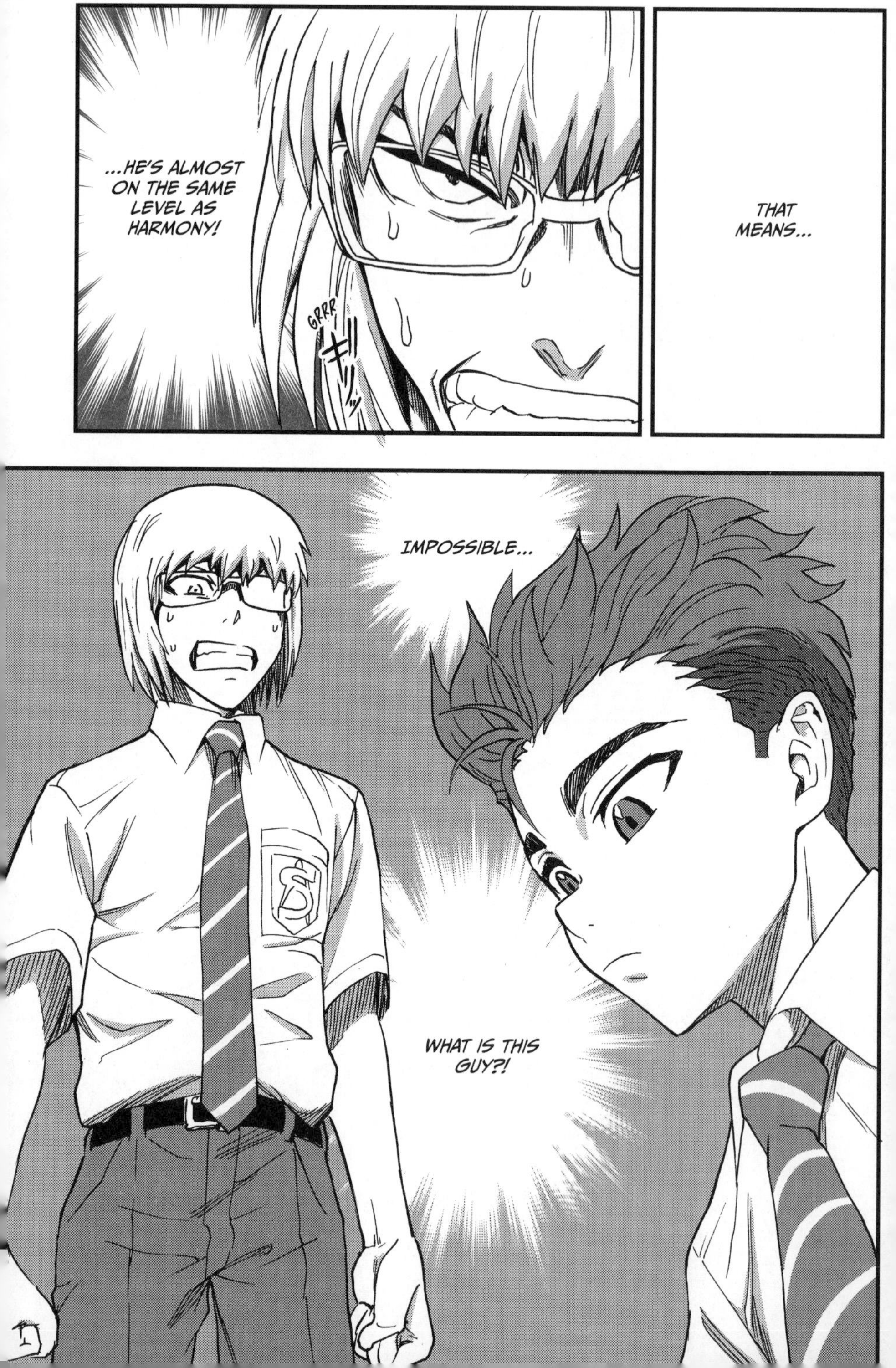
THAT MEANS...
...HE'S ALMOST ON THE SAME LEVEL AS HARMONY!
GRRR
IMPOSSIBLE...
WHAT IS THIS GUY?!

BLITZ

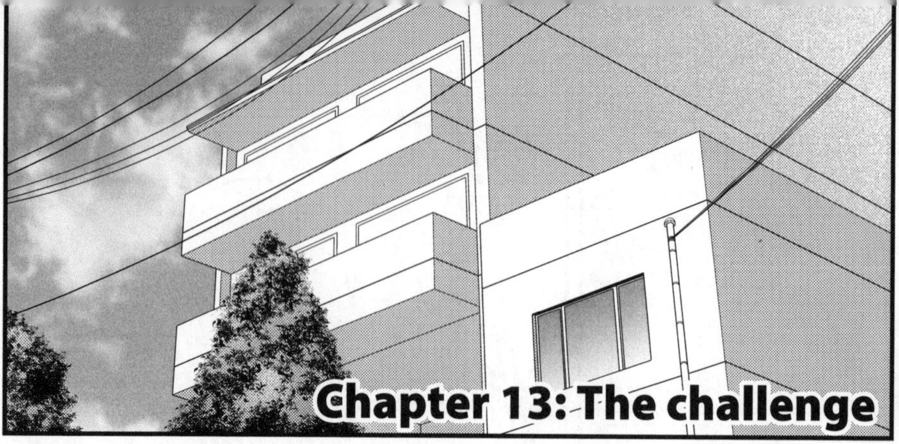
Chapter 13: The challenge

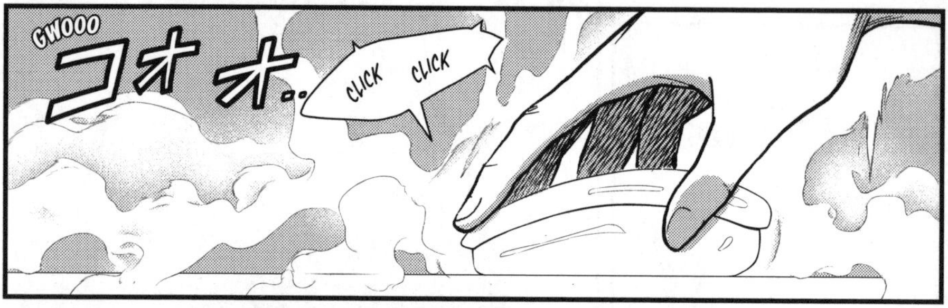
GWOOO
コオオ..
CLICK CLICK

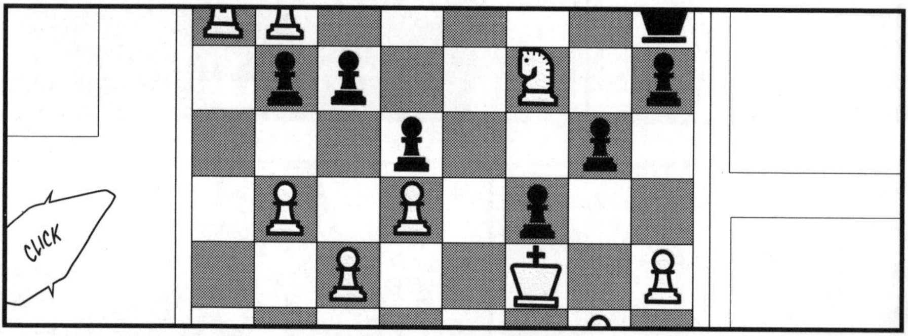
CLICK

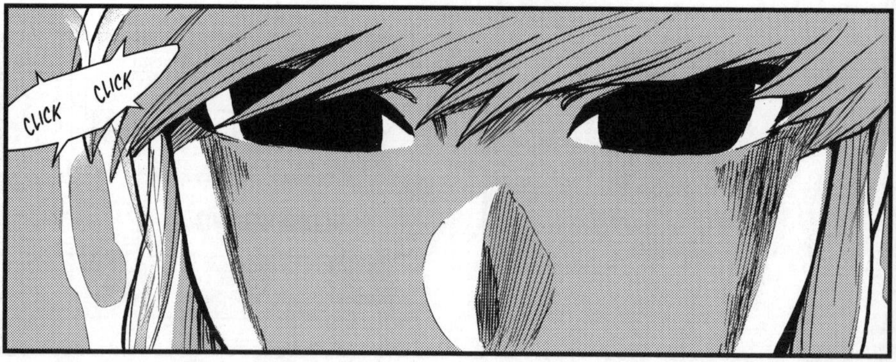
CLICK CLICK

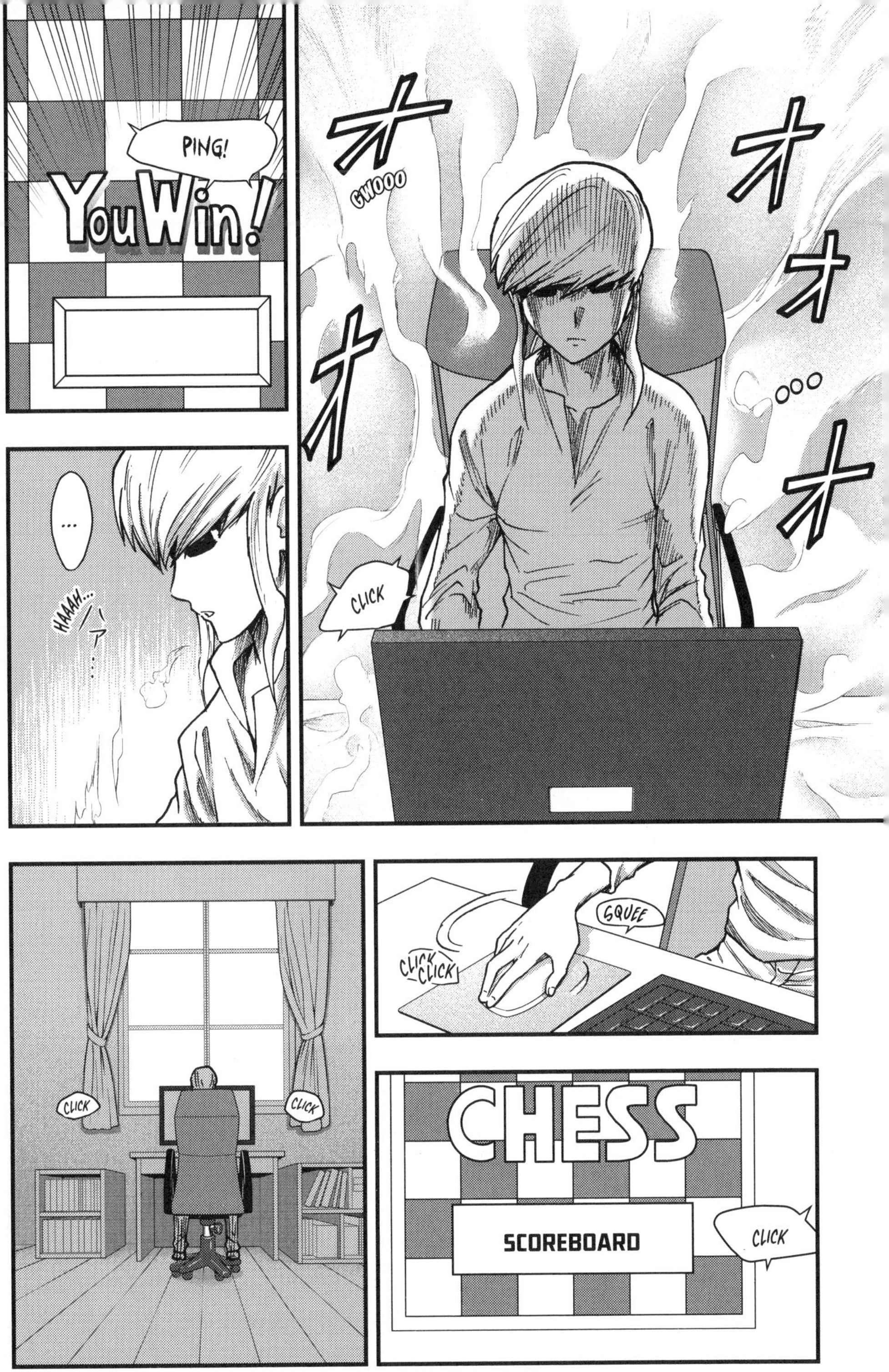
オ
オ
オ
オ
GWOOO
オ
...OOO
CLICK
PING!
YouWin!
...
HAAAH...
ハァ...
SQUEE
CLICK CLICK
CHESS
SCOREBOARD
CLICK
CLICK
CLICK

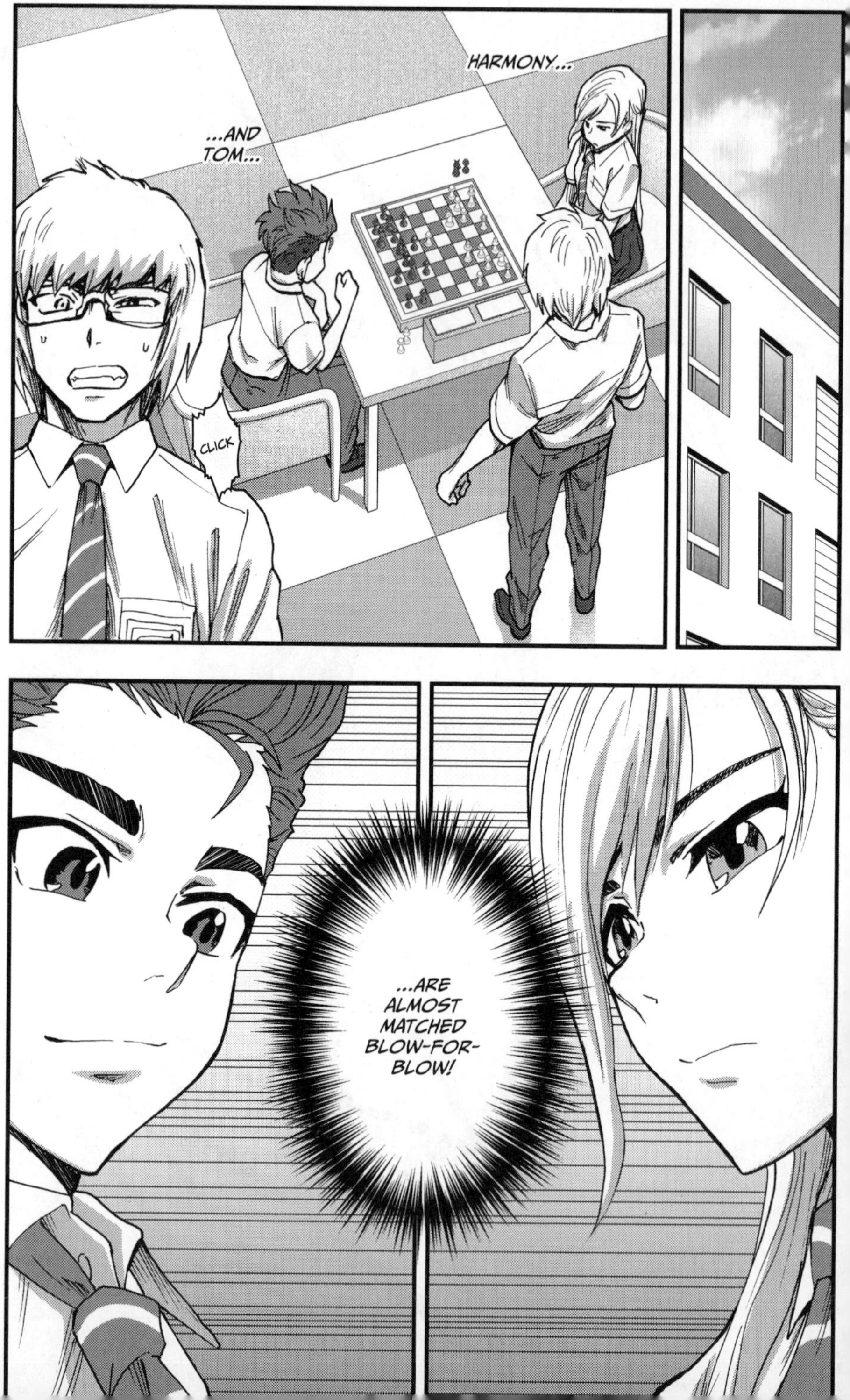
HARMONY...
...AND TOM...
CLICK
...ARE ALMOST MATCHED BLOW-FOR-BLOW!

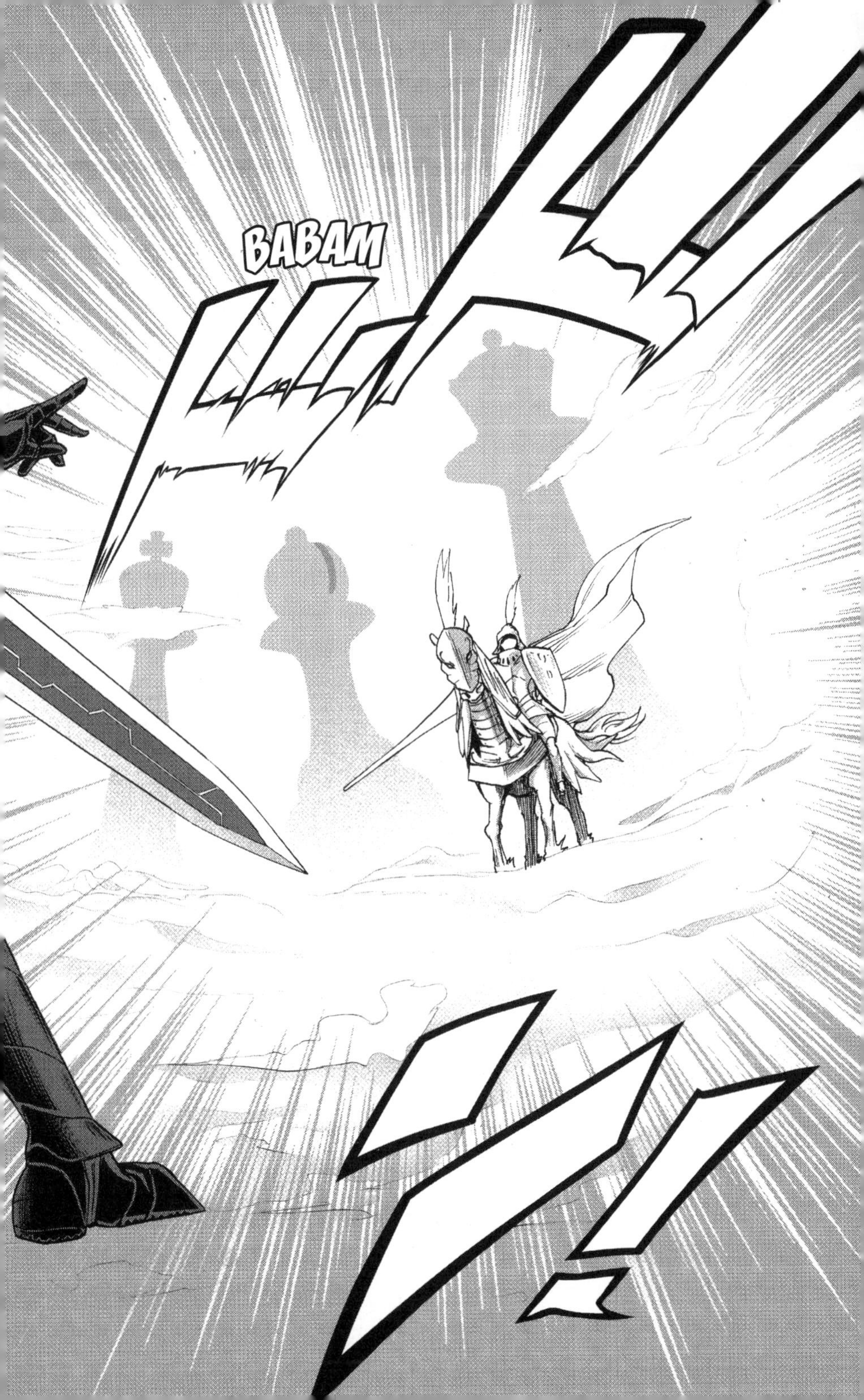
BABAM

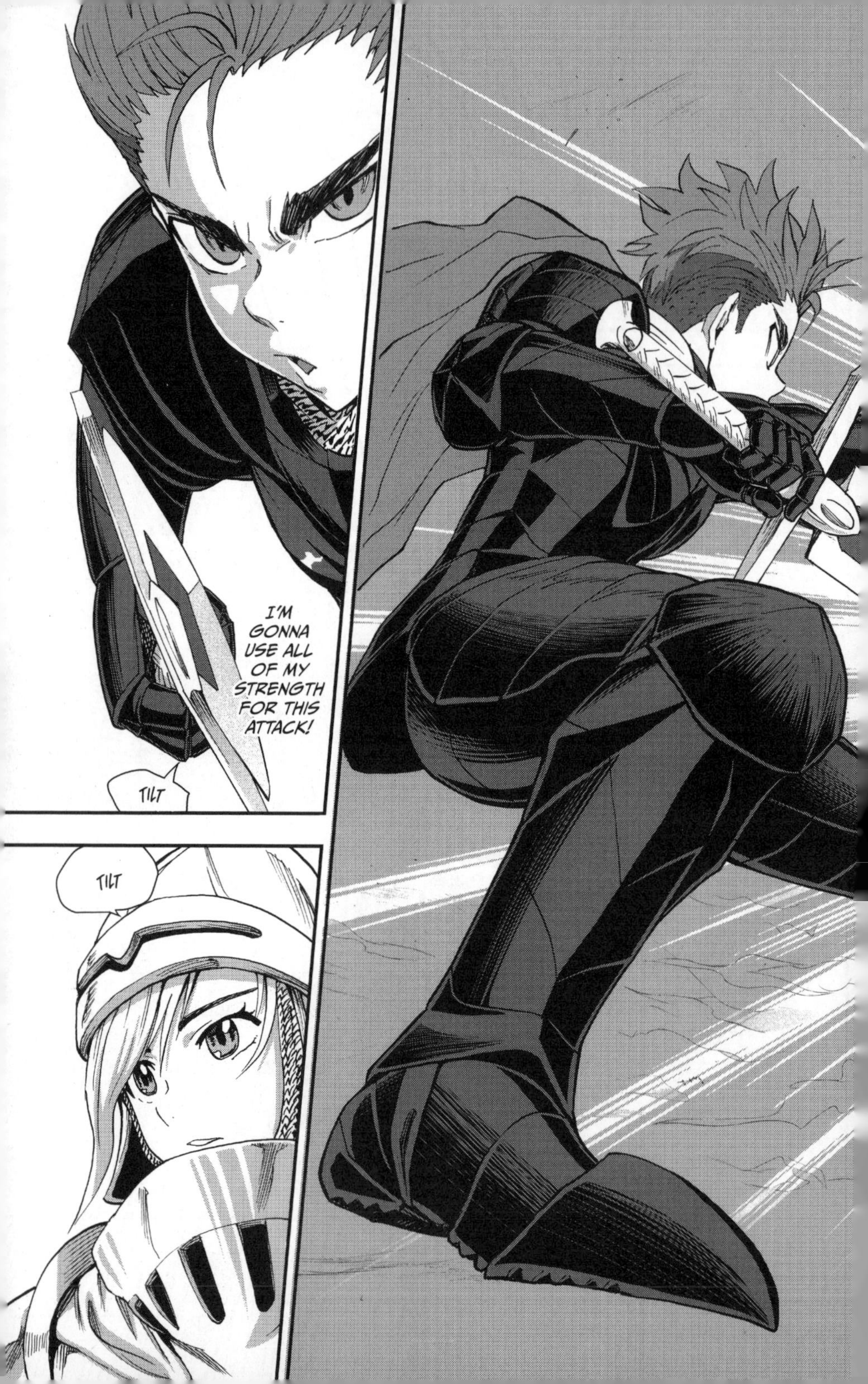
I'M GONNA USE ALL OF MY STRENGTH FOR THIS ATTACK!
TILT
TILT

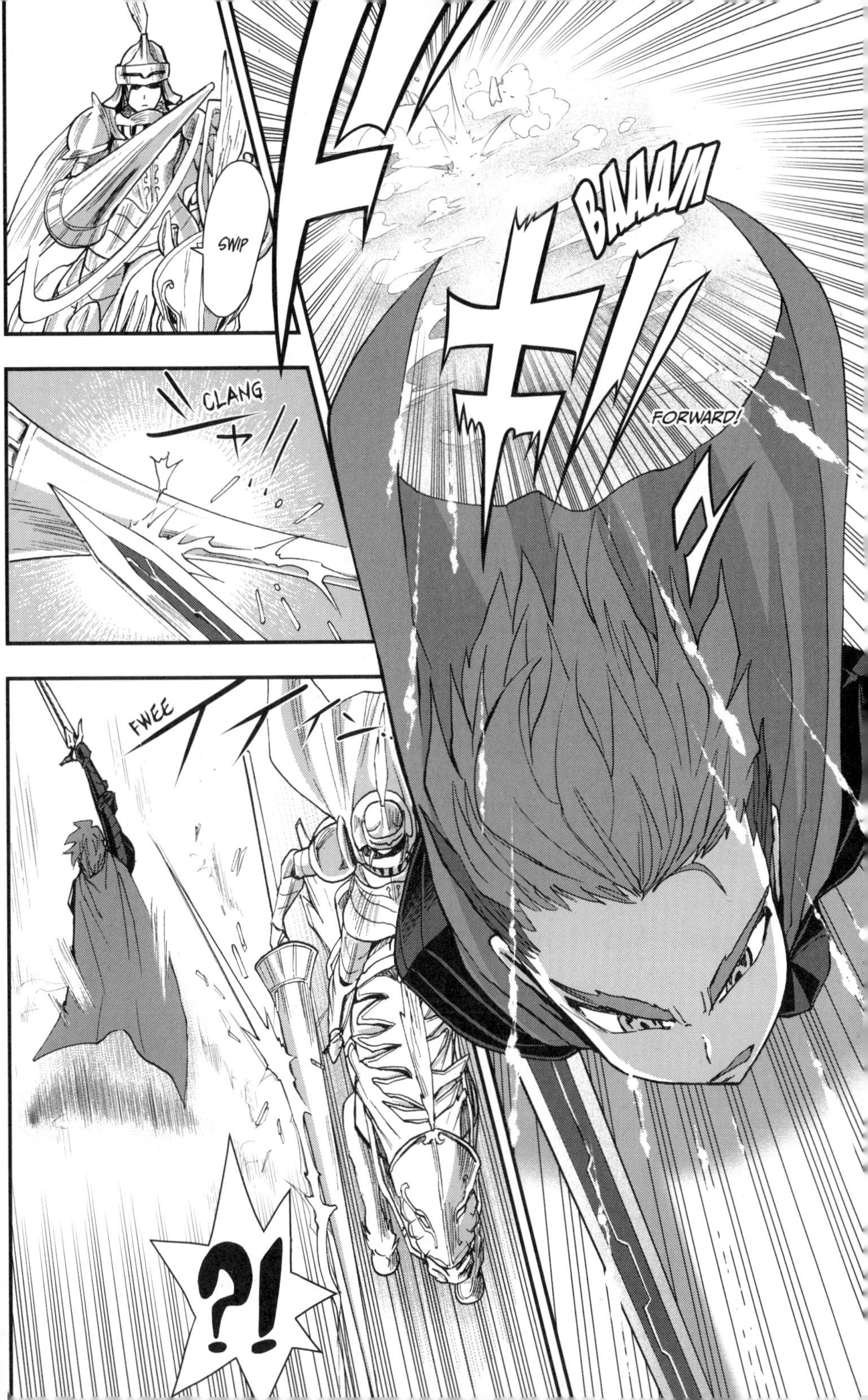
BAAAM
FORWARD!
SWIP
CLANG
FWEE
?!

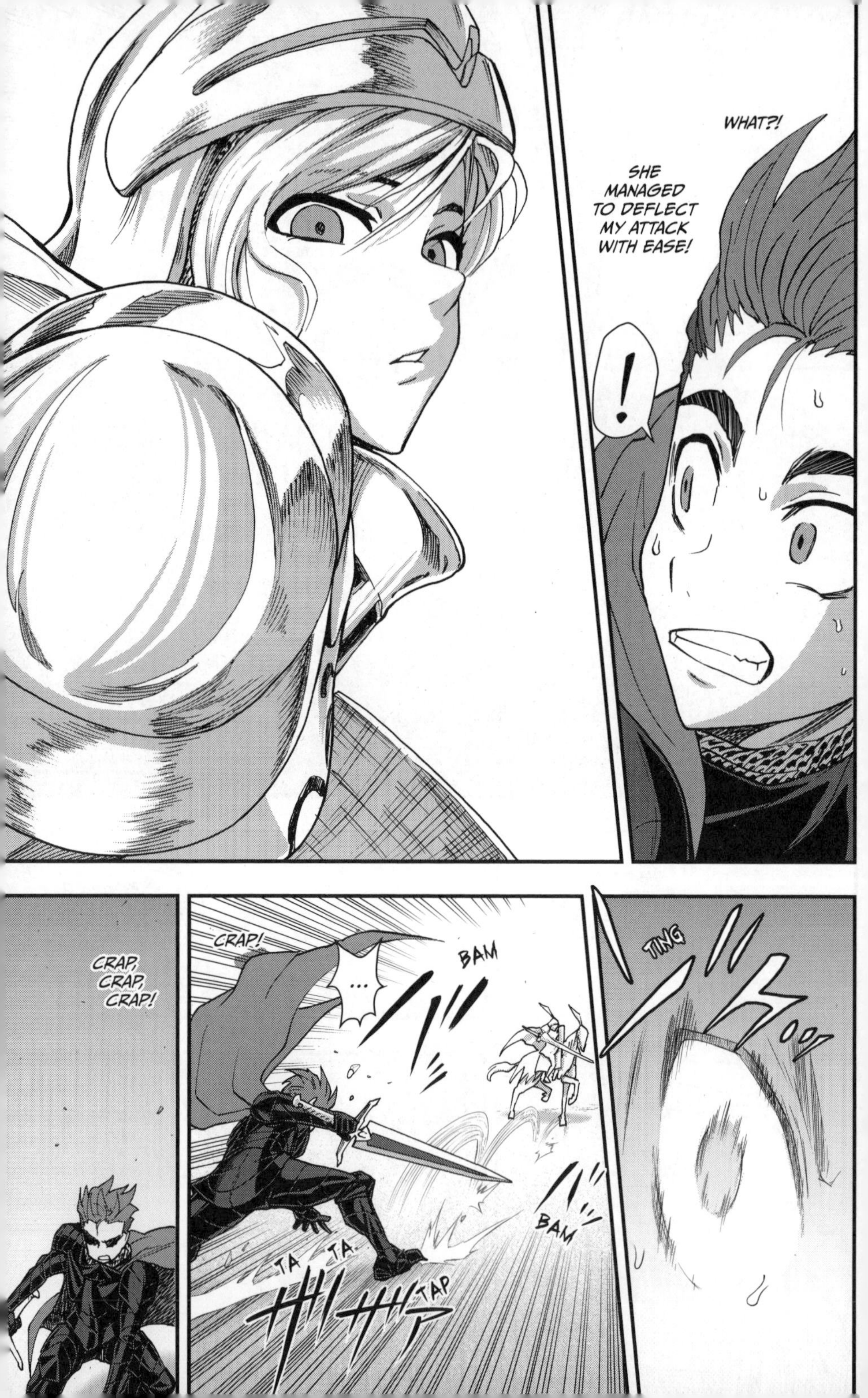
WHAT?!
SHE MANAGED TO DEFLECT MY ATTACK WITH EASE!
!
TING
CRAP!
...
BAM
BAM
TA TA
TAP
CRAP, CRAP, CRAP!

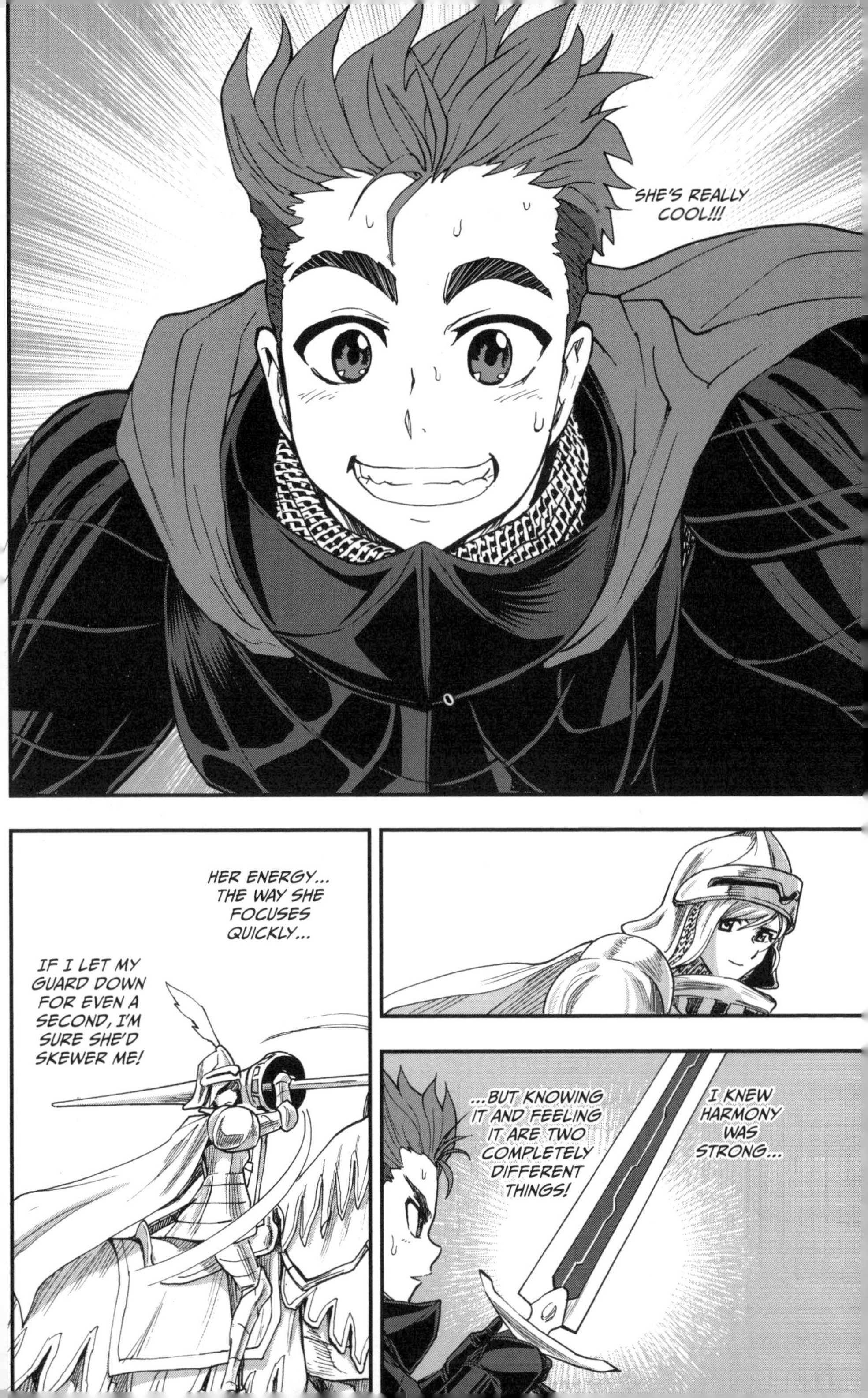
SHE'S REALLY COOL!!!
I KNEW HARMONY WAS STRONG...
...BUT KNOWING IT AND FEELING IT ARE TWO COMPLETELY DIFFERENT THINGS!
HER ENERGY... THE WAY SHE FOCUSES QUICKLY...
IF I LET MY GUARD DOWN FOR EVEN A SECOND, I'M SURE SHE'D SKEWER ME!

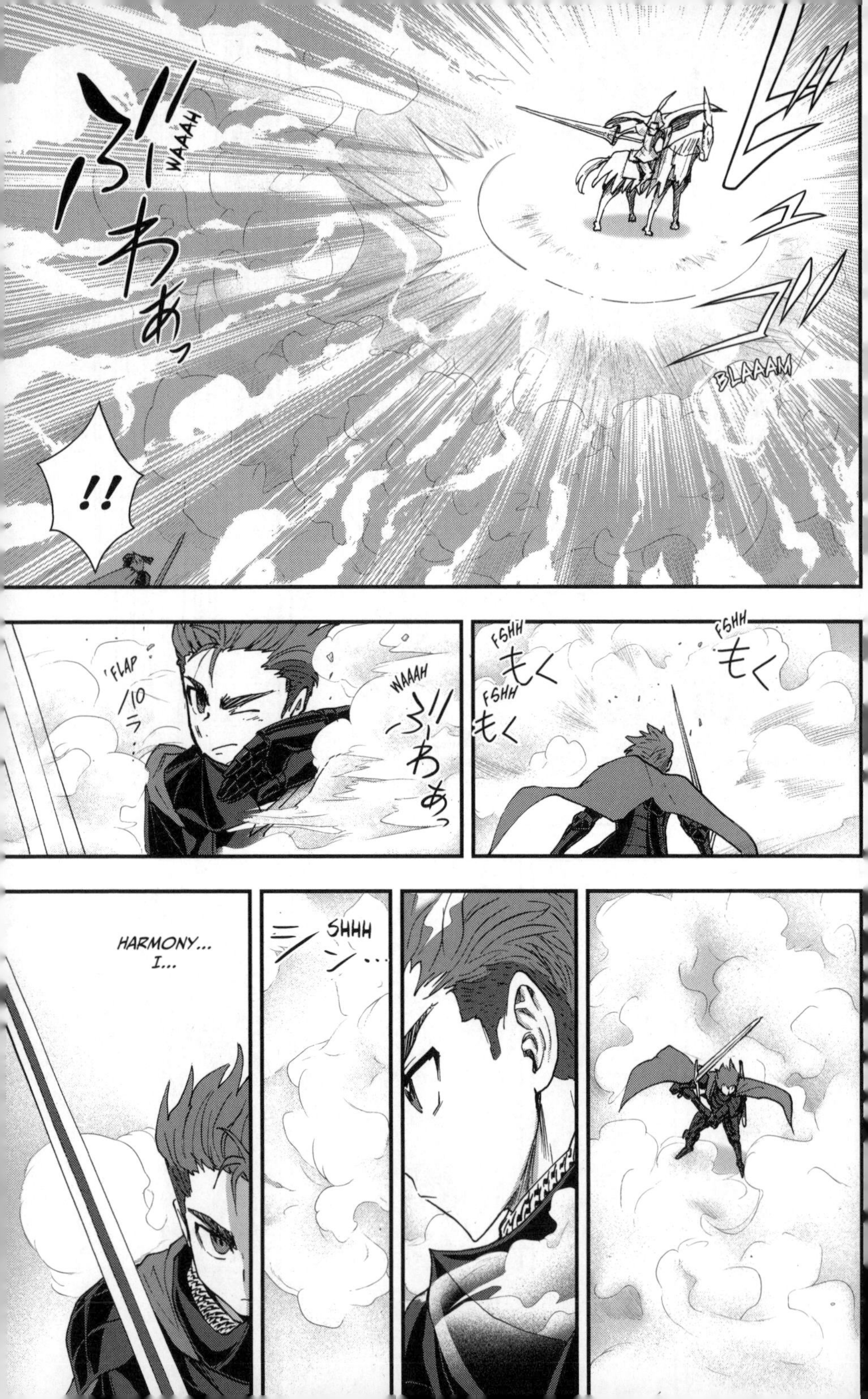
BLAAAM
ぶわぁっ
WAAAH
!!
もく
FSHH
もく
FSHH
もく
FSHH
ぶわぁっ
WAAAH
FLAP
シン…
SHHH
HARMONY... I...

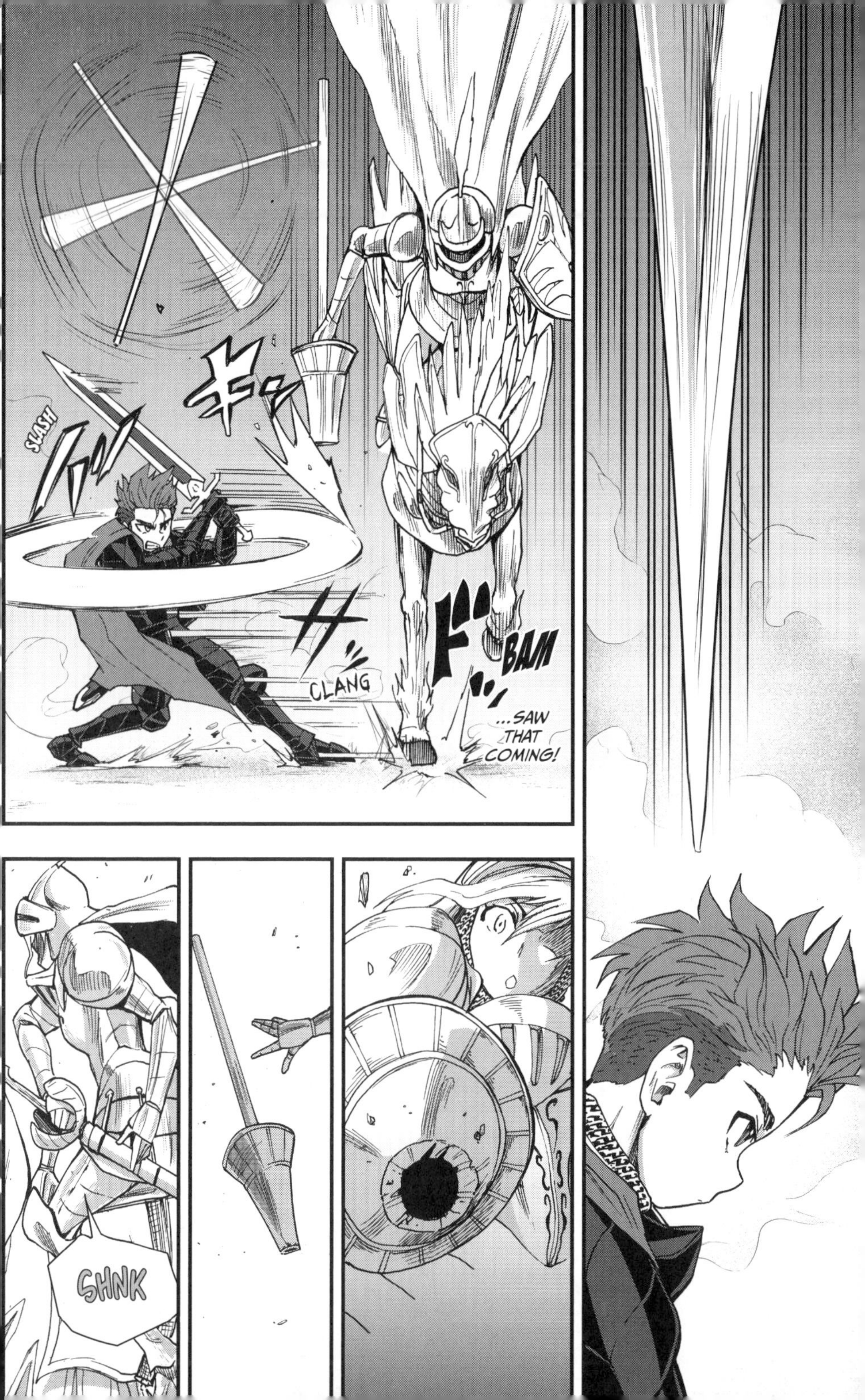
BAM
...SAW THAT COMING!
SLASH
CLANG
SHNK

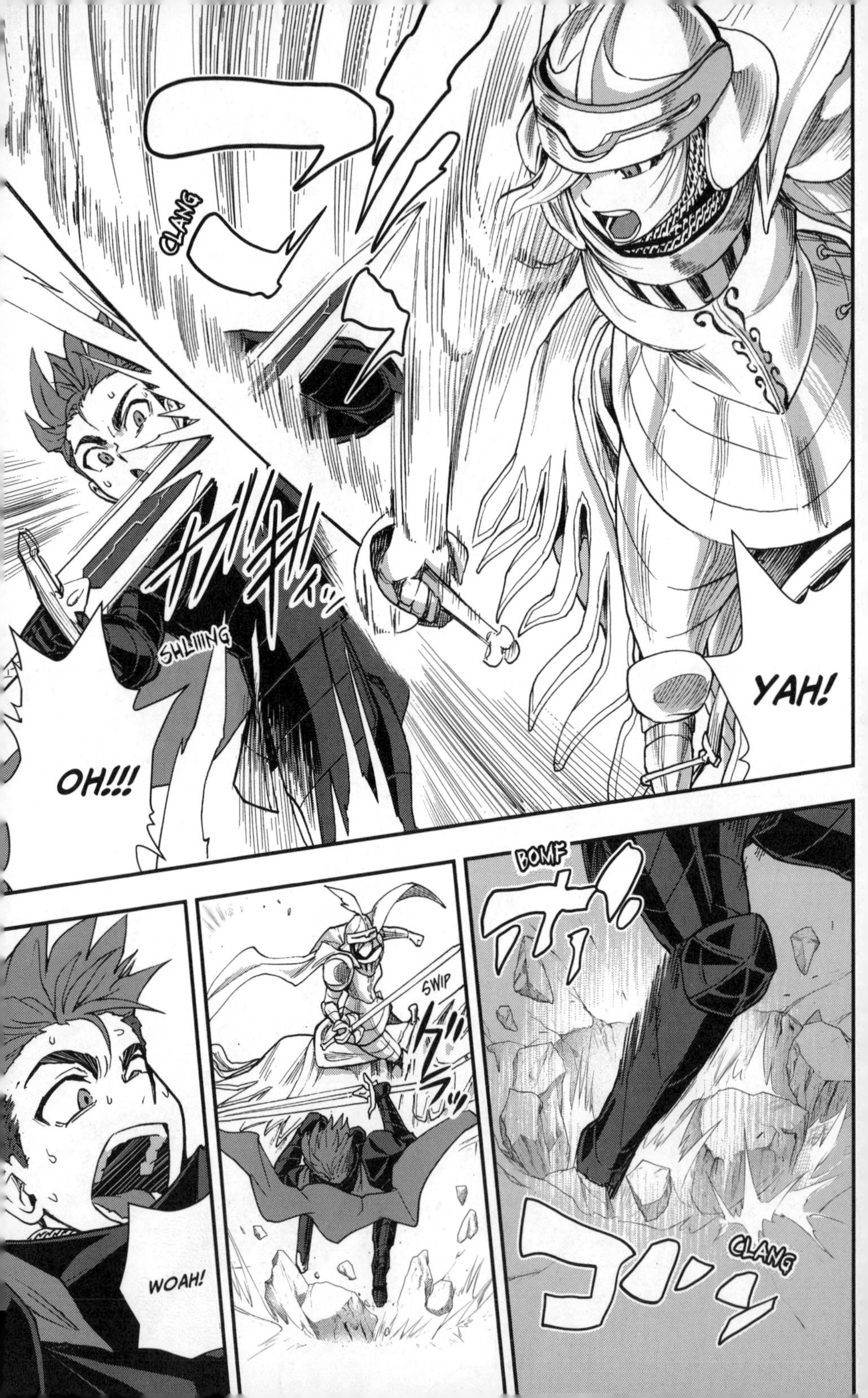
CLANG
YAH!
SHLIIING
OH!!!
BOMF
CLANG
SWIP
WOAH!

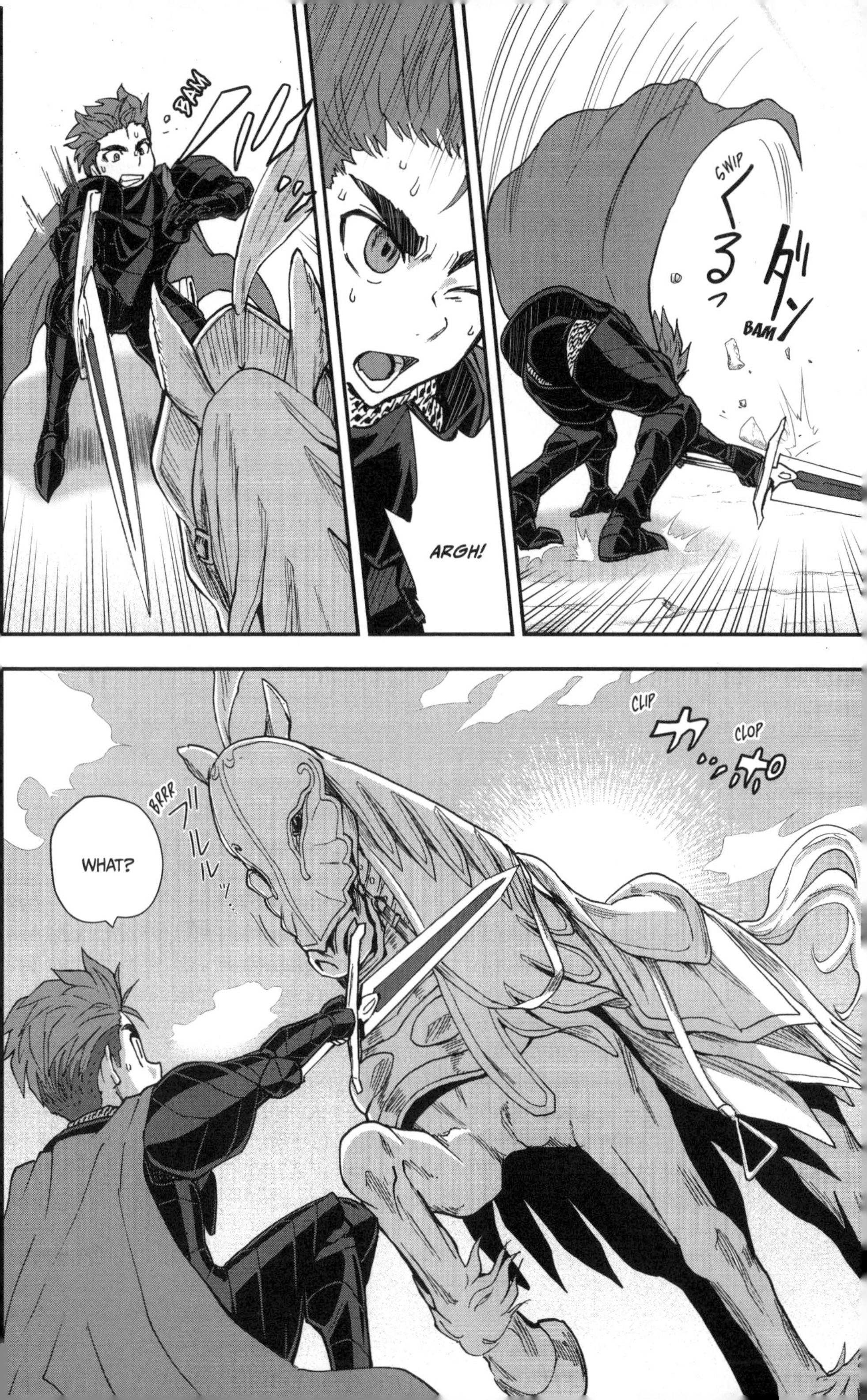
SWIP
くるっ
ダン
BAM
ARGH!
BAM
CLIP
カッ
CLOP
ポッ
BRRR
ブルルッ…
WHAT?

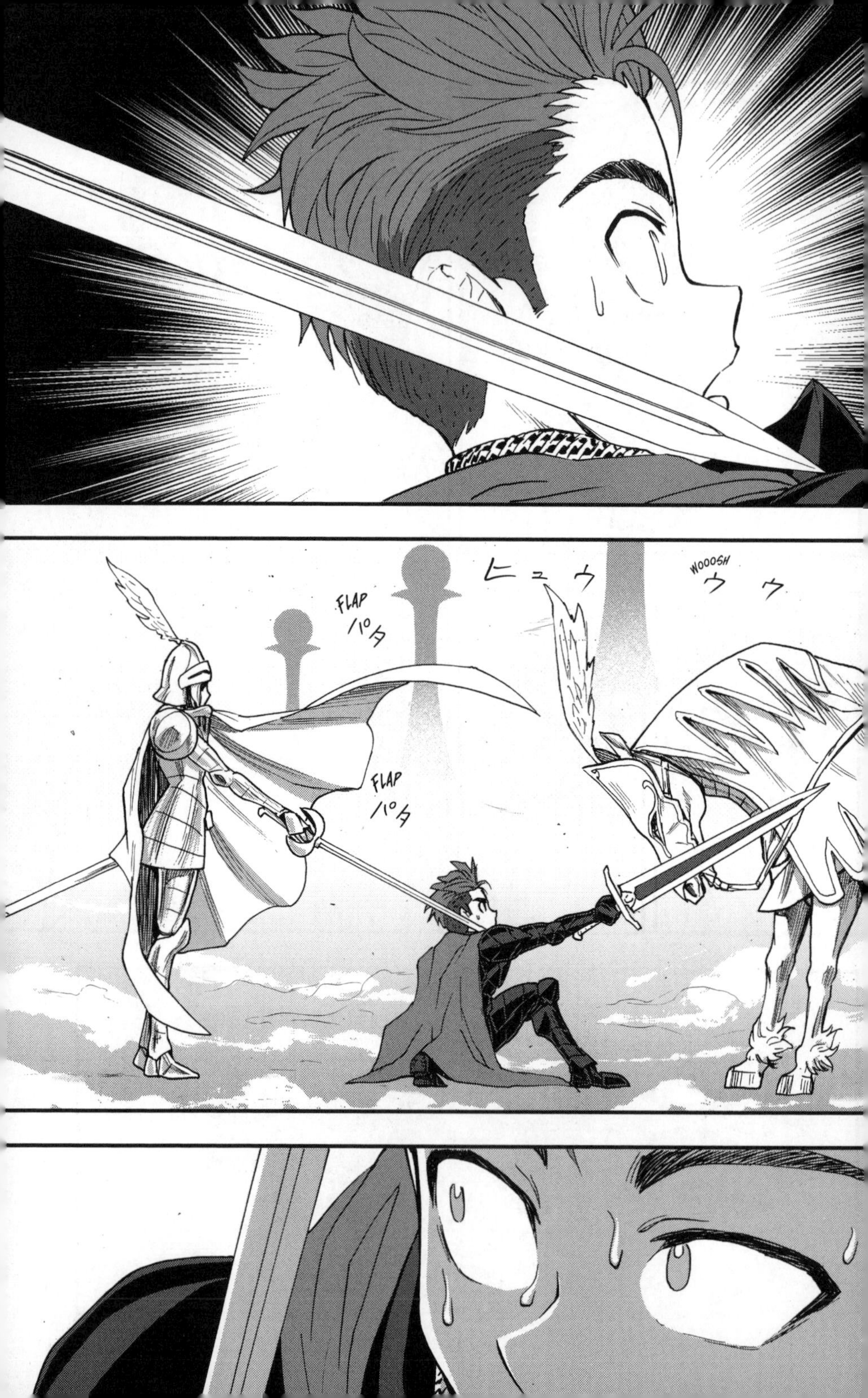
WOOOSH
ヒュウウウ
FLAP
パタ
FLAP
パタ

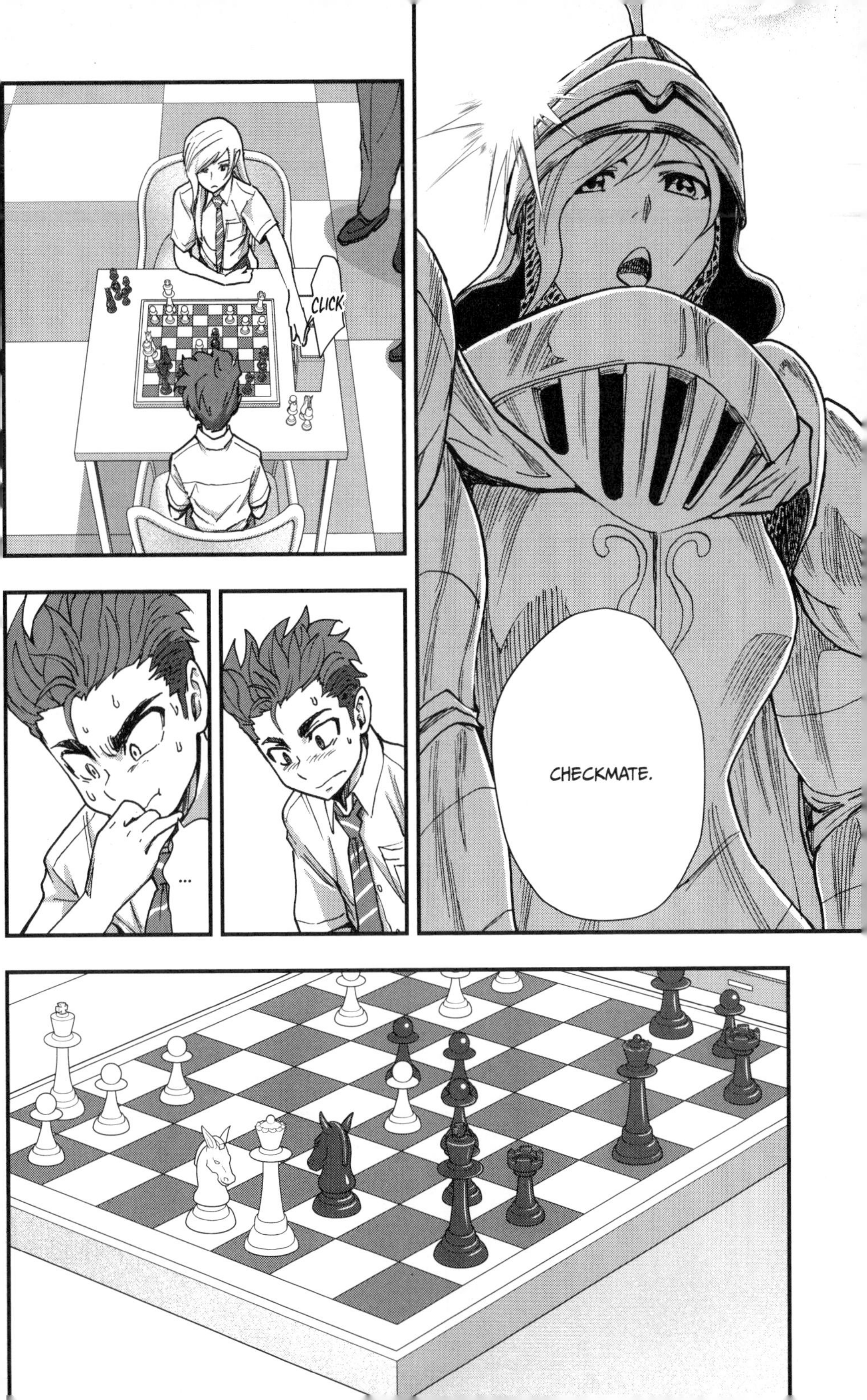
CHECKMATE.
CLICK
...

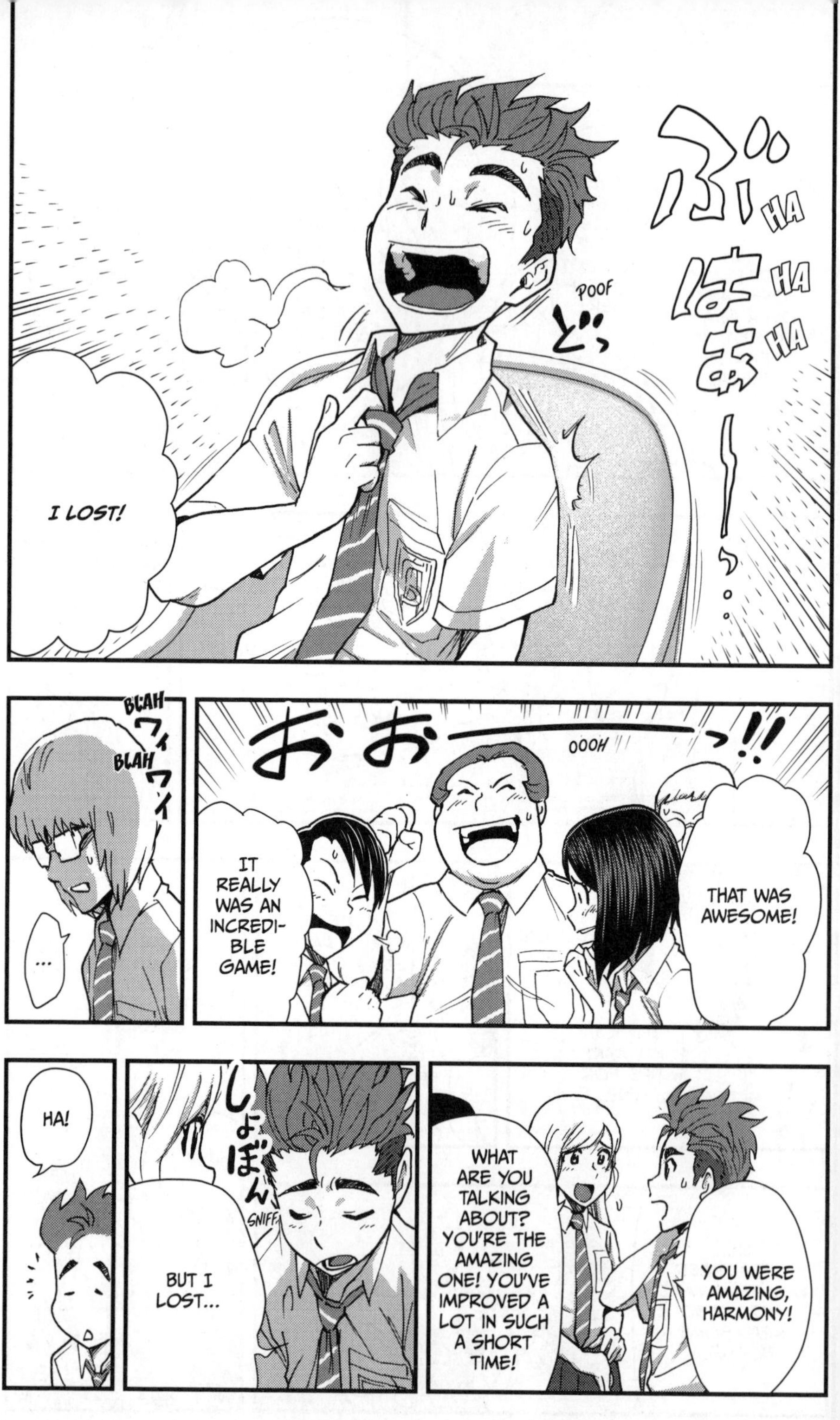

ぶはぁ～～っ。。。
HA
HA
HA
POOF
どっ
I LOST!
おおーーーっ!!
OOOH
THAT WAS AWESOME!
IT REALLY WAS AN INCREDI-BLE GAME!
BLAH
ワィ
BLAH
ワイ
...
YOU WERE AMAZING, HARMONY!
WHAT ARE YOU TALKING ABOUT? YOU'RE THE AMAZING ONE! YOU'VE IMPROVED A LOT IN SUCH A SHORT TIME!
しょぼん
SNIFF
BUT I LOST...
HA!

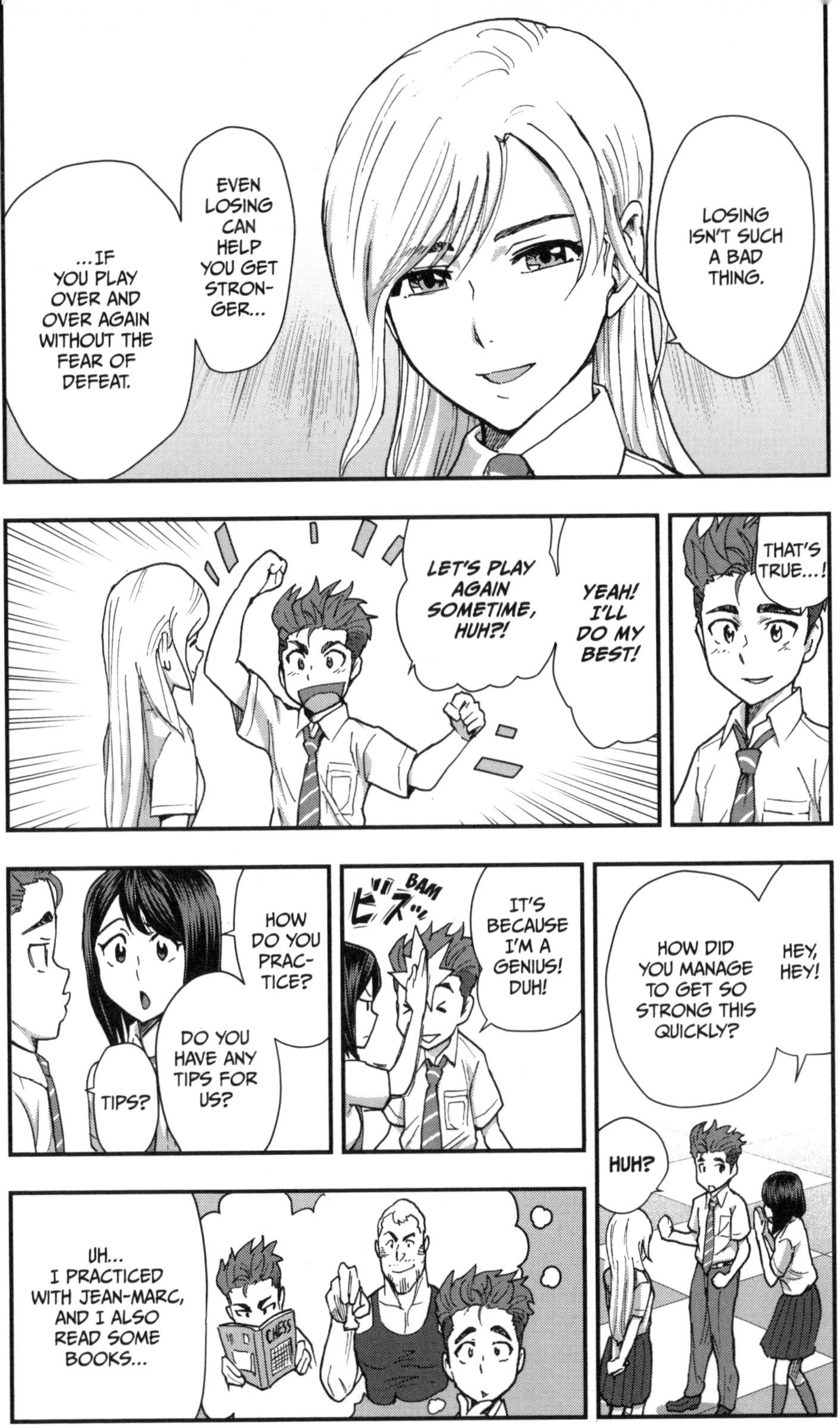
LOSING ISN'T SUCH A BAD THING.
EVEN LOSING CAN HELP YOU GET STRONGER...
...IF YOU PLAY OVER AND OVER AGAIN WITHOUT THE FEAR OF DEFEAT.
THAT'S TRUE...!
YEAH! I'LL DO MY BEST!
LET'S PLAY AGAIN SOMETIME, HUH?!
HEY, HEY!
HOW DID YOU MANAGE TO GET SO STRONG THIS QUICKLY?
HUH?
BAM
IT'S BECAUSE I'M A GENIUS! DUH!
HOW DO YOU PRACTICE?
DO YOU HAVE ANY TIPS FOR US?
TIPS?
UH... I PRACTICED WITH JEAN-MARC, AND I ALSO READ SOME BOOKS...
CHESS

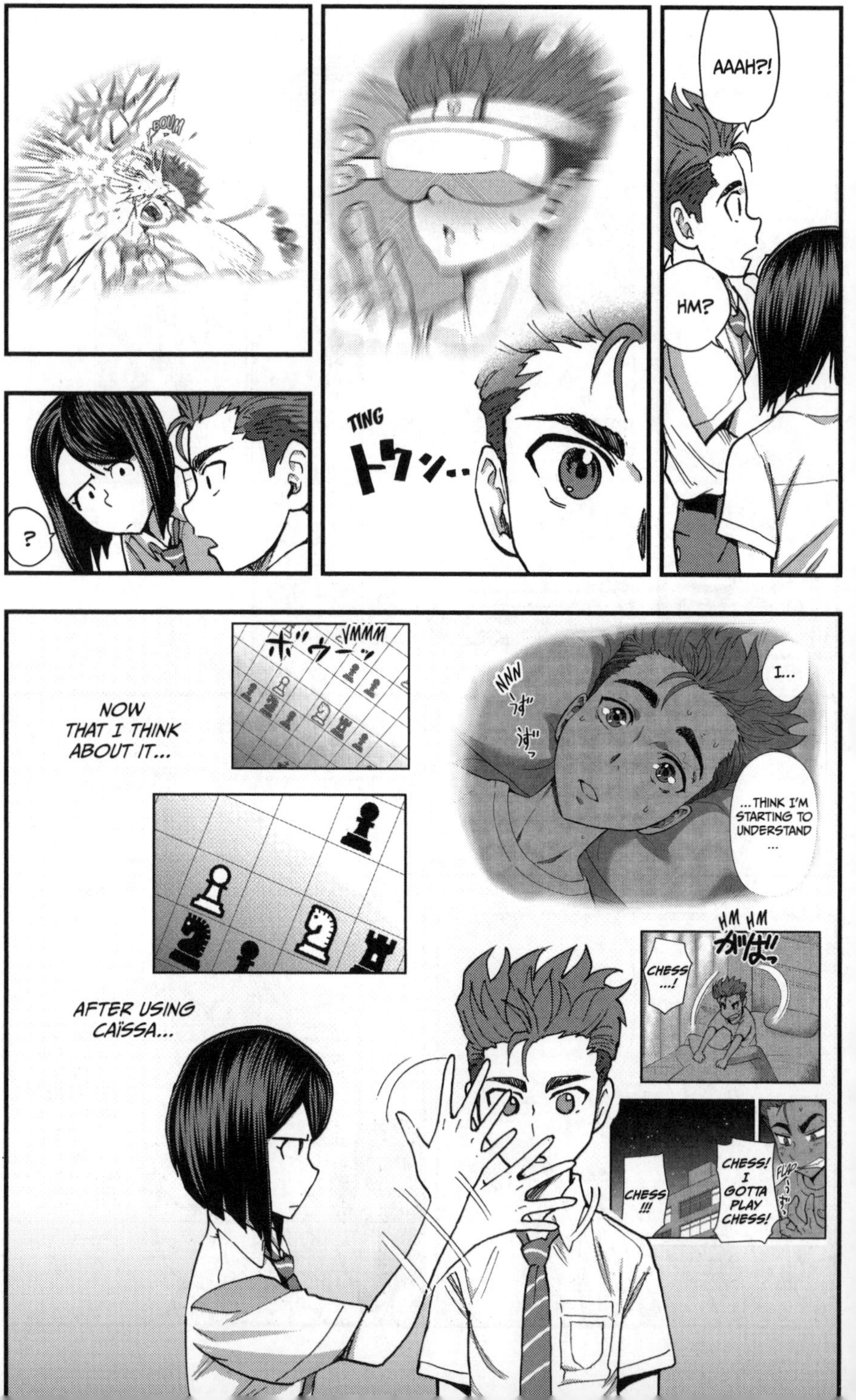
AAAH?!
HM?
TING
トクン…
BOUM
?
I…
…THINK I'M STARTING TO UNDERSTAND …
NNN
うず
うずっ
VMMM
ボウーッ
NOW THAT I THINK ABOUT IT…
HM HM
がばっ
CHESS …!
CHESS! I GOTTA PLAY CHESS!
FLAP
CHESS !!!
AFTER USING CAÏSSA…

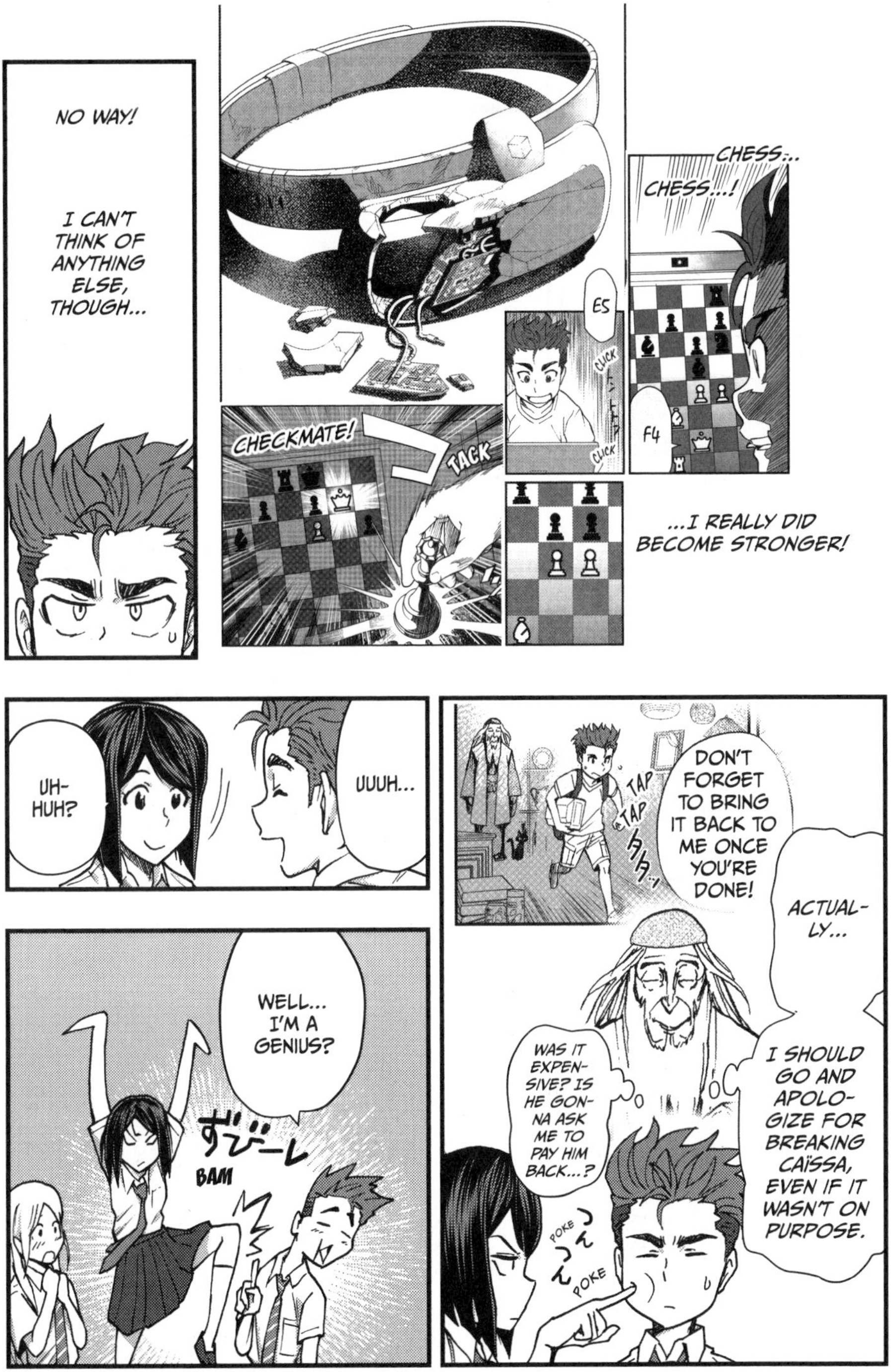
CHESS...
CHESS...!
E5
CLICK
CLICK
F4
...I REALLY DID BECOME STRONGER!
CHECKMATE!
TACK
NO WAY!
I CAN'T THINK OF ANYTHING ELSE, THOUGH...
DON'T FORGET TO BRING IT BACK TO ME ONCE YOU'RE DONE!
TAP
TAP
ACTUAL-LY...
I SHOULD GO AND APOLO-GIZE FOR BREAKING CAÏSSA, EVEN IF IT WASN'T ON PURPOSE.
WAS IT EXPEN-SIVE? IS HE GON-NA ASK ME TO PAY HIM BACK...?
POKE
POKE
UUUH...
UH-HUH?
WELL... I'M A GENIUS?
BAM

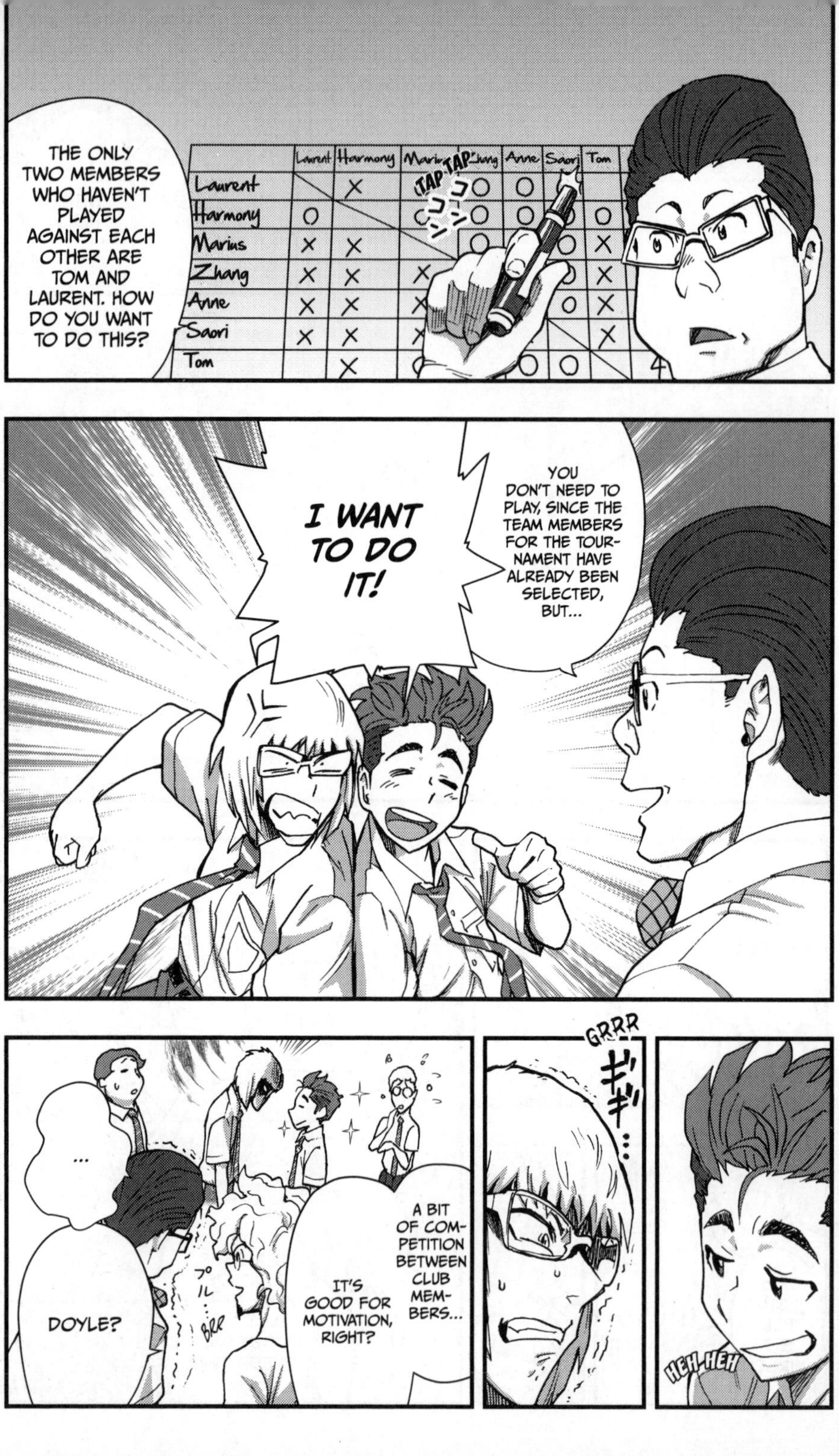
THE ONLY TWO MEMBERS WHO HAVEN'T PLAYED AGAINST EACH OTHER ARE TOM AND LAURENT. HOW DO YOU WANT TO DO THIS?
TAP TAP
YOU DON'T NEED TO PLAY, SINCE THE TEAM MEMBERS FOR THE TOURNAMENT HAVE ALREADY BEEN SELECTED, BUT...
I WANT TO DO IT!
HEH-HEH
GRRR
A BIT OF COMPETITION BETWEEN CLUB MEMBERS...
IT'S GOOD FOR MOTIVATION, RIGHT?
BRR
...
DOYLE?

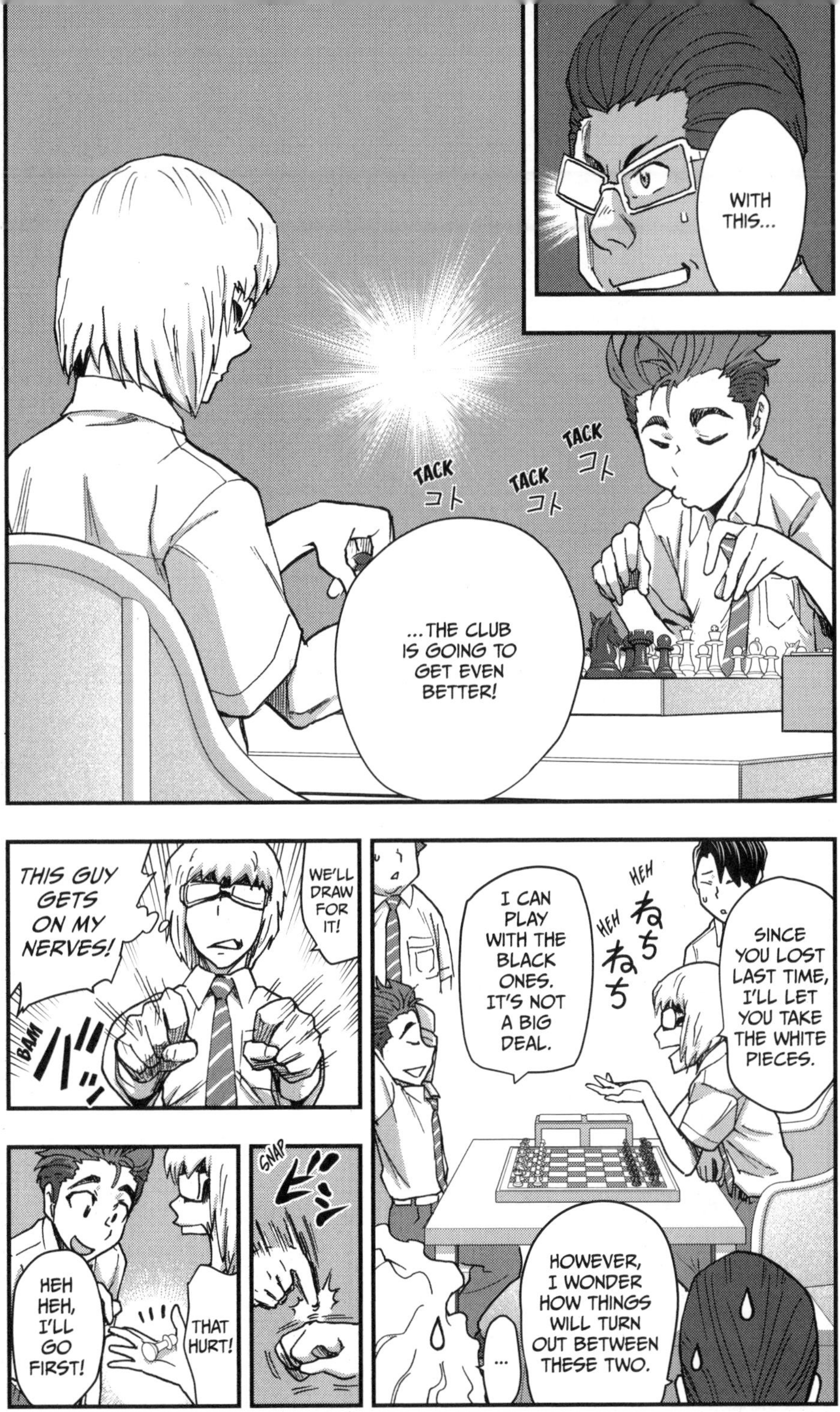
WITH THIS...
TACK コト
TACK コト
TACK コト
...THE CLUB IS GOING TO GET EVEN BETTER!
SINCE YOU LOST LAST TIME, I'LL LET YOU TAKE THE WHITE PIECES.
HEH ねち
HEH ねち
I CAN PLAY WITH THE BLACK ONES. IT'S NOT A BIG DEAL.
HOWEVER, I WONDER HOW THINGS WILL TURN OUT BETWEEN THESE TWO.
...
WE'LL DRAW FOR IT!
THIS GUY GETS ON MY NERVES!
BAM
SNAP
THAT HURT!
HEH HEH, I'LL GO FIRST!

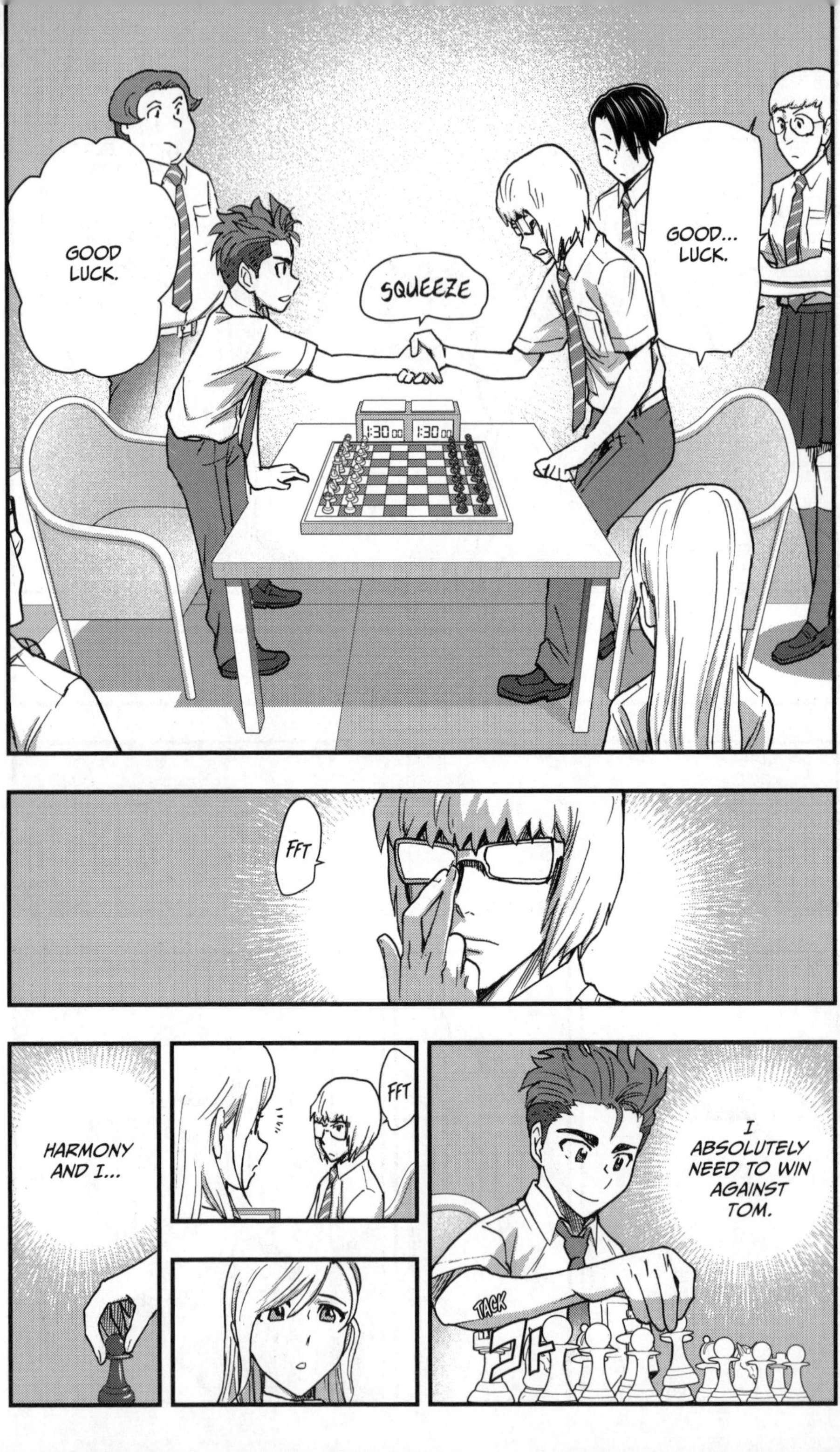
GOOD LUCK.
SQUEEZE
GOOD... LUCK.
1:30 00
1:30 00
FFT
HARMONY AND I...
FFT
I ABSOLUTELY NEED TO WIN AGAINST TOM.
TACK

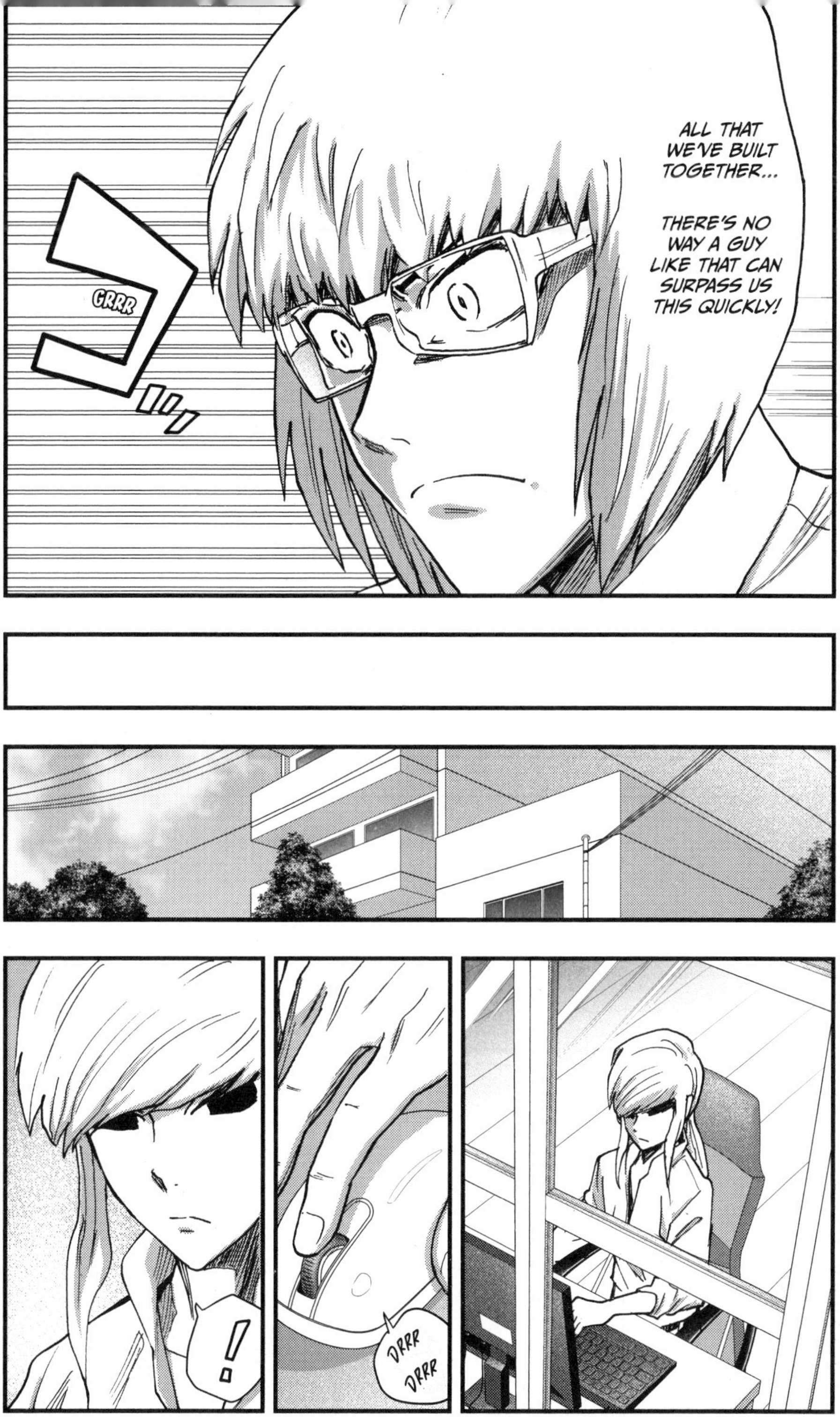
ALL THAT WE'VE BUILT TOGETHER...
THERE'S NO WAY A GUY LIKE THAT CAN SURPASS US THIS QUICKLY!
GRRR
DRRR DRRR
!

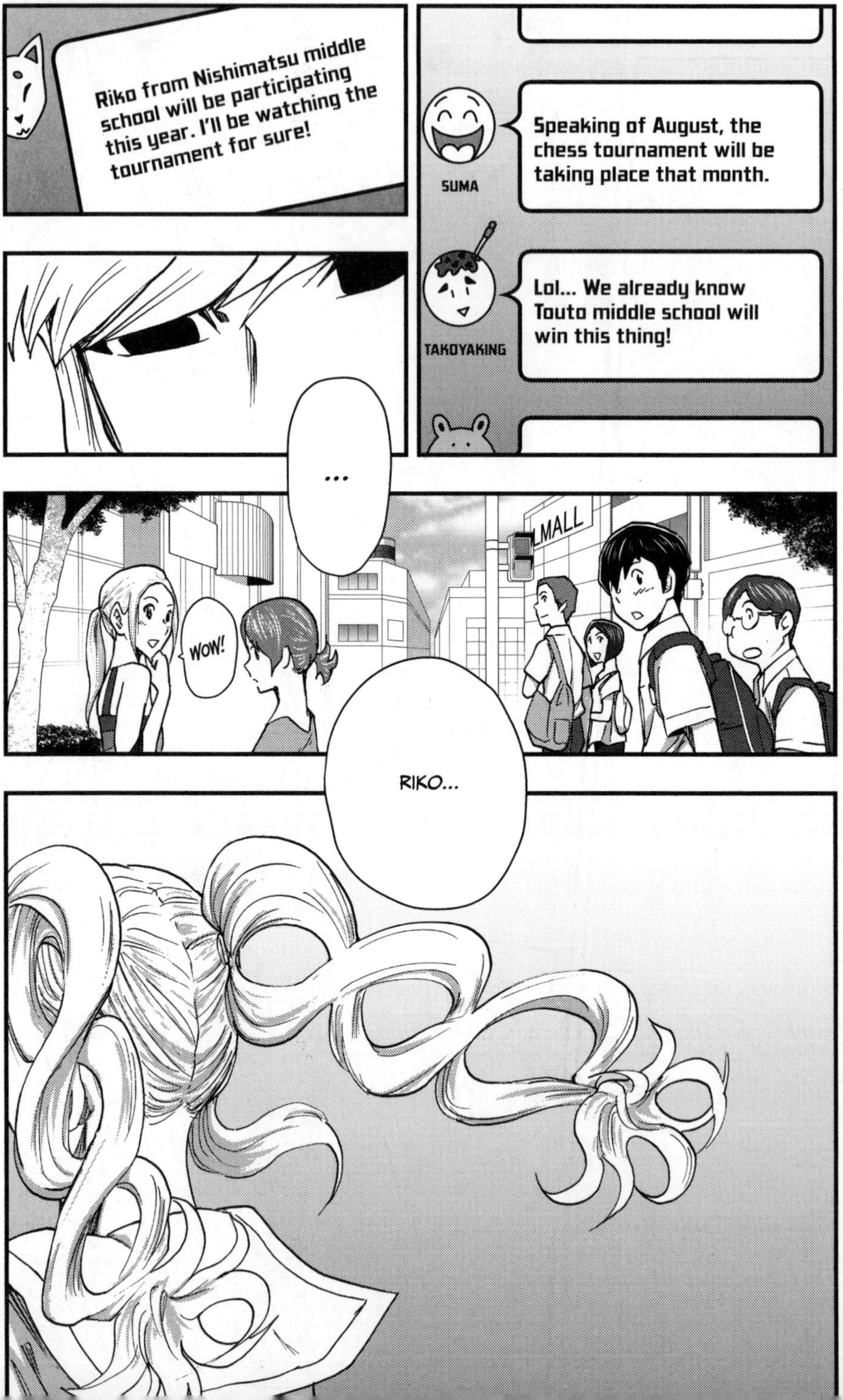
SUMA
Speaking of August, the chess tournament will be taking place that month.
TAKOYAKING
Lol... We already know Touto middle school will win this thing!
Riko from Nishimatsu middle school will be participating this year. I'll be watching the tournament for sure!
...
LMALL
WOW!
RIKO...

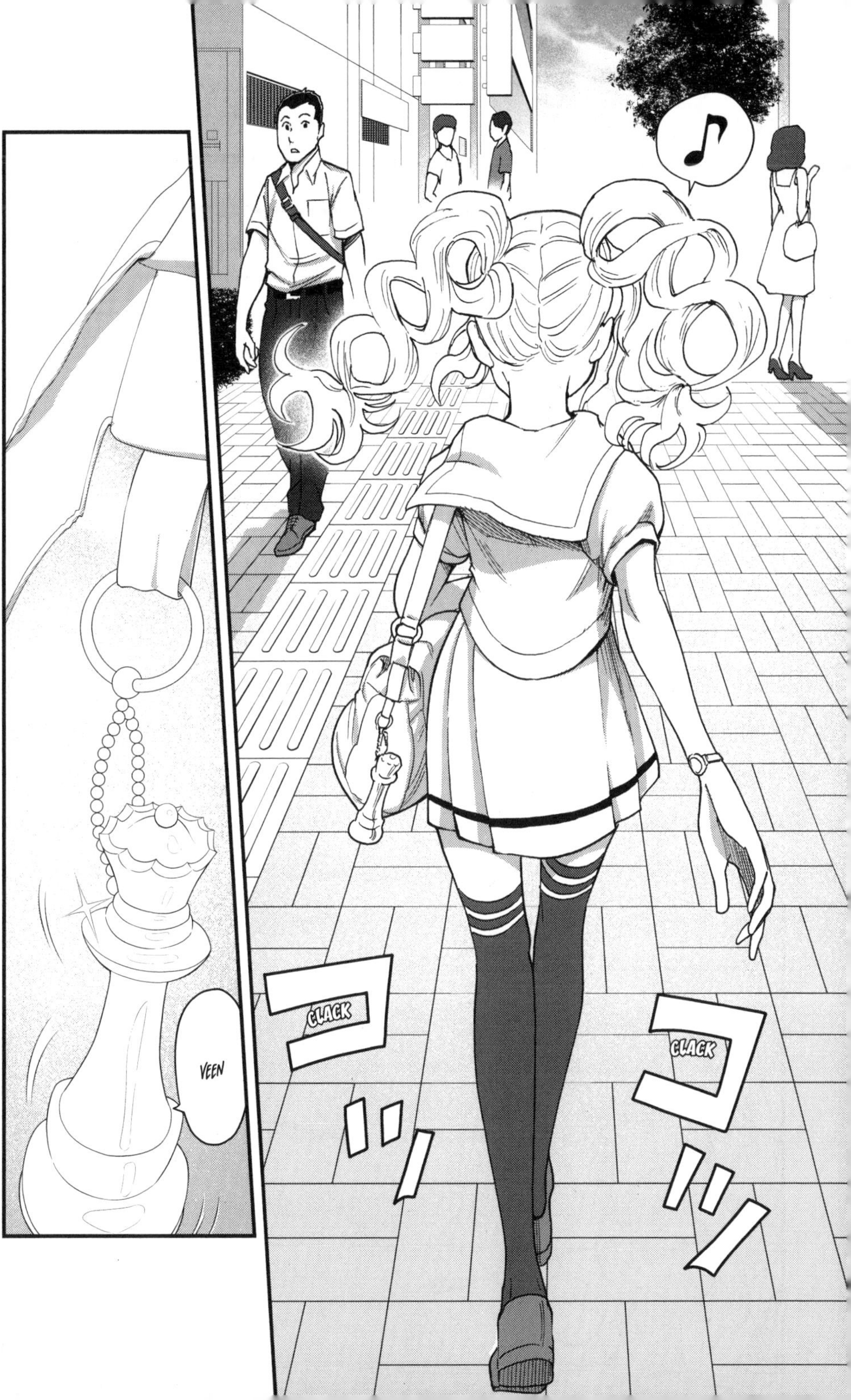
♪
CLACK
CLACK
VEEN

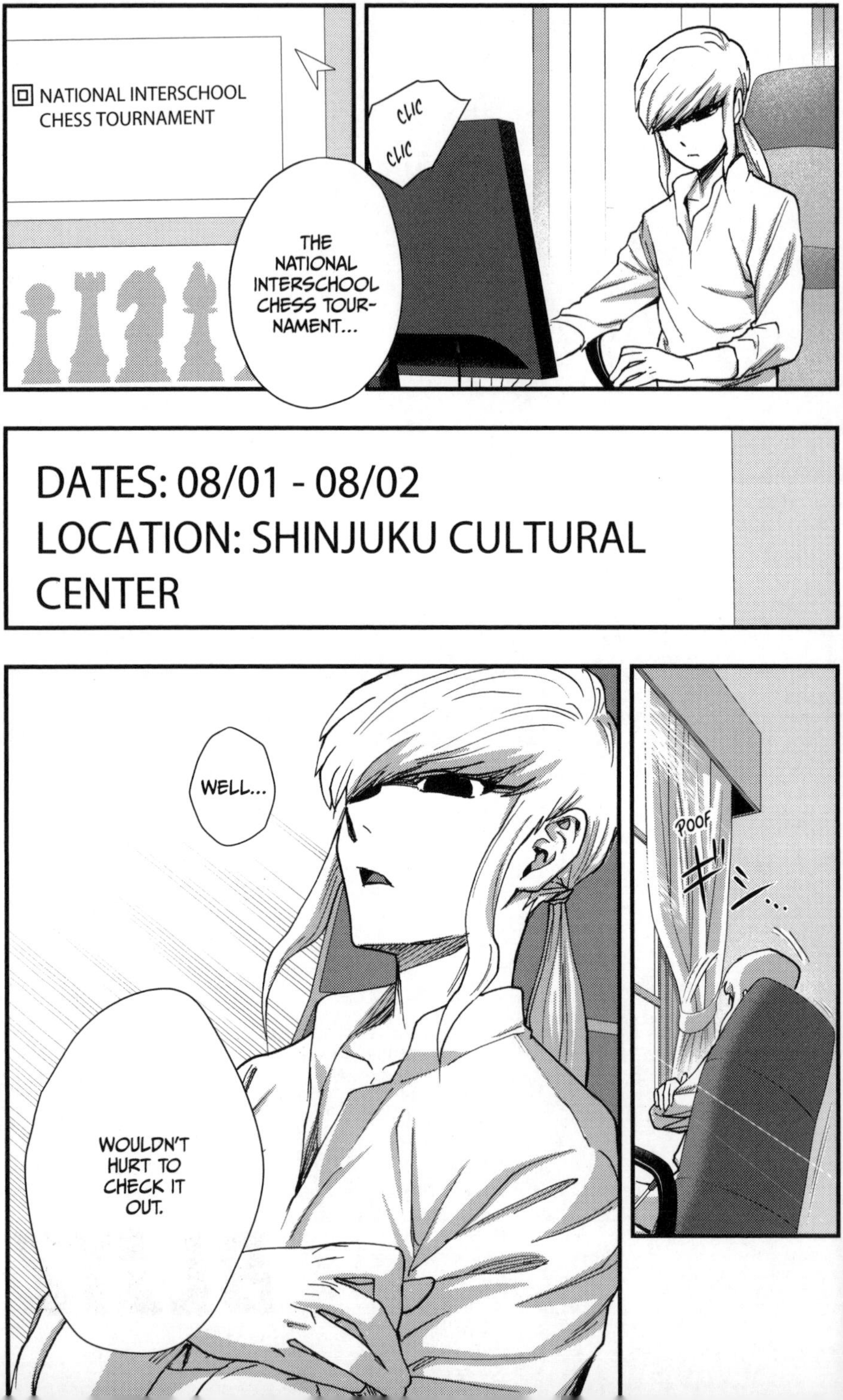
CLIC
CLIC
THE NATIONAL INTERSCHOOL CHESS TOUR-NAMENT...
NATIONAL INTERSCHOOL CHESS TOURNAMENT
DATES: 08/01 - 08/02
LOCATION: SHINJUKU CULTURAL CENTER
POOF
...
WELL...
WOULDN'T HURT TO CHECK IT OUT.

BLiTZ

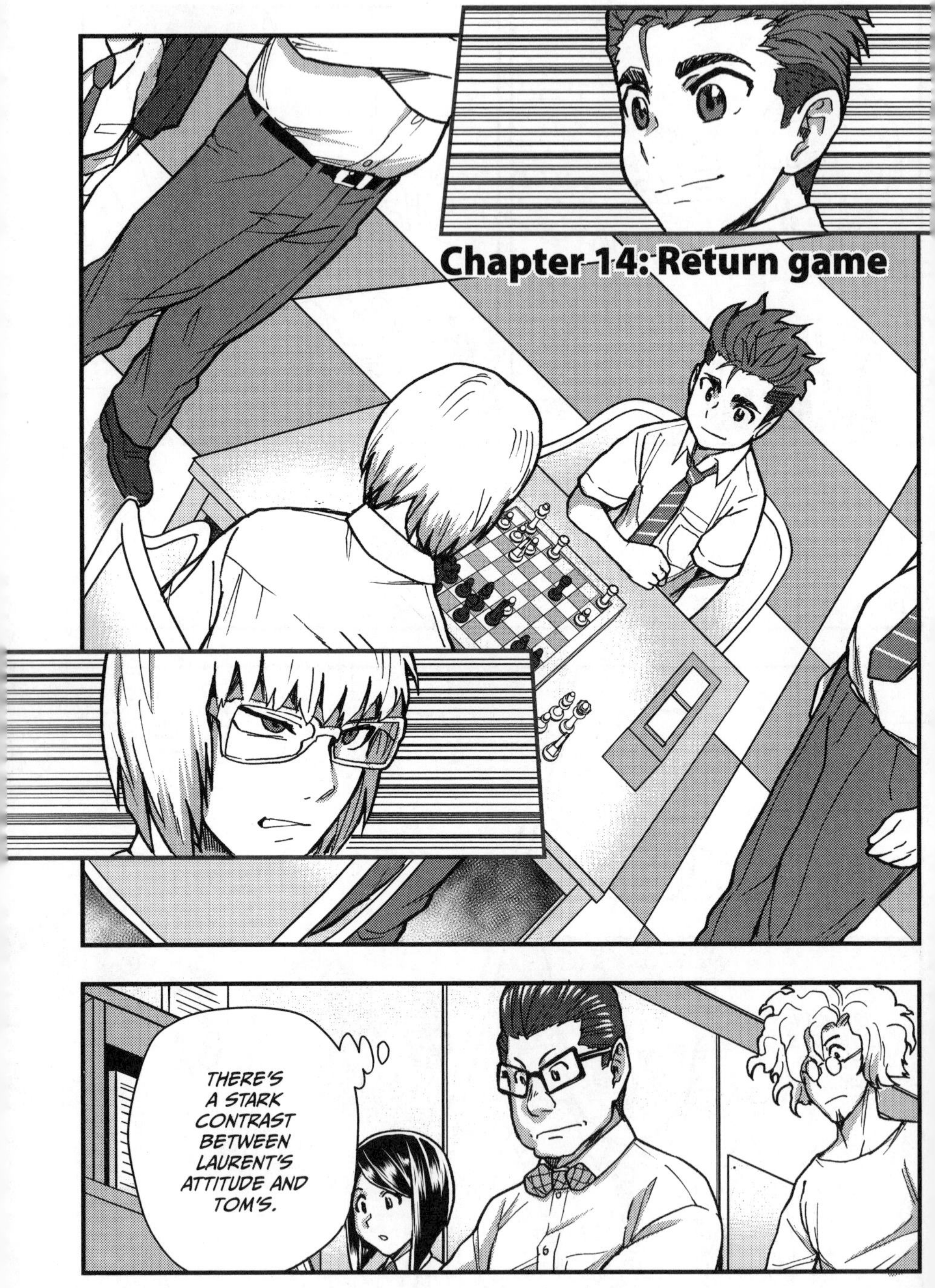
Chapter 14: Return game
THERE'S A STARK CONTRAST BETWEEN LAURENT'S ATTITUDE AND TOM'S.

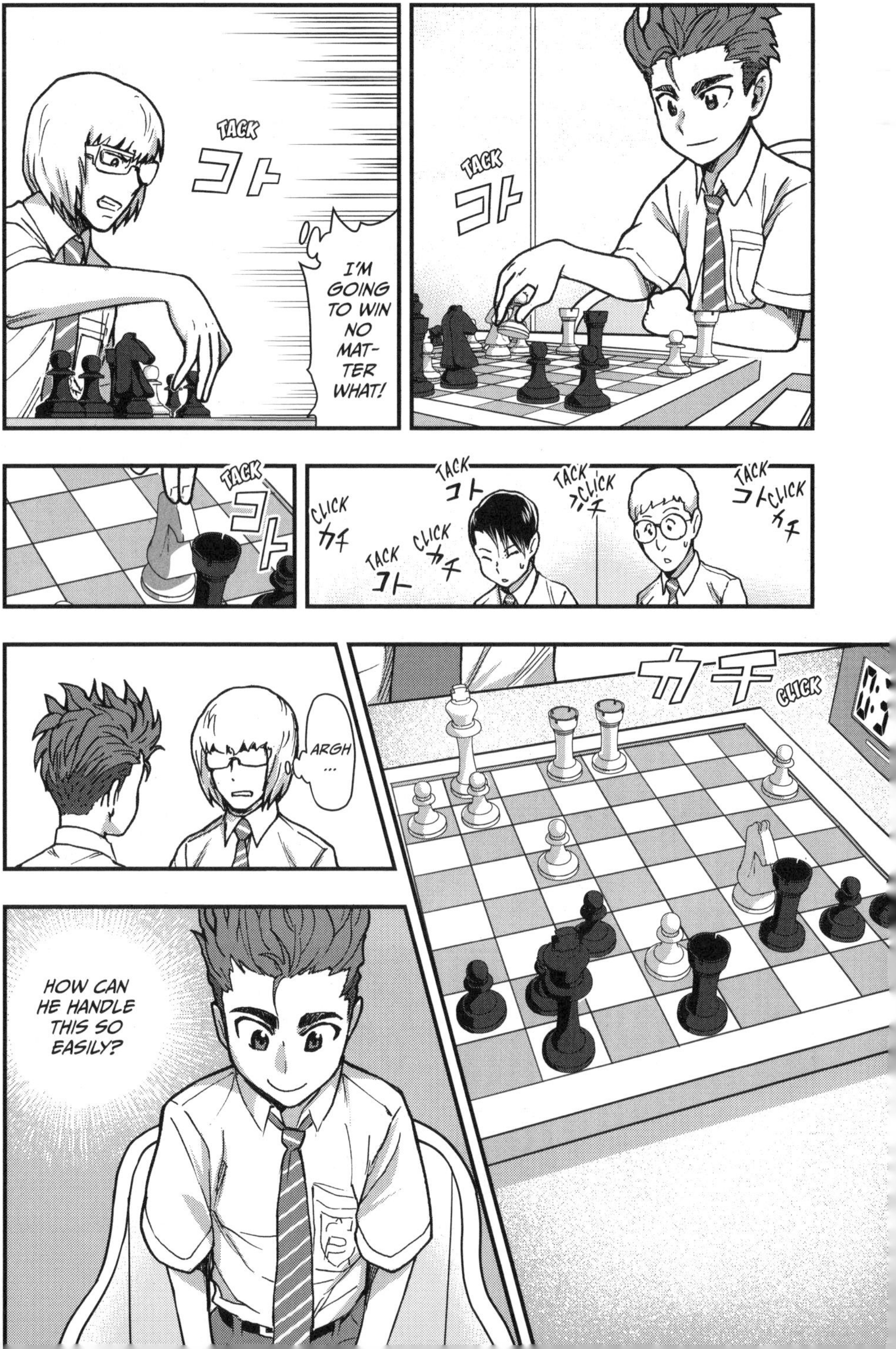
TACK
コト
TACK
コト
I'M GOING TO WIN NO MATTER WHAT!
TACK
コト
CLICK
カチ
TACK
CLICK
カチ
TACK
コト
CLICK
カチ
CLICK
カチ
TACK
コト
TACK
コト
カチ
CLICK
ARGH...
HOW CAN HE HANDLE THIS SO EASILY?

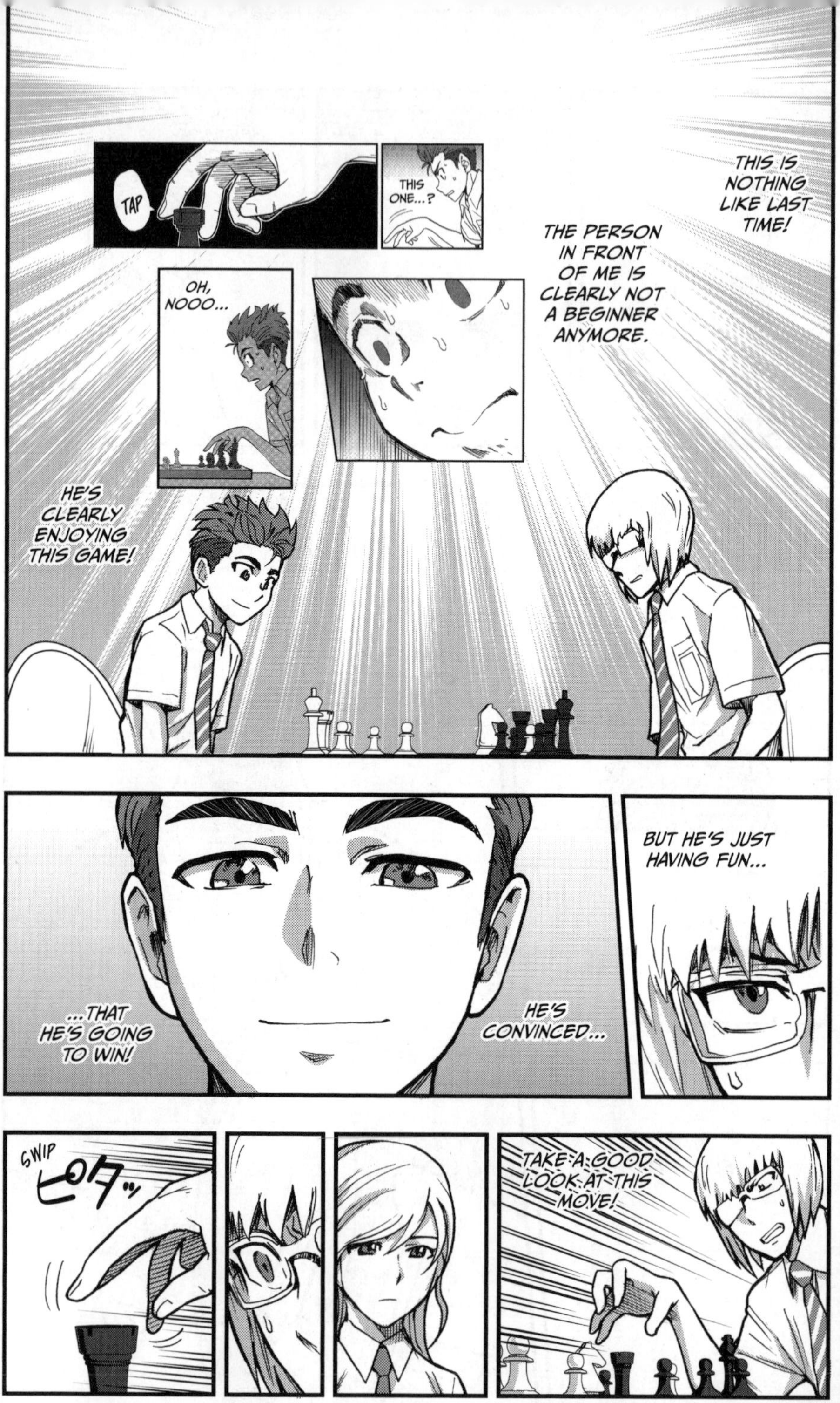
THIS IS NOTHING LIKE LAST TIME!
THIS ONE...?
TAP
THE PERSON IN FRONT OF ME IS CLEARLY NOT A BEGINNER ANYMORE.
OH, NOOO...
HE'S CLEARLY ENJOYING THIS GAME!
BUT HE'S JUST HAVING FUN...
HE'S CONVINCED...
...THAT HE'S GOING TO WIN!
TAKE A GOOD LOOK AT THIS MOVE!
SWIP
ピクッ

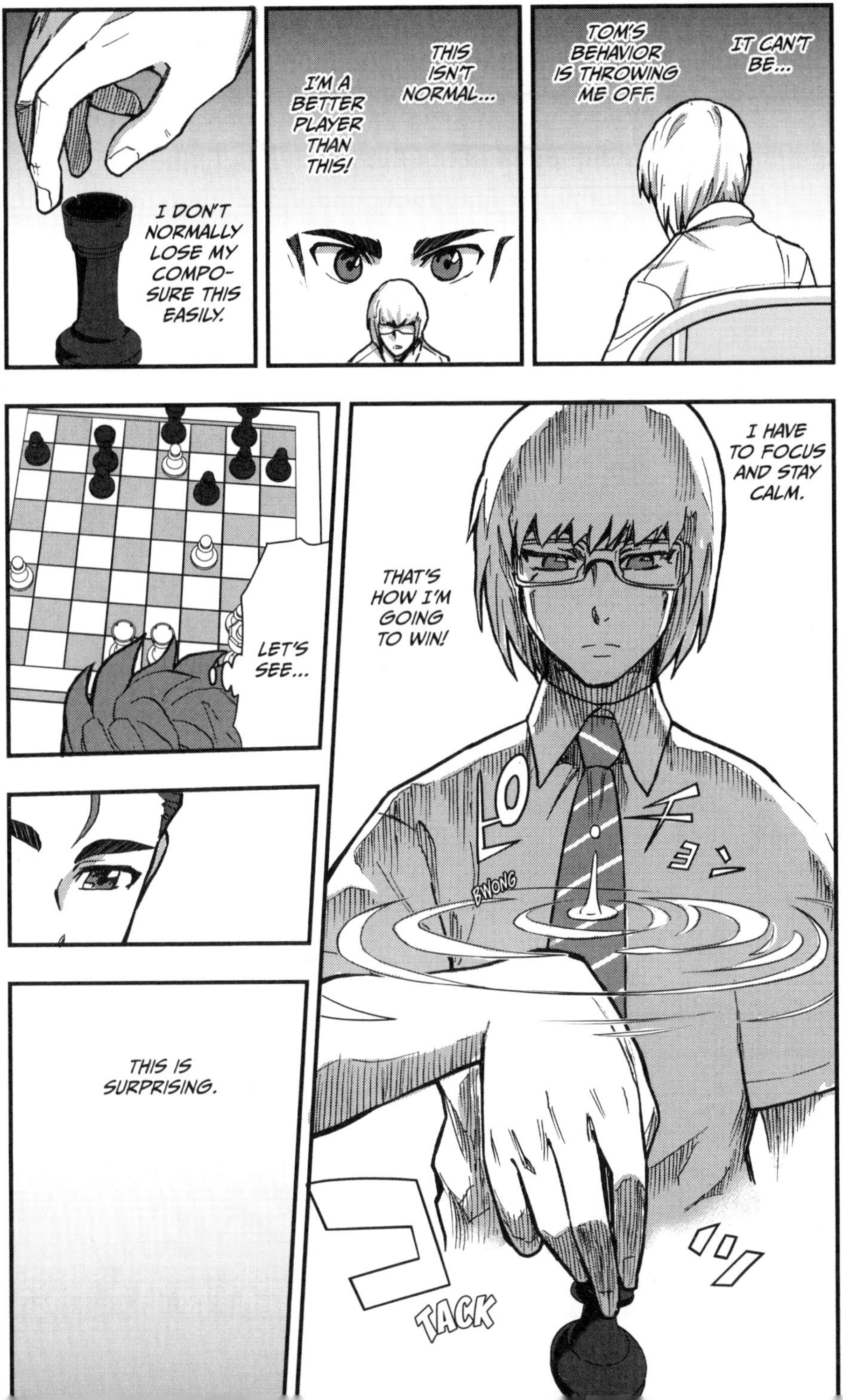
IT CAN'T BE...
TOM'S BEHAVIOR IS THROWING ME OFF.
THIS ISN'T NORMAL...
I'M A BETTER PLAYER THAN THIS!
I DON'T NORMALLY LOSE MY COMPOSURE THIS EASILY.
I HAVE TO FOCUS AND STAY CALM.
THAT'S HOW I'M GOING TO WIN!
BWONG
TACK
LET'S SEE...
THIS IS SURPRISING.

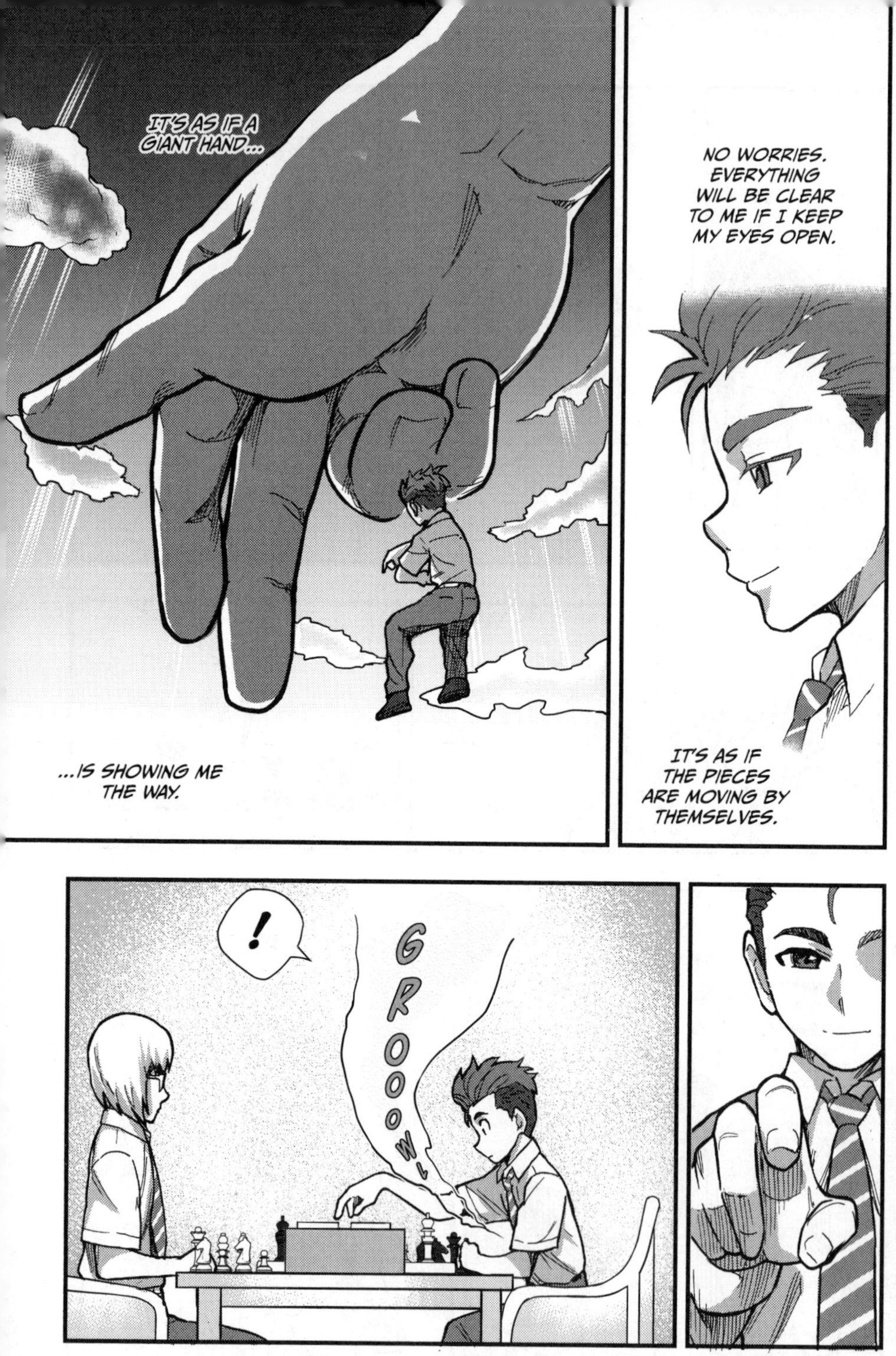
NO WORRIES. EVERYTHING WILL BE CLEAR TO ME IF I KEEP MY EYES OPEN.
IT'S AS IF THE PIECES ARE MOVING BY THEMSELVES.
IT'S AS IF A GIANT HAND...
...IS SHOWING ME THE WAY.
!
GROOOWL

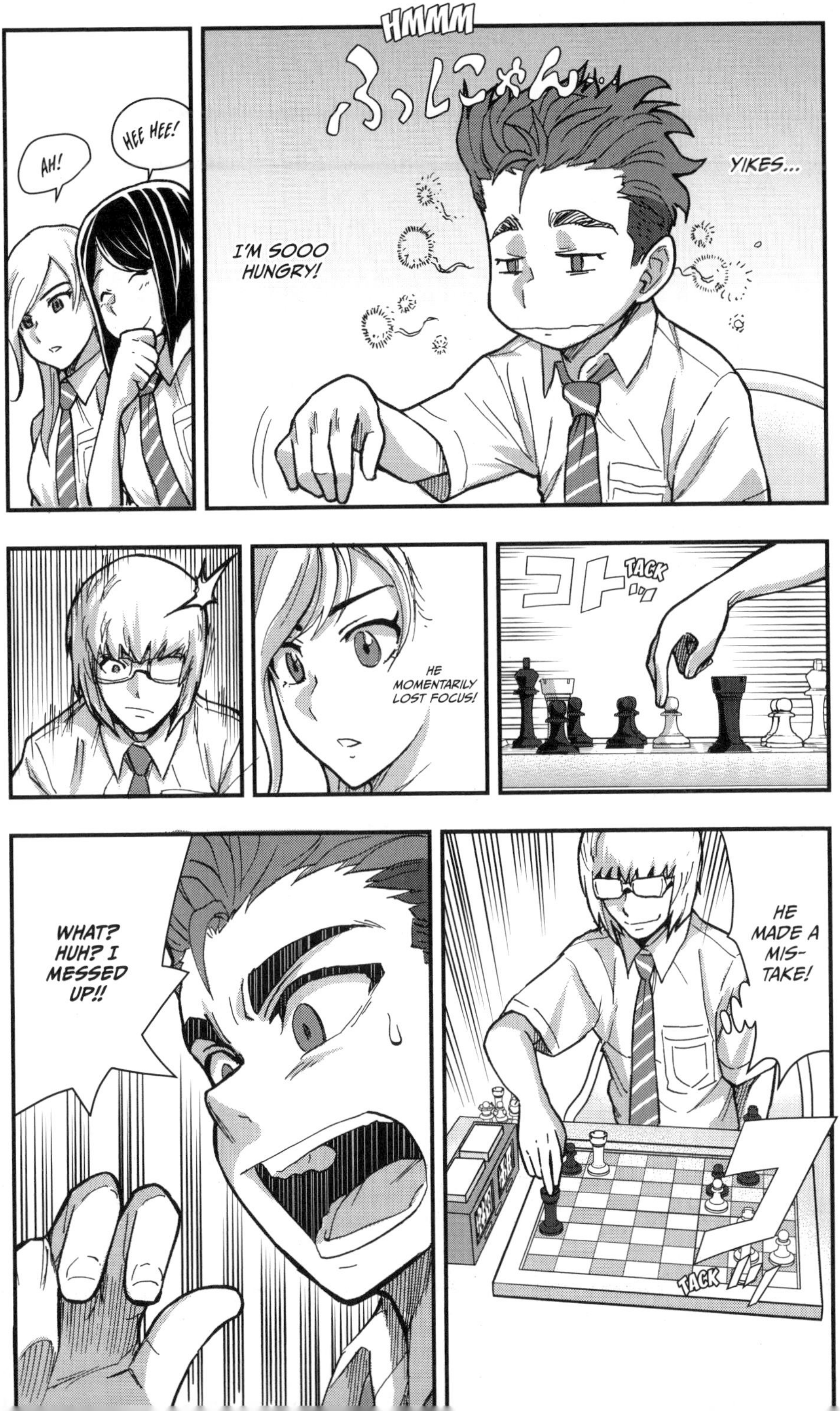
HMMM
YIKES...
I'M SOOO HUNGRY!
HEE HEE!
AH!
コト
TACK
HE MOMENTARILY LOST FOCUS!
HE MADE A MIS-TAKE!
TACK
WHAT? HUH? I MESSED UP!!

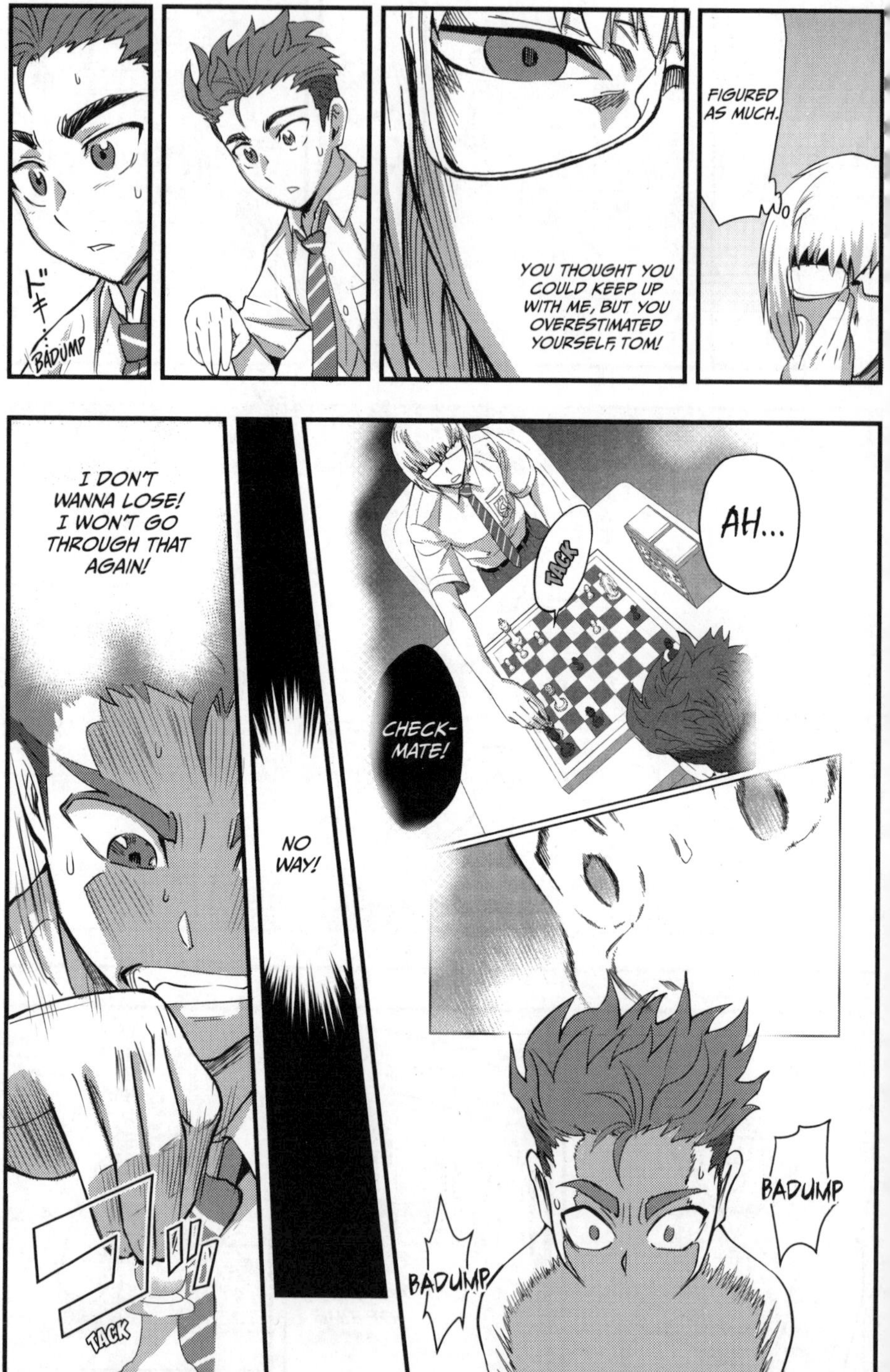
FIGURED AS MUCH.
YOU THOUGHT YOU COULD KEEP UP WITH ME, BUT YOU OVERESTIMATED YOURSELF, TOM!
ドキ…
BADUMP
AH...
TACK
CHECKMATE!
BADUMP
BADUMP
NO WAY!
I DON'T WANNA LOSE! I WON'T GO THROUGH THAT AGAIN!
TACK

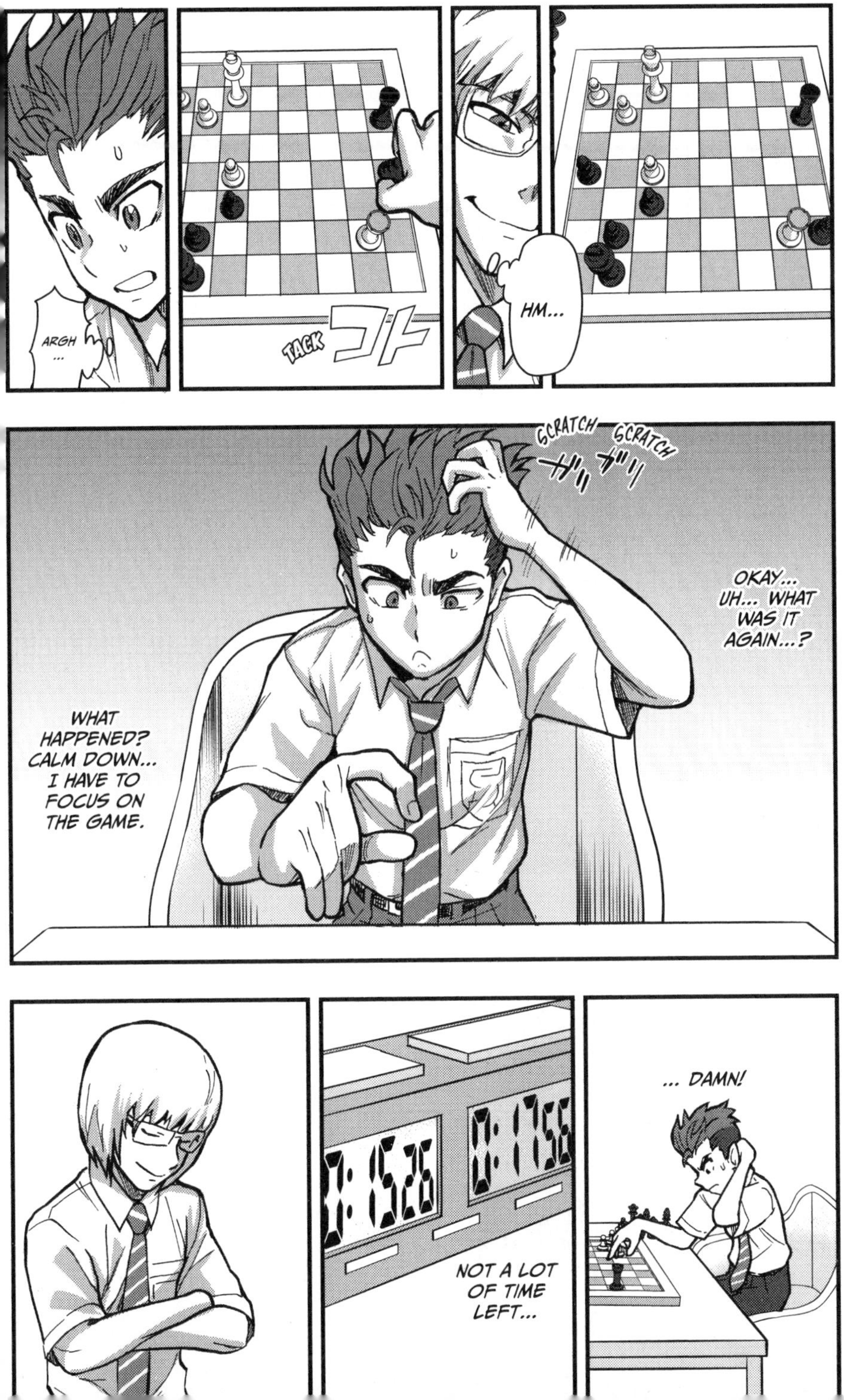
HM...
TACK
コト
ARGH ...
SCRATCH
SCRATCH
ガリ ガリ
OKAY... UH... WHAT WAS IT AGAIN...?
WHAT HAPPENED? CALM DOWN... I HAVE TO FOCUS ON THE GAME.
... DAMN!
NOT A LOT OF TIME LEFT...

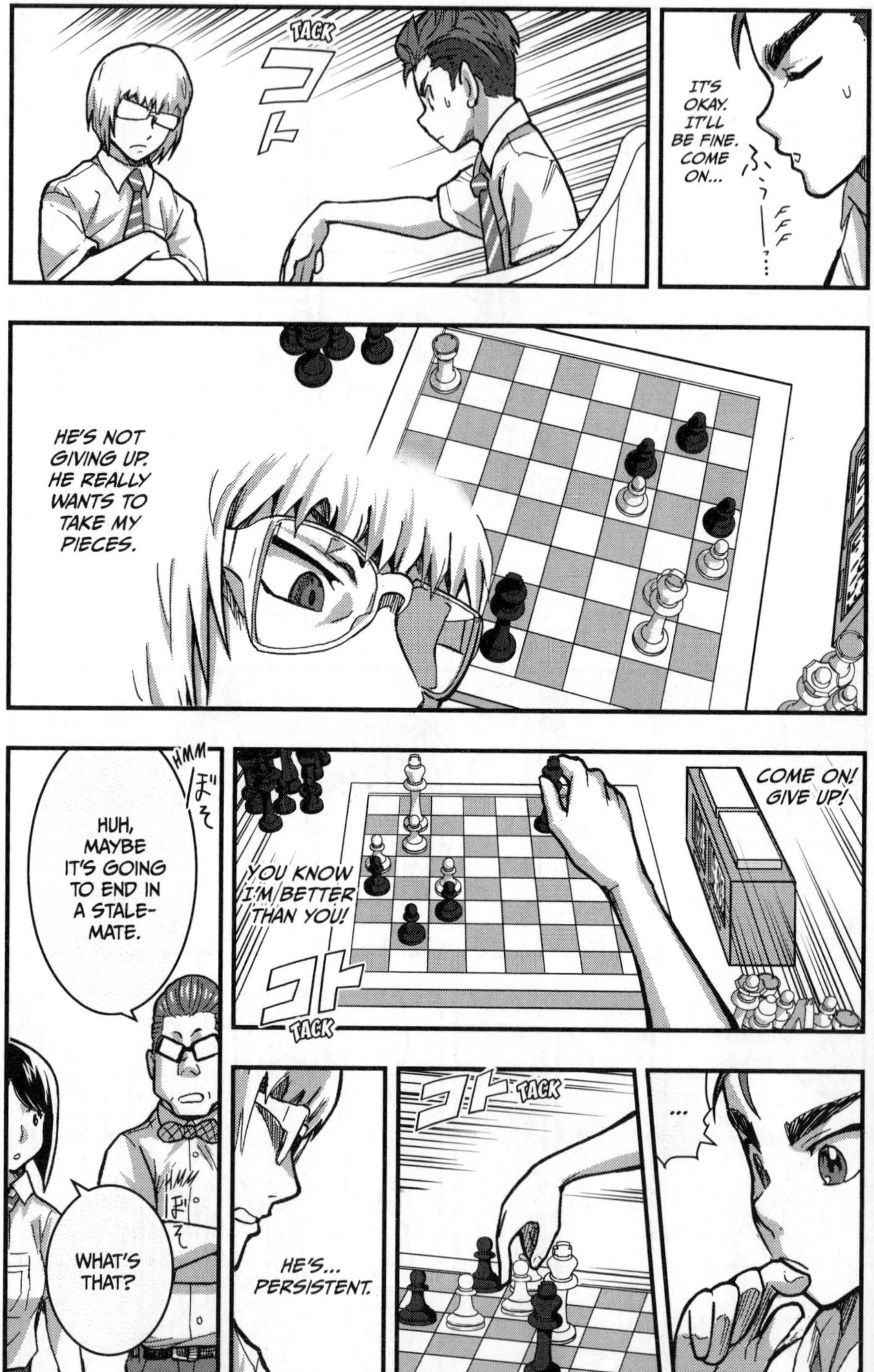
IT'S OKAY. IT'LL BE FINE. COME ON...
FFF
TACK
コト
HE'S NOT GIVING UP. HE REALLY WANTS TO TAKE MY PIECES.
COME ON! GIVE UP!
YOU KNOW I'M BETTER THAN YOU!
コト
TACK
...
コト
TACK
HE'S... PERSISTENT.
HMM
ぼそ
HUH, MAYBE IT'S GOING TO END IN A STALE-MATE.
HMM
ぼそ
WHAT'S THAT?

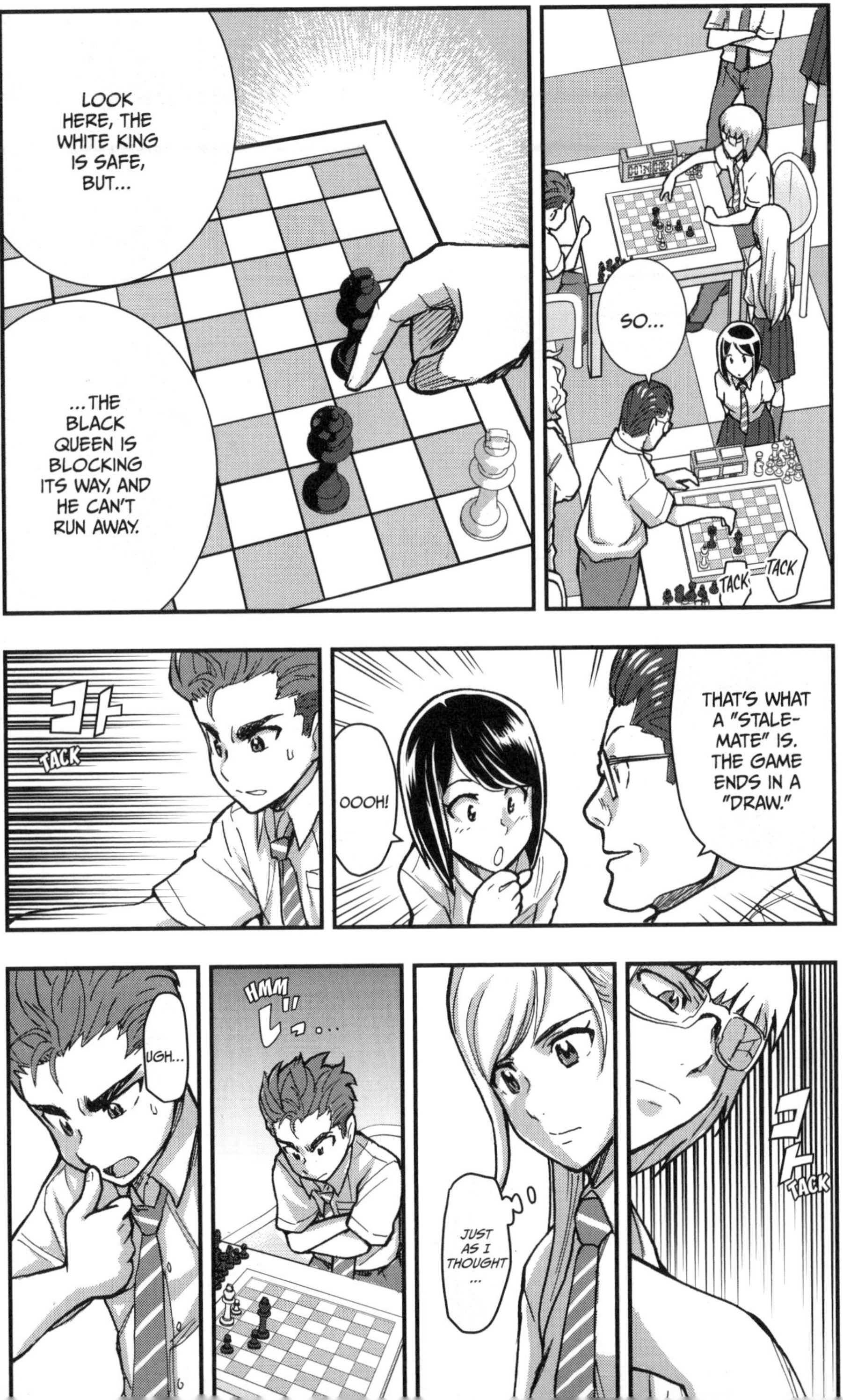
SO...
TACK
TACK
LOOK HERE, THE WHITE KING IS SAFE, BUT...
...THE BLACK QUEEN IS BLOCKING ITS WAY, AND HE CAN'T RUN AWAY.
THAT'S WHAT A "STALE-MATE" IS. THE GAME ENDS IN A "DRAW."
OOOH!
コト
TACK
コト
TACK
JUST AS I THOUGHT...
HMM
じっ...
UGH...

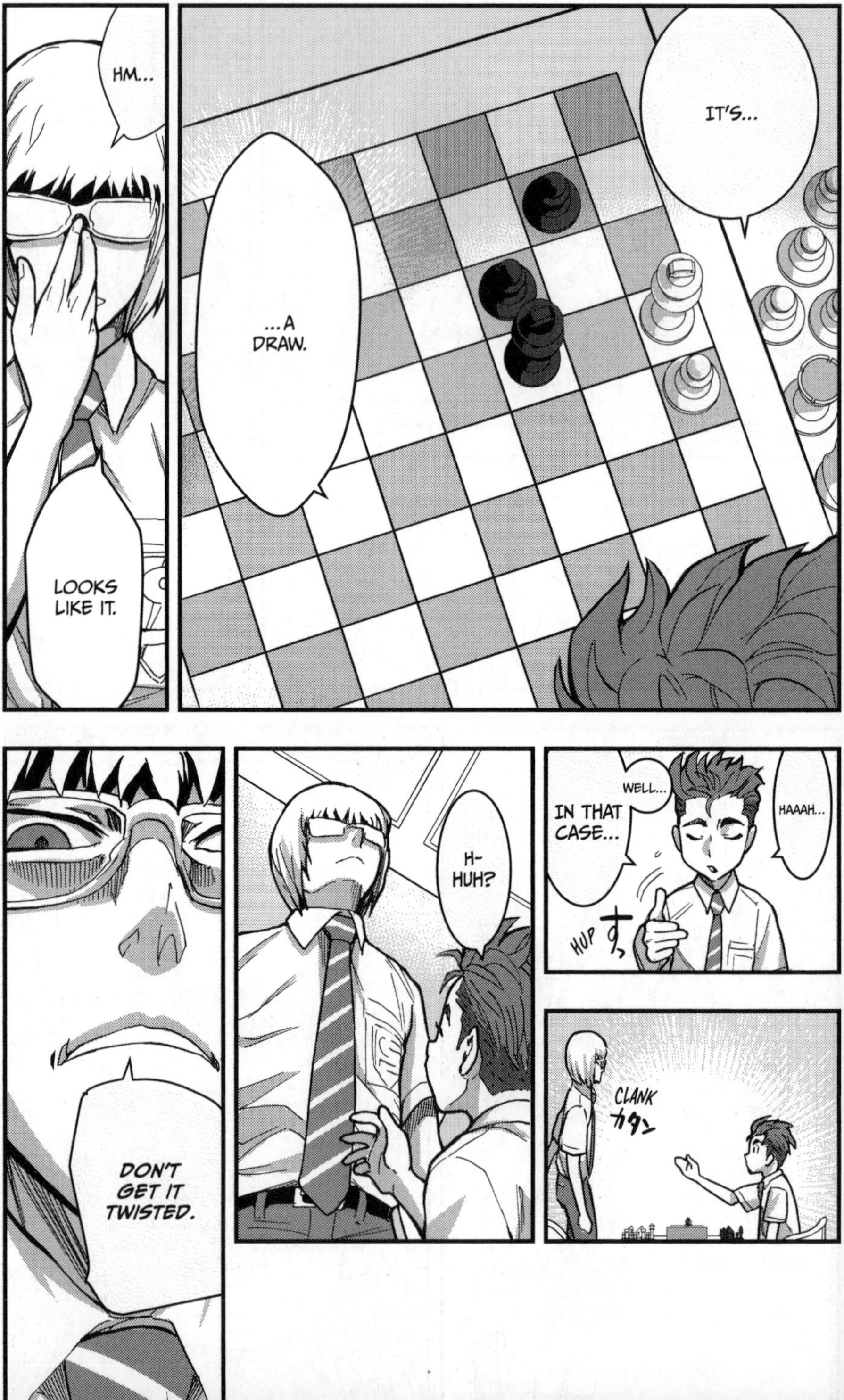
IT'S...
...A DRAW.
HM...
LOOKS LIKE IT.
HAAAH...
WELL...
IN THAT CASE...
HUP
すっ
CLANK
カタン
H-HUH?
DON'T GET IT TWISTED.

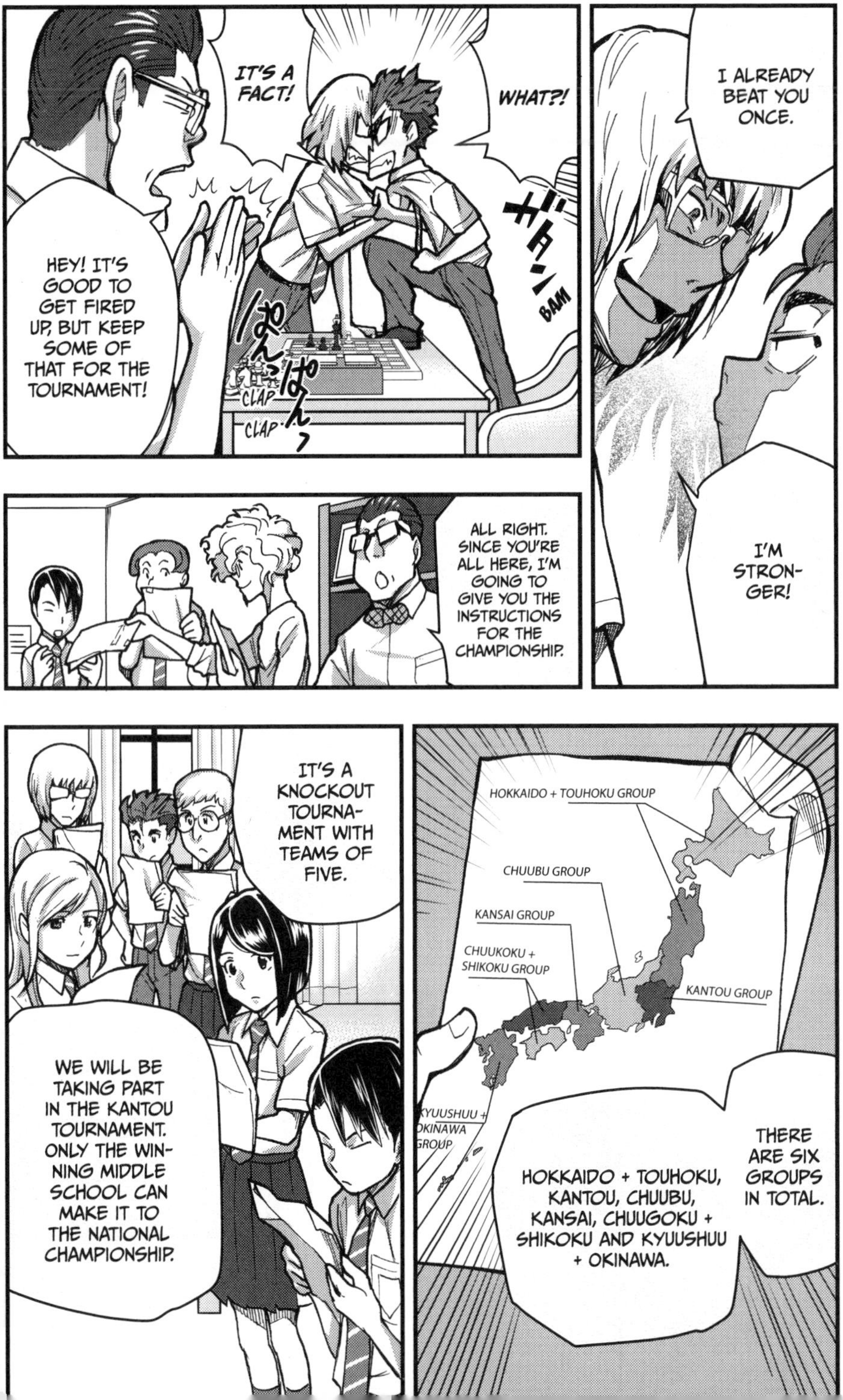
I ALREADY BEAT YOU ONCE.
I'M STRON-GER!
WHAT?!
IT'S A FACT!
BAM
CLAP
CLAP
HEY! IT'S GOOD TO GET FIRED UP, BUT KEEP SOME OF THAT FOR THE TOURNAMENT!
ALL RIGHT. SINCE YOU'RE ALL HERE, I'M GOING TO GIVE YOU THE INSTRUCTIONS FOR THE CHAMPIONSHIP.
HOKKAIDO + TOUHOKU GROUP
CHUUBU GROUP
KANSAI GROUP
CHUUKOKU + SHIKOKU GROUP
KANTOU GROUP
THERE ARE SIX GROUPS IN TOTAL.
HOKKAIDO + TOUHOKU, KANTOU, CHUUBU, KANSAI, CHUUGOKU + SHIKOKU AND KYUUSHUU + OKINAWA.
IT'S A KNOCKOUT TOURNA-MENT WITH TEAMS OF FIVE.
WE WILL BE TAKING PART IN THE KANTOU TOURNAMENT. ONLY THE WIN-NING MIDDLE SCHOOL CAN MAKE IT TO THE NATIONAL CHAMPIONSHIP.

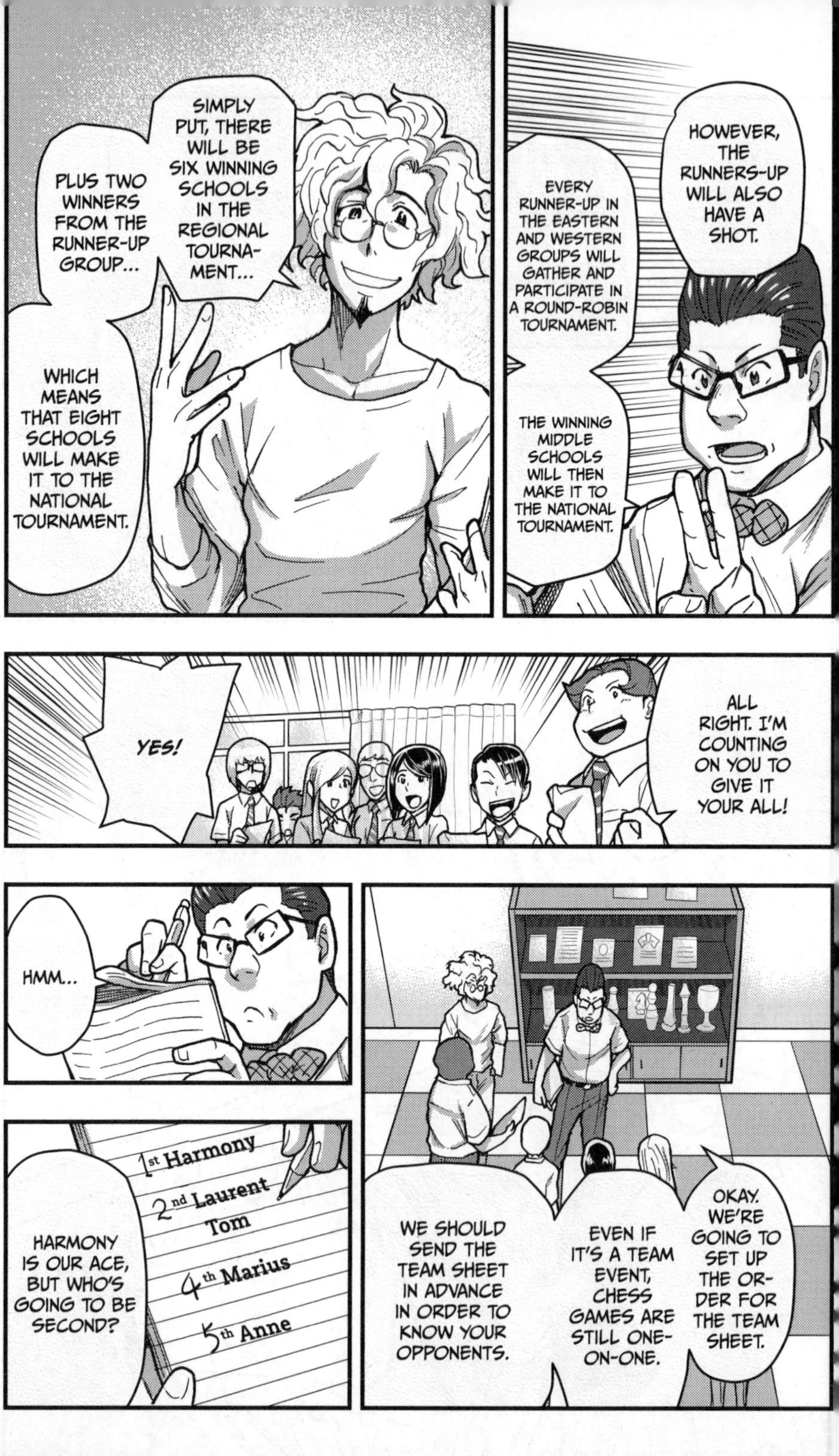
HOWEVER, THE RUNNERS-UP WILL ALSO HAVE A SHOT.
EVERY RUNNER-UP IN THE EASTERN AND WESTERN GROUPS WILL GATHER AND PARTICIPATE IN A ROUND-ROBIN TOURNAMENT.
THE WINNING MIDDLE SCHOOLS WILL THEN MAKE IT TO THE NATIONAL TOURNAMENT.
SIMPLY PUT, THERE WILL BE SIX WINNING SCHOOLS IN THE REGIONAL TOURNA-MENT...
PLUS TWO WINNERS FROM THE RUNNER-UP GROUP...
WHICH MEANS THAT EIGHT SCHOOLS WILL MAKE IT TO THE NATIONAL TOURNAMENT.
ALL RIGHT. I'M COUNTING ON YOU TO GIVE IT YOUR ALL!
YES!
OKAY. WE'RE GOING TO SET UP THE OR-DER FOR THE TEAM SHEET.
EVEN IF IT'S A TEAM EVENT, CHESS GAMES ARE STILL ONE-ON-ONE.
WE SHOULD SEND THE TEAM SHEET IN ADVANCE IN ORDER TO KNOW YOUR OPPONENTS.
HMM...
1st Harmony
2nd Laurent
Tom
4th Marius
5th Anne
HARMONY IS OUR ACE, BUT WHO'S GOING TO BE SECOND?

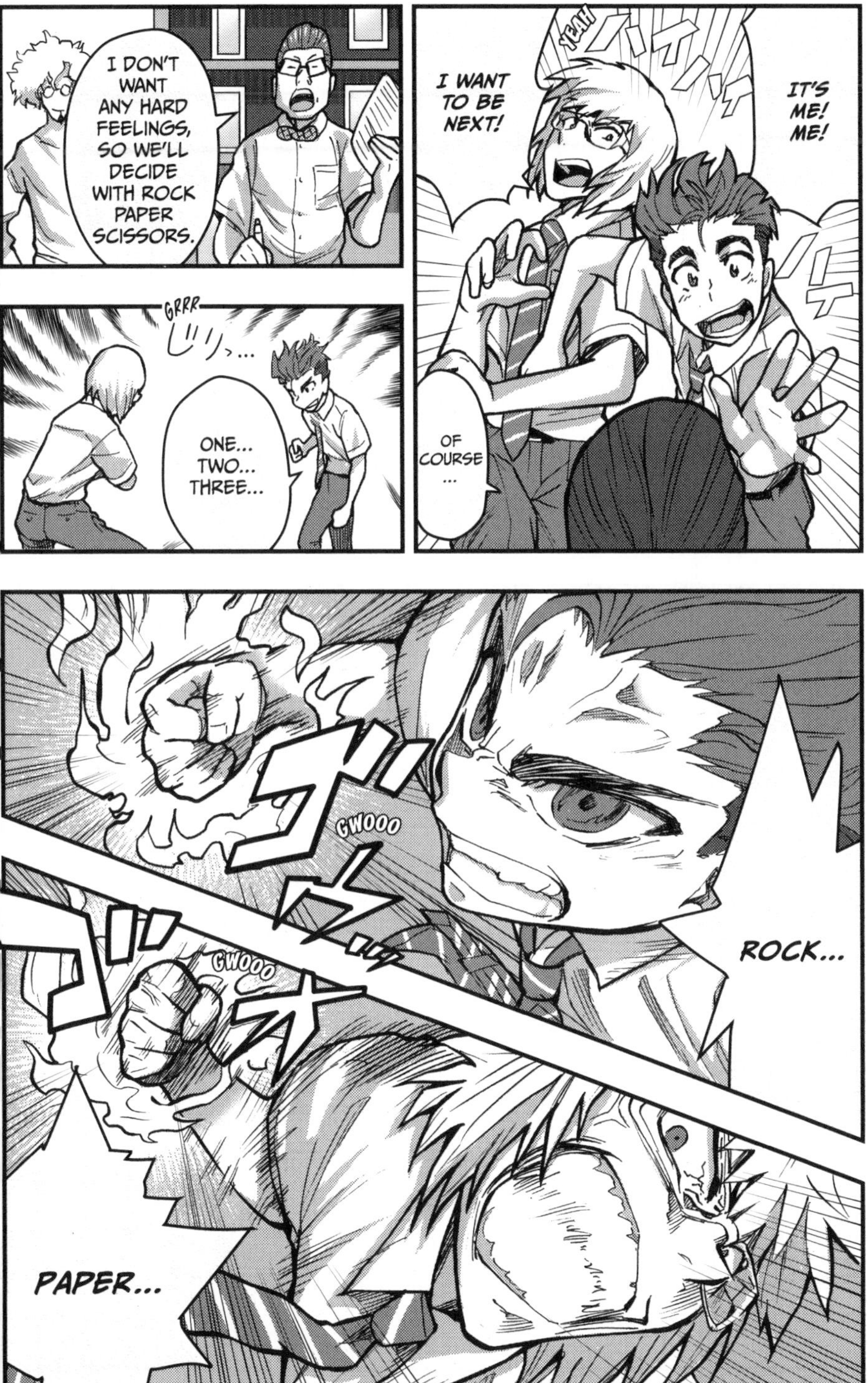
YEAH!
IT'S ME! ME!
I WANT TO BE NEXT!
OF COURSE...
I DON'T WANT ANY HARD FEELINGS, SO WE'LL DECIDE WITH ROCK PAPER SCISSORS.
GRRR
ONE... TWO... THREE...
GWOOO
ROCK...
GWOOO
PAPER...

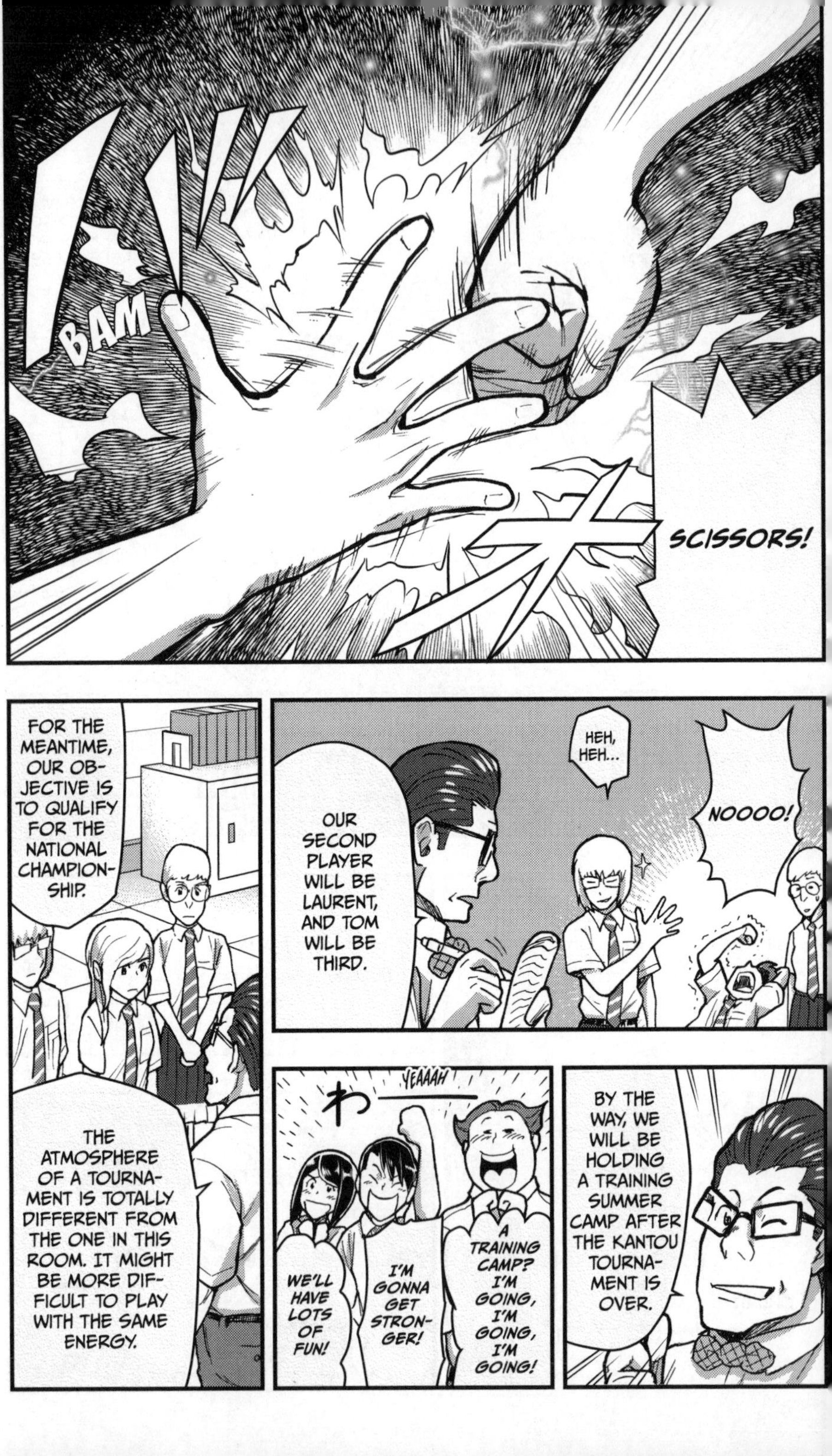
BAM
SCISSORS!
OUR SECOND PLAYER WILL BE LAURENT, AND TOM WILL BE THIRD.
HEH, HEH...
NOOOO!
BY THE WAY, WE WILL BE HOLDING A TRAINING SUMMER CAMP AFTER THE KANTOU TOURNAMENT IS OVER.
YEAAAH
わ
A TRAINING CAMP? I'M GOING, I'M GOING, I'M GOING!
I'M GONNA GET STRONGER!
WE'LL HAVE LOTS OF FUN!
FOR THE MEANTIME, OUR OBJECTIVE IS TO QUALIFY FOR THE NATIONAL CHAMPIONSHIP.
THE ATMOSPHERE OF A TOURNAMENT IS TOTALLY DIFFERENT FROM THE ONE IN THIS ROOM. IT MIGHT BE MORE DIFFICULT TO PLAY WITH THE SAME ENERGY.

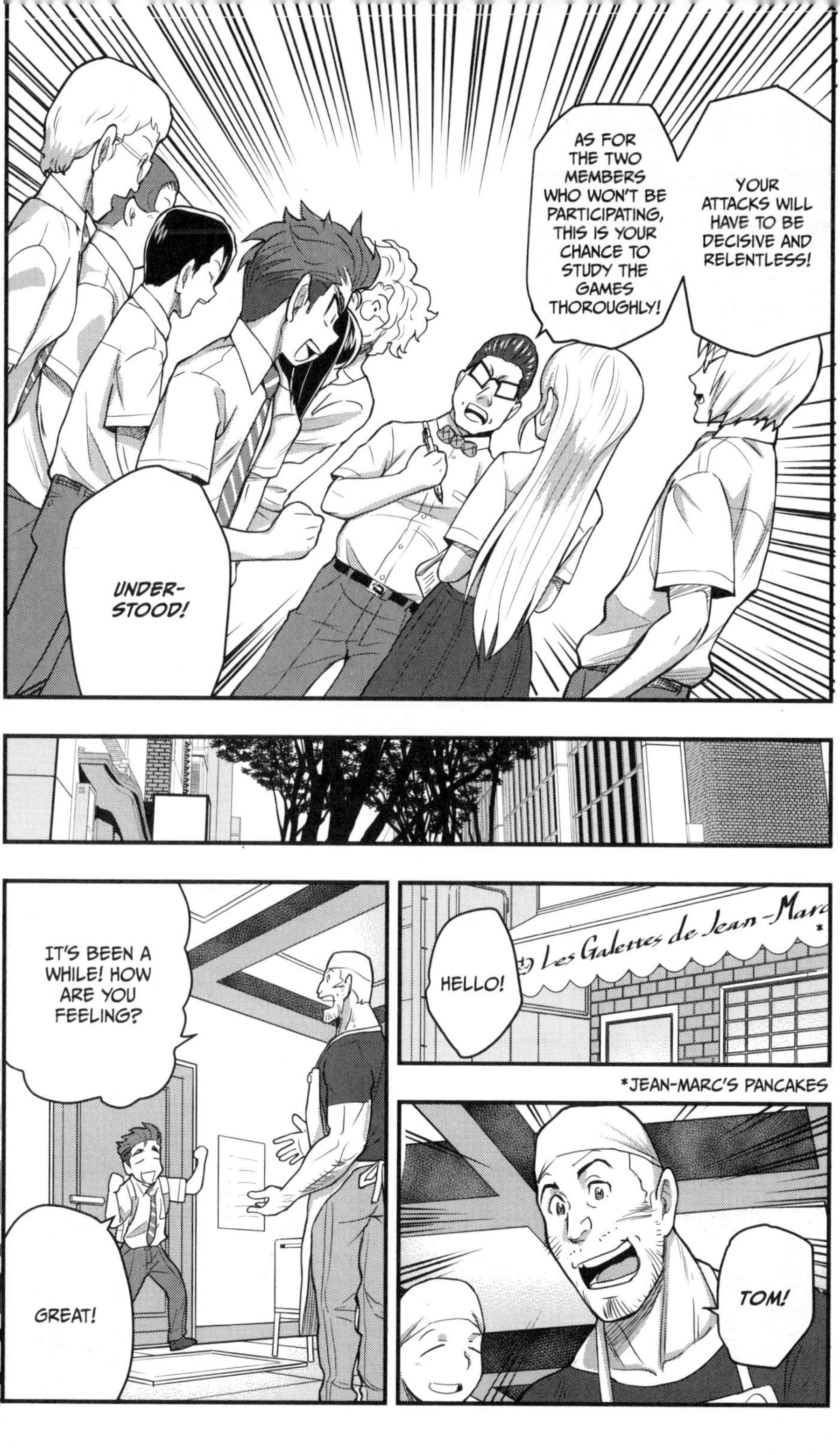
YOUR ATTACKS WILL HAVE TO BE DECISIVE AND RELENTLESS!
AS FOR THE TWO MEMBERS WHO WON'T BE PARTICIPATING, THIS IS YOUR CHANCE TO STUDY THE GAMES THOROUGHLY!
UNDER-STOOD!
Les Galettes de Jean-Marc *
HELLO!
*JEAN-MARC'S PANCAKES
TOM!
IT'S BEEN A WHILE! HOW ARE YOU FEELING?
GREAT!

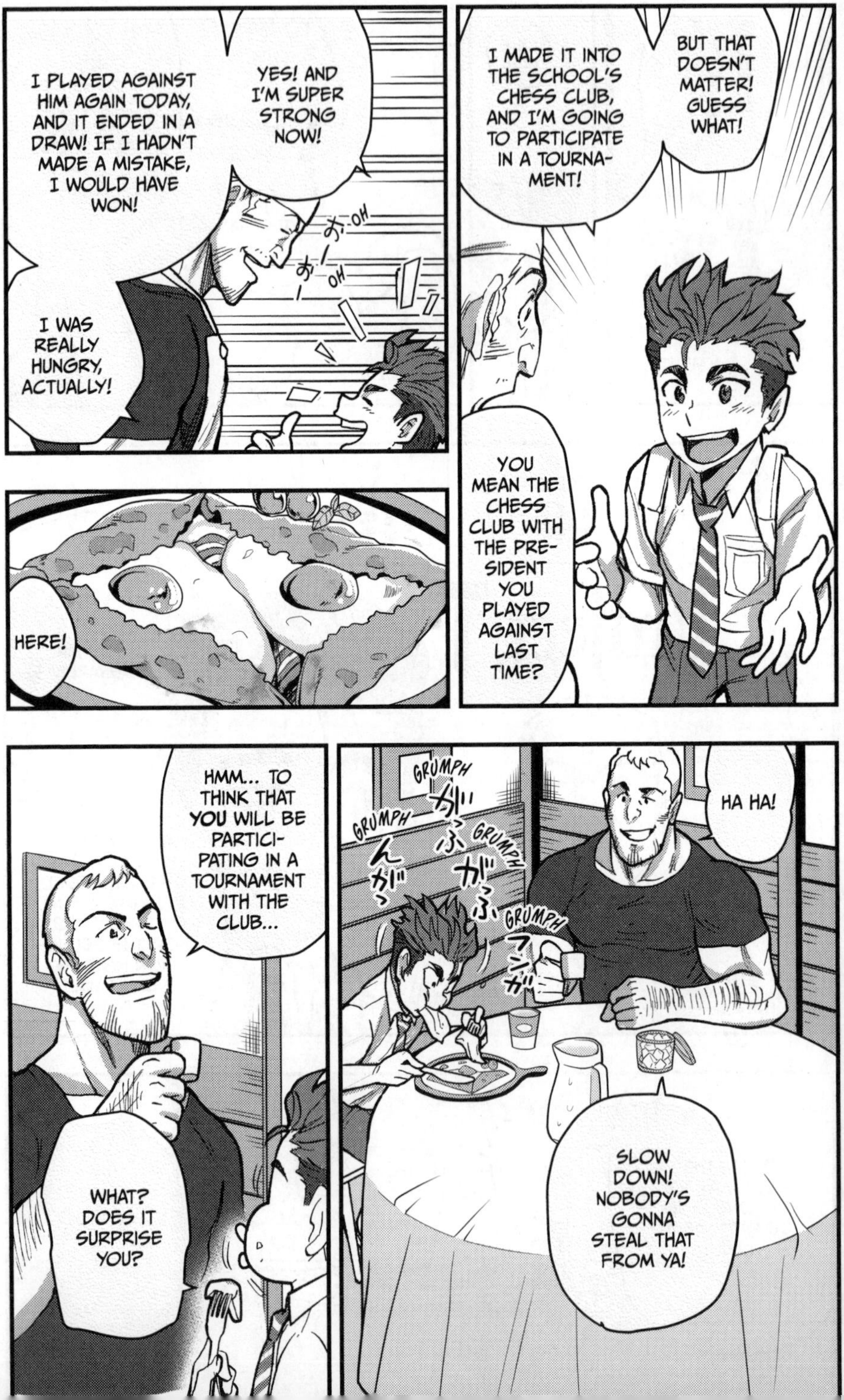
BUT THAT DOESN'T MATTER! GUESS WHAT!
I MADE IT INTO THE SCHOOL'S CHESS CLUB, AND I'M GOING TO PARTICIPATE IN A TOURNAMENT!
YOU MEAN THE CHESS CLUB WITH THE PRESIDENT YOU PLAYED AGAINST LAST TIME?
YES! AND I'M SUPER STRONG NOW!
OH
OH
I PLAYED AGAINST HIM AGAIN TODAY, AND IT ENDED IN A DRAW! IF I HADN'T MADE A MISTAKE, I WOULD HAVE WON!
I WAS REALLY HUNGRY, ACTUALLY!
HERE!
HA HA!
GRUMPH
GRUMPH
GRUMPH
GRUMPH
SLOW DOWN! NOBODY'S GONNA STEAL THAT FROM YA!
HMM... TO THINK THAT **YOU** WILL BE PARTICIPATING IN A TOURNAMENT WITH THE CLUB...
WHAT? DOES IT SURPRISE YOU?

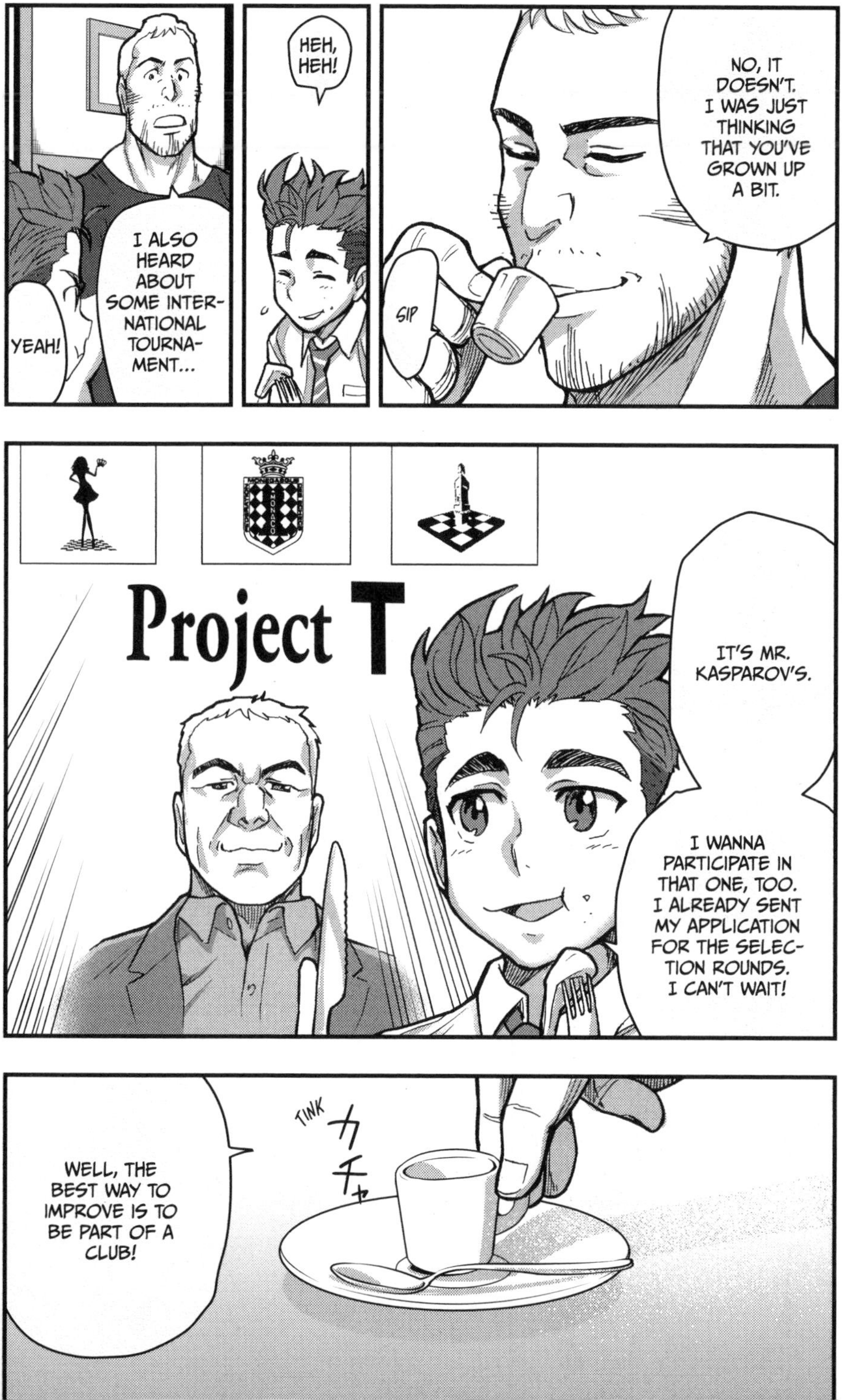
NO, IT DOESN'T. I WAS JUST THINKING THAT YOU'VE GROWN UP A BIT.
SIP
HEH, HEH!
I ALSO HEARD ABOUT SOME INTER-NATIONAL TOURNA-MENT...
YEAH!
IT'S MR. KASPAROV'S.
I WANNA PARTICIPATE IN THAT ONE, TOO. I ALREADY SENT MY APPLICATION FOR THE SELEC-TION ROUNDS. I CAN'T WAIT!
Project T
TINK
カチャ
WELL, THE BEST WAY TO IMPROVE IS TO BE PART OF A CLUB!

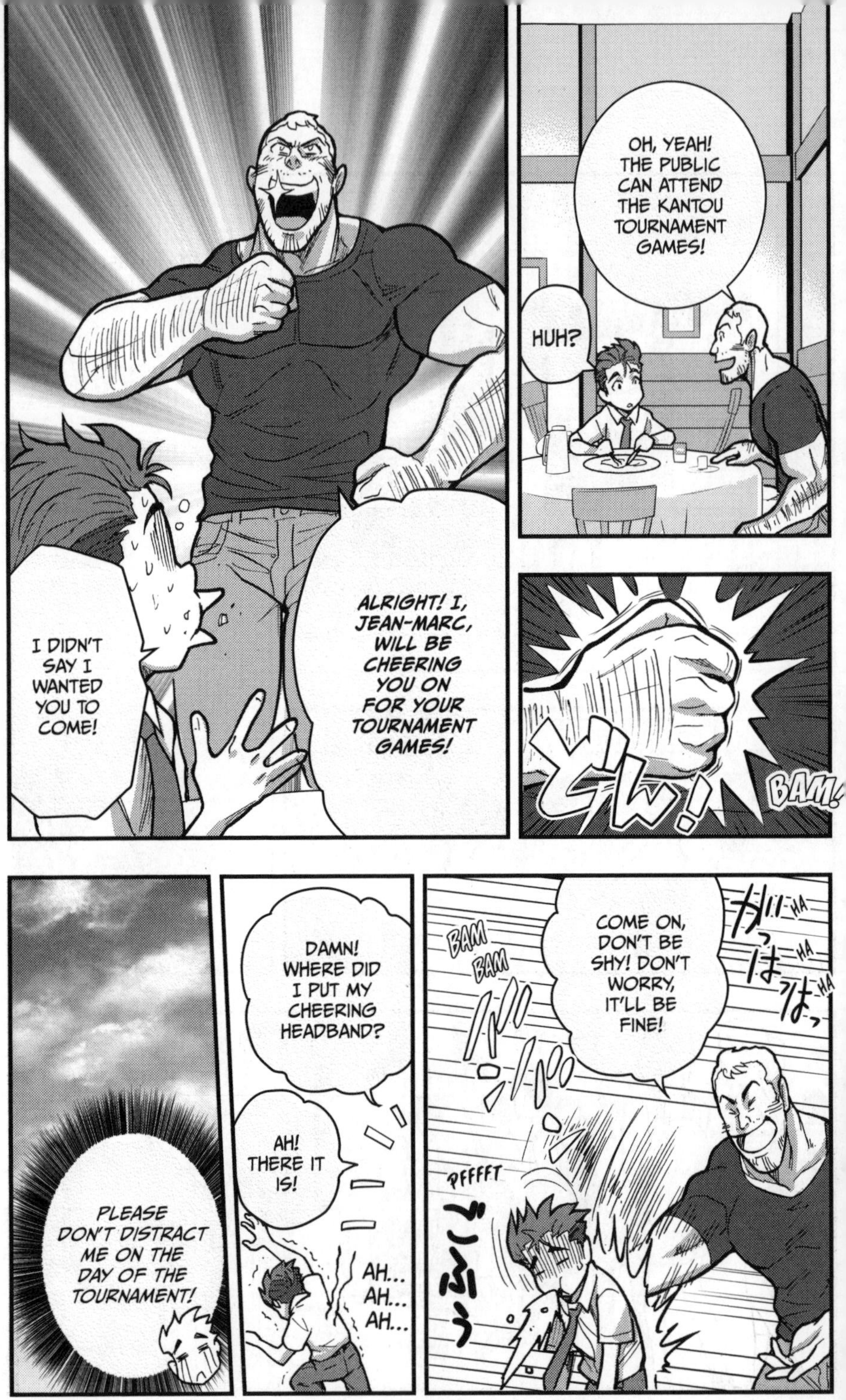

OH, YEAH! THE PUBLIC CAN ATTEND THE KANTOU TOURNAMENT GAMES!
HUH?
どん!
BAM!
ALRIGHT! I, JEAN-MARC, WILL BE CHEERING YOU ON FOR YOUR TOURNAMENT GAMES!
I DIDN'T SAY I WANTED YOU TO COME!
HA
HA
HA
COME ON, DON'T BE SHY! DON'T WORRY, IT'LL BE FINE!
BAM
BAM
PFFFFT
DAMN! WHERE DID I PUT MY CHEERING HEADBAND?
AH! THERE IT IS!
AH... AH... AH...
PLEASE DON'T DISTRACT ME ON THE DAY OF THE TOURNAMENT!

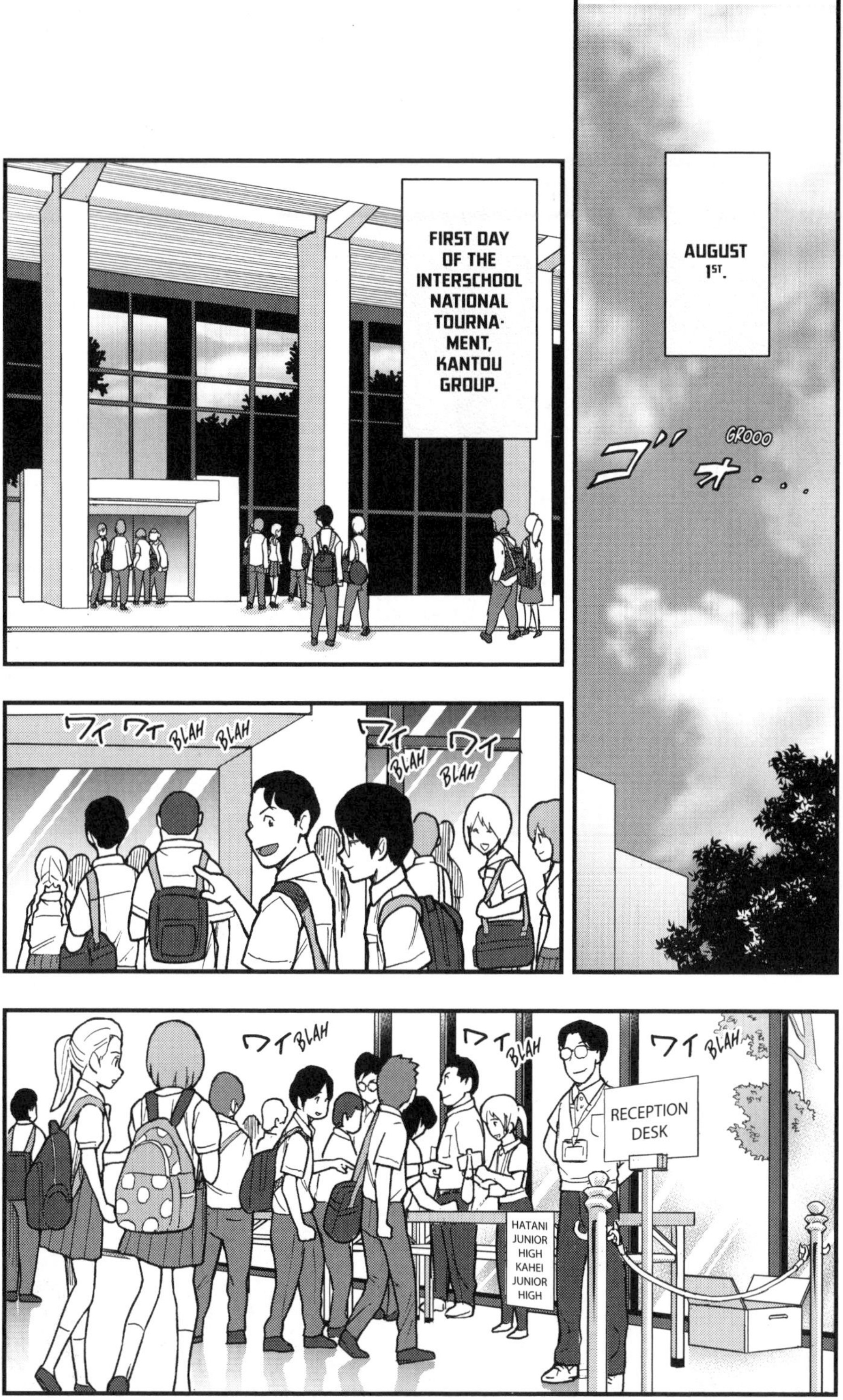
AUGUST 1ST.
ゴオ...
GROOO
FIRST DAY OF THE INTERSCHOOL NATIONAL TOURNAMENT, KANTOU GROUP.
ワイ ワイ BLAH BLAH
ワイ ワイ BLAH BLAH
ワイ BLAH
ワイ BLAH
ワイ BLAH
RECEPTION DESK
HATANI JUNIOR HIGH
KAHEI JUNIOR HIGH

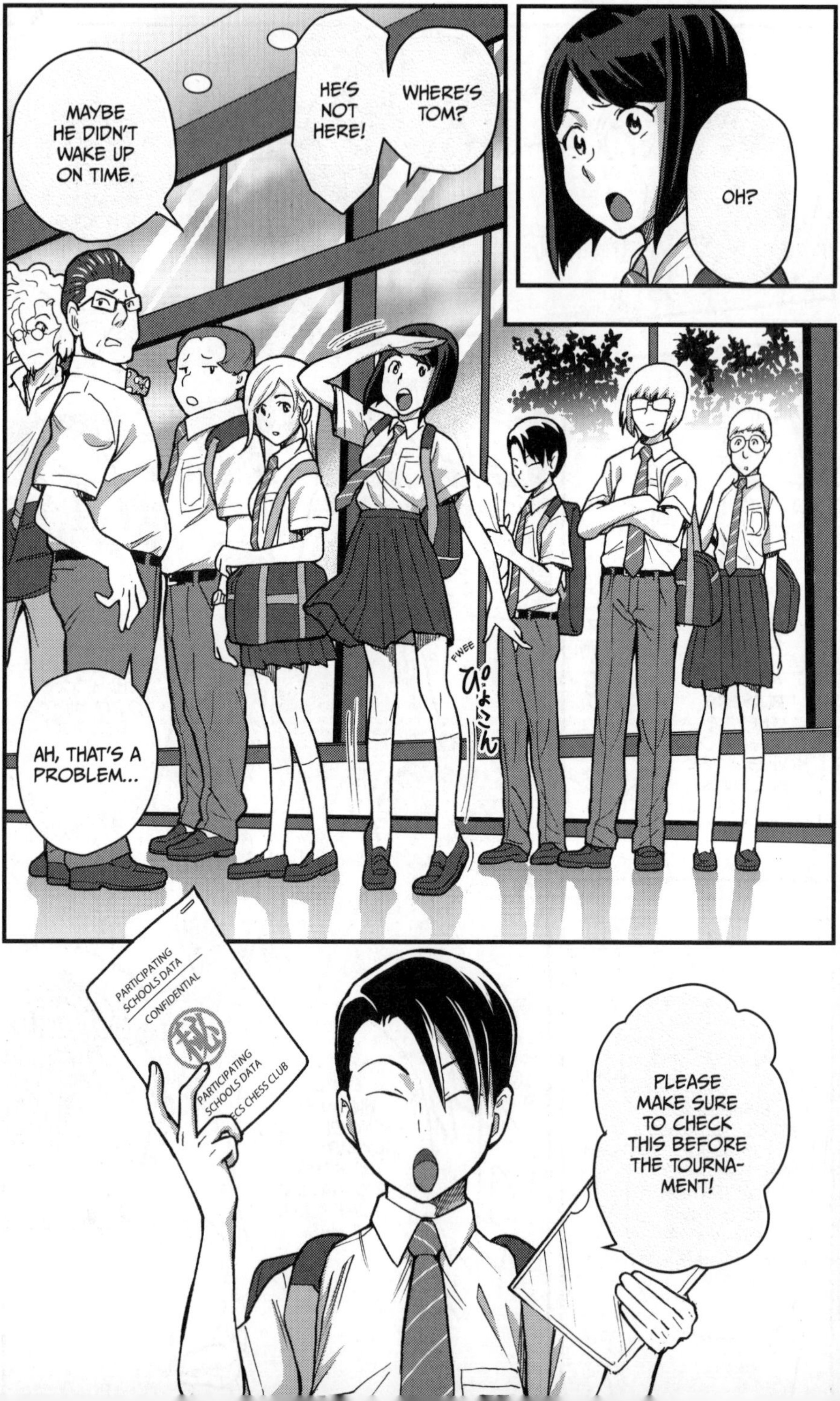
OH?
WHERE'S TOM?
HE'S NOT HERE!
MAYBE HE DIDN'T WAKE UP ON TIME.
FWEE
ぴょこん
AH, THAT'S A PROBLEM...
PARTICIPATING SCHOOLS DATA
CONFIDENTIAL
PARTICIPATING SCHOOLS DATA
PLEASE MAKE SURE TO CHECK THIS BEFORE THE TOURNA-MENT!

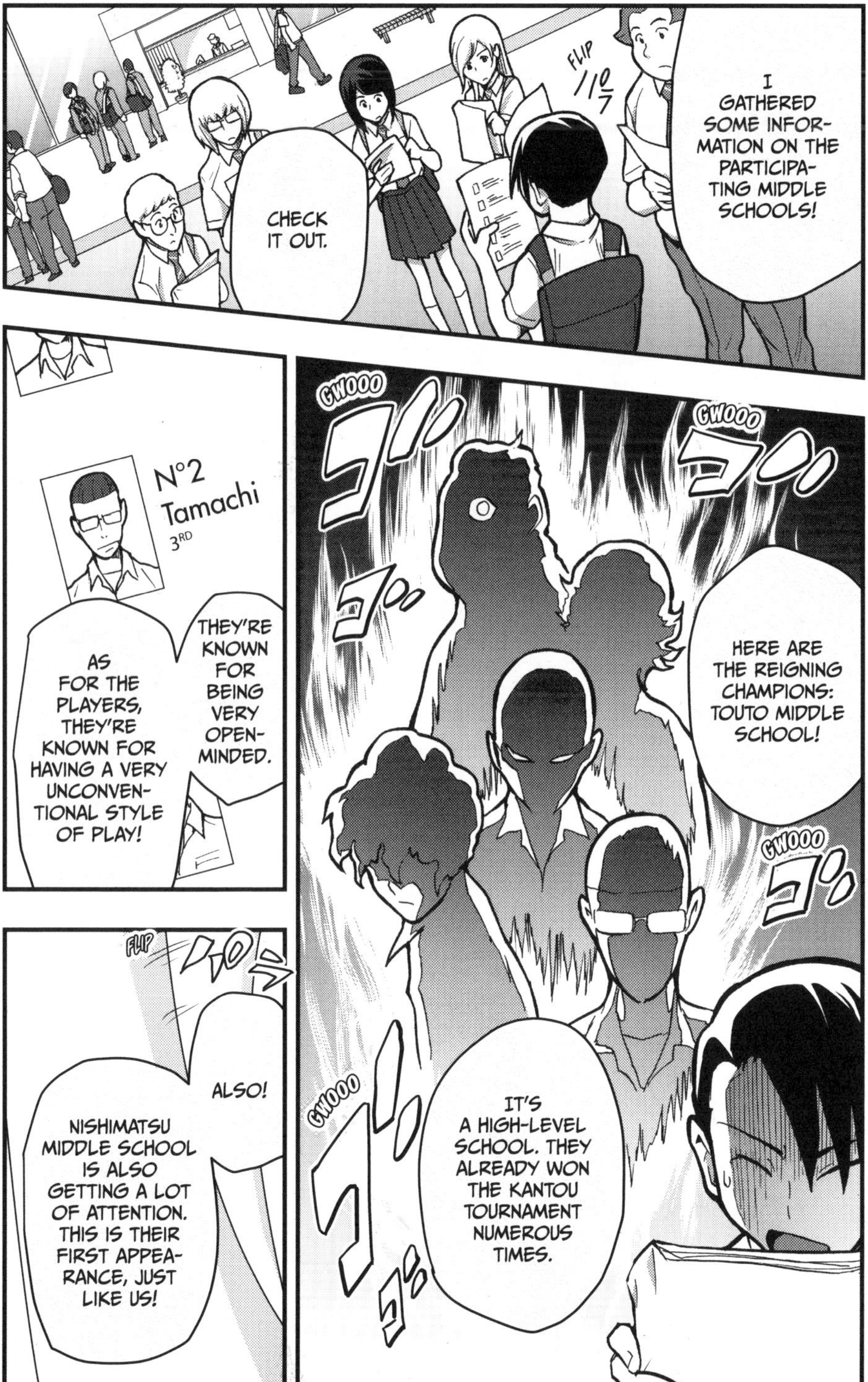
I GATHERED SOME INFORMATION ON THE PARTICIPATING MIDDLE SCHOOLS!
FLIP
CHECK IT OUT.
GWOOO
GWOOO
HERE ARE THE REIGNING CHAMPIONS: TOUTO MIDDLE SCHOOL!
GWOOO
GWOOO
IT'S A HIGH-LEVEL SCHOOL. THEY ALREADY WON THE KANTOU TOURNAMENT NUMEROUS TIMES.
N°2 Tamachi 3RD
THEY'RE KNOWN FOR BEING VERY OPEN-MINDED.
AS FOR THE PLAYERS, THEY'RE KNOWN FOR HAVING A VERY UNCONVENTIONAL STYLE OF PLAY!
FLIP
ALSO!
NISHIMATSU MIDDLE SCHOOL IS ALSO GETTING A LOT OF ATTENTION. THIS IS THEIR FIRST APPEARANCE, JUST LIKE US!

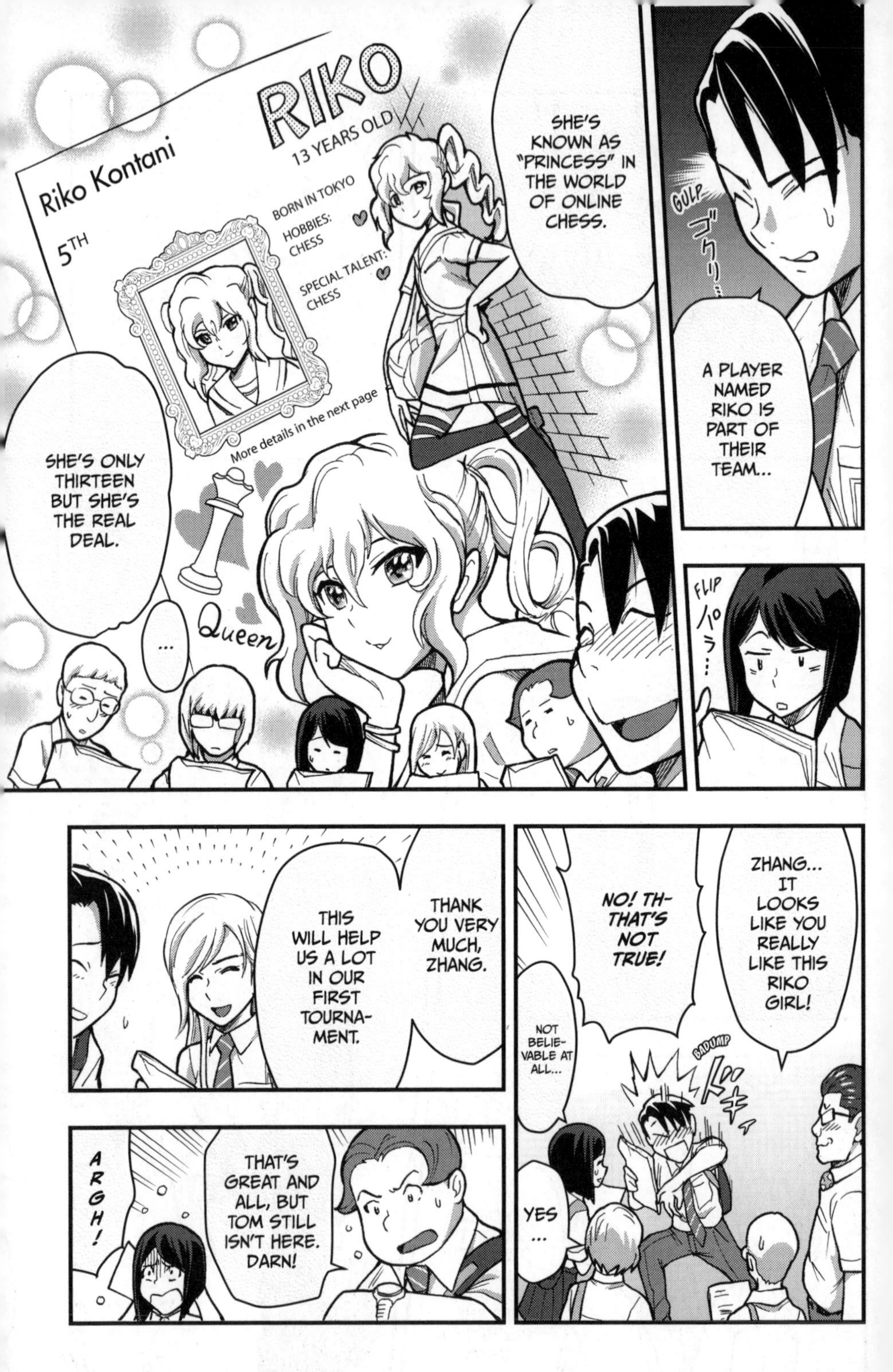
GULP ゴクリ…
A PLAYER NAMED RIKO IS PART OF THEIR TEAM...
FLIP パラ…
SHE'S KNOWN AS "PRINCESS" IN THE WORLD OF ONLINE CHESS.
RIKO
13 YEARS OLD
Riko Kontani
5TH
BORN IN TOKYO
HOBBIES: CHESS
SPECIAL TALENT: CHESS
More details in the next page
Queen
SHE'S ONLY THIRTEEN BUT SHE'S THE REAL DEAL.
...
ZHANG... IT LOOKS LIKE YOU REALLY LIKE THIS RIKO GIRL!
NO! TH-THAT'S NOT TRUE!
BADUMP ドキィ
NOT BELIEVABLE AT ALL...
YES ...
THANK YOU VERY MUCH, ZHANG.
THIS WILL HELP US A LOT IN OUR FIRST TOURNAMENT.
THAT'S GREAT AND ALL, BUT TOM STILL ISN'T HERE. DARN!
ARGH!

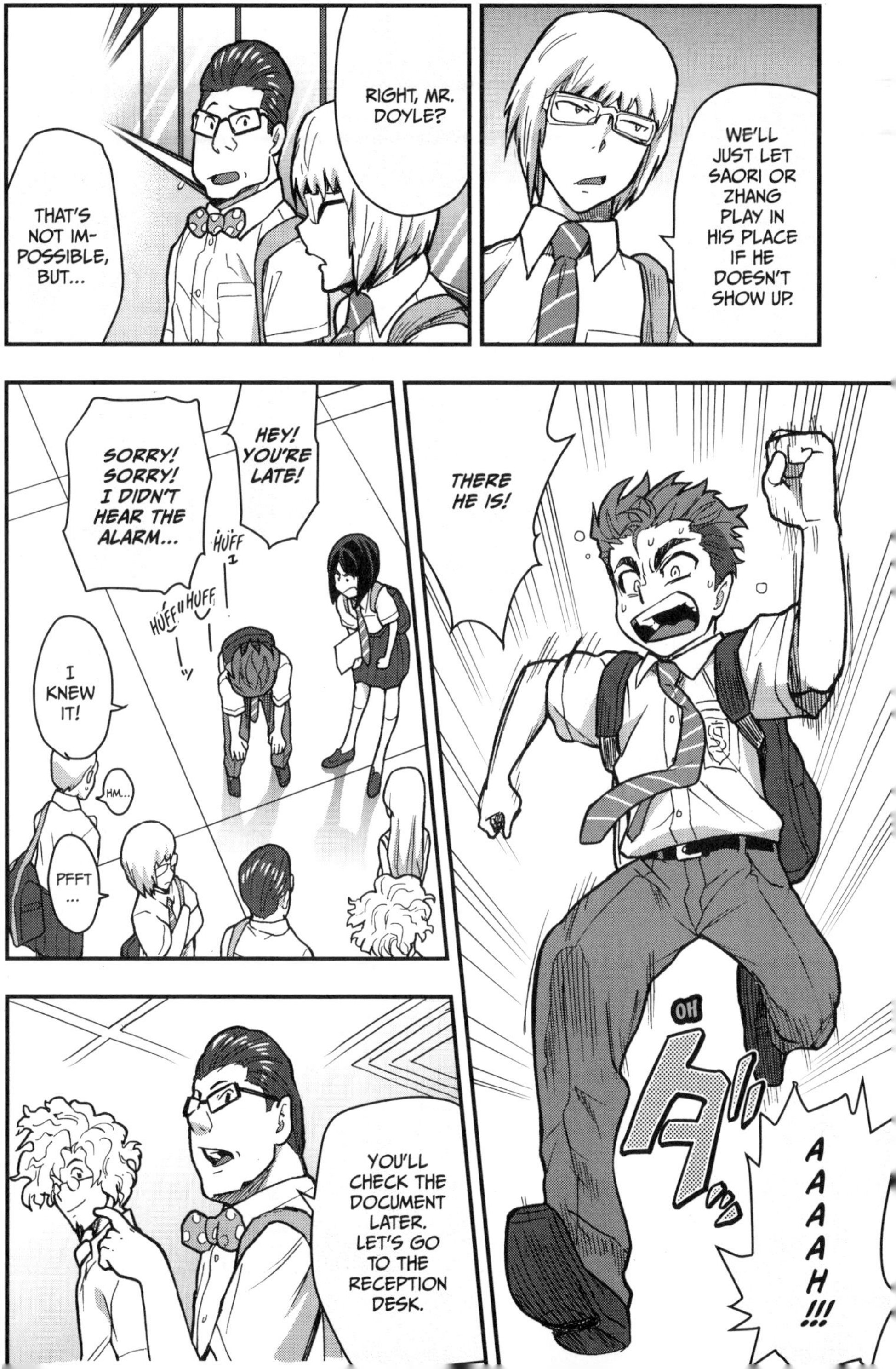
WE'LL JUST LET SAORI OR ZHANG PLAY IN HIS PLACE IF HE DOESN'T SHOW UP.
RIGHT, MR. DOYLE?
THAT'S NOT IM-POSSIBLE, BUT...
THERE HE IS!
OH
AAAAAAH!!!
HEY! YOU'RE LATE!
SORRY! SORRY! I DIDN'T HEAR THE ALARM...
HUFF
HUFF HUFF
I KNEW IT!
HM...
PFFT ...
YOU'LL CHECK THE DOCUMENT LATER. LET'S GO TO THE RECEPTION DESK.

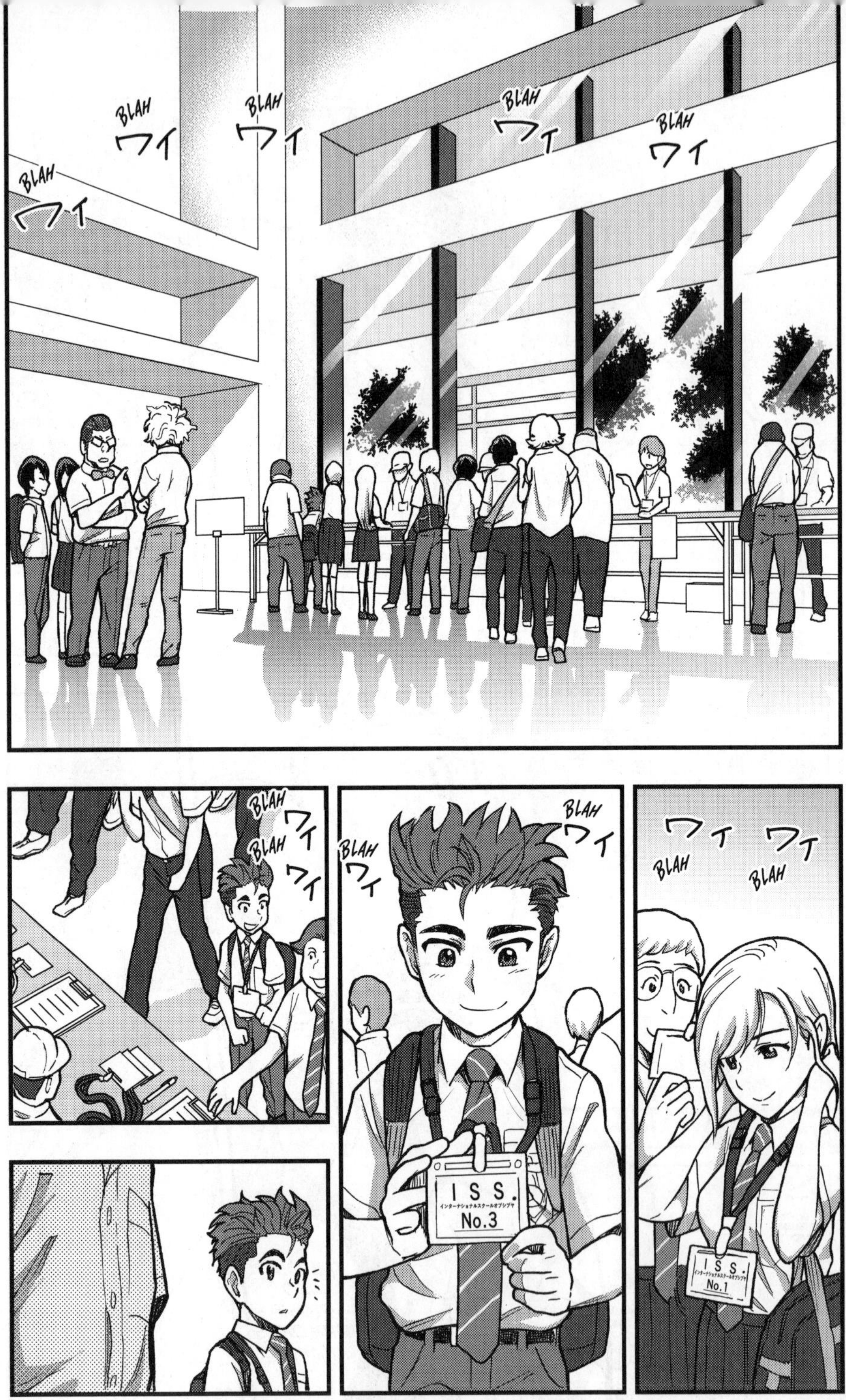
BLAH ワイ
BLAH ワイ
BLAH ワイ
BLAH ワイ
BLAH ワイ
ワイ BLAH
ワイ BLAH
I S S.
No.1
BLAH ワイ
BLAH ワイ
I S S.
No.3
BLAH ワイ
BLAH ワイ

*INTERNATIONAL SCHOOL OF SHIBUYA

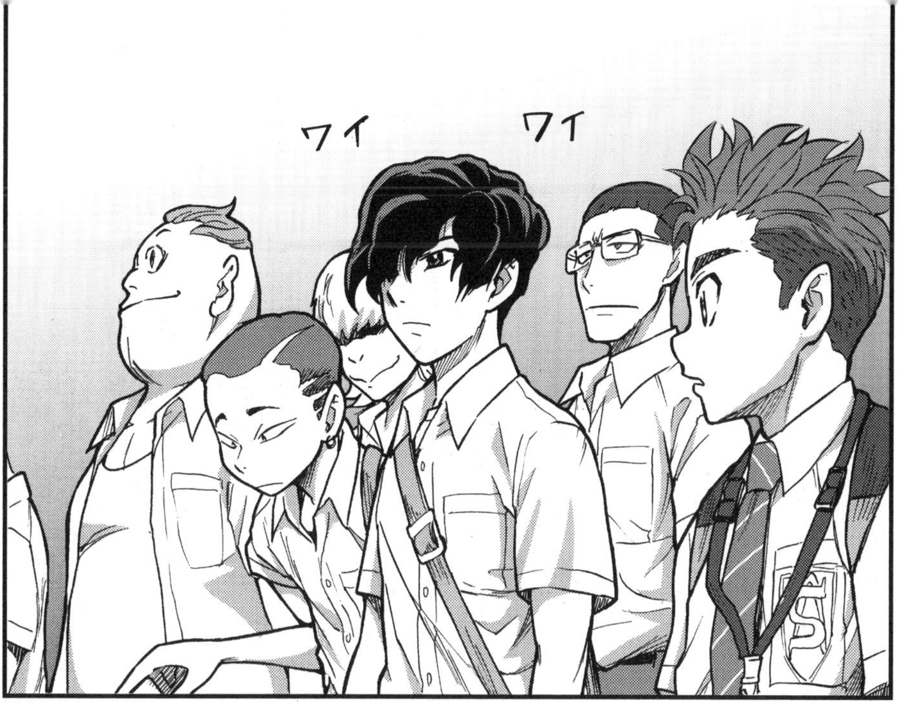
ワイ
ワイ

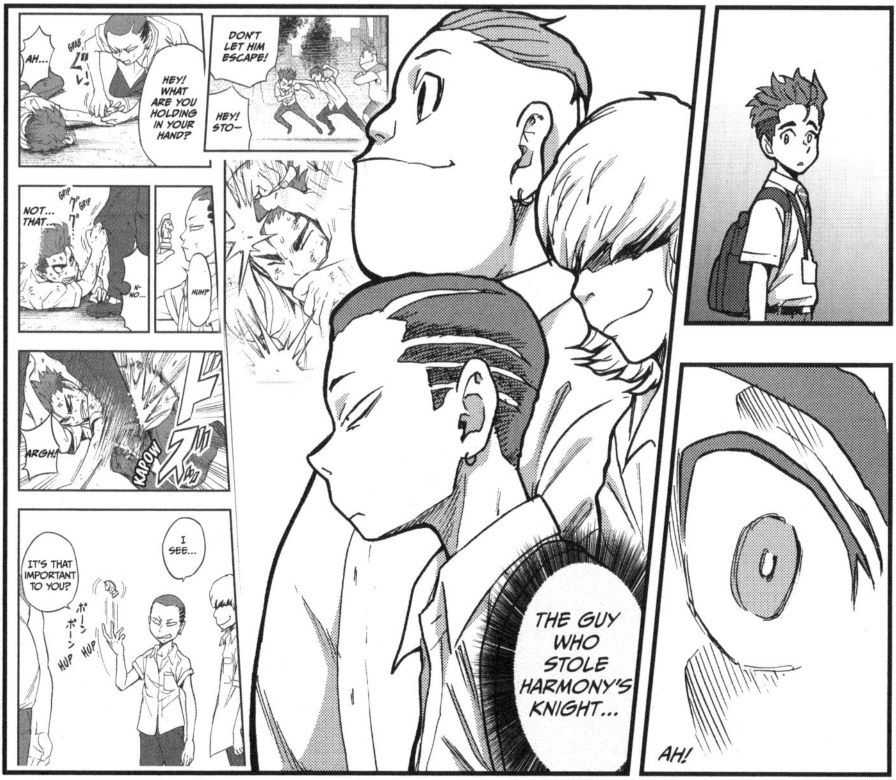
AH!
THE GUY WHO STOLE HARMONY'S KNIGHT...
DON'T LET HIM ESCAPE!
HEY! STO—
AH...
GRAB
HEY! WHAT ARE YOU HOLDING IN YOUR HAND?
HUMP
NOT... THAT...
GRIP GRIP
N-NO...
KAPOW
ARGH!
I SEE...
IT'S THAT IMPORTANT TO YOU?
ポーン ポーン
HUP HUP

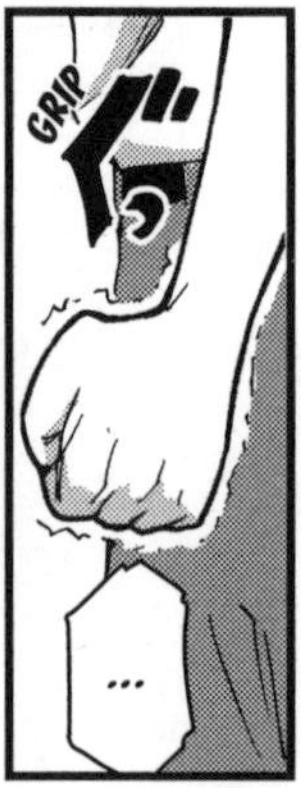
GRIP
...

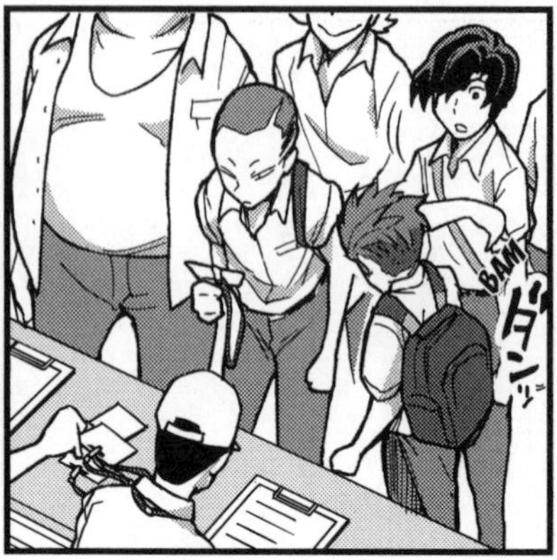
BAM

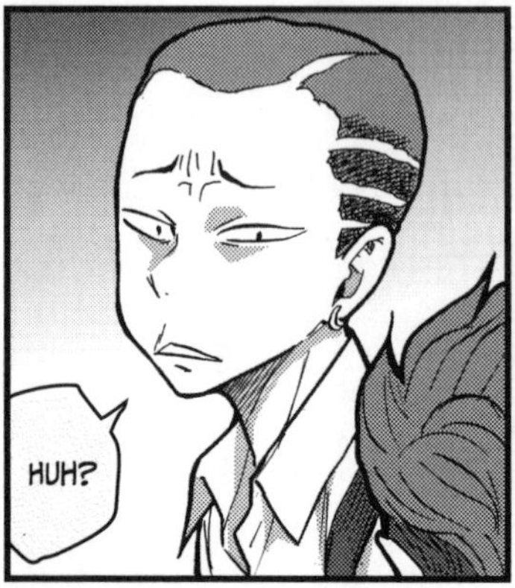
HUH?

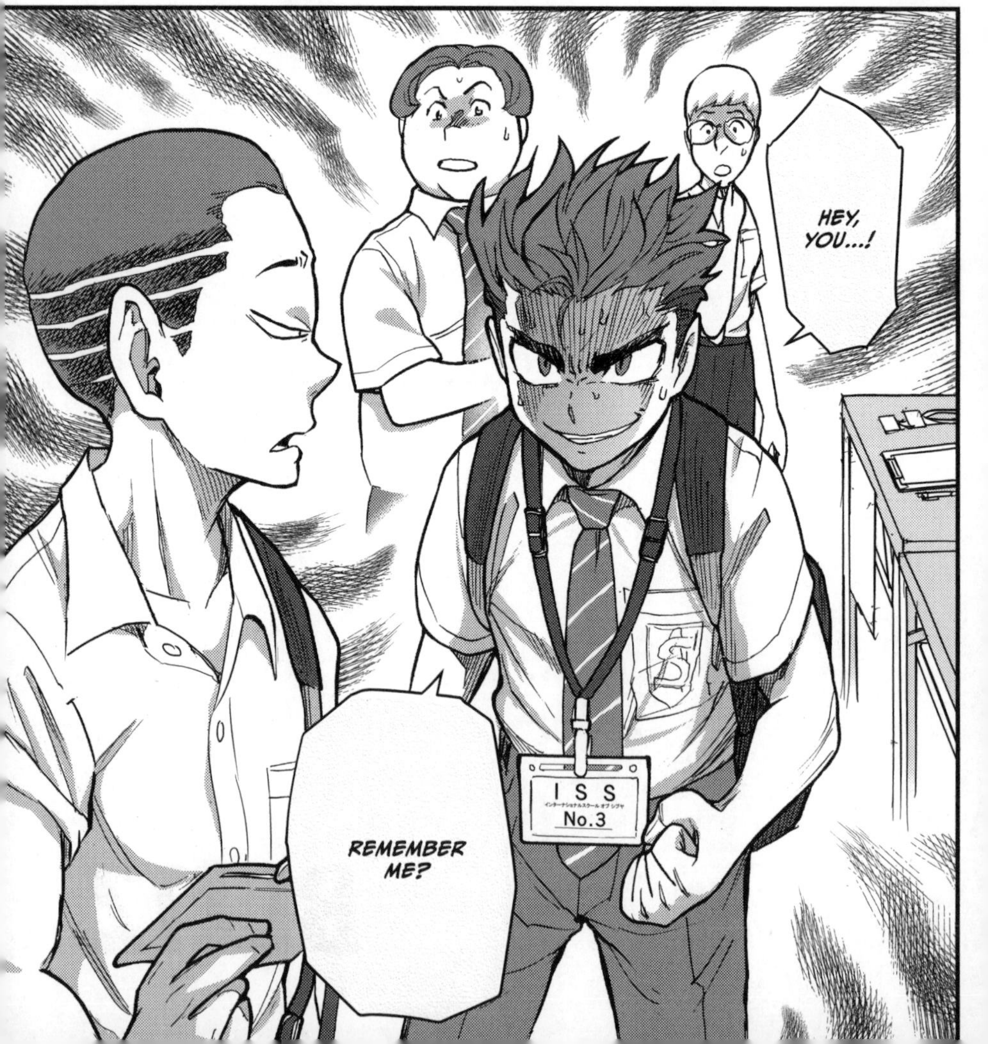
HEY, YOU...!
I S S
No.3
REMEMBER ME?

BLITZ

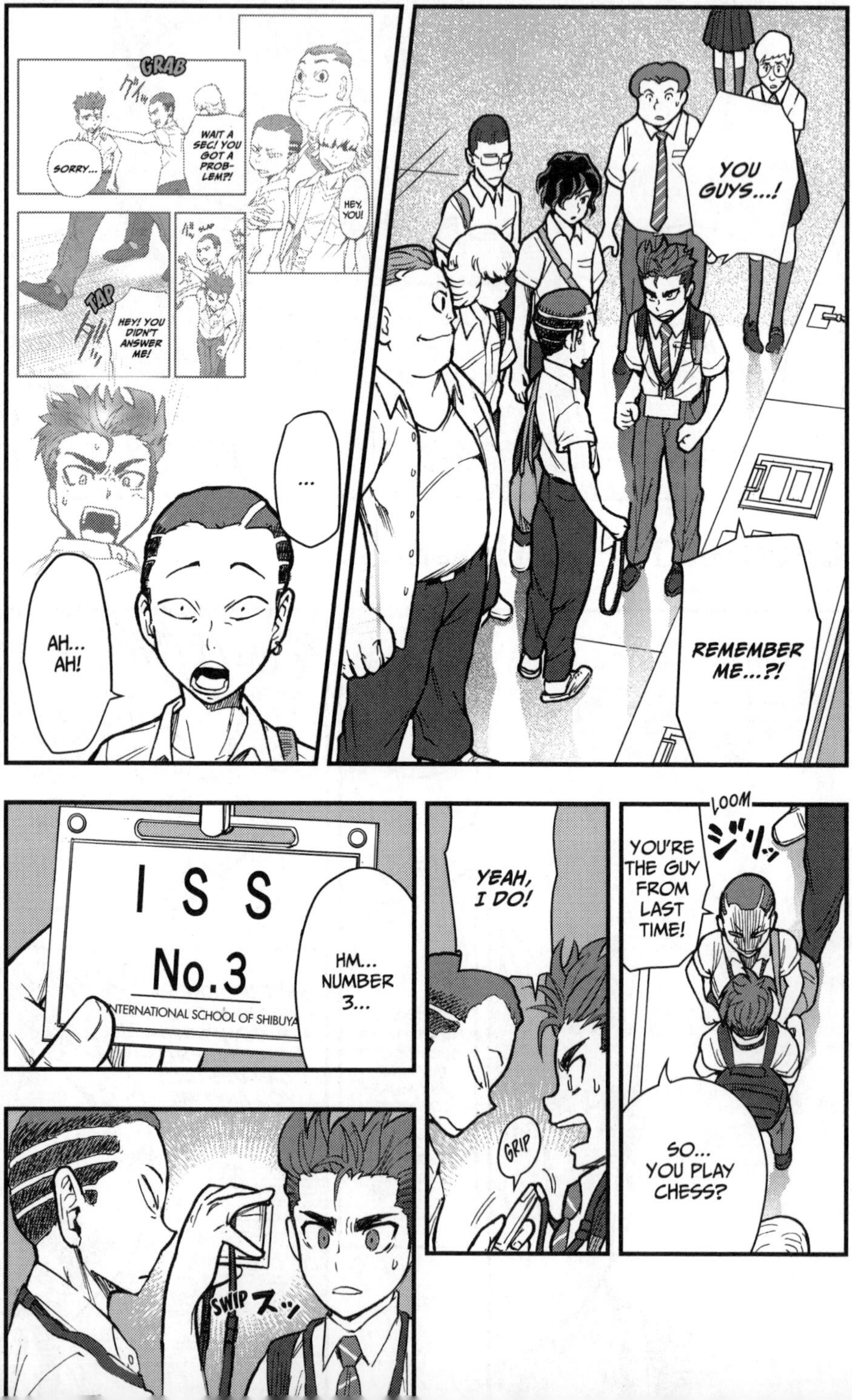
YOU GUYS...!
REMEMBER ME...?!
HEY, YOU!
WAIT A SEC! YOU GOT A PROBLEM?!
GRAB
SORRY...
SLAP
HEY! YOU DIDN'T ANSWER ME!
TAP
...
AH... AH!
LOOM
YOU'RE THE GUY FROM LAST TIME!
SO... YOU PLAY CHESS?
YEAH, I DO!
GRIP
ISS
No.3
INTERNATIONAL SCHOOL OF SHIBUYA
HM... NUMBER 3...
SWIP

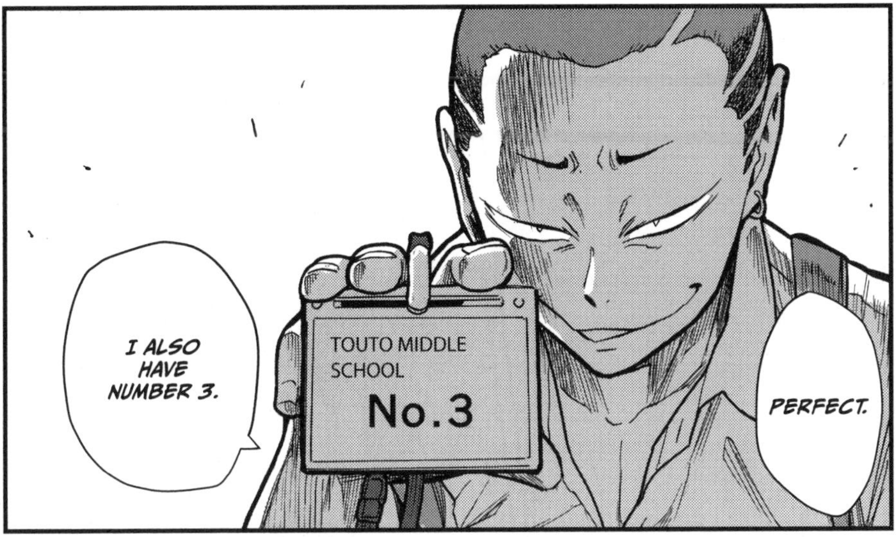
PERFECT.
TOUTO MIDDLE SCHOOL
No.3
I ALSO HAVE NUMBER 3.

Chapter 15: Restlessness

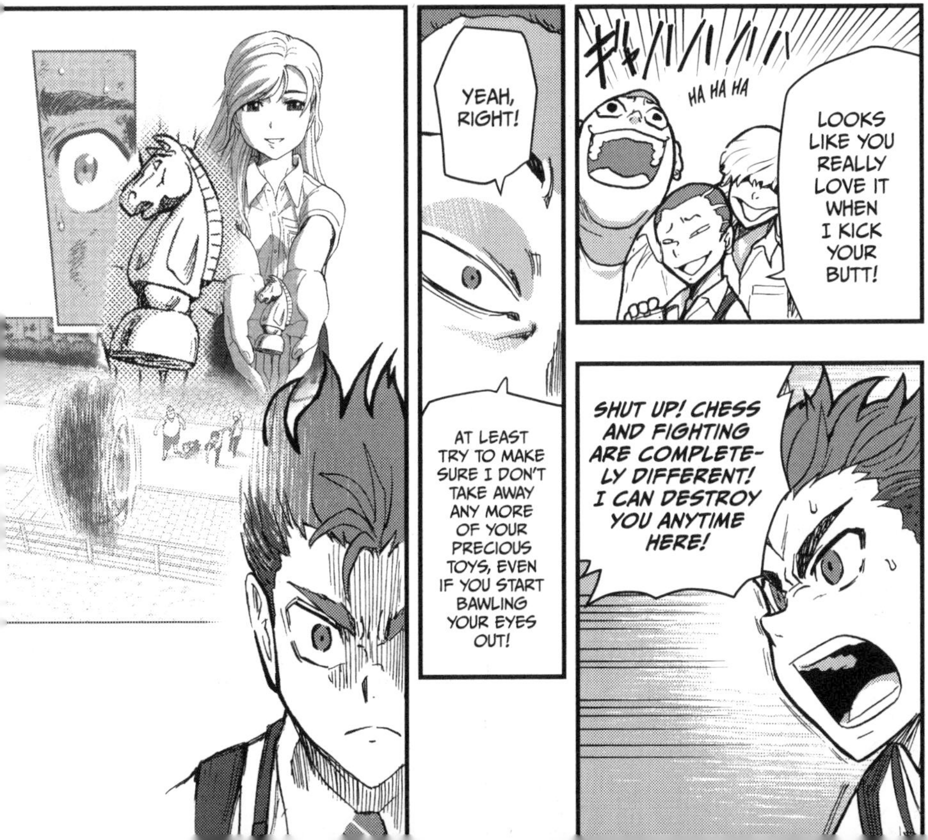
HA HA HA
LOOKS LIKE YOU REALLY LOVE IT WHEN I KICK YOUR BUTT!
SHUT UP! CHESS AND FIGHTING ARE COMPLETE-LY DIFFERENT! I CAN DESTROY YOU ANYTIME HERE!
YEAH, RIGHT!
AT LEAST TRY TO MAKE SURE I DON'T TAKE AWAY ANY MORE OF YOUR PRECIOUS TOYS, EVEN IF YOU START BAWLING YOUR EYES OUT!

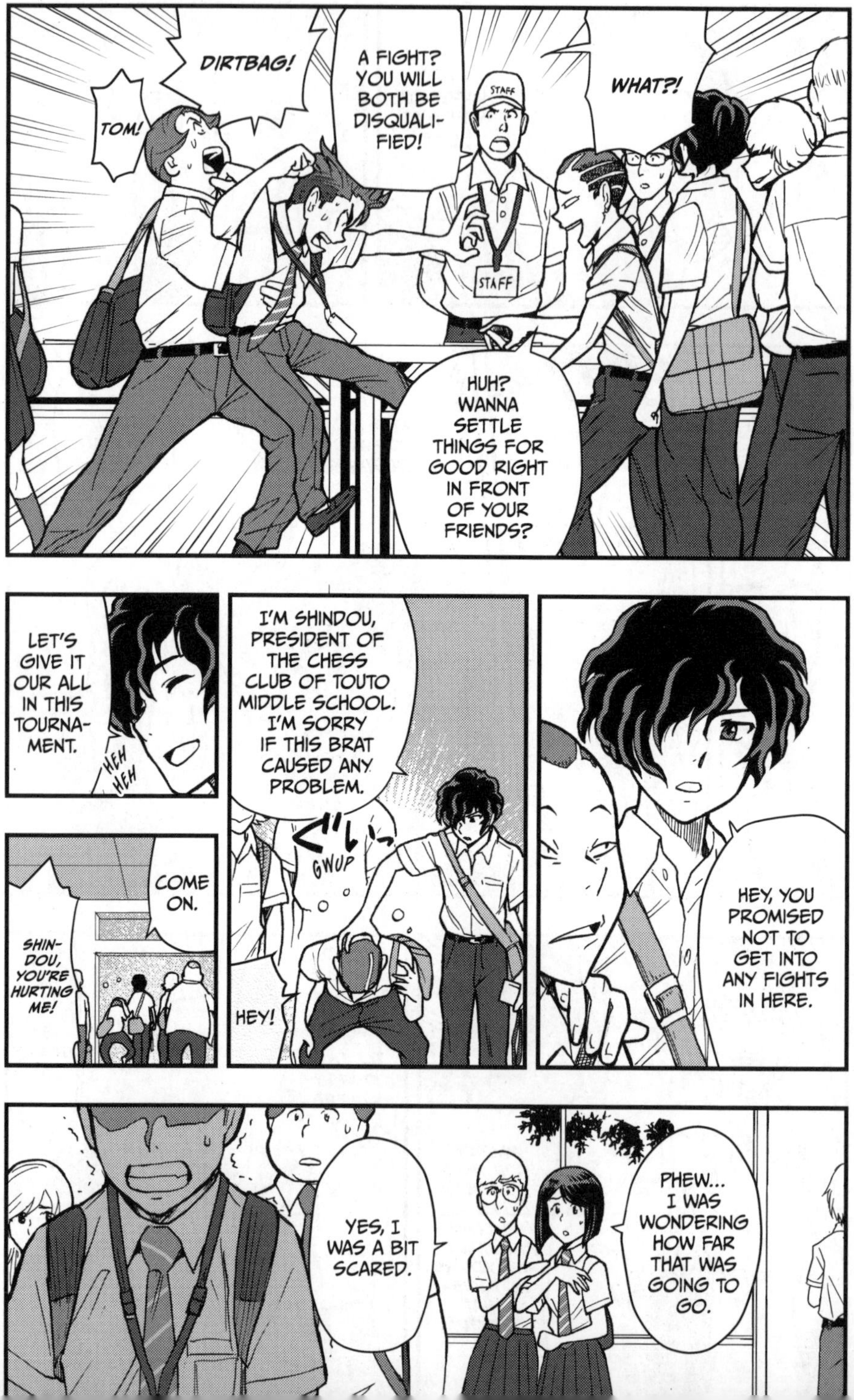
WHAT?!
A FIGHT? YOU WILL BOTH BE DISQUALI-FIED!
STAFF
DIRTBAG!
TOM!
STAFF
HUH? WANNA SETTLE THINGS FOR GOOD RIGHT IN FRONT OF YOUR FRIENDS?
HEY, YOU PROMISED NOT TO GET INTO ANY FIGHTS IN HERE.
I'M SHINDOU, PRESIDENT OF THE CHESS CLUB OF TOUTO MIDDLE SCHOOL. I'M SORRY IF THIS BRAT CAUSED ANY PROBLEM.
GWUP
HEY!
LET'S GIVE IT OUR ALL IN THIS TOURNA-MENT.
HEH HEH
COME ON.
SHIN-DOU, YOU'RE HURTING ME!
PHEW... I WAS WONDERING HOW FAR THAT WAS GOING TO GO.
YES, I WAS A BIT SCARED.

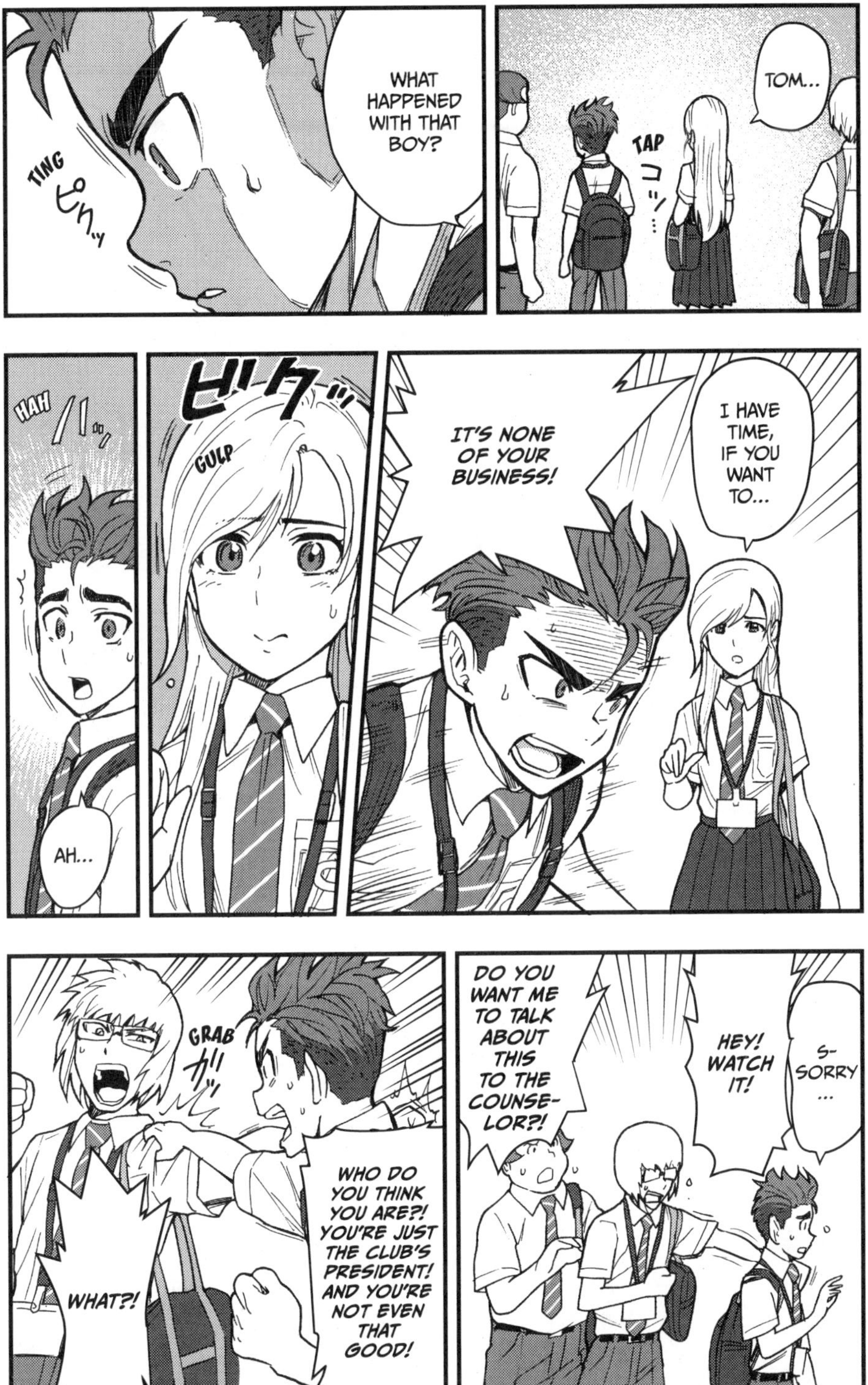
TOM...
TAP
WHAT HAPPENED WITH THAT BOY?
TING
I HAVE TIME, IF YOU WANT TO...
IT'S NONE OF YOUR BUSINESS!
GULP
HAH
AH...
HEY! WATCH IT!
S-SORRY...
DO YOU WANT ME TO TALK ABOUT THIS TO THE COUNSE-LOR?!
WHO DO YOU THINK YOU ARE?! YOU'RE JUST THE CLUB'S PRESIDENT! AND YOU'RE NOT EVEN THAT GOOD!
GRAB
WHAT?!

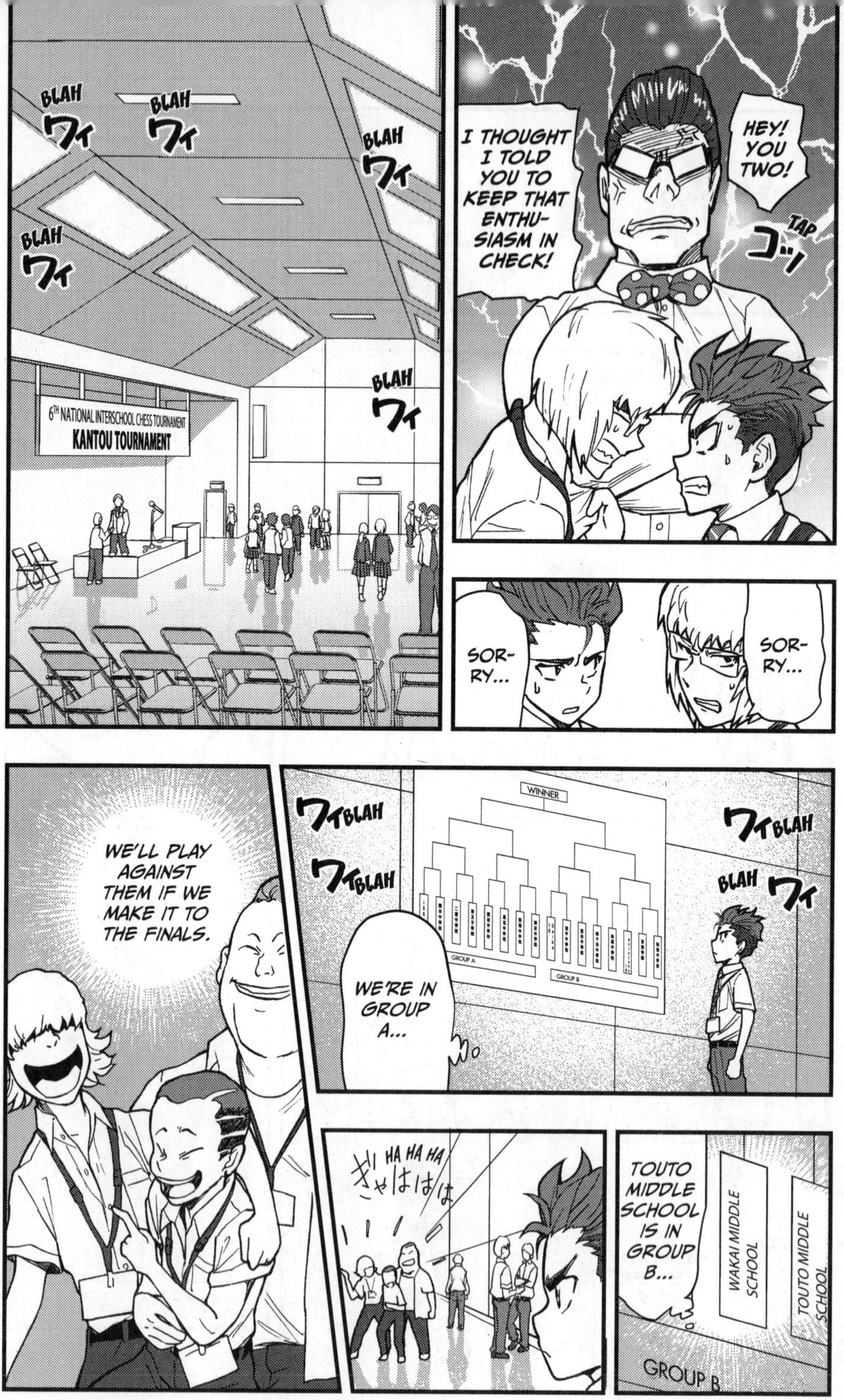
HEY! YOU TWO!
I THOUGHT I TOLD YOU TO KEEP THAT ENTHUSIASM IN CHECK!
TAP ゴッ
SORRY...
SORRY...
BLAH ワイ
BLAH ワイ
BLAH ワイ
BLAH ワイ
BLAH ワイ
6TH NATIONAL INTERSCHOOL CHESS TOURNAMENT
KANTOU TOURNAMENT
ワイ BLAH
BLAH ワイ
ワイ BLAH
WINNER
GROUP A
GROUP B
WE'RE IN GROUP A...
ワイ BLAH
TOUTO MIDDLE SCHOOL IS IN GROUP B...
WAKAI MIDDLE SCHOOL
TOUTO MIDDLE SCHOOL
GROUP B
HA HA HA ぎゃははは
WE'LL PLAY AGAINST THEM IF WE MAKE IT TO THE FINALS.

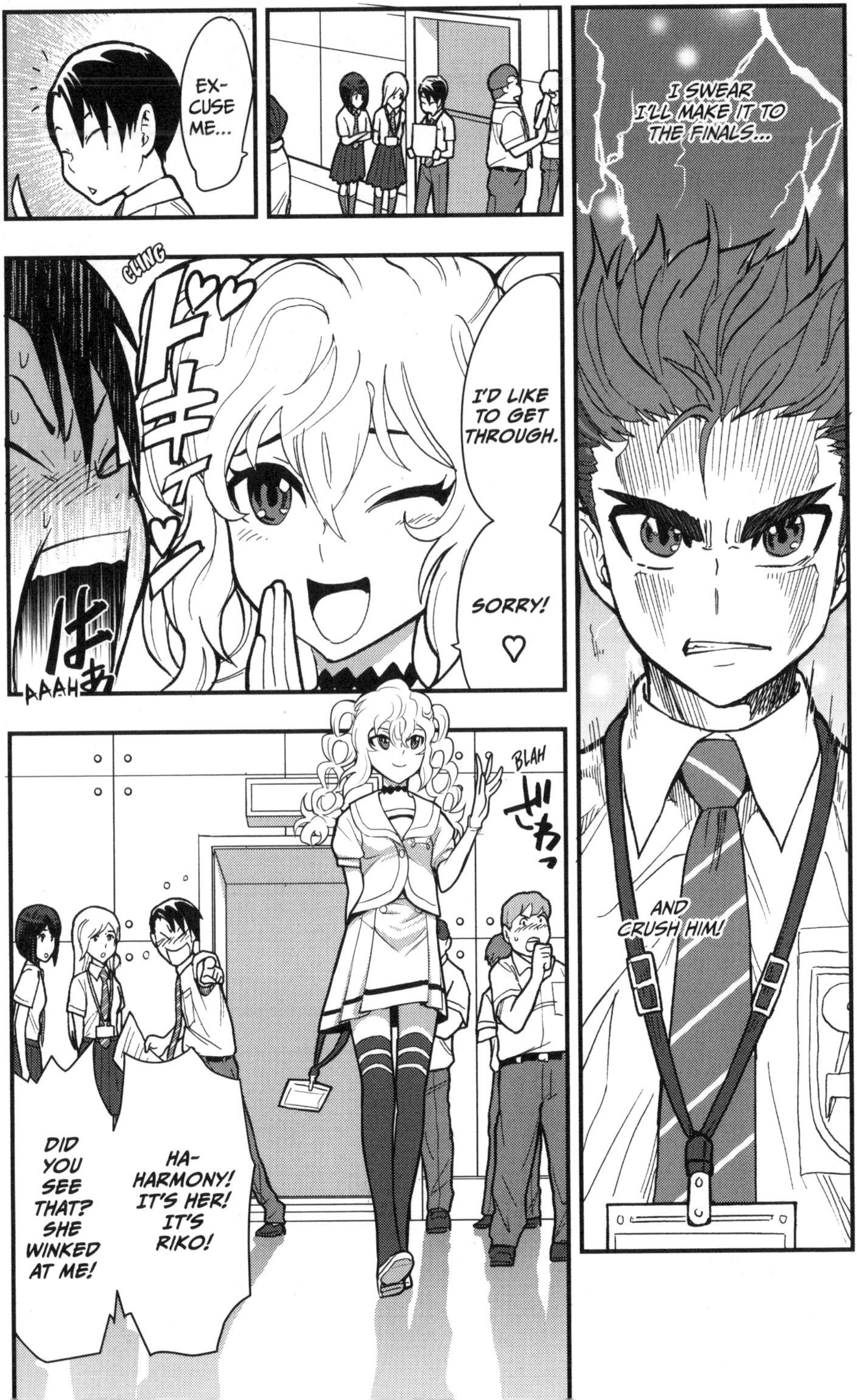
I SWEAR I'LL MAKE IT TO THE FINALS...
AND CRUSH HIM!
EX-CUSE ME...
CLING
I'D LIKE TO GET THROUGH.
SORRY! ♥
AAAH
BLAH
HA-HARMONY! IT'S HER! IT'S RIKO!
DID YOU SEE THAT? SHE WINKED AT ME!

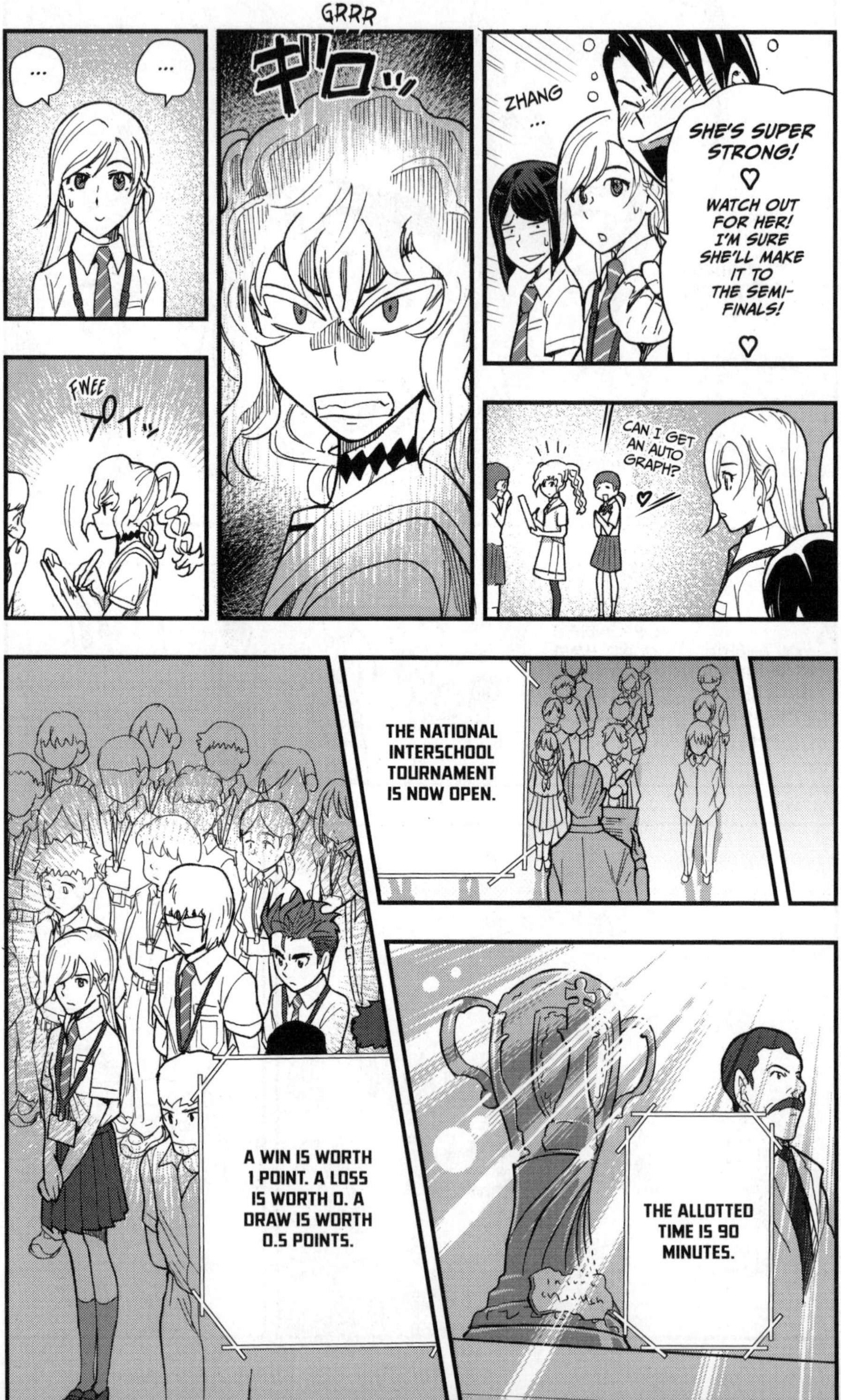
ZHANG ...
SHE'S SUPER STRONG! ♡ WATCH OUT FOR HER! I'M SURE SHE'LL MAKE IT TO THE SEMI-FINALS! ♡
CAN I GET AN AUTO GRAPH?
GRRR
ギロッ
...
...
FWEE
プイッ
THE NATIONAL INTERSCHOOL TOURNAMENT IS NOW OPEN.
THE ALLOTTED TIME IS 90 MINUTES.
A WIN IS WORTH 1 POINT. A LOSS IS WORTH 0. A DRAW IS WORTH 0.5 POINTS.

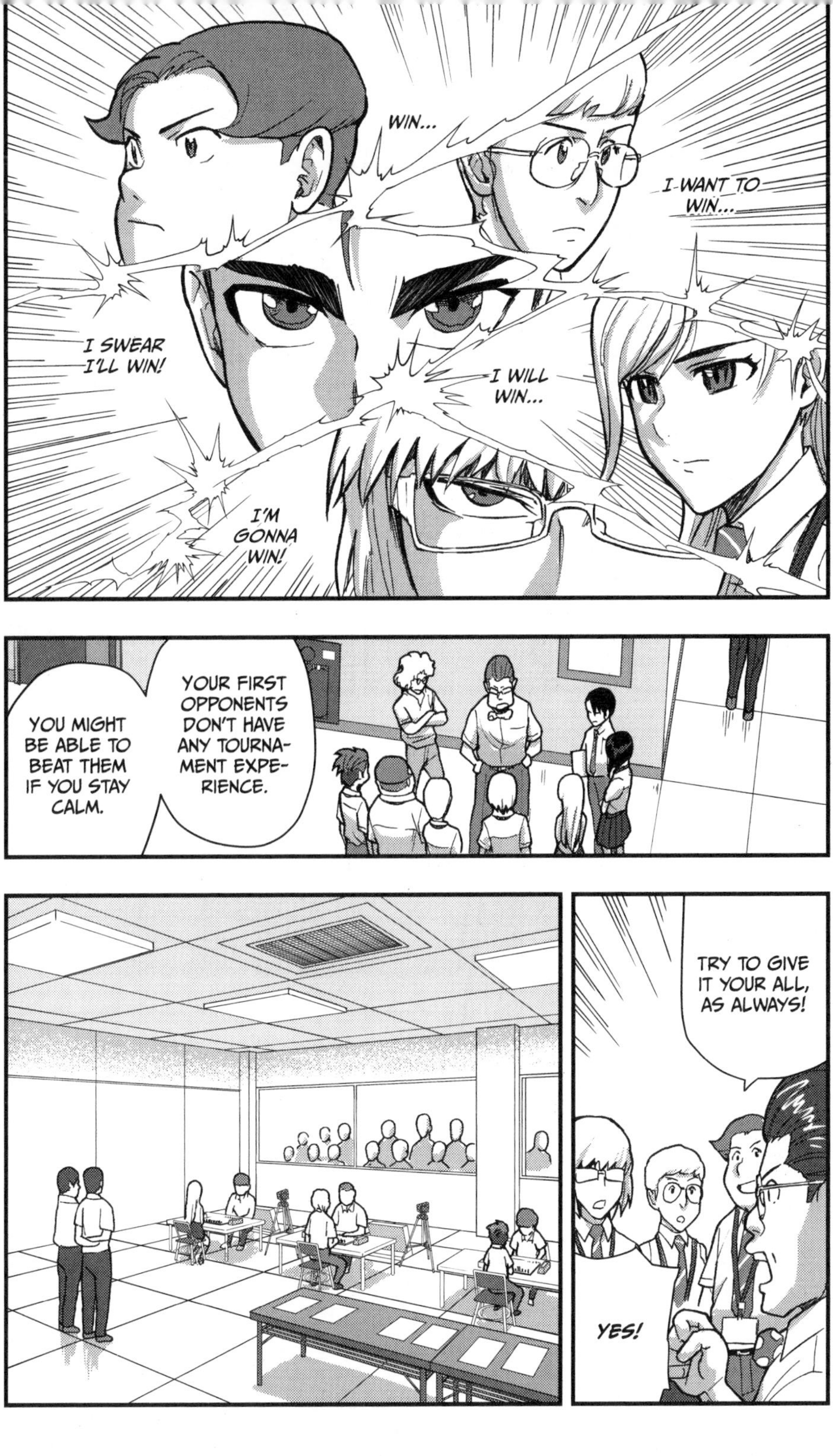
I WANT TO WIN...
WIN...
I WILL WIN...
I SWEAR I'LL WIN!
I'M GONNA WIN!
YOUR FIRST OPPONENTS DON'T HAVE ANY TOURNAMENT EXPERIENCE.
YOU MIGHT BE ABLE TO BEAT THEM IF YOU STAY CALM.
TRY TO GIVE IT YOUR ALL, AS ALWAYS!
YES!

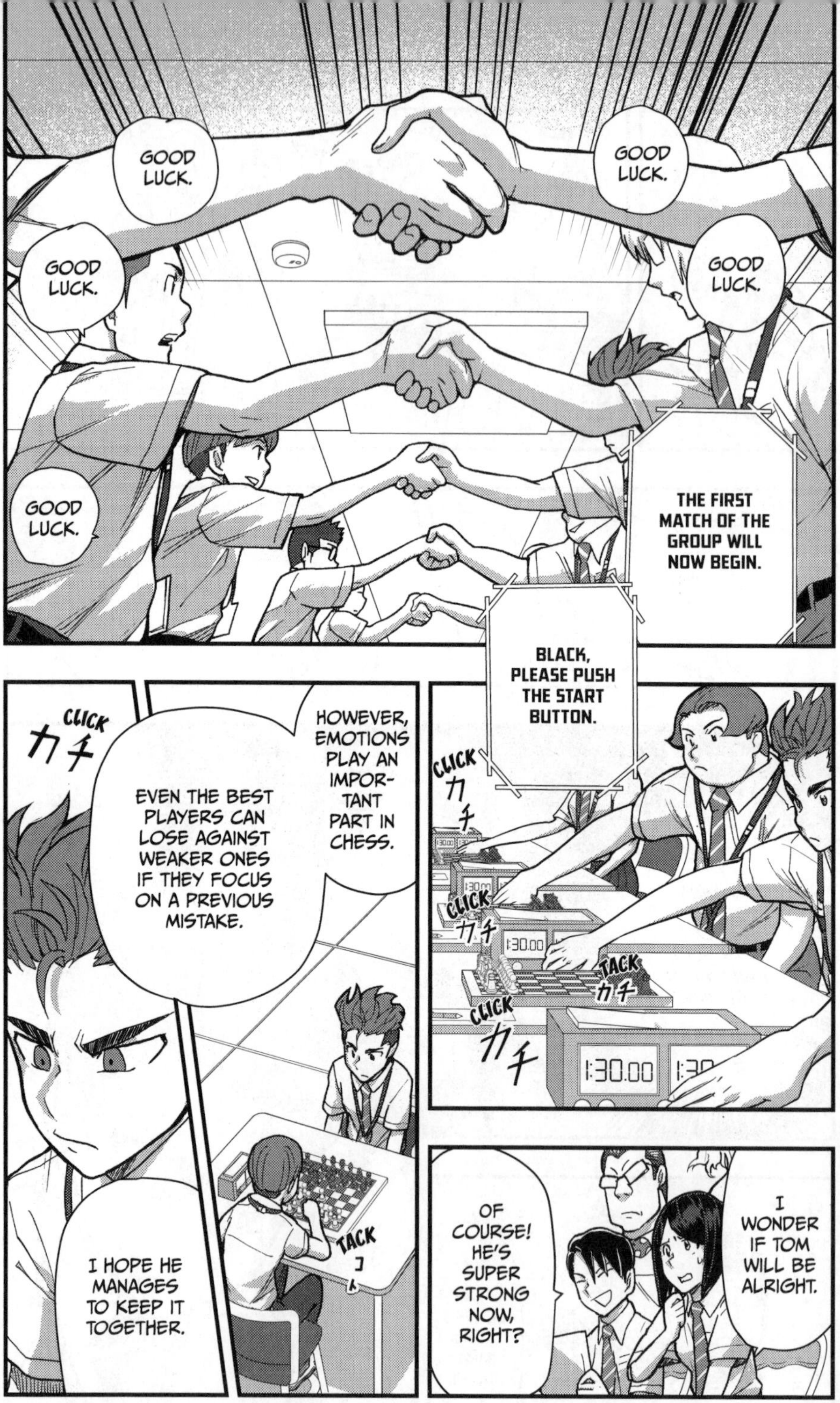
GOOD LUCK.
GOOD LUCK.
GOOD LUCK.
GOOD LUCK.
GOOD LUCK.
THE FIRST MATCH OF THE GROUP WILL NOW BEGIN.
BLACK, PLEASE PUSH THE START BUTTON.
CLICK カチ
CLICK カチ
TACK カチ
CLICK カチ
1:30.00
I WONDER IF TOM WILL BE ALRIGHT.
OF COURSE! HE'S SUPER STRONG NOW, RIGHT?
HOWEVER, EMOTIONS PLAY AN IMPOR-TANT PART IN CHESS.
TACK コト
CLICK カチ
EVEN THE BEST PLAYERS CAN LOSE AGAINST WEAKER ONES IF THEY FOCUS ON A PREVIOUS MISTAKE.
I HOPE HE MANAGES TO KEEP IT TOGETHER.

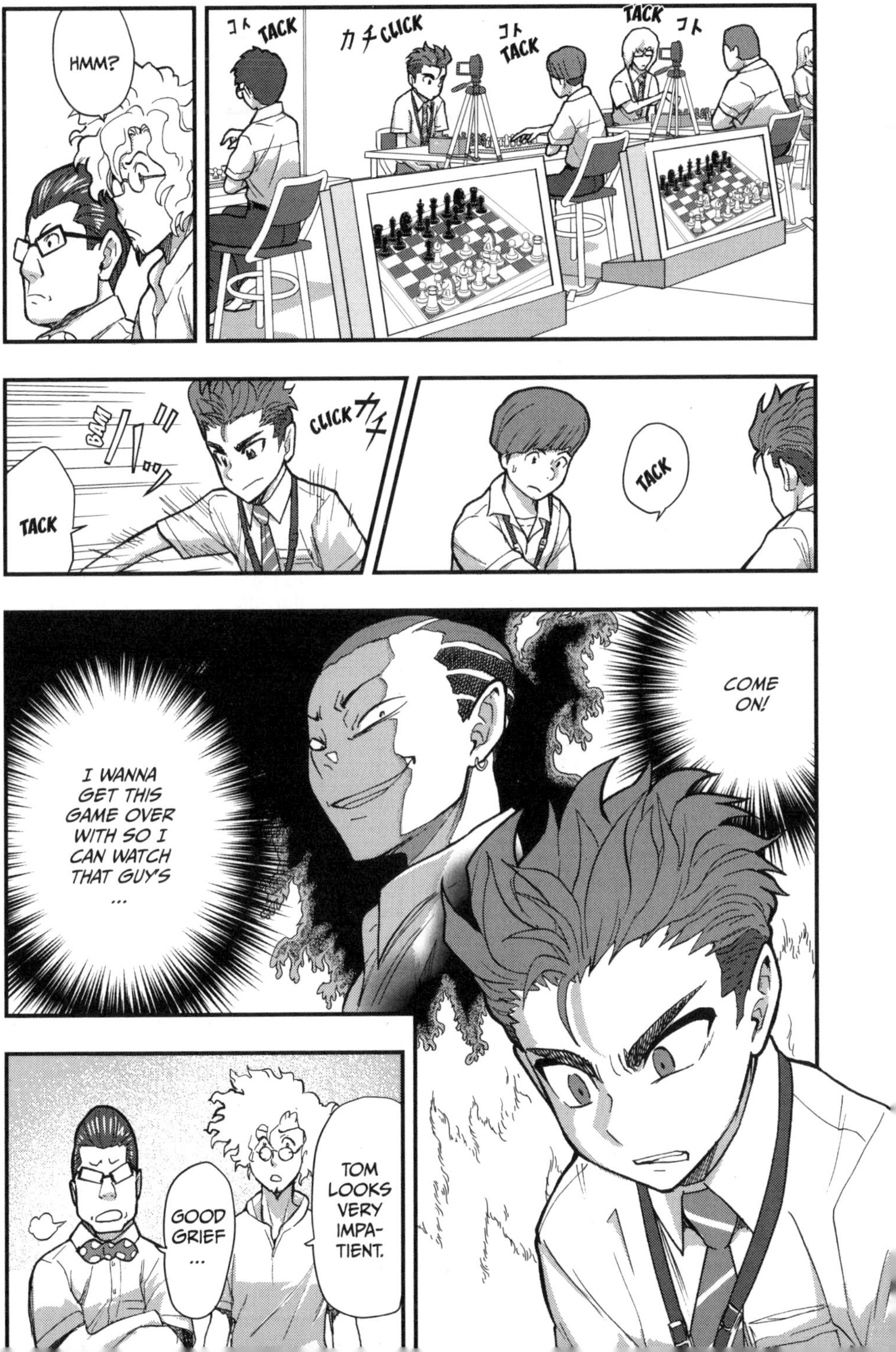
コト
TACK
コト
TACK
カチ
CLICK
コト
TACK
HMM?
TACK
CLICK
カチ
BAM
TACK
COME ON!
I WANNA GET THIS GAME OVER WITH SO I CAN WATCH THAT GUY'S ...
TOM LOOKS VERY IMPA-TIENT.
GOOD GRIEF ...

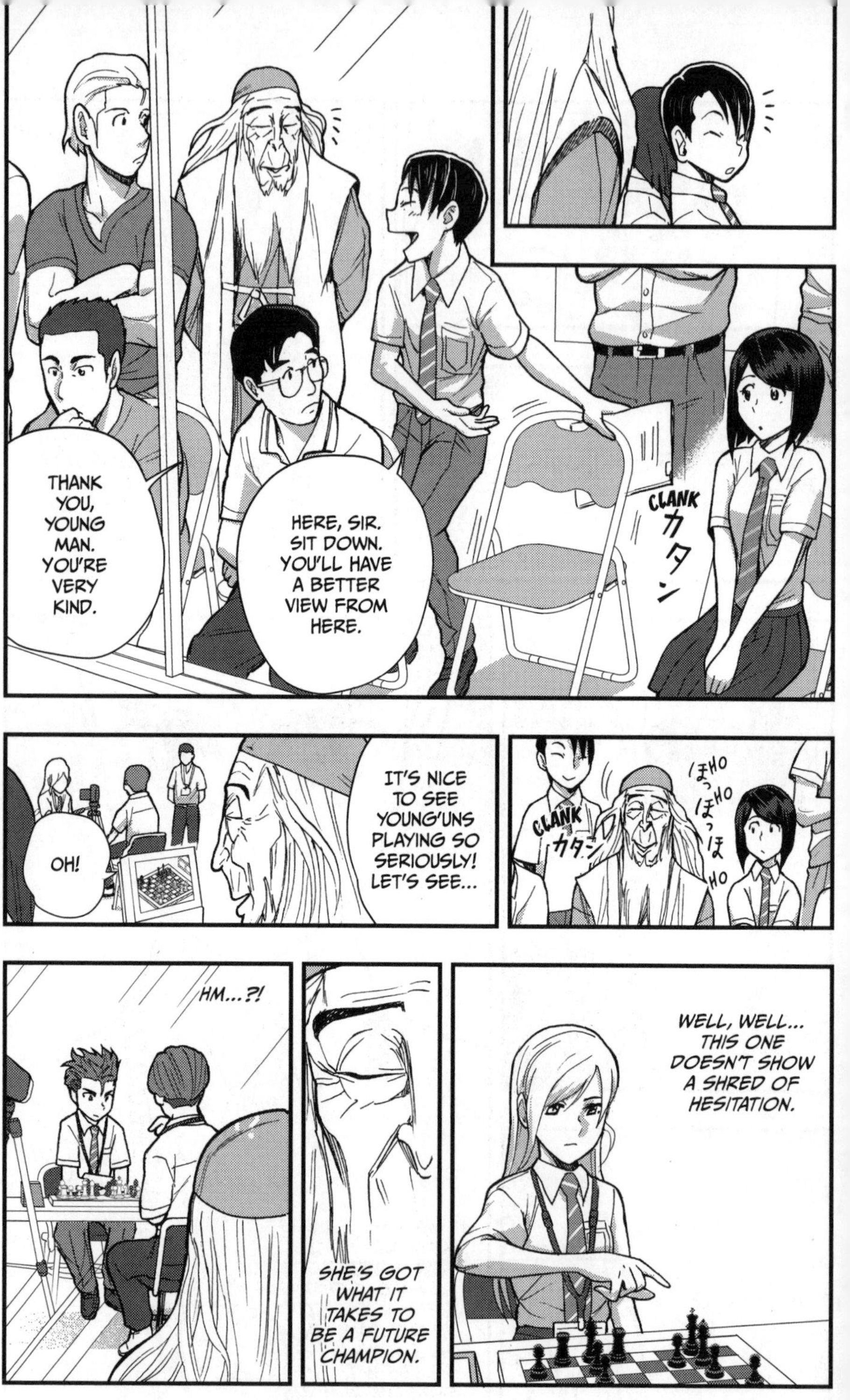
CLANK カタン
HERE, SIR. SIT DOWN. YOU'LL HAVE A BETTER VIEW FROM HERE.
THANK YOU, YOUNG MAN. YOU'RE VERY KIND.
HO HO HO ほっほっほ
CLANK カタン
IT'S NICE TO SEE YOUNG'UNS PLAYING SO SERIOUSLY! LET'S SEE...
OH!
WELL, WELL... THIS ONE DOESN'T SHOW A SHRED OF HESITATION.
SHE'S GOT WHAT IT TAKES TO BE A FUTURE CHAMPION.
HM...?!

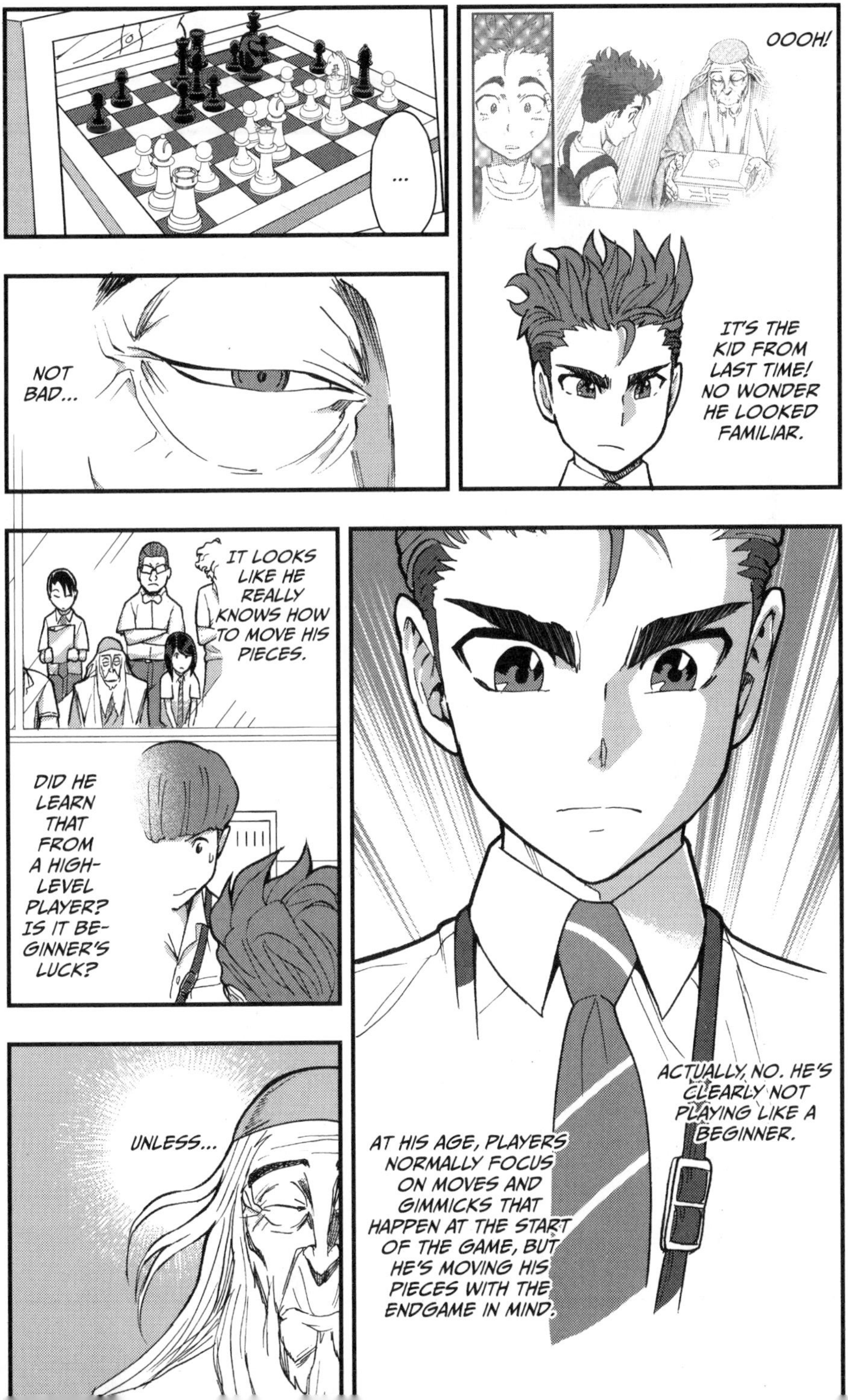
...
NOT BAD...
OOOH!
IT'S THE KID FROM LAST TIME! NO WONDER HE LOOKED FAMILIAR.
IT LOOKS LIKE HE REALLY KNOWS HOW TO MOVE HIS PIECES.
DID HE LEARN THAT FROM A HIGH-LEVEL PLAYER? IS IT BE-GINNER'S LUCK?
ACTUALLY, NO. HE'S CLEARLY NOT PLAYING LIKE A BEGINNER.
AT HIS AGE, PLAYERS NORMALLY FOCUS ON MOVES AND GIMMICKS THAT HAPPEN AT THE START OF THE GAME, BUT HE'S MOVING HIS PIECES WITH THE ENDGAME IN MIND.
UNLESS...

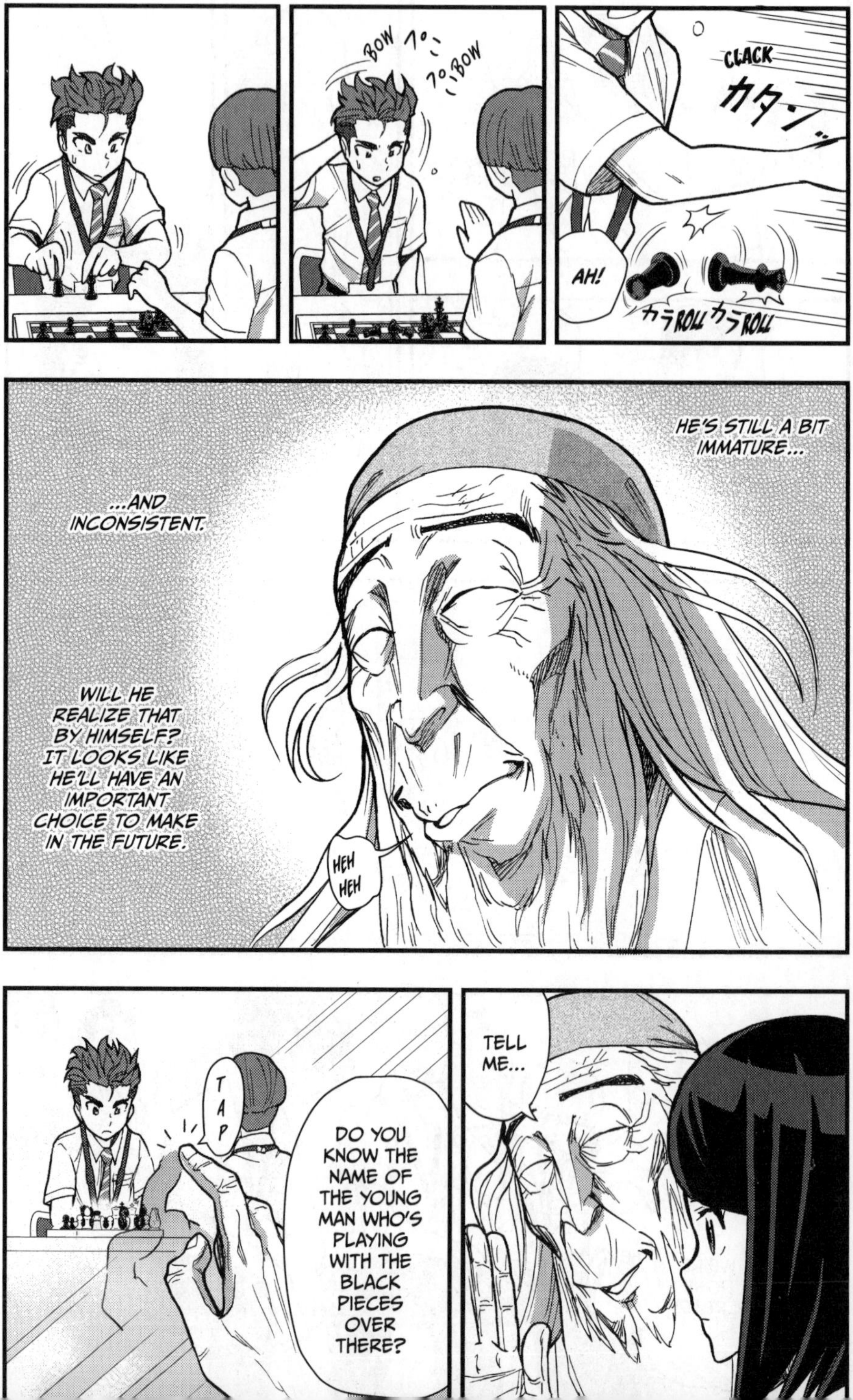
CLACK
カタンッ
AH!
カラ ROLL カラ ROLL
BOW ペこ
ペこ BOW
HE'S STILL A BIT IMMATURE...
...AND INCONSISTENT.
WILL HE REALIZE THAT BY HIMSELF? IT LOOKS LIKE HE'LL HAVE AN IMPORTANT CHOICE TO MAKE IN THE FUTURE.
HEH HEH
TELL ME...
DO YOU KNOW THE NAME OF THE YOUNG MAN WHO'S PLAYING WITH THE BLACK PIECES OVER THERE?
TAP

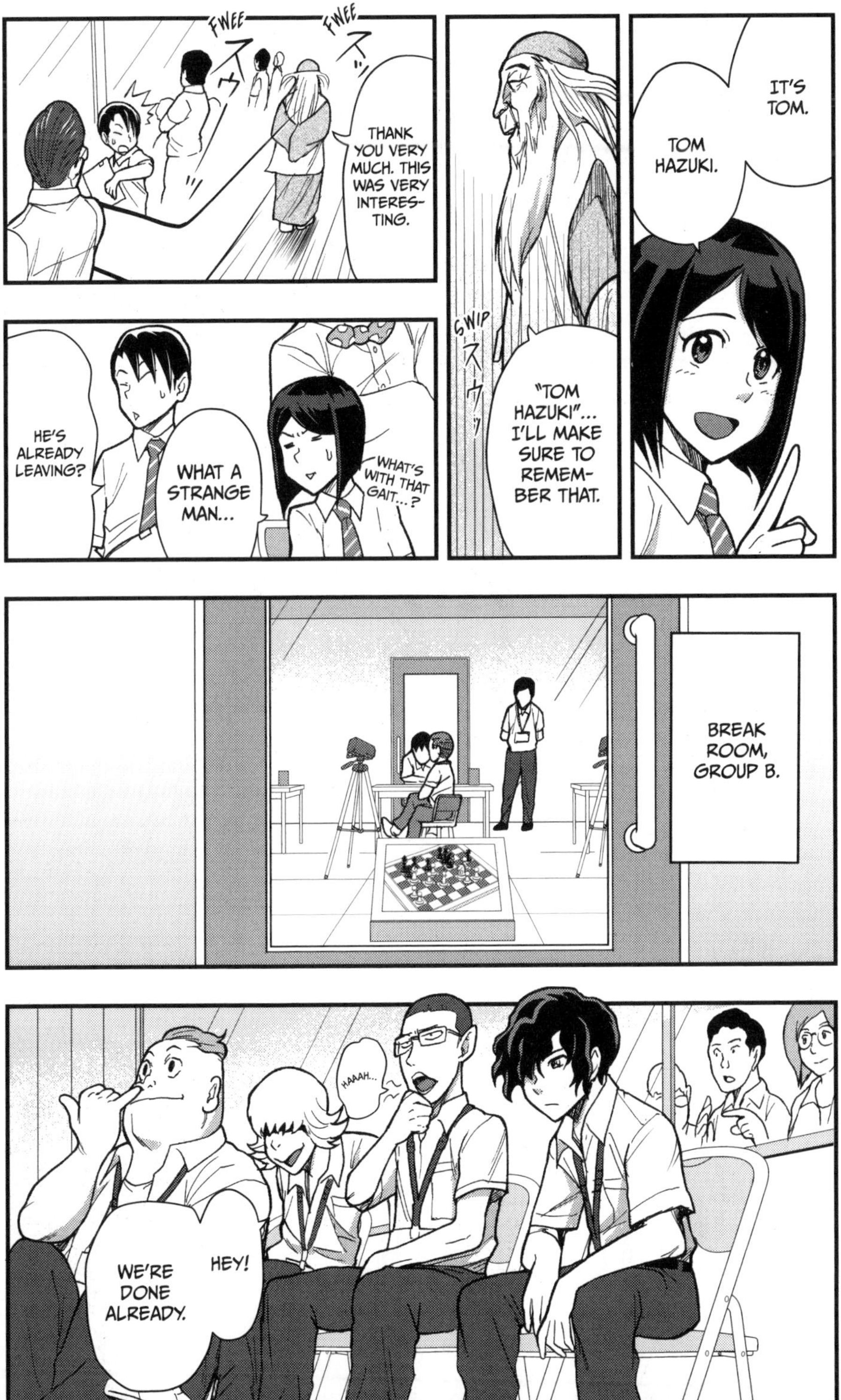

IT'S TOM.
TOM HAZUKI.
"TOM HAZUKI"... I'LL MAKE SURE TO REMEMBER THAT.
SWIP
FWEE
FWEE
THANK YOU VERY MUCH. THIS WAS VERY INTERESTING.
WHAT'S WITH THAT GAIT...?
WHAT A STRANGE MAN...
HE'S ALREADY LEAVING?
BREAK ROOM, GROUP B.
HAAAH...
HEY!
WE'RE DONE ALREADY.

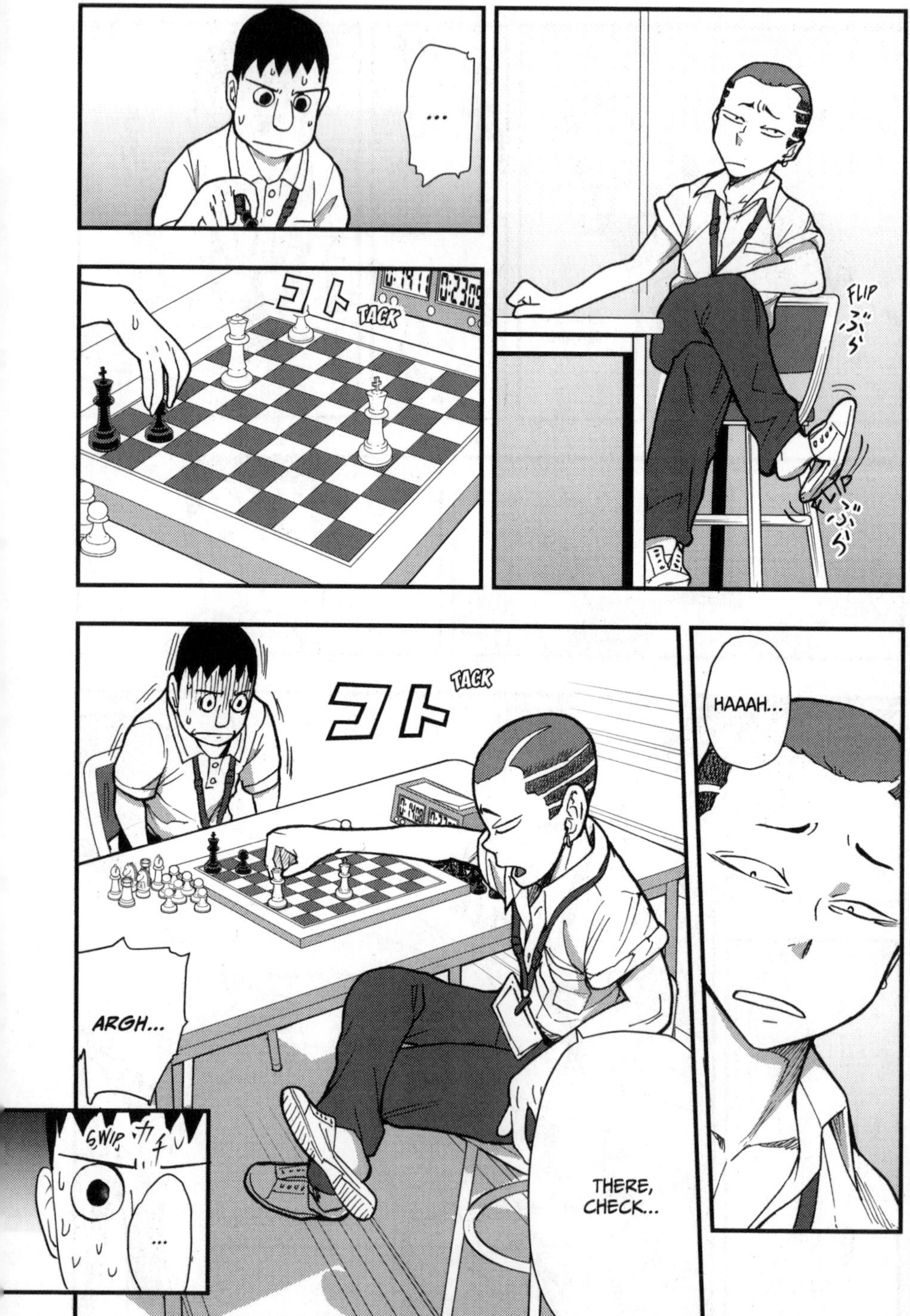
FLIP
ぶぶ
FLIP
ぶぶ
...
コト
TACK
HAAAH...
コト
TACK
THERE, CHECK...
ARGH...
SWIP
カチ
...

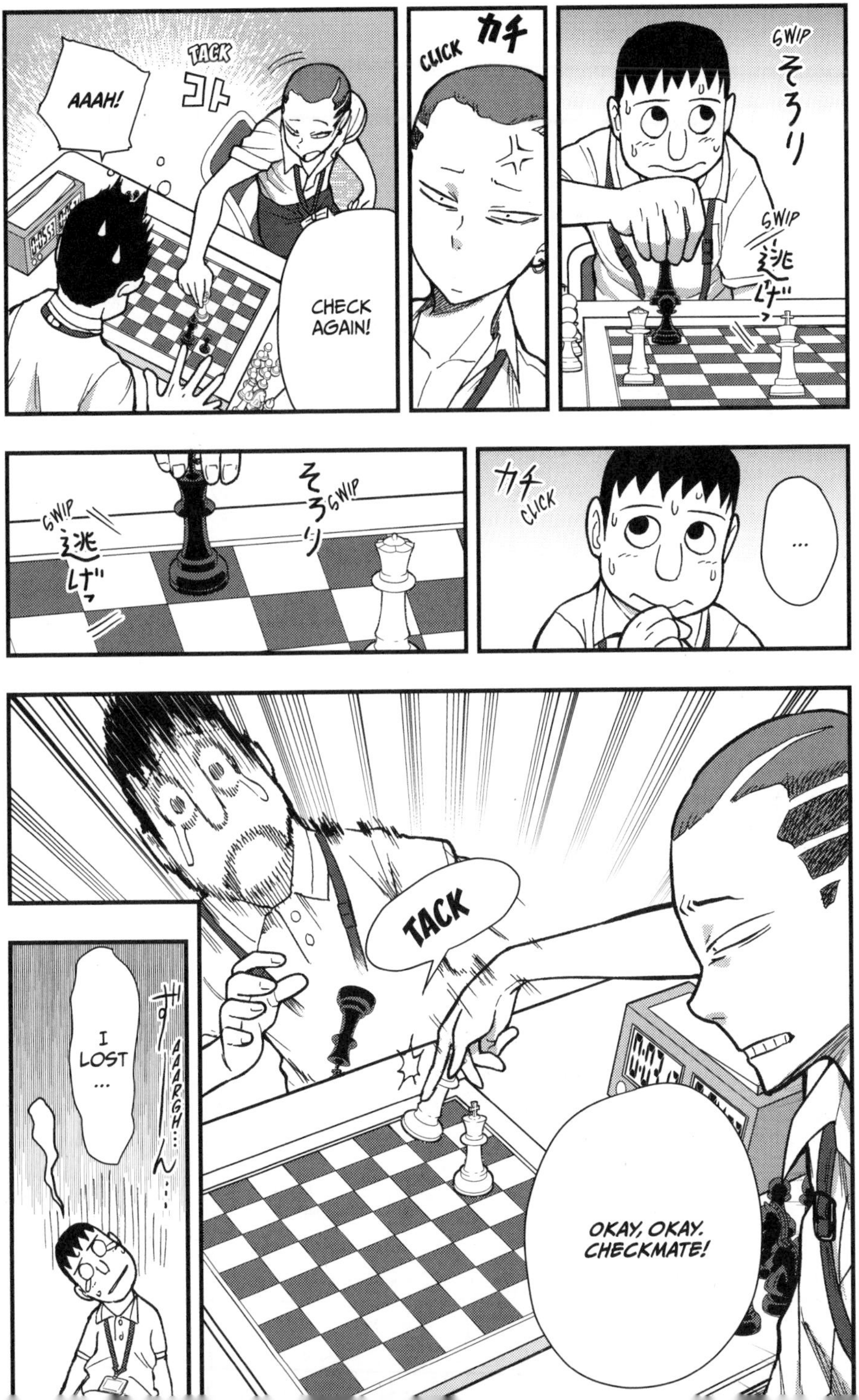
SWIP
そろり
SWIP
逃げ
CLICK
カチ
TACK
コト
AAAH!
CHECK AGAIN!
カチ
CLICK
...
そろり
SWIP
SWIP
逃げ
TACK
OKAY, OKAY. CHECKMATE!
ずーん…
AAARGH...
I LOST ...

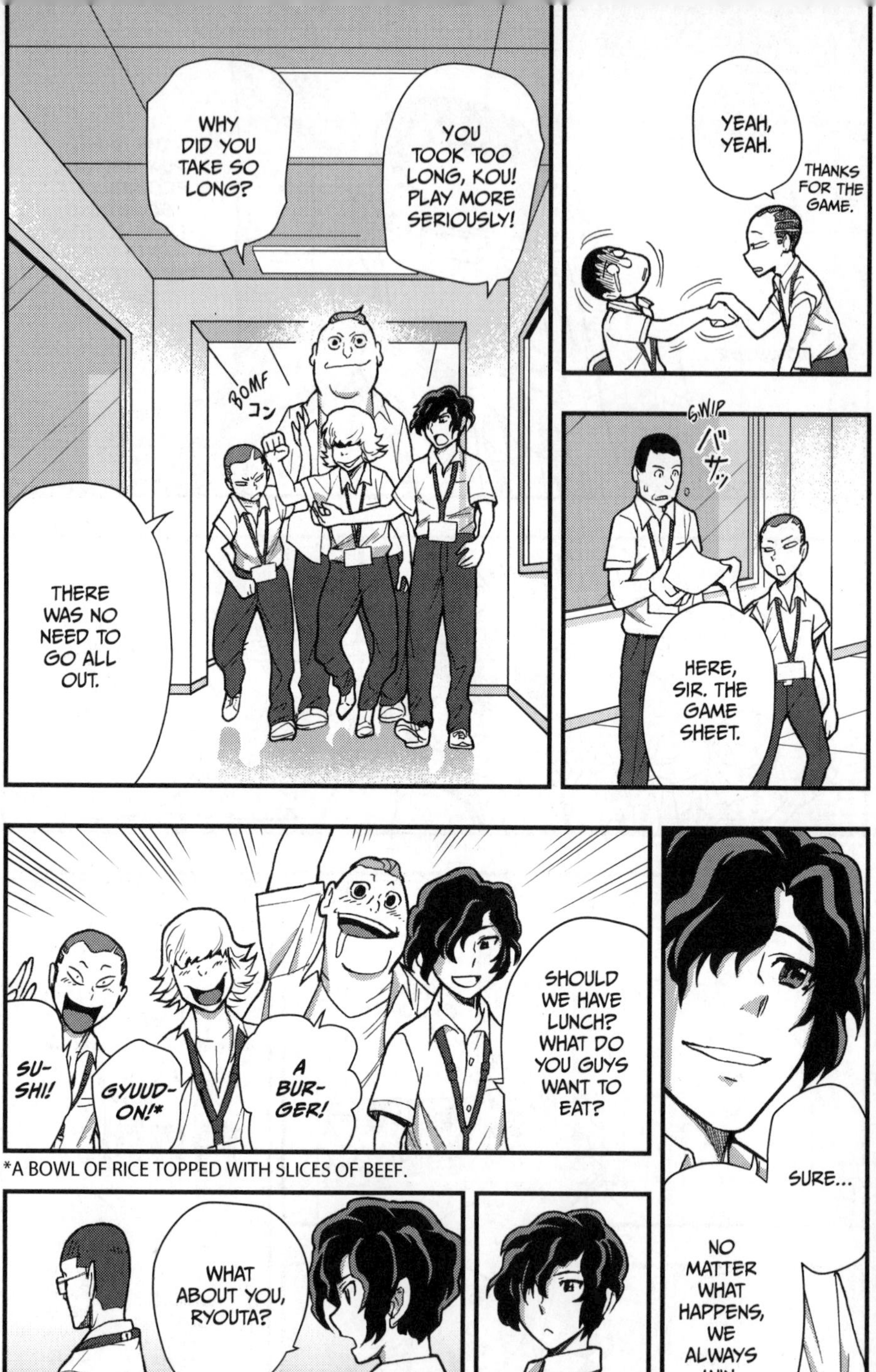
YEAH, YEAH.
THANKS FOR THE GAME.
SWIP バサッ
HERE, SIR. THE GAME SHEET.
YOU TOOK TOO LONG, KOU! PLAY MORE SERIOUSLY!
WHY DID YOU TAKE SO LONG?
BOMF コン
THERE WAS NO NEED TO GO ALL OUT.
SURE...
NO MATTER WHAT HAPPENS, WE ALWAYS WIN.
SHOULD WE HAVE LUNCH? WHAT DO YOU GUYS WANT TO EAT?
A BUR-GER!
GYUUD-ON!*
SU-SHI!
WHAT ABOUT YOU, RYOUTA?

*A BOWL OF RICE TOPPED WITH SLICES OF BEEF.

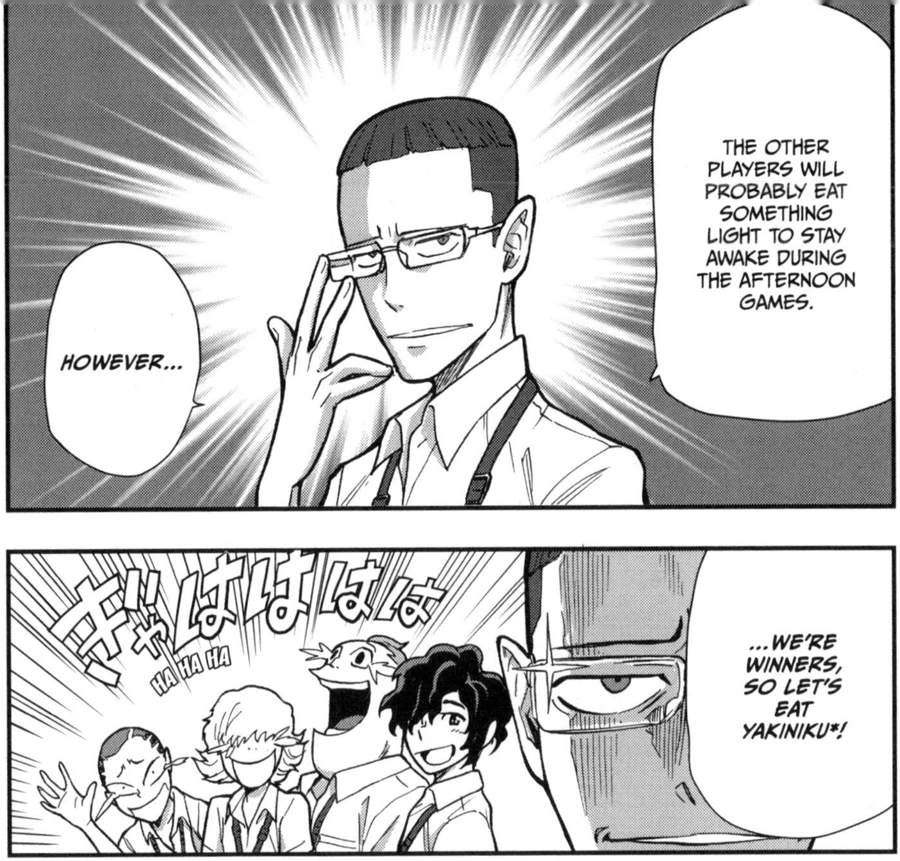
THE OTHER PLAYERS WILL PROBABLY EAT SOMETHING LIGHT TO STAY AWAKE DURING THE AFTERNOON GAMES.
HOWEVER...
...WE'RE WINNERS, SO LET'S EAT YAKINIKU*!
ぎゃはははは
HA HA HA

*KOREAN BARBECUE.

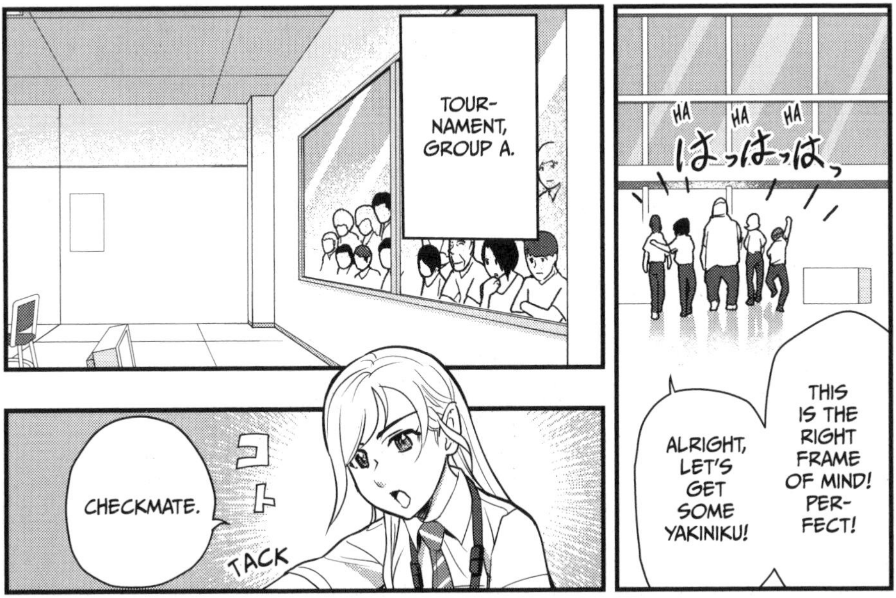
HA HA HA
はっはっはっ
THIS IS THE RIGHT FRAME OF MIND! PER-FECT!
ALRIGHT, LET'S GET SOME YAKINIKU!
TOUR-NAMENT, GROUP A.
コト
TACK
CHECKMATE.

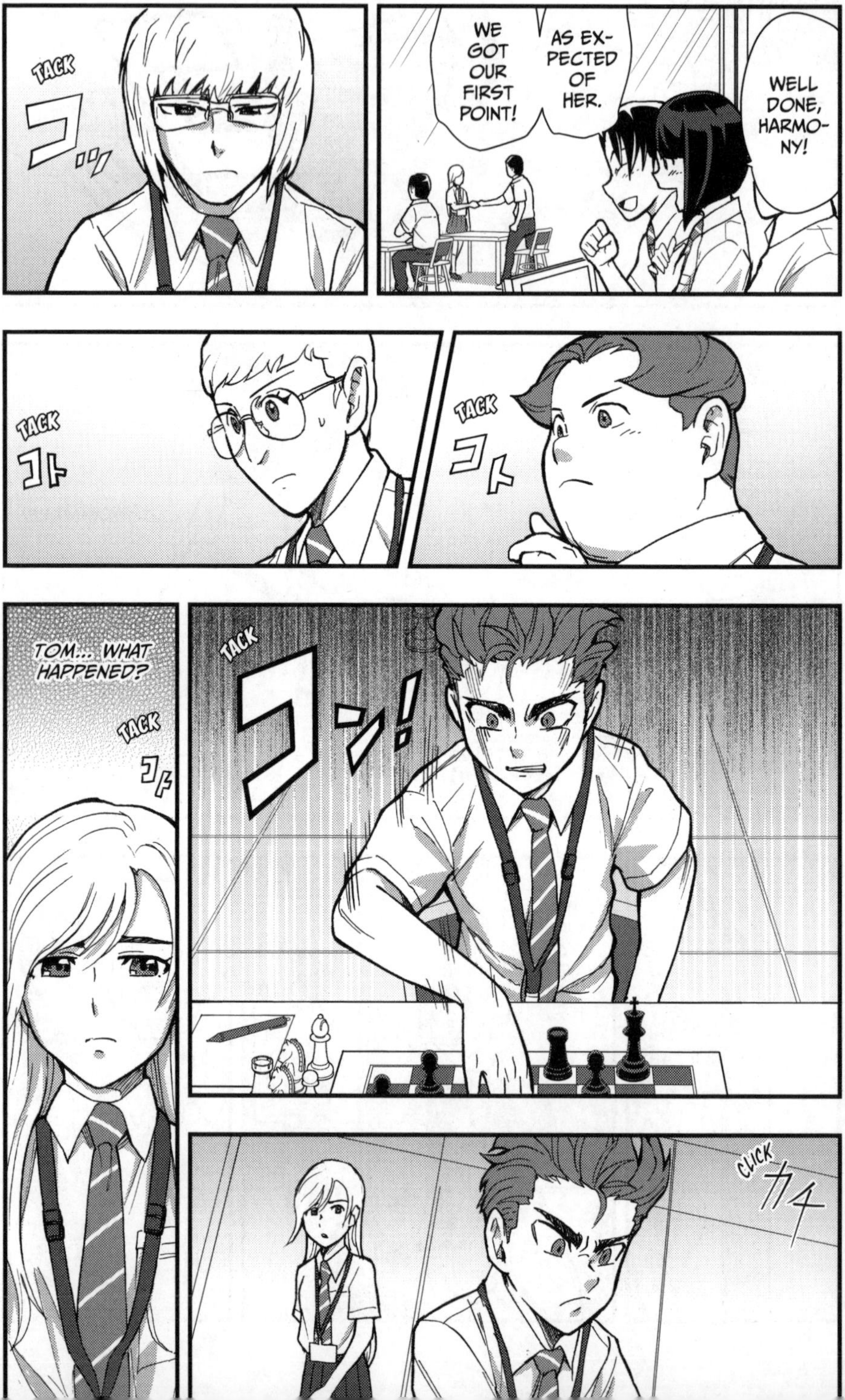
WELL DONE, HARMONY!
AS EXPECTED OF HER.
WE GOT OUR FIRST POINT!
TACK
TACK
TACK
TACK
CLICK
TOM... WHAT HAPPENED?
TACK

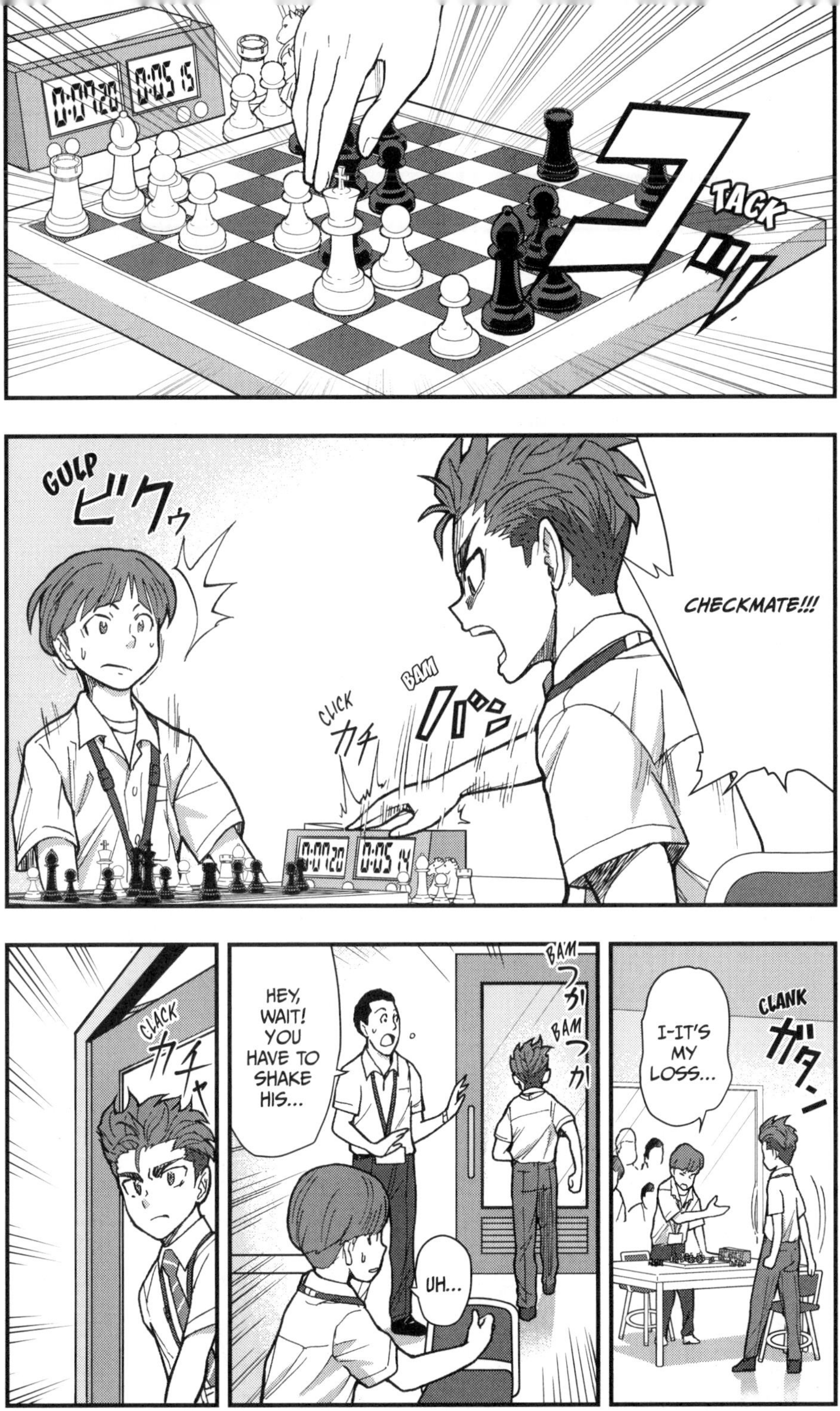
TACK
CHECKMATE!!!
BAM
パン
CLICK
カチ
GULP
ビクゥ
CLANK
ガタン
I-IT'S MY LOSS...
BAM
つか
BAM
つか
HEY, WAIT! YOU HAVE TO SHAKE HIS...
UH...
CLACK
カチャ

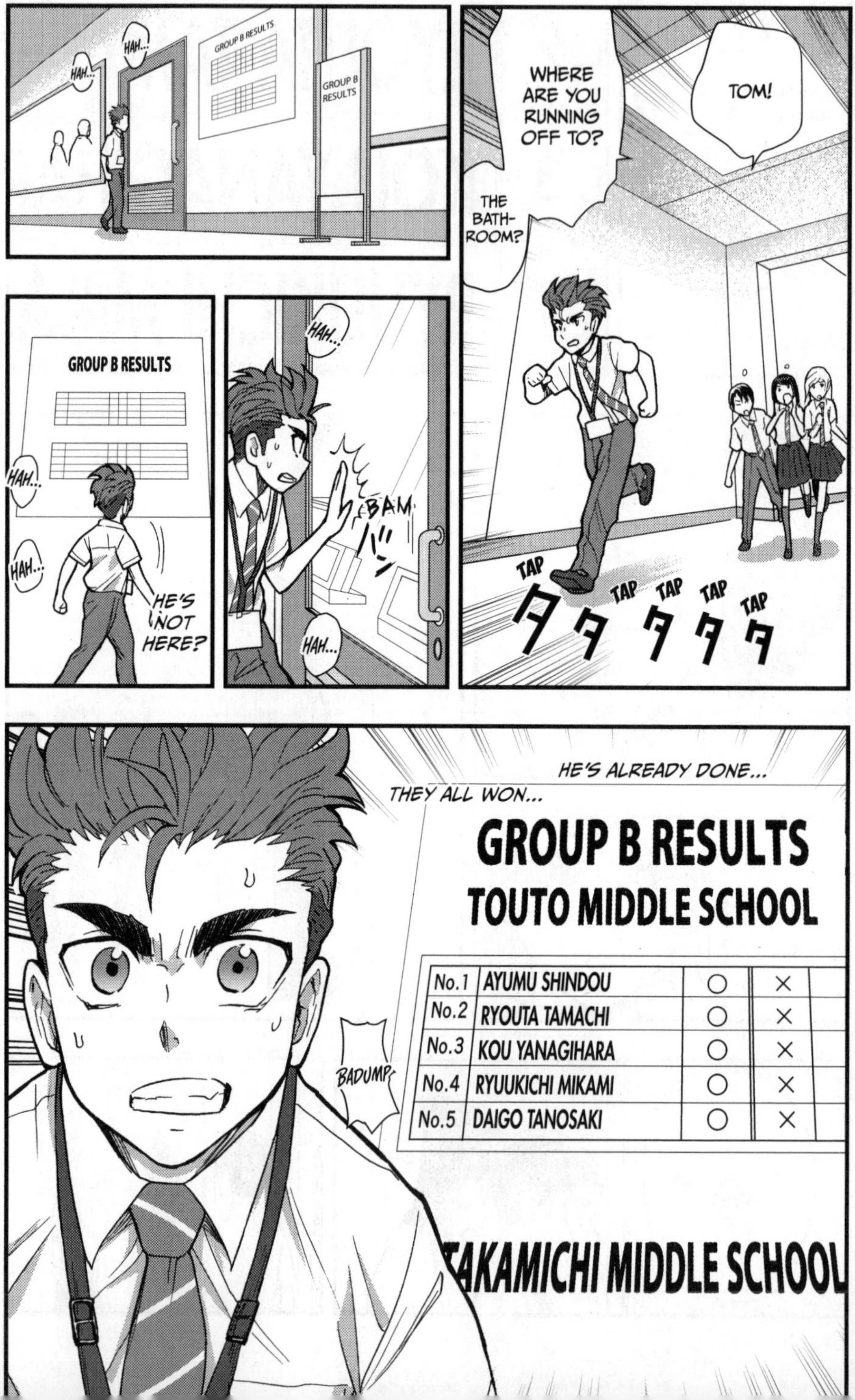
TOM!
WHERE ARE YOU RUNNING OFF TO?
THE BATH-ROOM?
TAP
タ
TAP
タ
TAP
タ
TAP
タ
TAP
タ
HAH...
HAH...
GROUP B RESULTS
GROUP B RESULTS
HAH...
BAM
バン
HAH...
GROUP B RESULTS
HAH...
HAH...
HE'S NOT HERE?
HE'S ALREADY DONE...
THEY ALL WON...
GROUP B RESULTS
TOUTO MIDDLE SCHOOL
No.1 AYUMU SHINDOU ○ ×
No.2 RYOUTA TAMACHI ○ ×
No.3 KOU YANAGIHARA ○ ×
No.4 RYUUKICHI MIKAMI ○ ×
No.5 DAIGO TANOSAKI ○ ×
BADUMP
TAKAMICHI MIDDLE SCHOOL

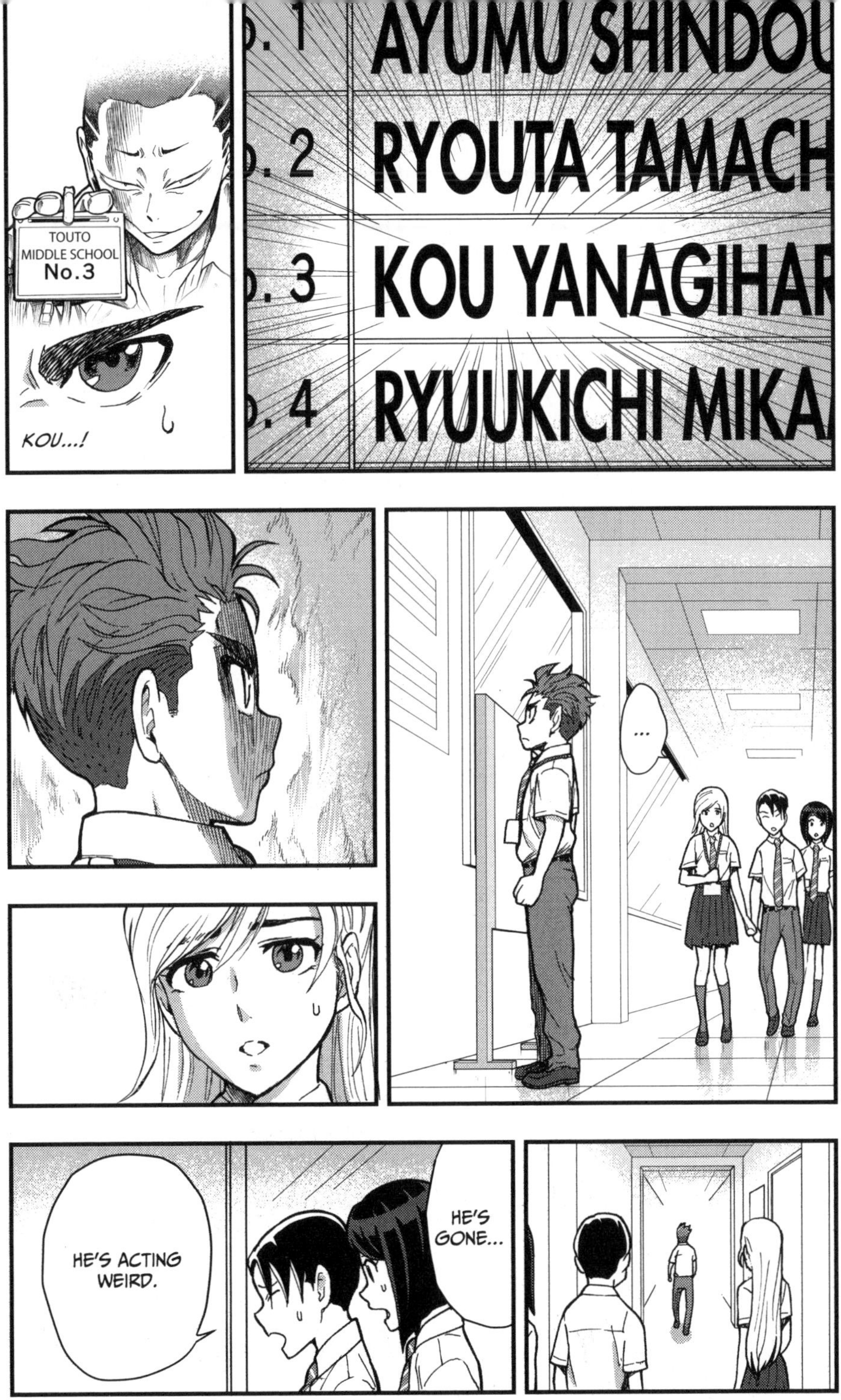
1 AYUMU SHINDOU
2 RYOUTA TAMACH
3 KOU YANAGIHAR
4 RYUUKICHI MIKA
TOUTO MIDDLE SCHOOL No.3
KOU...!
...
HE'S GONE...
HE'S ACTING WEIRD.

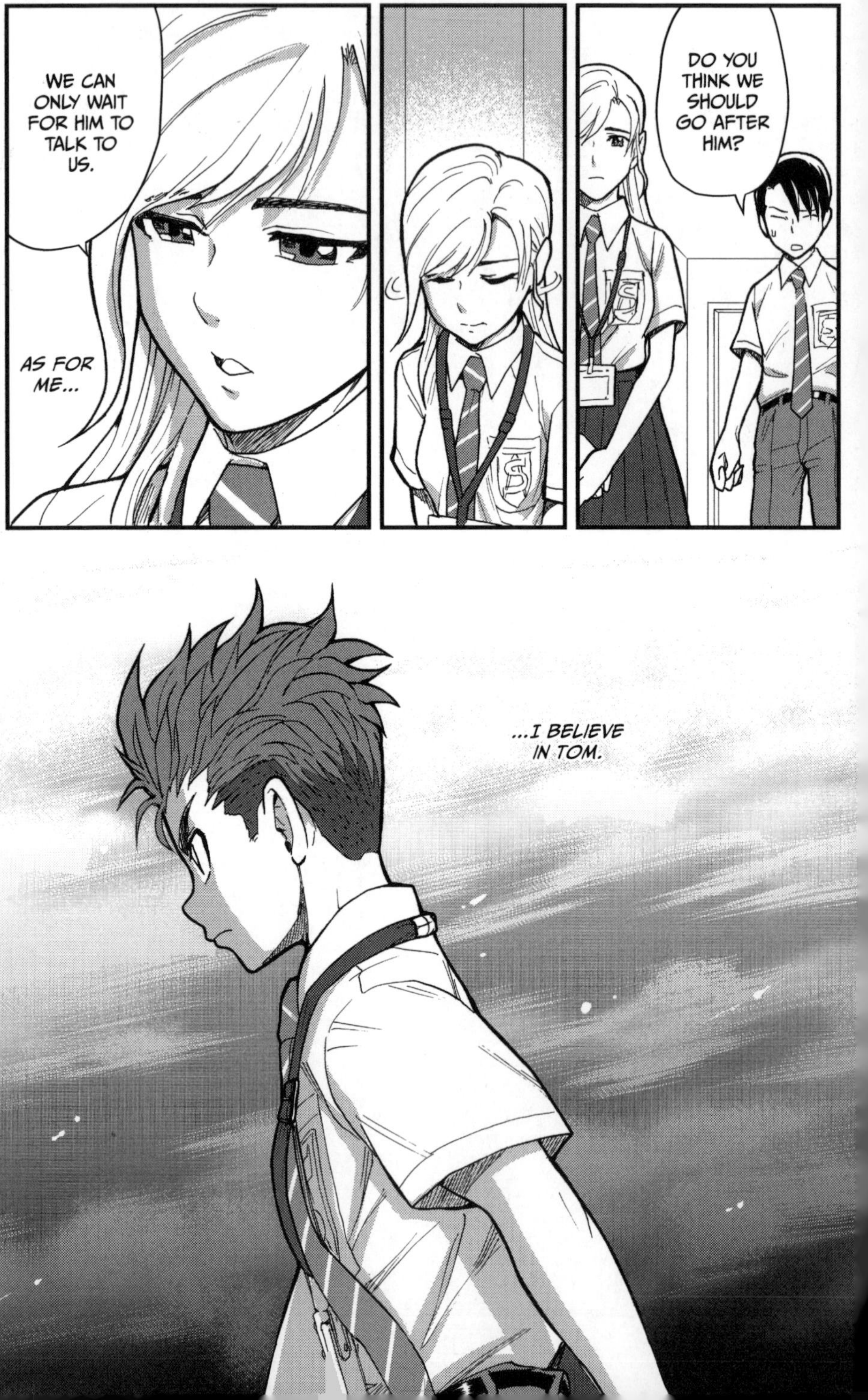
DO YOU THINK WE SHOULD GO AFTER HIM?
WE CAN ONLY WAIT FOR HIM TO TALK TO US.
AS FOR ME...
...I BELIEVE IN TOM.

BLiTZ

Chapter 16: Friends

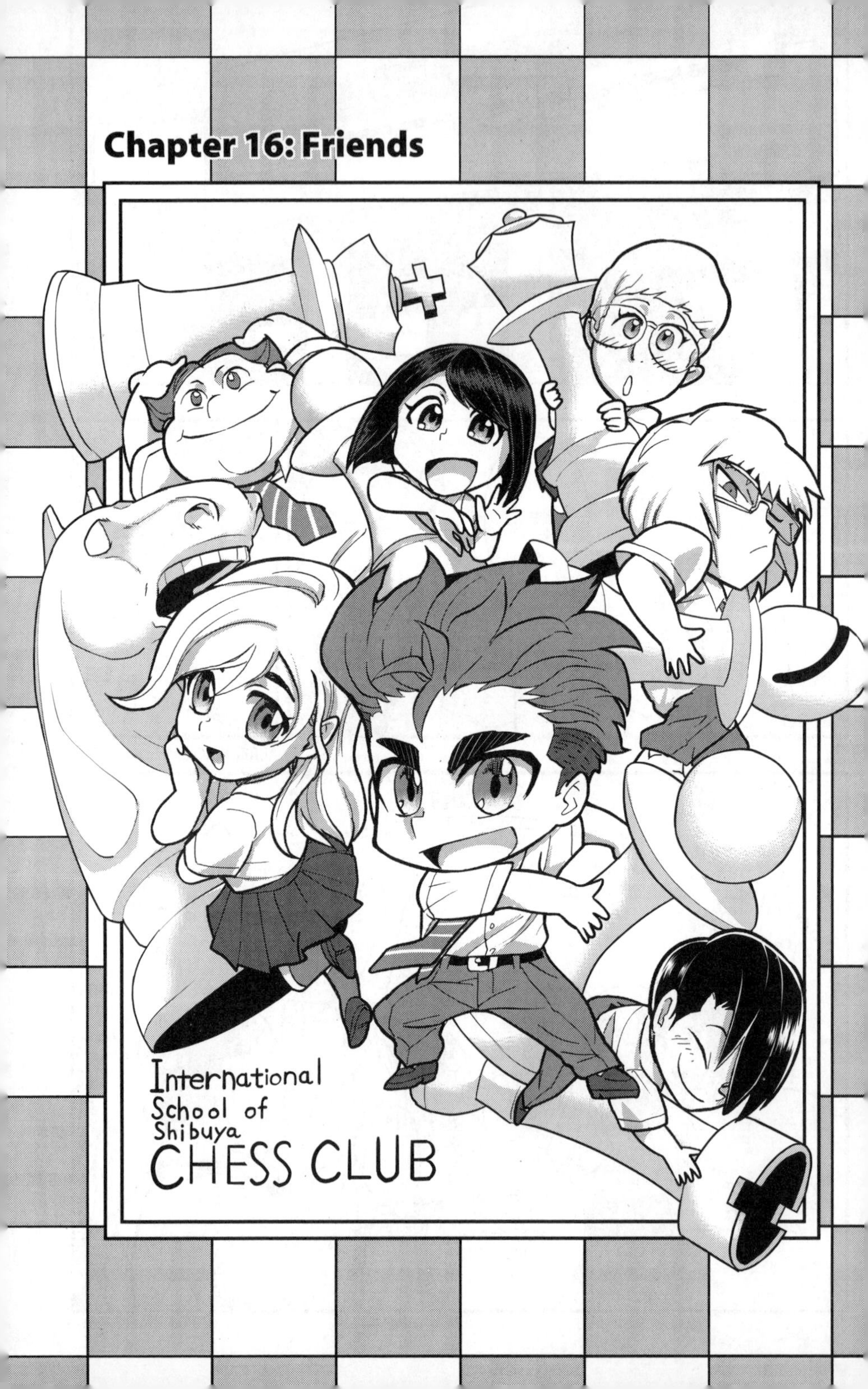
International
School of
Shibuya
CHESS CLUB

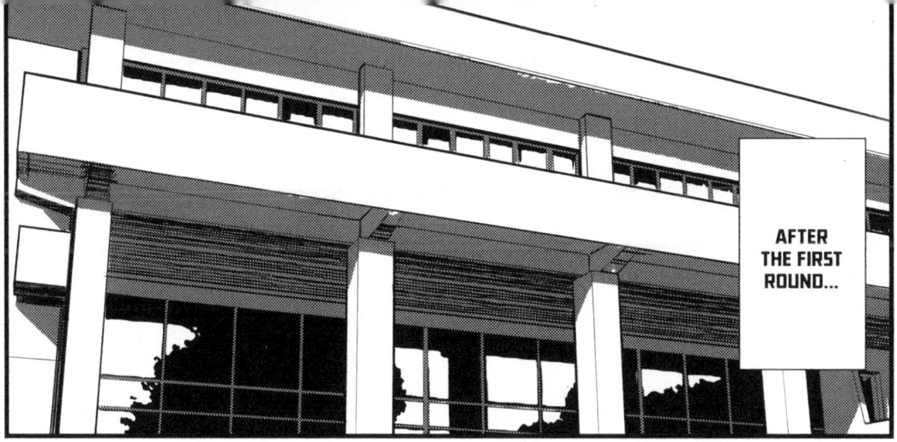
AFTER THE FIRST ROUND...

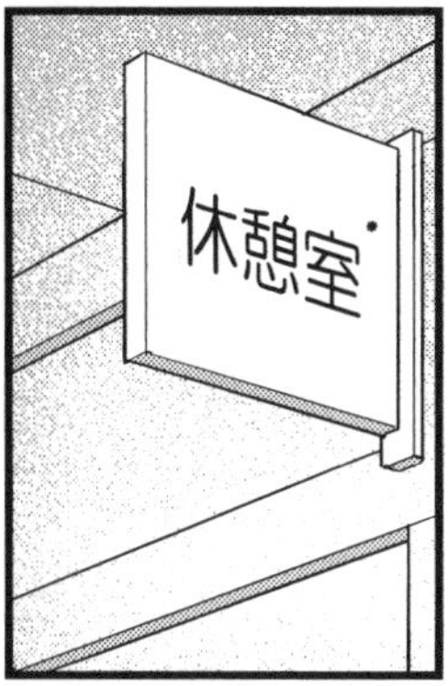
休憩室*

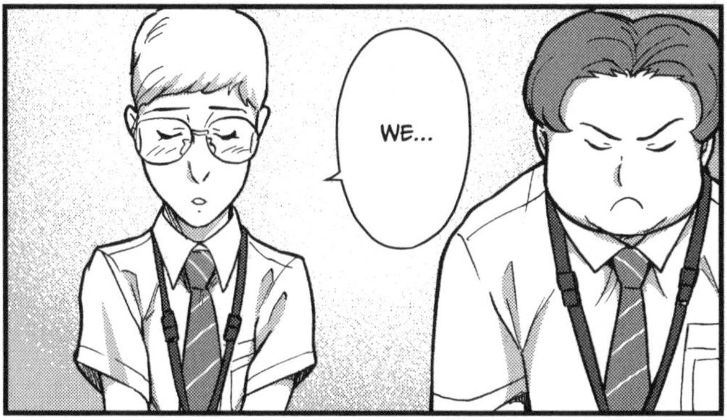
WE...

*BREAK ROOM.

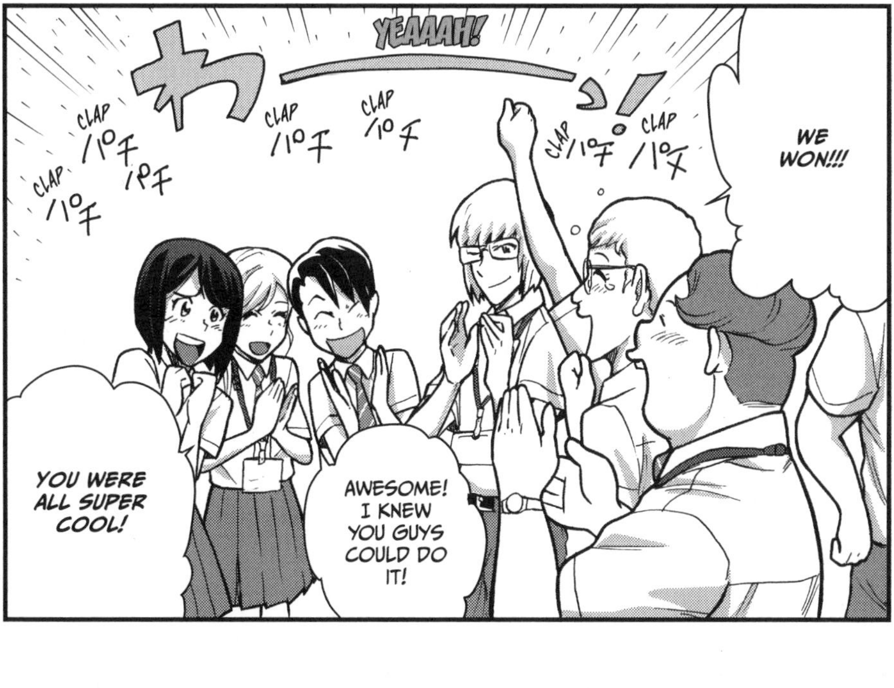
YEAAAH!
わーっ!
CLAP パチ
CLAP パチ
CLAP パチ
CLAP パチ
パチ
WE WON!!!
AWESOME! I KNEW YOU GUYS COULD DO IT!
YOU WERE ALL SUPER COOL!

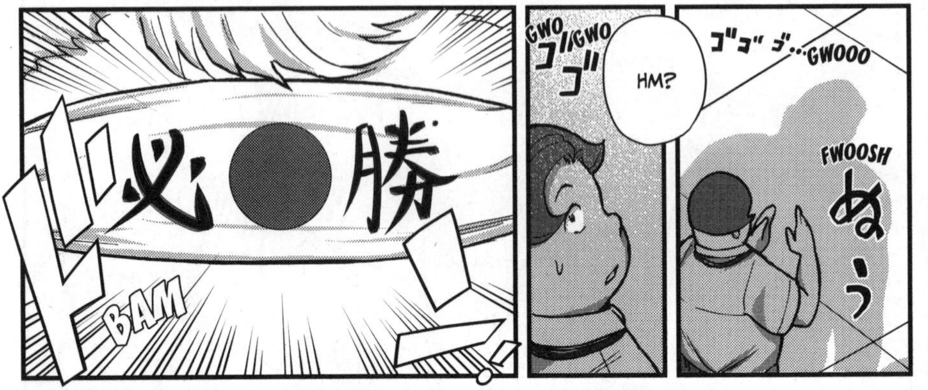
GWOOO
FWOOSH
GWO GWO
HM?
必●勝
BAM

*VICTORY.

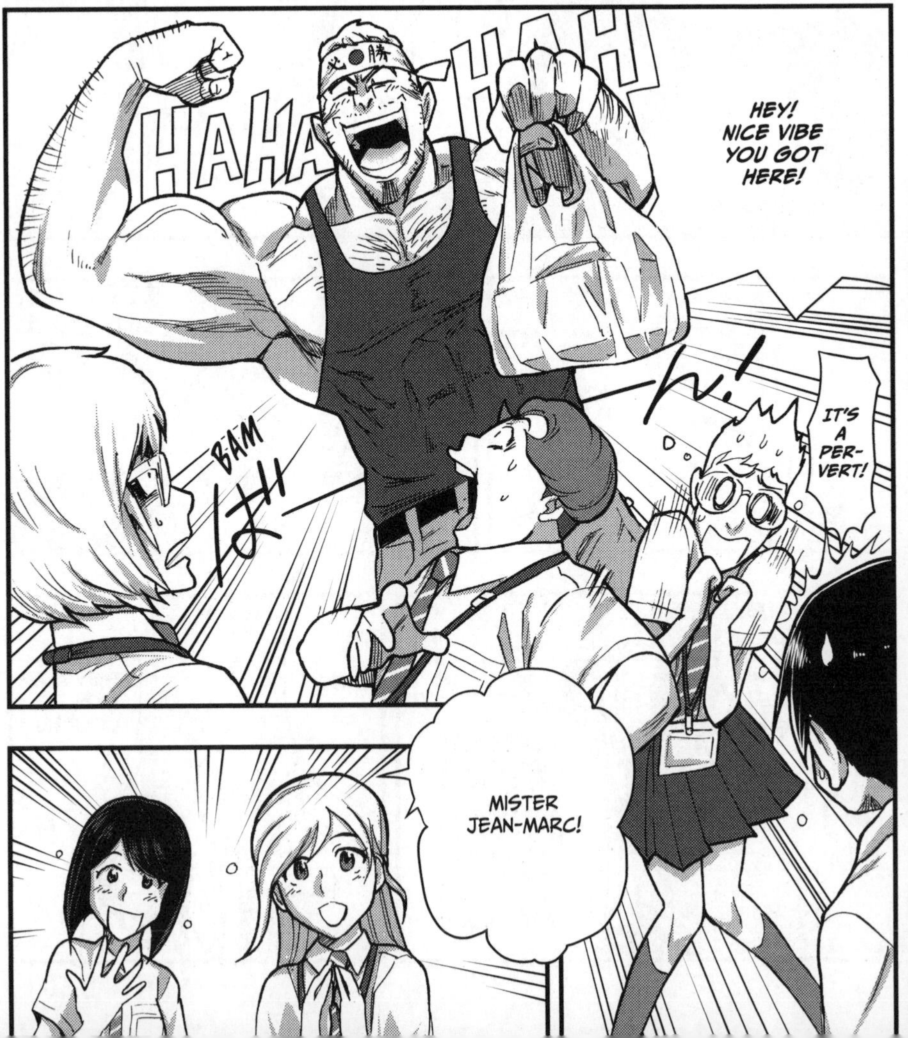
HEY! NICE VIBE YOU GOT HERE!
IT'S A PER-VERT!
HAHAHAHAH
BAM
MISTER JEAN-MARC!

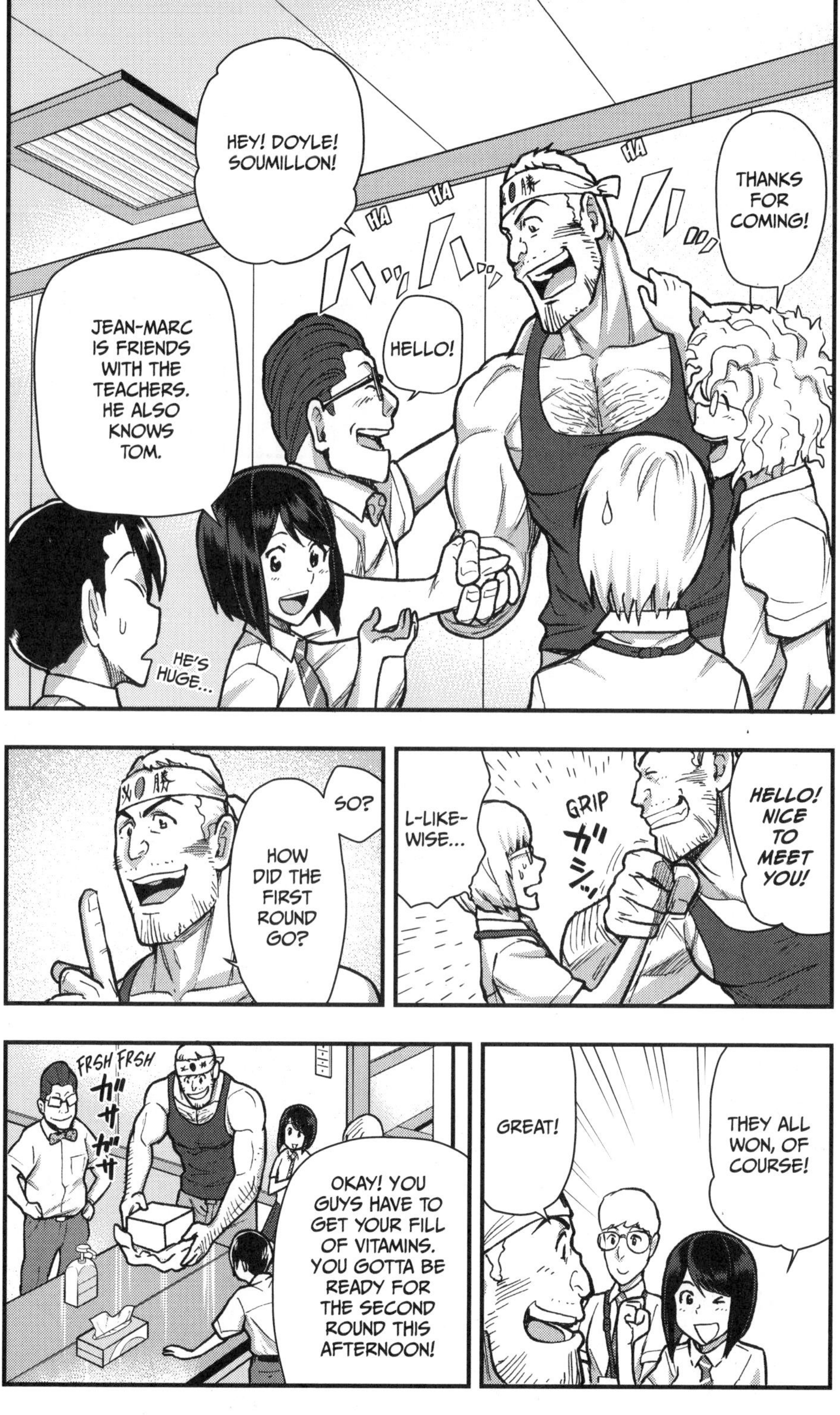
THANKS FOR COMING!
HA HA HA
HEY! DOYLE! SOUMILLON!
HELLO!
JEAN-MARC IS FRIENDS WITH THE TEACHERS. HE ALSO KNOWS TOM.
HE'S HUGE...
HELLO! NICE TO MEET YOU!
GRIP
L-LIKE-WISE...
SO?
HOW DID THE FIRST ROUND GO?
THEY ALL WON, OF COURSE!
GREAT!
FRSH FRSH
OKAY! YOU GUYS HAVE TO GET YOUR FILL OF VITAMINS. YOU GOTTA BE READY FOR THE SECOND ROUND THIS AFTERNOON!

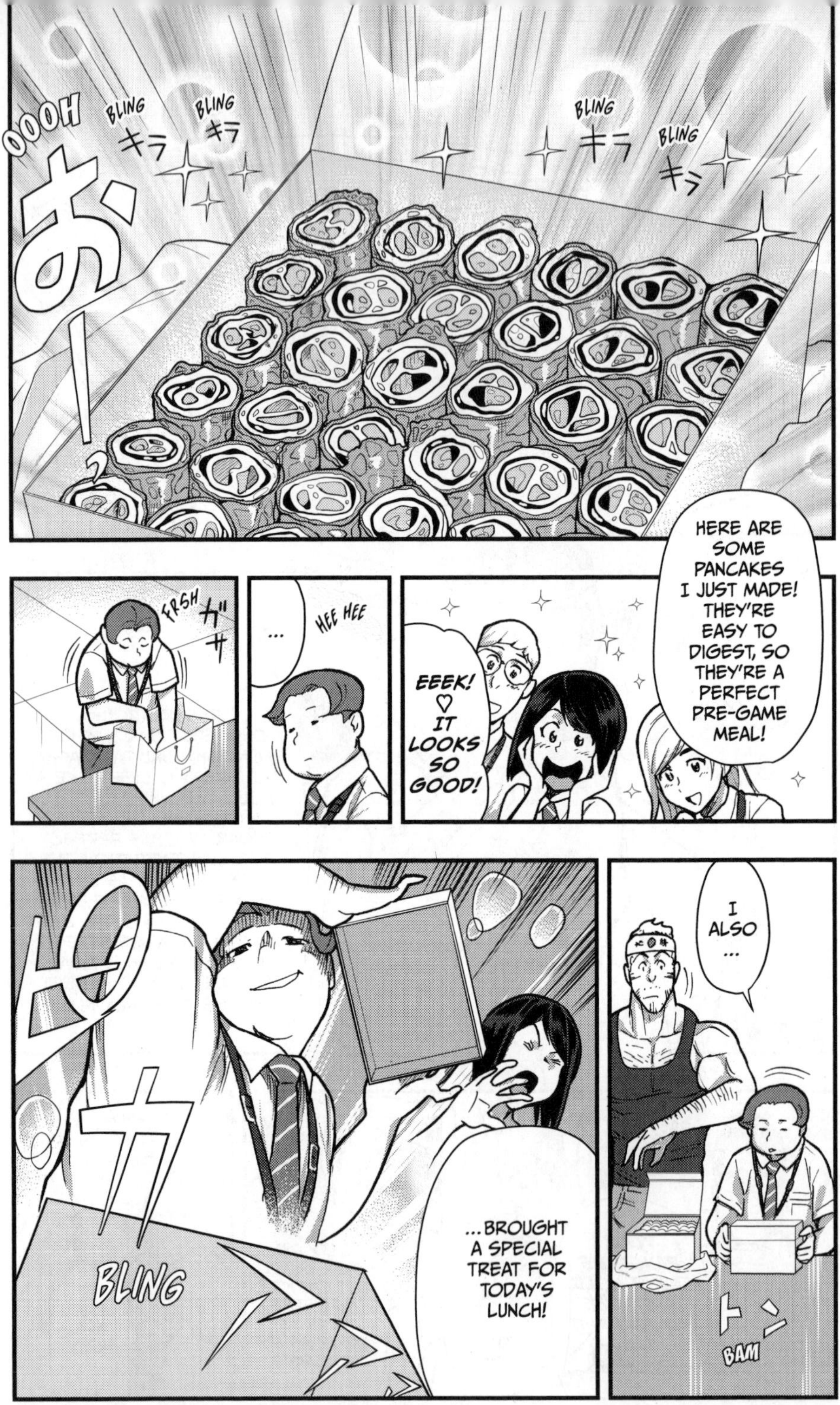
BLING
キラ
BLING
キラ
BLING
キラ
BLING
キラ
OOOH
おーっ
HERE ARE SOME PANCAKES I JUST MADE! THEY'RE EASY TO DIGEST, SO THEY'RE A PERFECT PRE-GAME MEAL!
EEEK! ♡ IT LOOKS SO GOOD!
HEE HEE
...
FRSH
ガサ
I ALSO ...
トン
BAM
...BROUGHT A SPECIAL TREAT FOR TODAY'S LUNCH!
ピカ
BLING

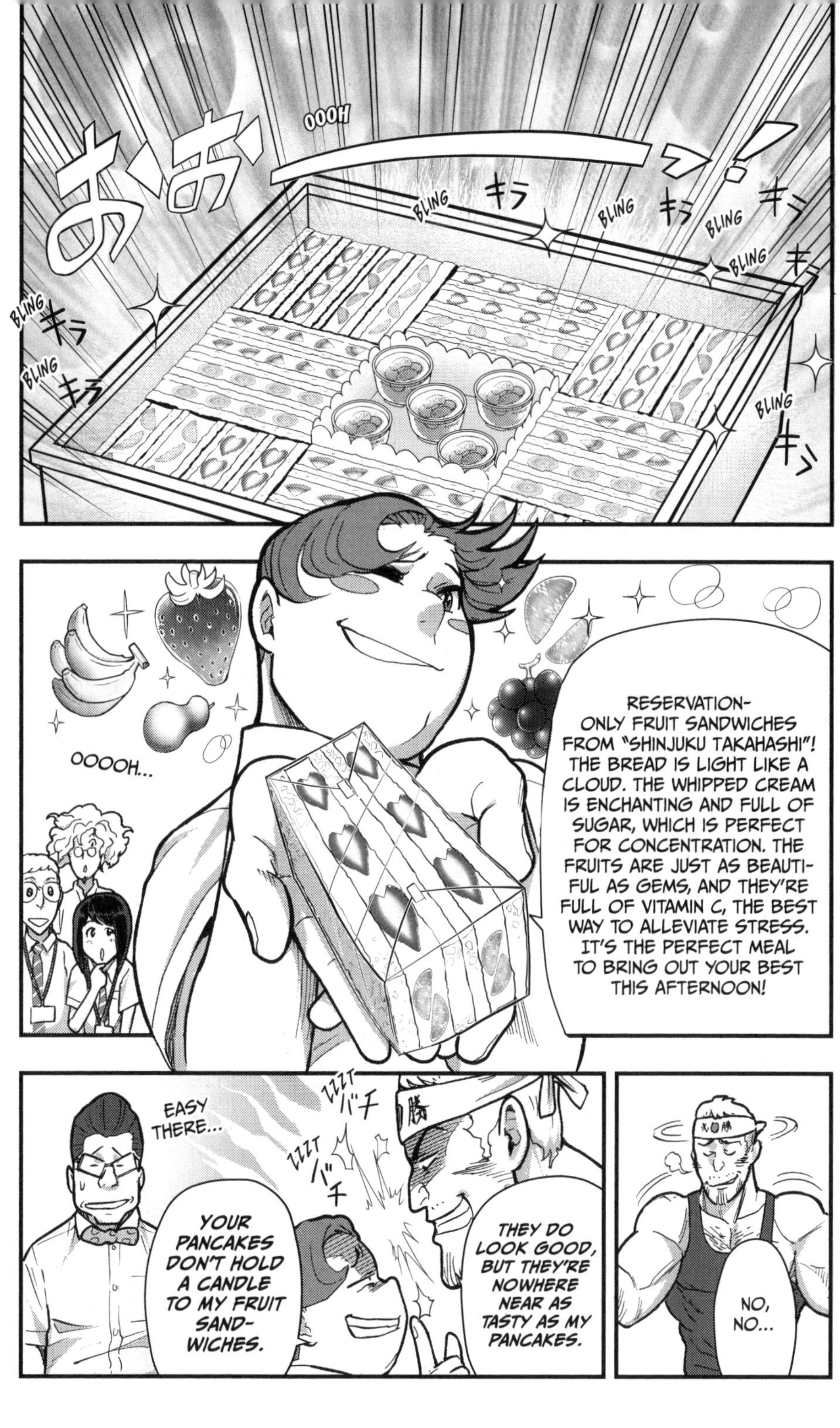
おおーーっ!
OOOH
BLING キラ
BLING キラ
BLING キラ
BLING キラ
BLING キラ
BLING キラ
BLING キラ
RESERVATION-ONLY FRUIT SANDWICHES FROM "SHINJUKU TAKAHASHI"! THE BREAD IS LIGHT LIKE A CLOUD. THE WHIPPED CREAM IS ENCHANTING AND FULL OF SUGAR, WHICH IS PERFECT FOR CONCENTRATION. THE FRUITS ARE JUST AS BEAUTIFUL AS GEMS, AND THEY'RE FULL OF VITAMIN C, THE BEST WAY TO ALLEVIATE STRESS. IT'S THE PERFECT MEAL TO BRING OUT YOUR BEST THIS AFTERNOON!
OOOOH...
NO, NO...
ZZZT バチ
ZZZT バチ
THEY DO LOOK GOOD, BUT THEY'RE NOWHERE NEAR AS TASTY AS MY PANCAKES.
YOUR PANCAKES DON'T HOLD A CANDLE TO MY FRUIT SANDWICHES.
EASY THERE...

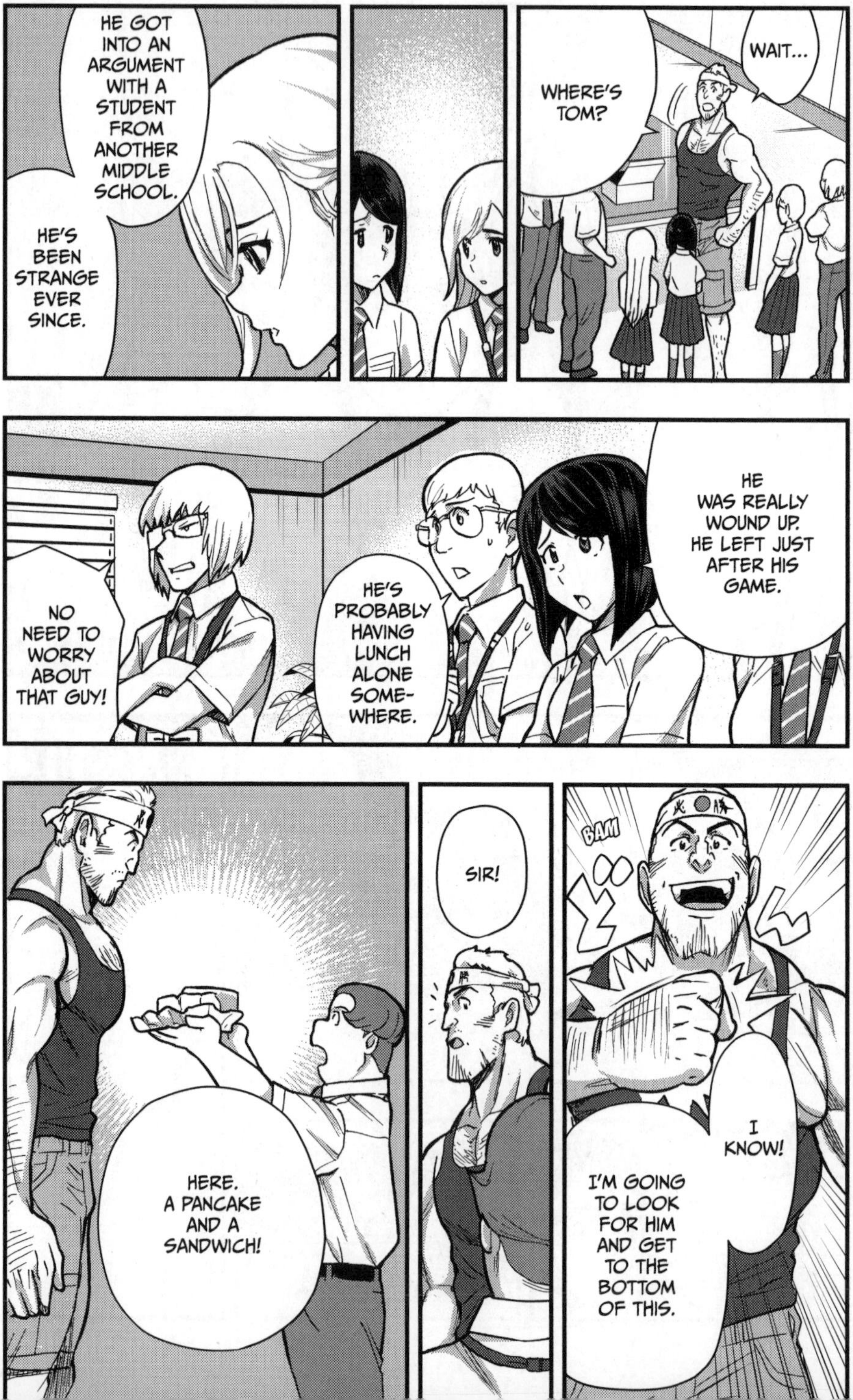
WAIT...
WHERE'S TOM?
HE GOT INTO AN ARGUMENT WITH A STUDENT FROM ANOTHER MIDDLE SCHOOL.
HE'S BEEN STRANGE EVER SINCE.
HE WAS REALLY WOUND UP. HE LEFT JUST AFTER HIS GAME.
HE'S PROBABLY HAVING LUNCH ALONE SOME-WHERE.
NO NEED TO WORRY ABOUT THAT GUY!
BAM
I KNOW!
I'M GOING TO LOOK FOR HIM AND GET TO THE BOTTOM OF THIS.
SIR!
HERE. A PANCAKE AND A SANDWICH!

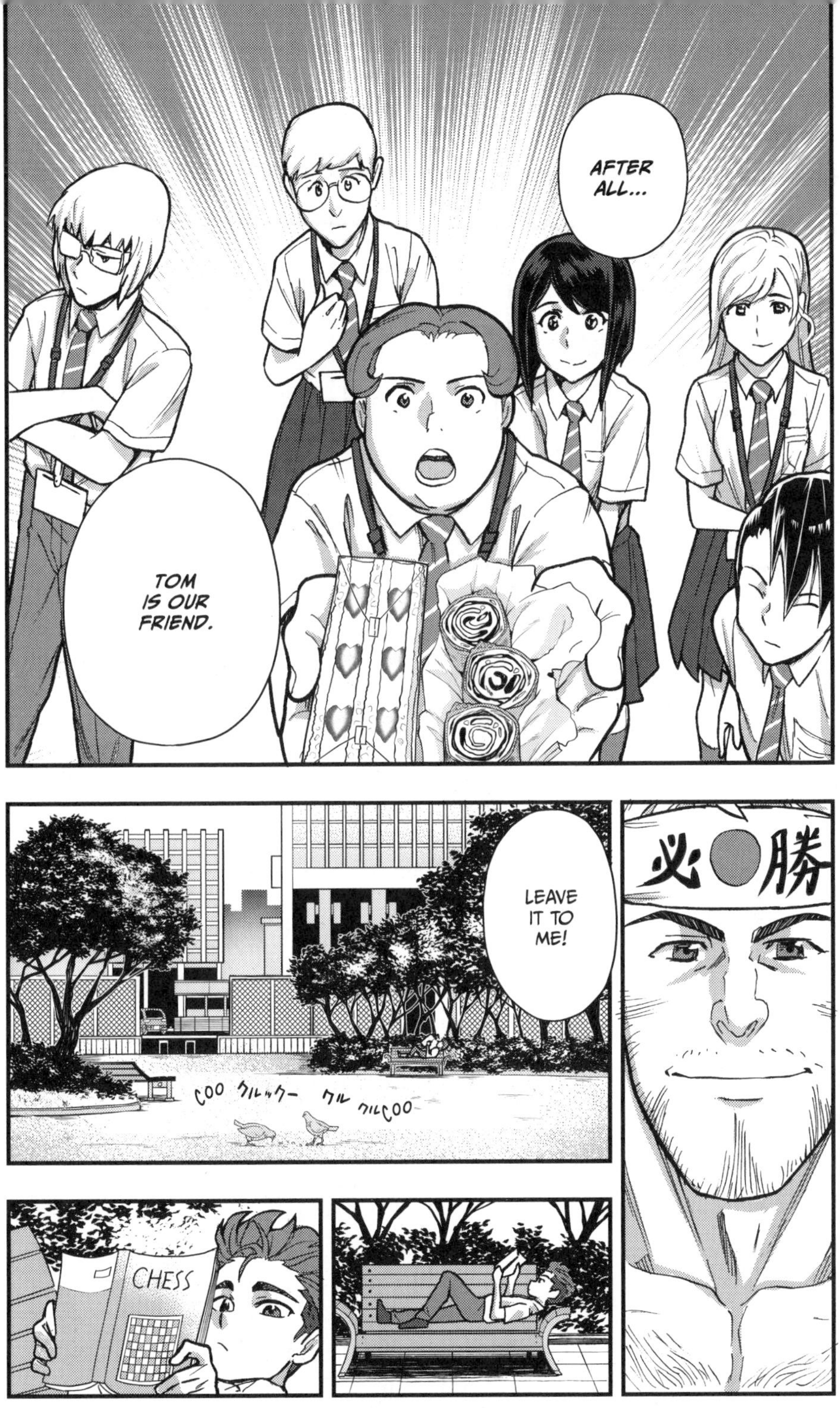
AFTER ALL...
TOM IS OUR FRIEND.
必勝
LEAVE IT TO ME!
COO クルックー クル クルCOO
CHESS

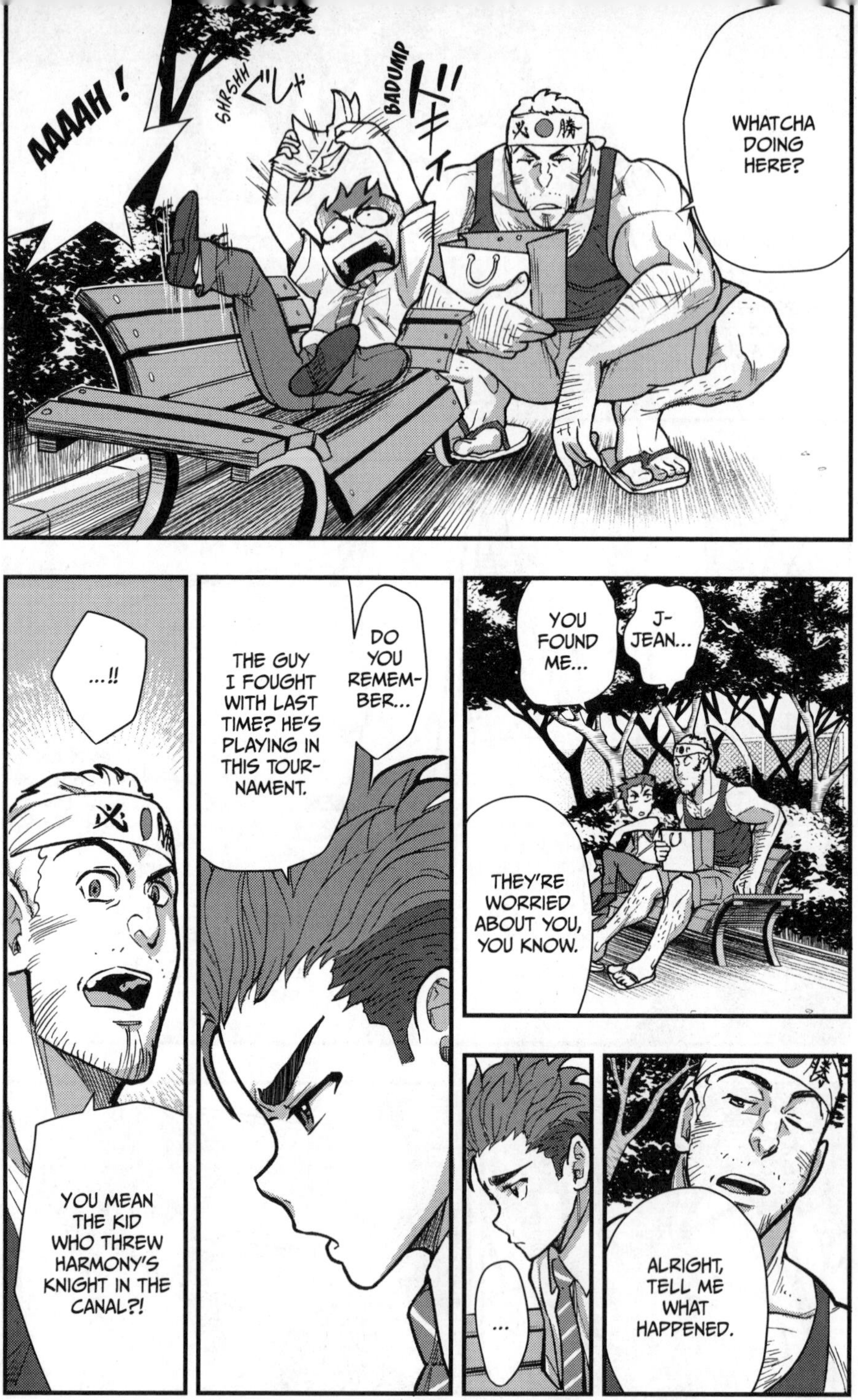
WHATCHA DOING HERE?
BADUMP
ドキィ
SHRSHH
ぐしゃ
AAAAH!
J- JEAN...
YOU FOUND ME...
THEY'RE WORRIED ABOUT YOU, YOU KNOW.
ALRIGHT, TELL ME WHAT HAPPENED.
...
DO YOU REMEMBER...
THE GUY I FOUGHT WITH LAST TIME? HE'S PLAYING IN THIS TOURNAMENT.
...!!
YOU MEAN THE KID WHO THREW HARMONY'S KNIGHT IN THE CANAL?!

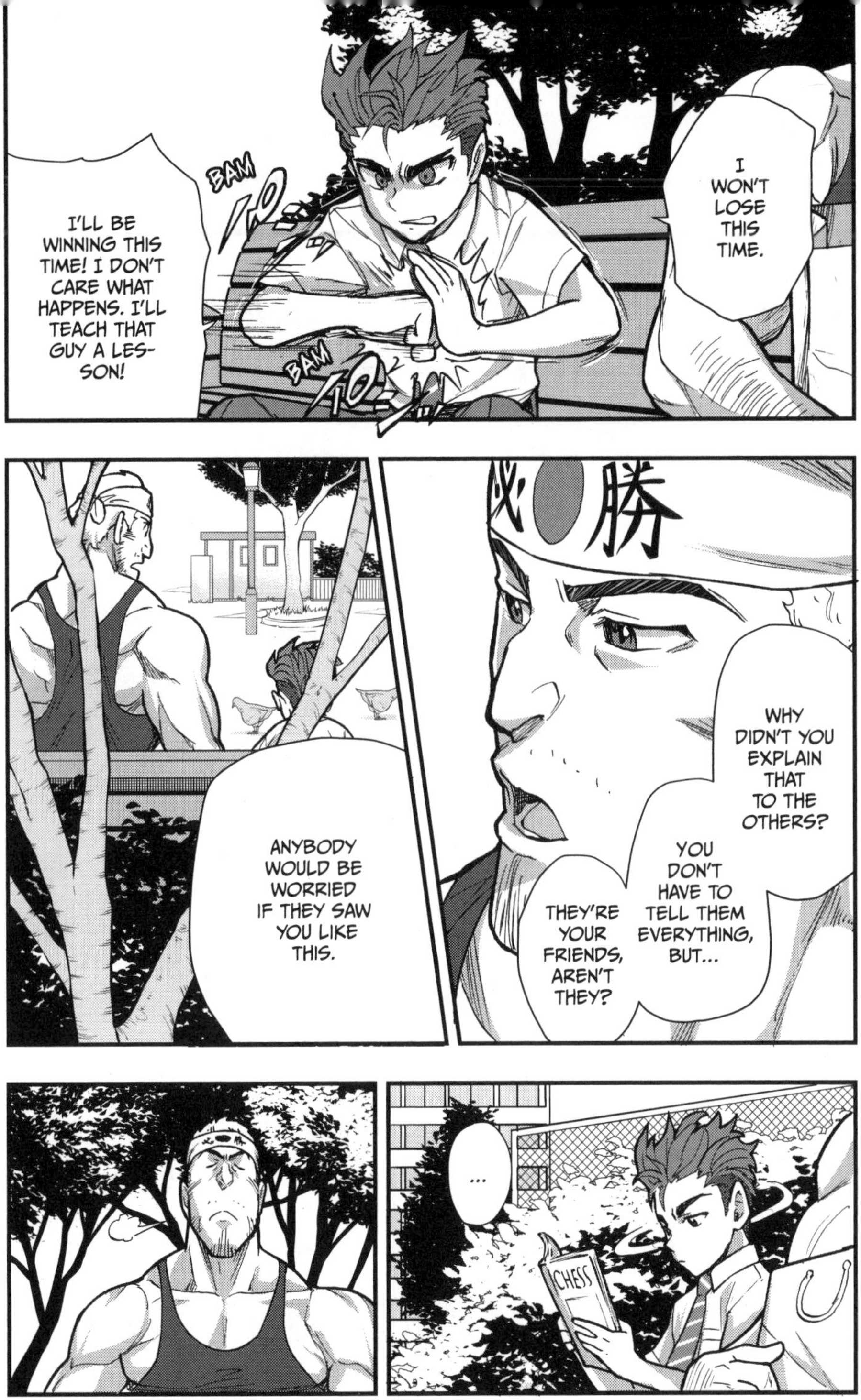
I WON'T LOSE THIS TIME.
BAM
I'LL BE WINNING THIS TIME! I DON'T CARE WHAT HAPPENS. I'LL TEACH THAT GUY A LES-SON!
BAM
勝
WHY DIDN'T YOU EXPLAIN THAT TO THE OTHERS?
YOU DON'T HAVE TO TELL THEM EVERYTHING, BUT...
THEY'RE YOUR FRIENDS, AREN'T THEY?
ANYBODY WOULD BE WORRIED IF THEY SAW YOU LIKE THIS.
...
CHESS

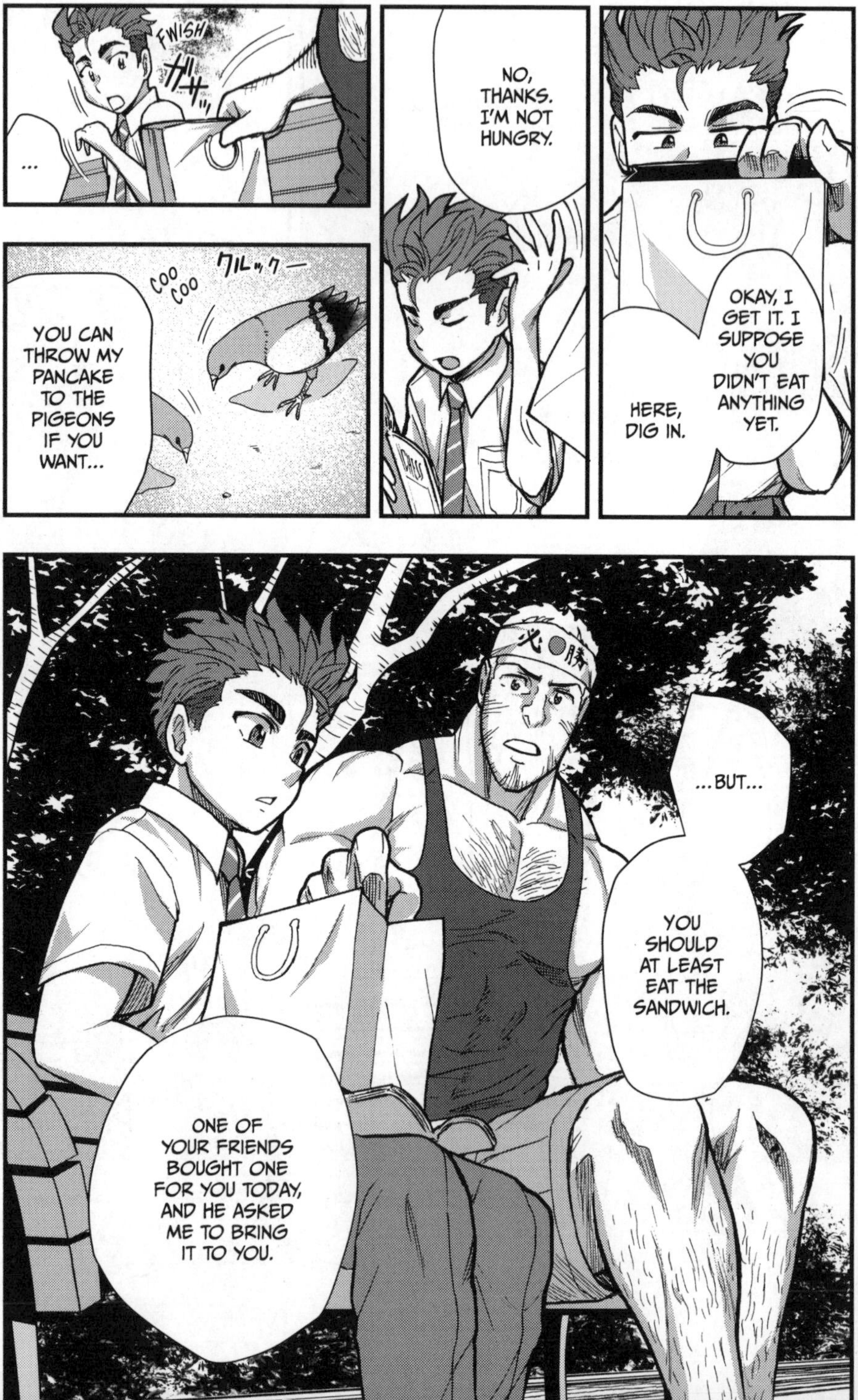
OKAY, I GET IT. I SUPPOSE YOU DIDN'T EAT ANYTHING YET.
HERE, DIG IN.
NO, THANKS. I'M NOT HUNGRY.
FWISH
...
COO COO
YOU CAN THROW MY PANCAKE TO THE PIGEONS IF YOU WANT...
...BUT...
YOU SHOULD AT LEAST EAT THE SANDWICH.
ONE OF YOUR FRIENDS BOUGHT ONE FOR YOU TODAY, AND HE ASKED ME TO BRING IT TO YOU.

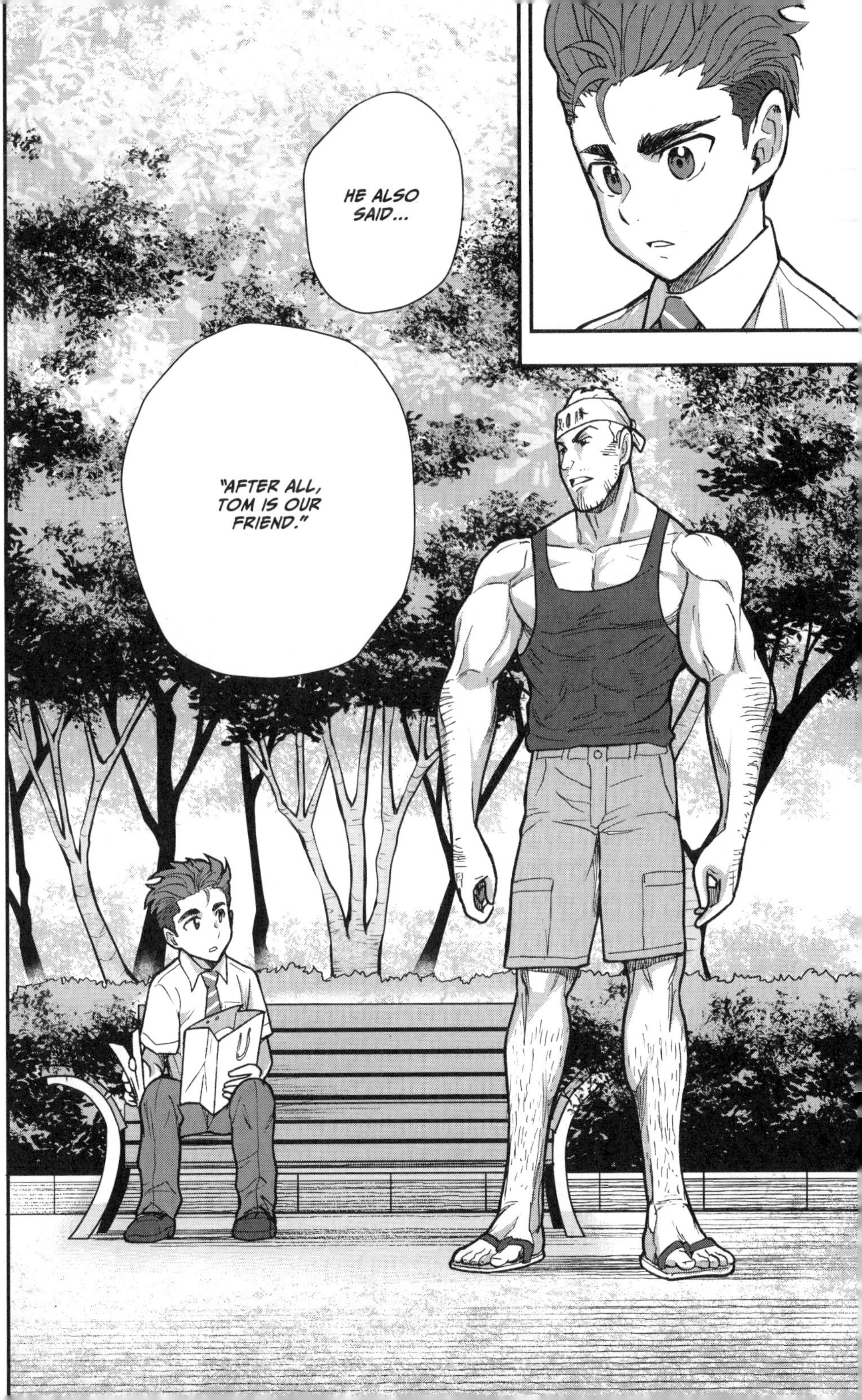
HE ALSO SAID...
"AFTER ALL, TOM IS OUR FRIEND."

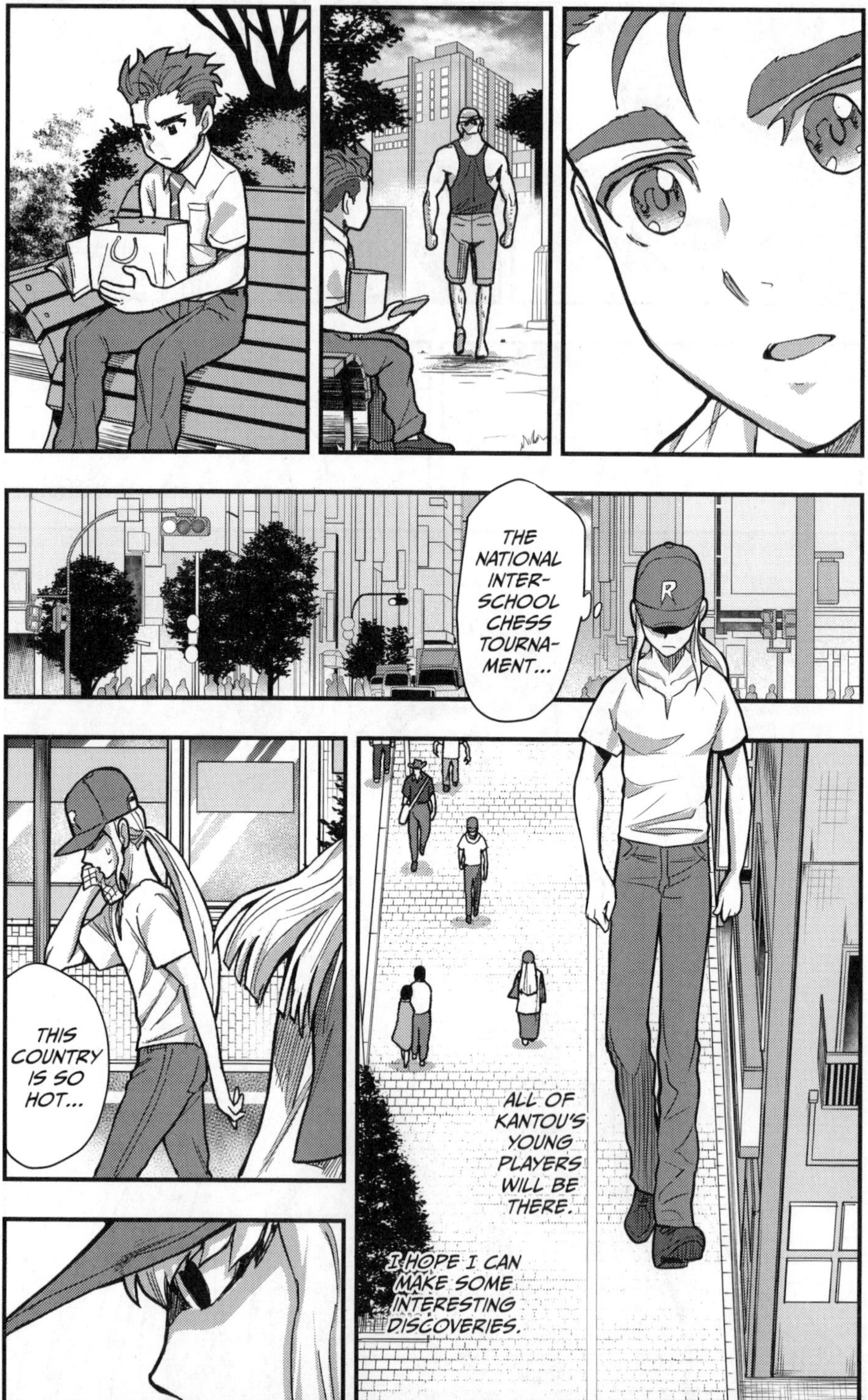
THE NATIONAL INTER-SCHOOL CHESS TOURNAMENT...
ALL OF KANTOU'S YOUNG PLAYERS WILL BE THERE.
I HOPE I CAN MAKE SOME INTERESTING DISCOVERIES.
THIS COUNTRY IS SO HOT...

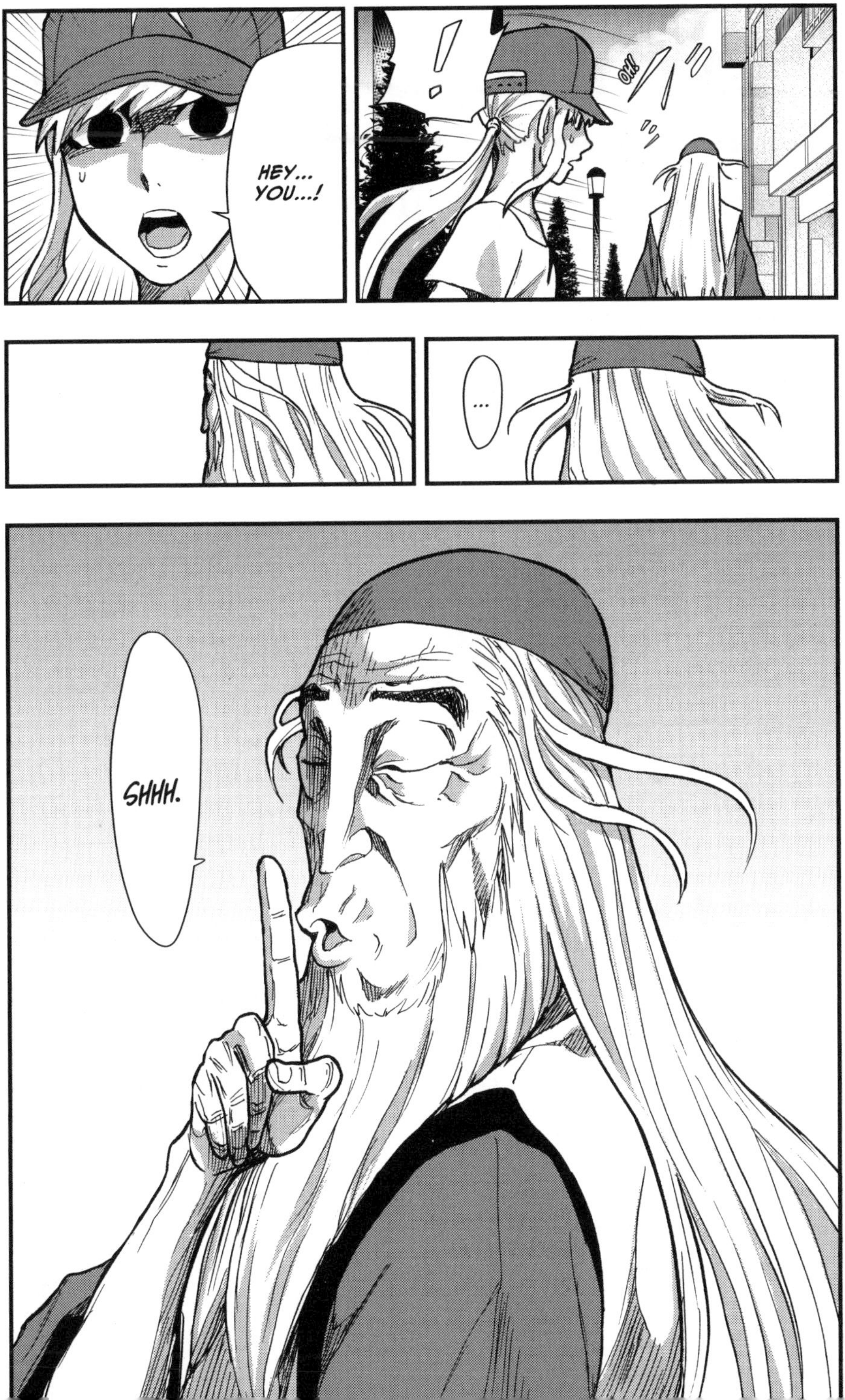
!
OH!!
HEY... YOU...!
...
SHHH.

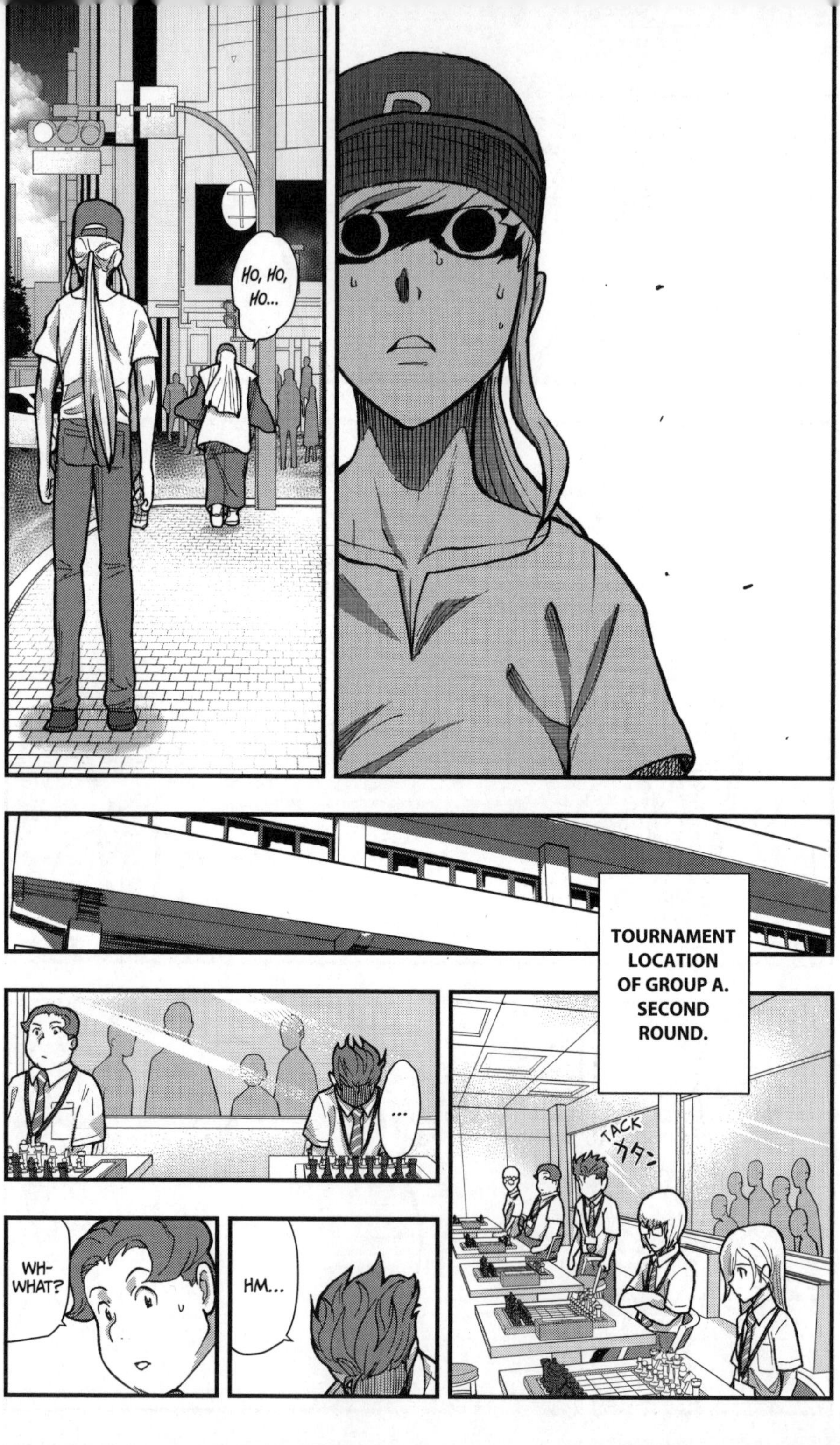
HO, HO, HO...
TOURNAMENT LOCATION OF GROUP A. SECOND ROUND.
TACK
カタン
...
HM...
WH-WHAT?

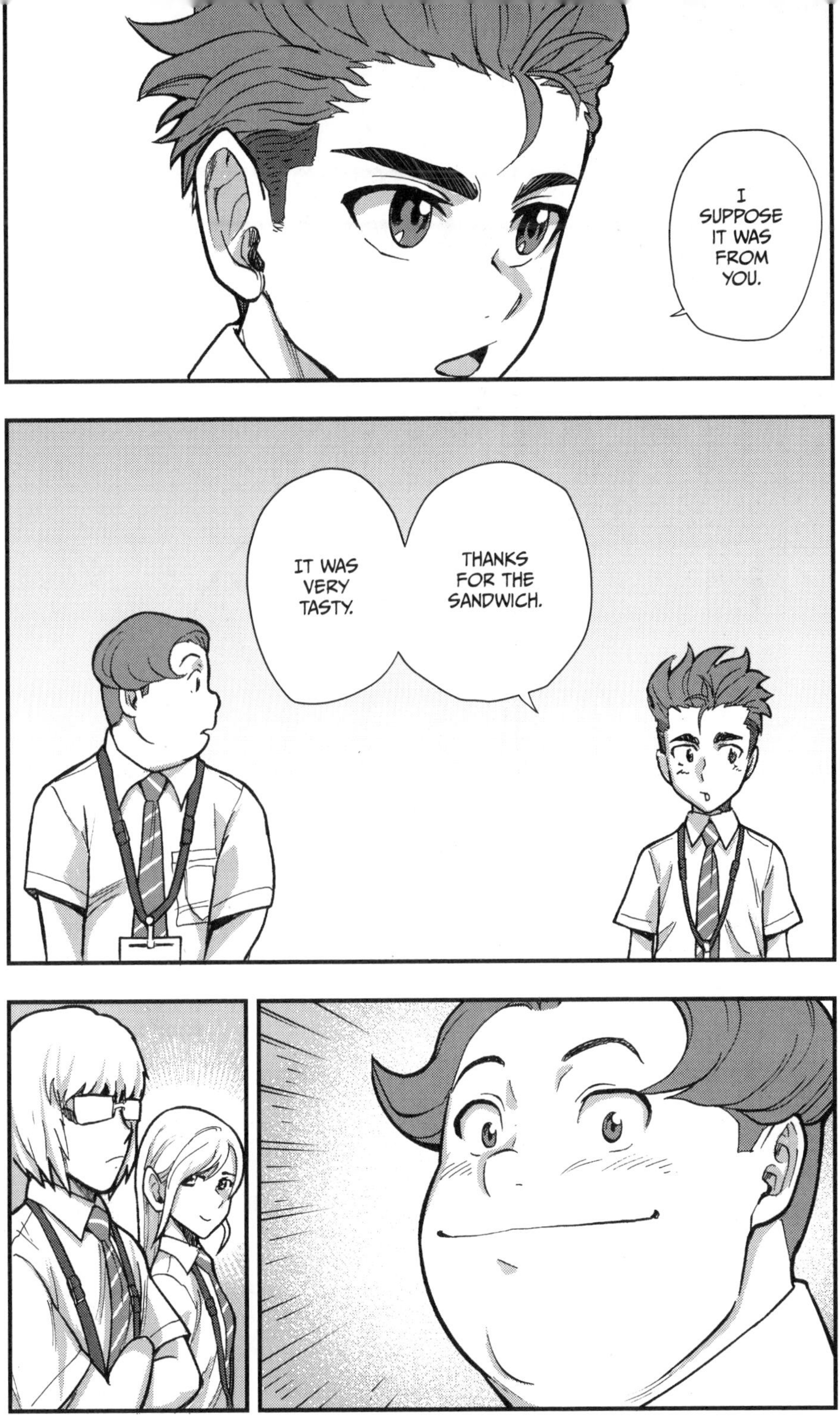
I SUPPOSE IT WAS FROM YOU.
THANKS FOR THE SANDWICH.
IT WAS VERY TASTY.

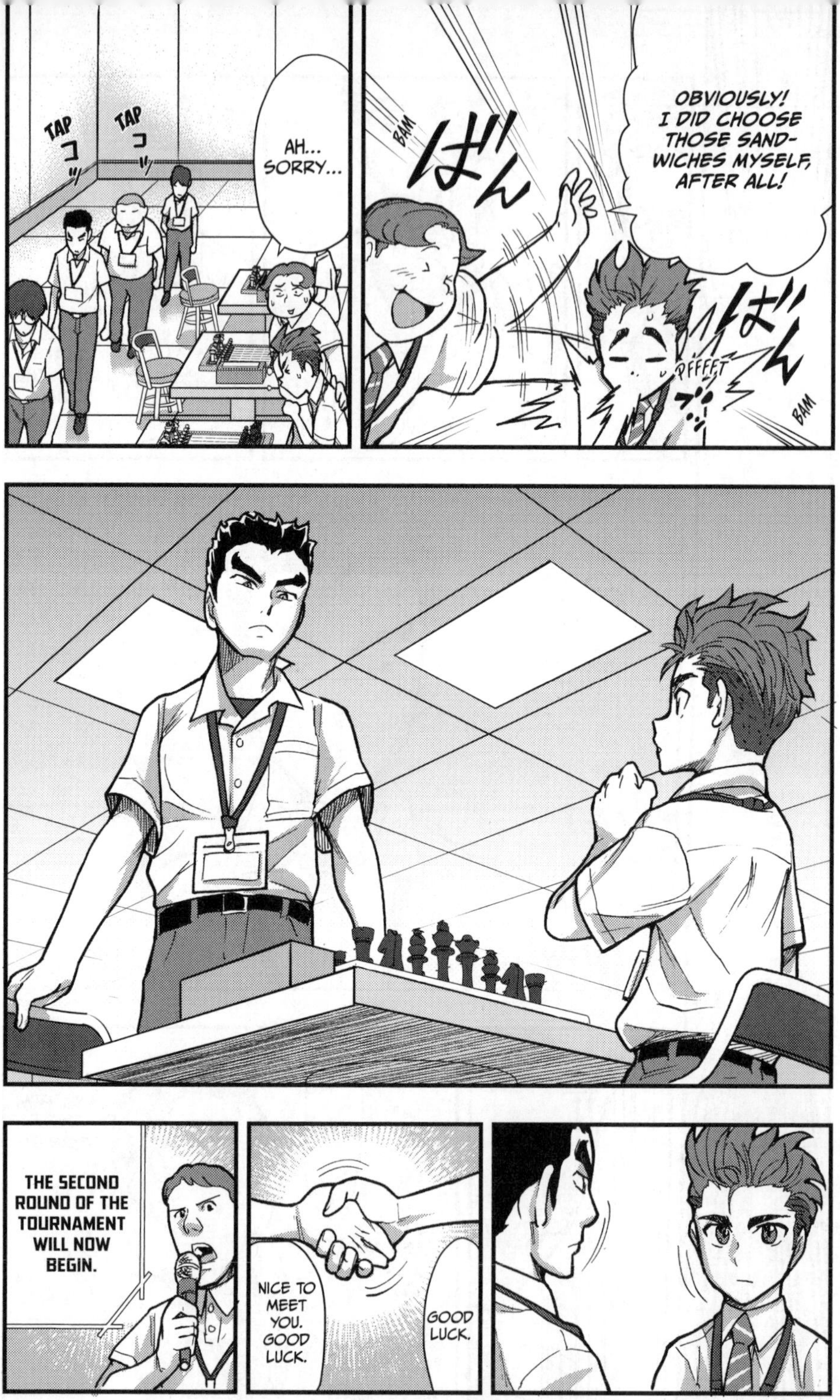

OBVIOUSLY! I DID CHOOSE THOSE SAND-WICHES MYSELF, AFTER ALL!
BAM
ばん
ばん
BAM
PFFFFT
ブッ
TAP
コッ
TAP
コッ
AH... SORRY...
NICE TO MEET YOU. GOOD LUCK.
GOOD LUCK.
THE SECOND ROUND OF THE TOURNAMENT WILL NOW BEGIN.

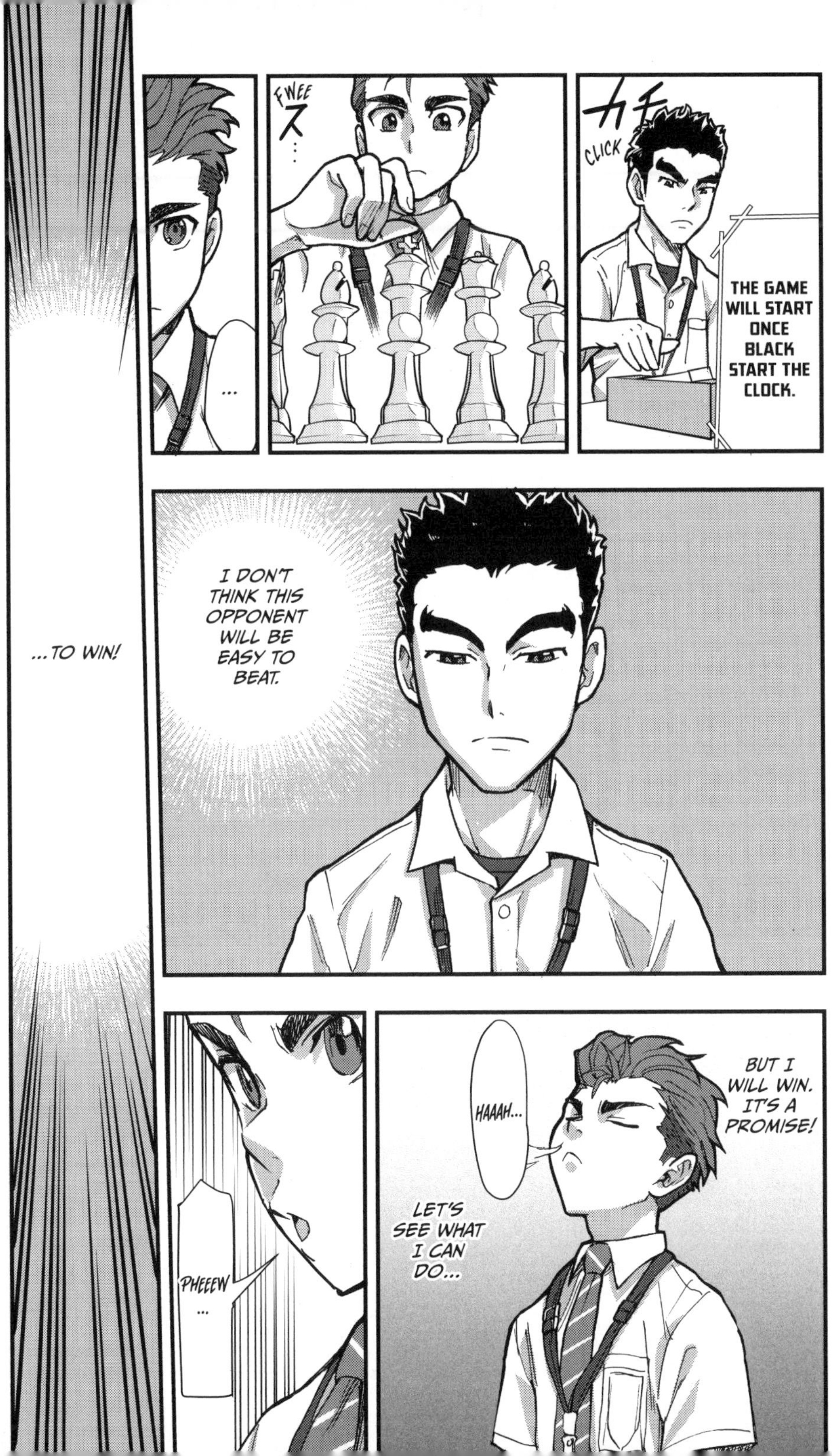

カチ
CLICK
THE GAME WILL START ONCE BLACK START THE CLOCK.
ス
FWEE
...
...
I DON'T THINK THIS OPPONENT WILL BE EASY TO BEAT.
BUT I WILL WIN. IT'S A PROMISE!
HAAAH...
LET'S SEE WHAT I CAN DO...
PHEEEW ...
...TO WIN!

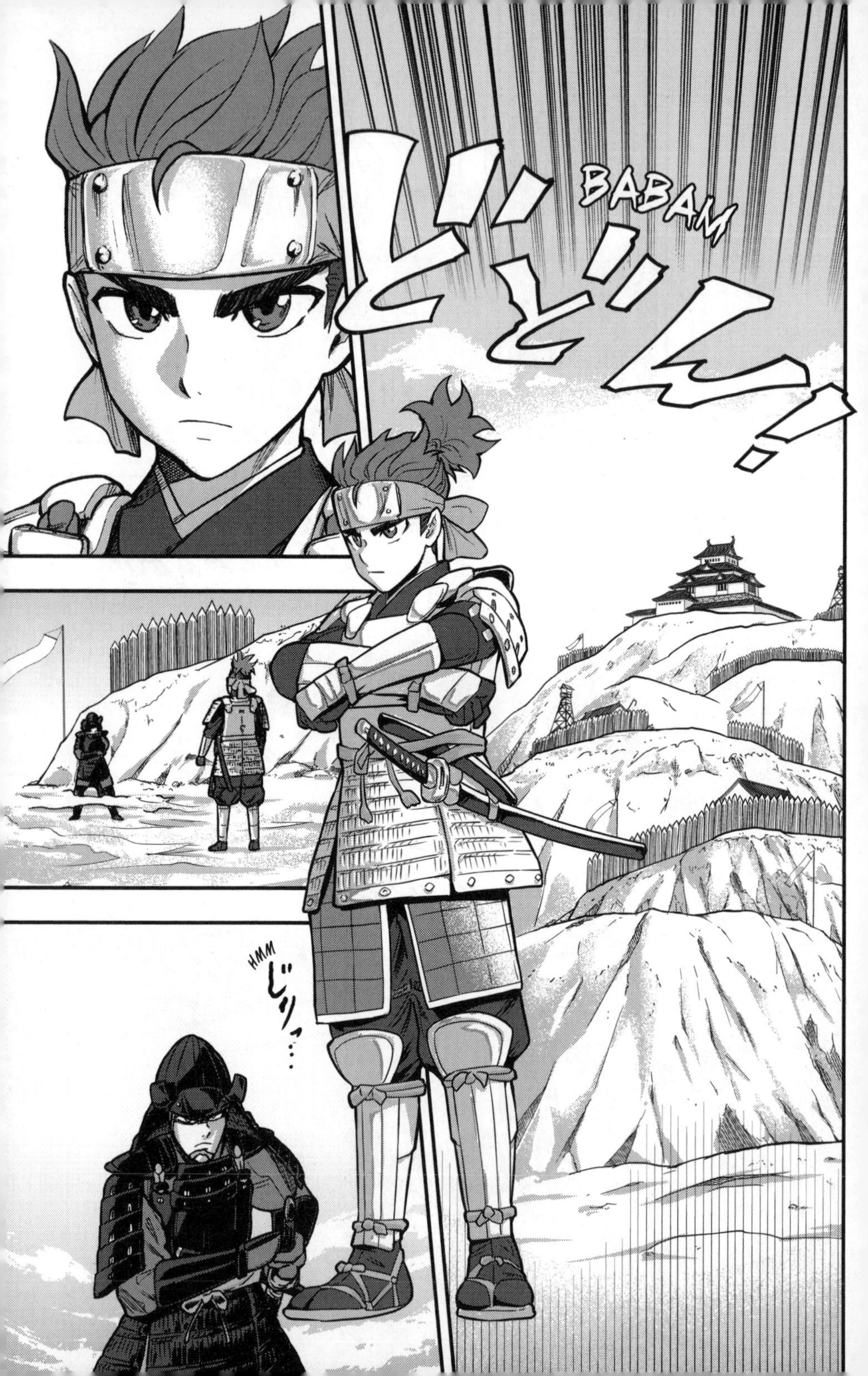
BABAM
HMM

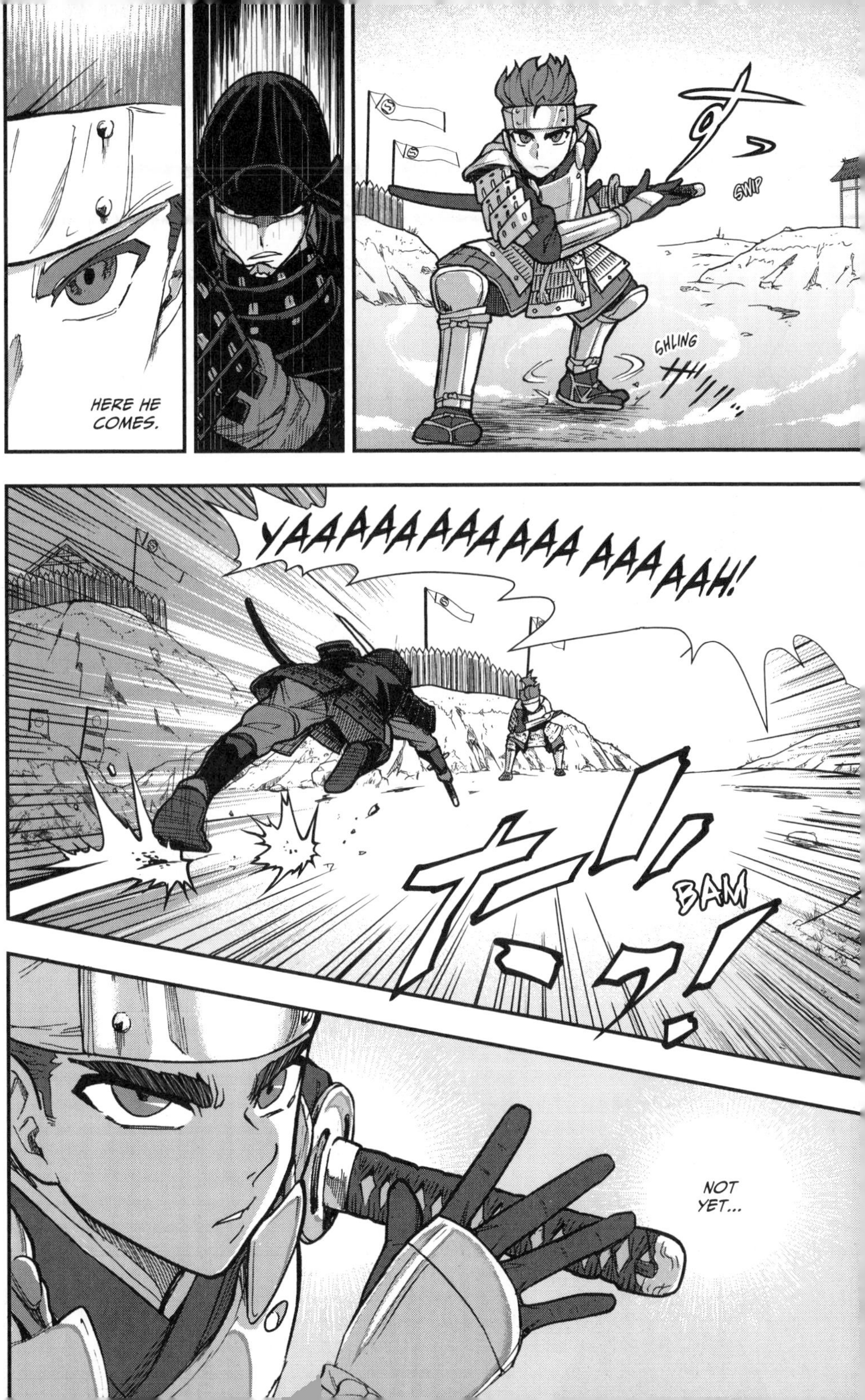
SWIP
SHLING
HERE HE COMES.
YAAAAAAAAAAAA AAAAAH!
BAM
NOT YET...

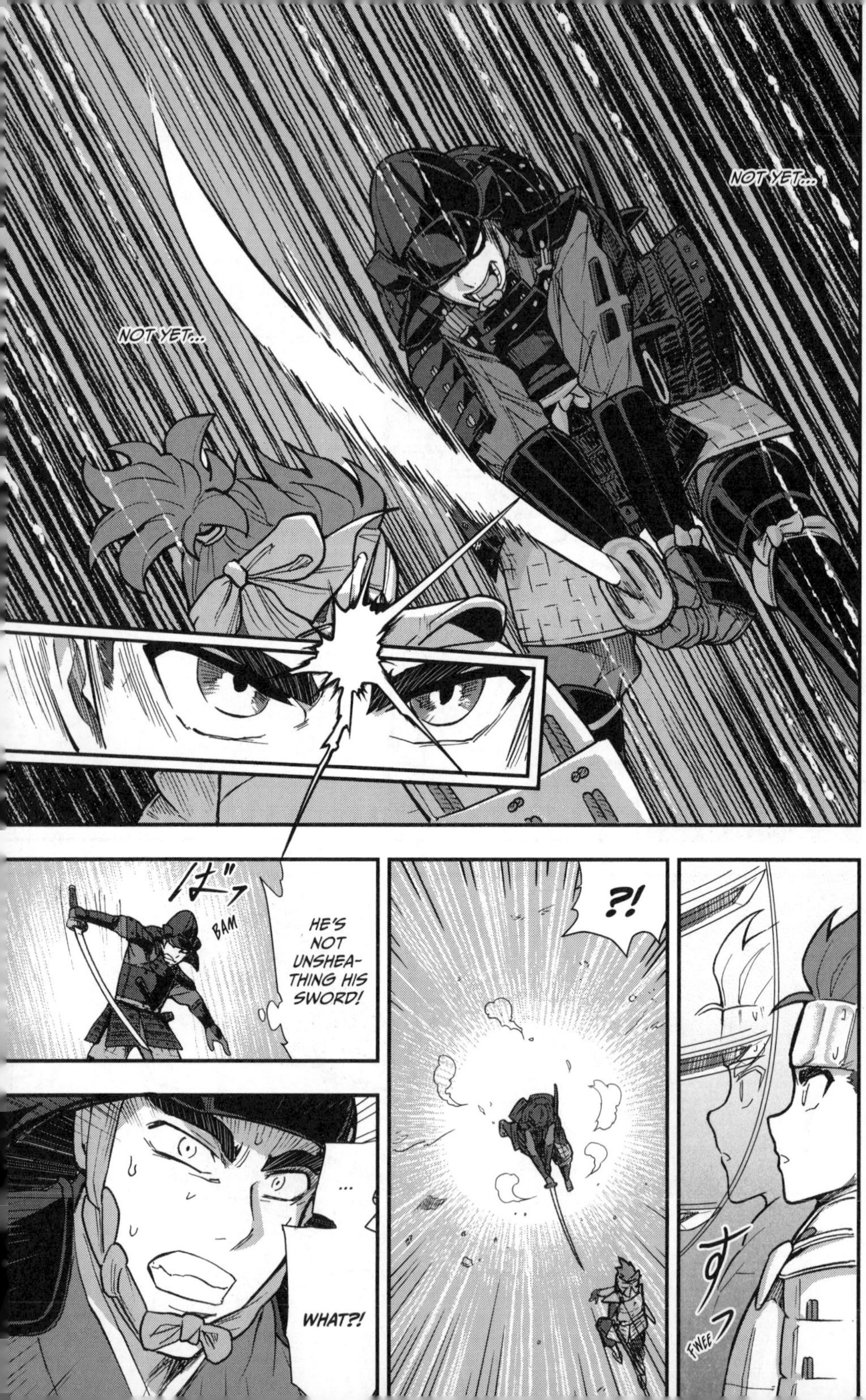
NOT YET...
NOT YET...
すっ
FWEE
?!
ばっ
BAM
HE'S NOT UNSHEATHING HIS SWORD!
...
WHAT?!

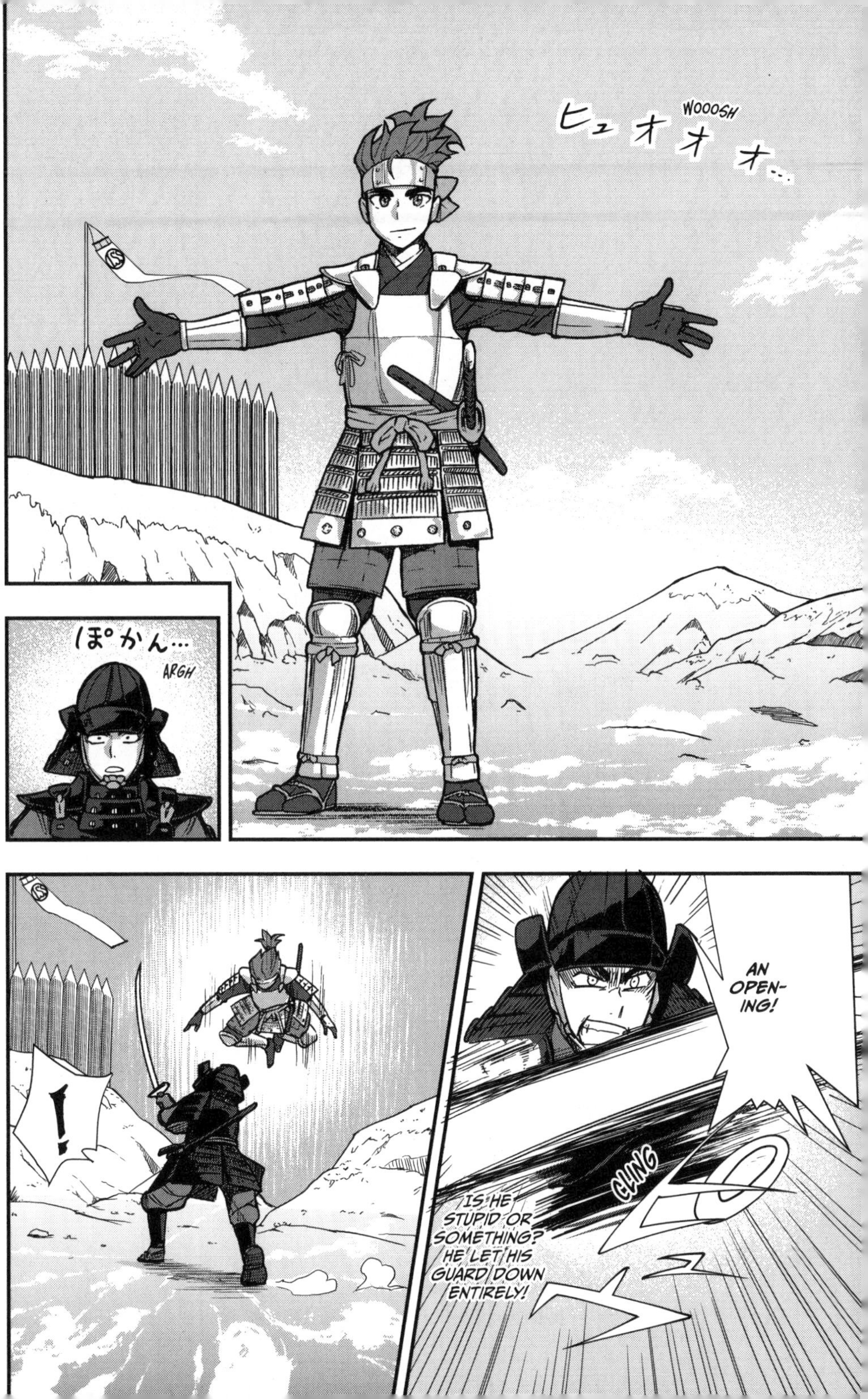
ヒュオオオ…
WOOOSH
ぽかん…
ARGH
AN OPEN-ING!
CLING
IS HE STUPID OR SOMETHING? HE LET HIS GUARD DOWN ENTIRELY!
!

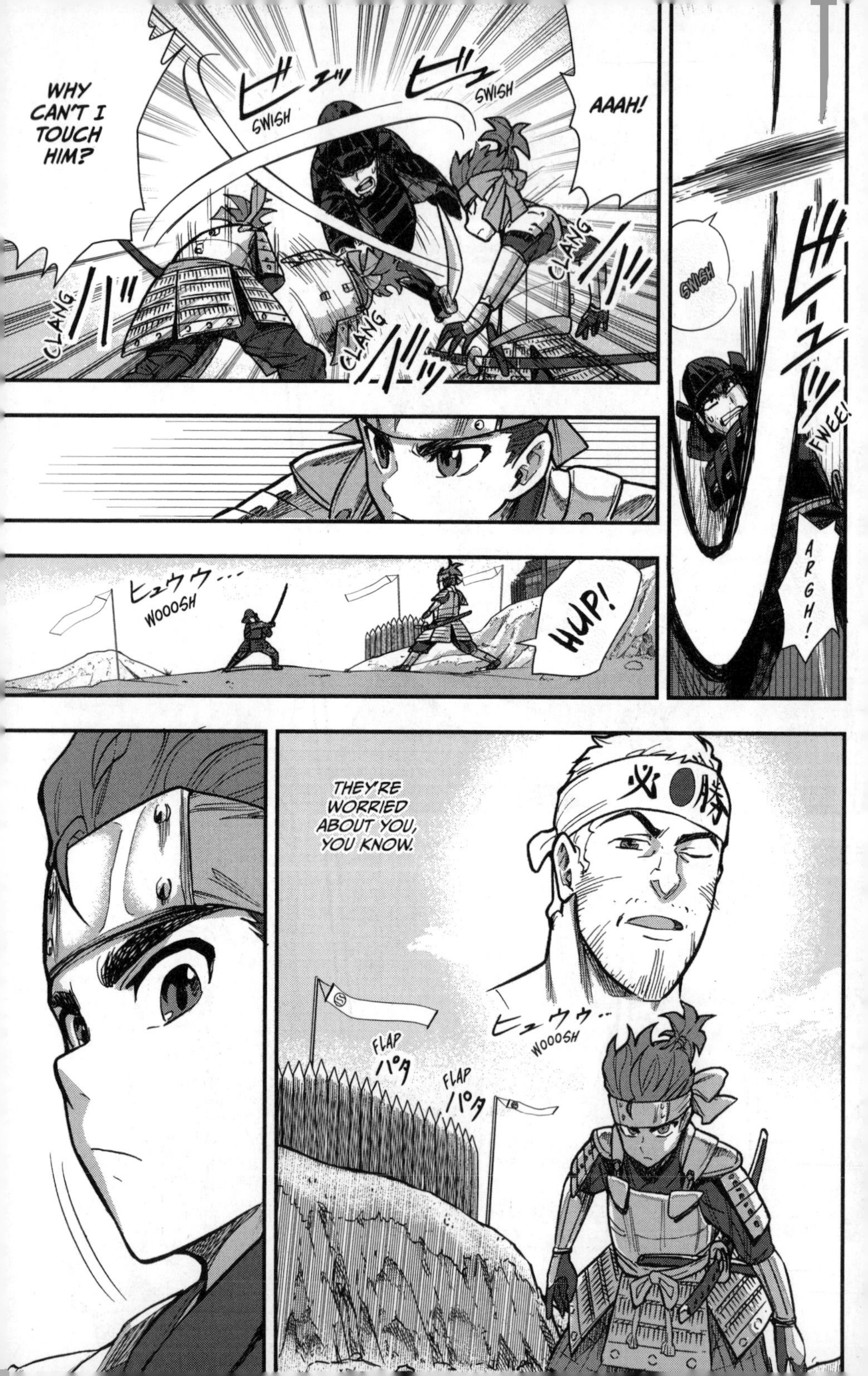

SWISH
FWEE!
ARGH!
AAAH!
SWISH
SWISH
WHY CAN'T I TOUCH HIM?
CLANG
CLANG
CLANG
ヒュウウ…
WOOOSH
HUP!
THEY'RE WORRIED ABOUT YOU, YOU KNOW.
必勝
ヒュウウ…
WOOOSH
FLAP
パタ
FLAP
パタ

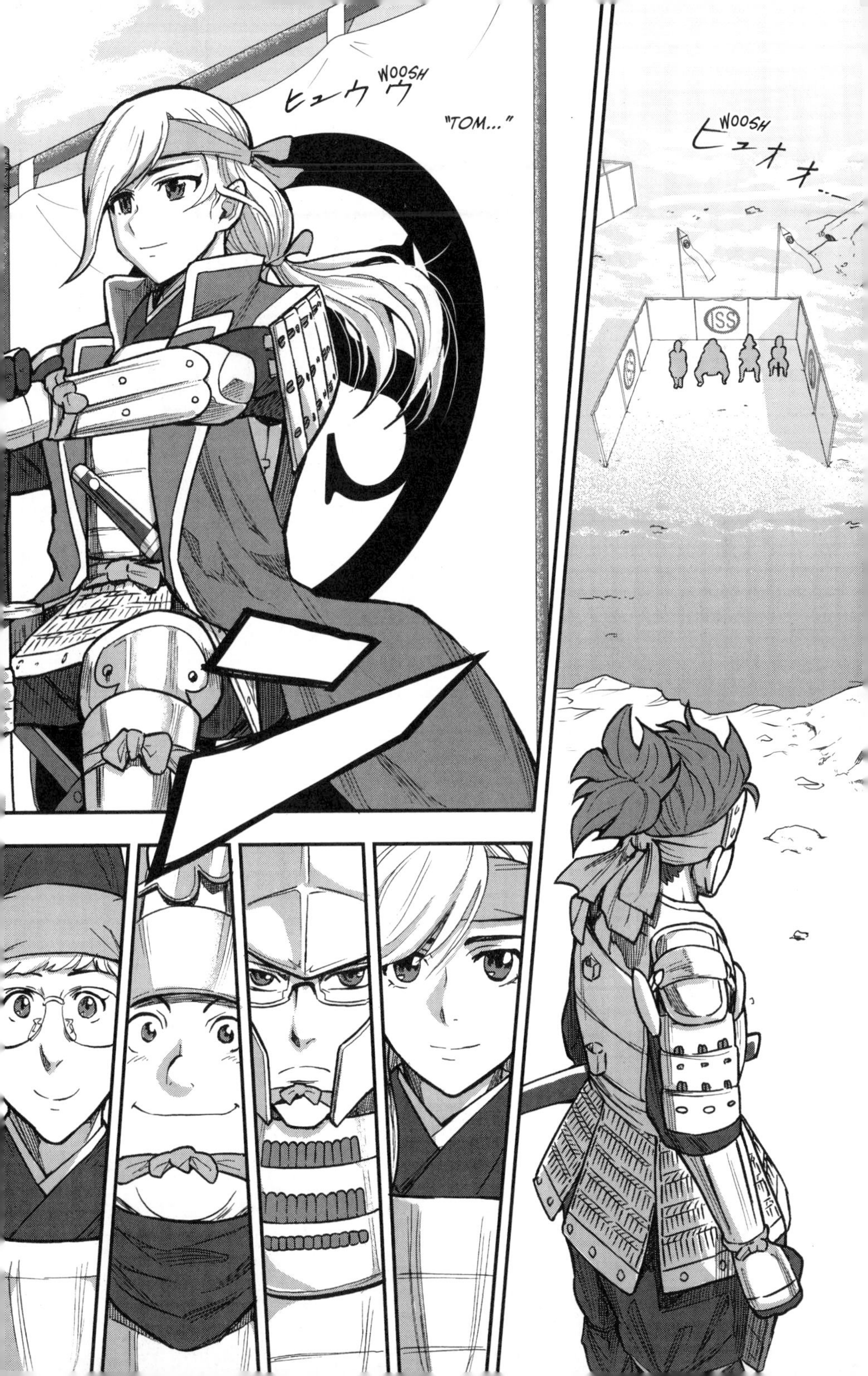
WOOSH
ヒュオオ…
WOOSH
ヒュウウ
"TOM..."

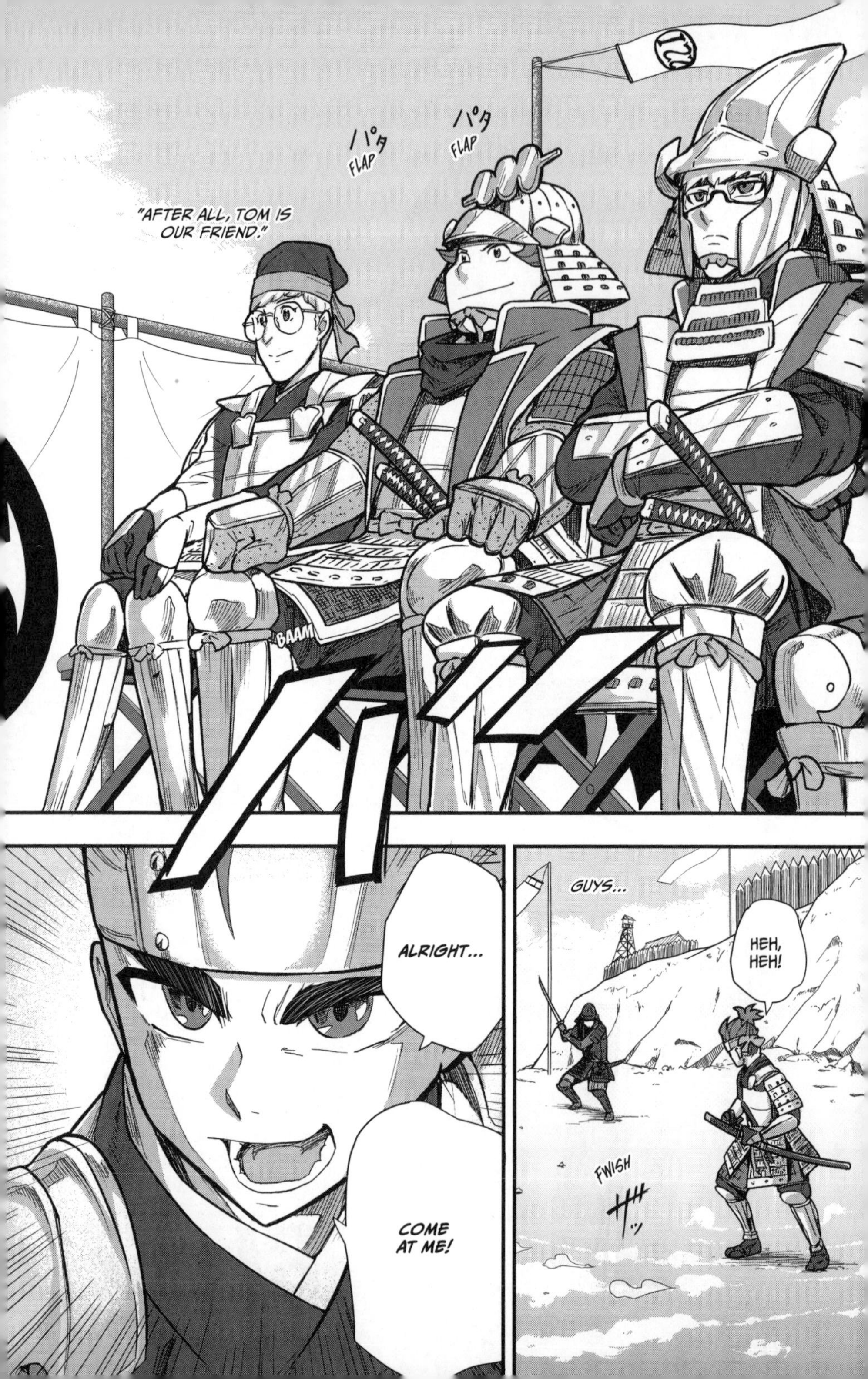

パタ
FLAP
パタ
FLAP
"AFTER ALL, TOM IS OUR FRIEND."
BAAM
GUYS...
HEH, HEH!
FWISH
ALRIGHT...
COME AT ME!

BLiTZ

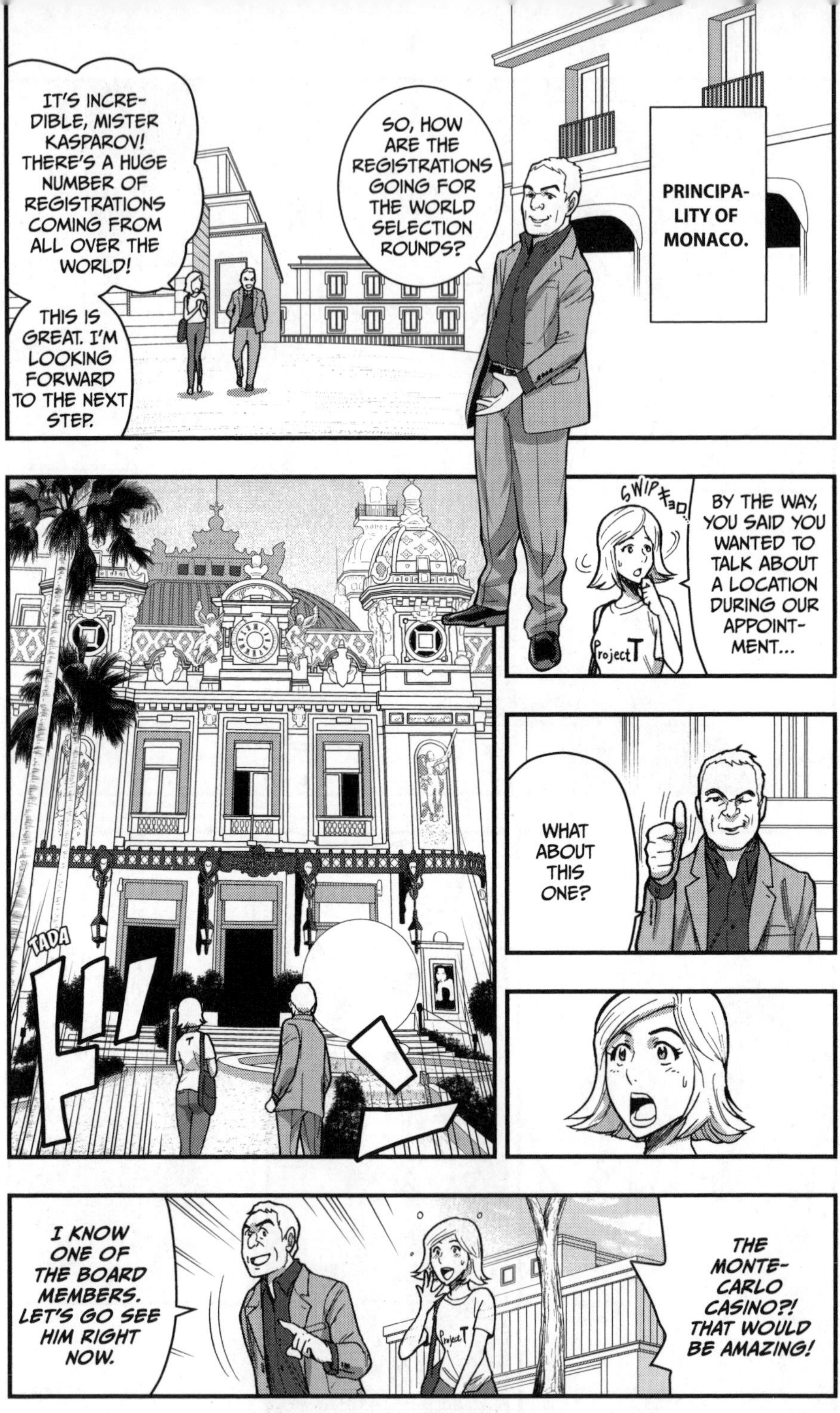
PRINCIPA-LITY OF MONACO.
SO, HOW ARE THE REGISTRATIONS GOING FOR THE WORLD SELECTION ROUNDS?
IT'S INCRE-DIBLE, MISTER KASPAROV! THERE'S A HUGE NUMBER OF REGISTRATIONS COMING FROM ALL OVER THE WORLD!
THIS IS GREAT. I'M LOOKING FORWARD TO THE NEXT STEP.
BY THE WAY, YOU SAID YOU WANTED TO TALK ABOUT A LOCATION DURING OUR APPOINT-MENT...
SWIP キョロ
Project T
WHAT ABOUT THIS ONE?
TADA
THE MONTE-CARLO CASINO?! THAT WOULD BE AMAZING!
I KNOW ONE OF THE BOARD MEMBERS. LET'S GO SEE HIM RIGHT NOW.

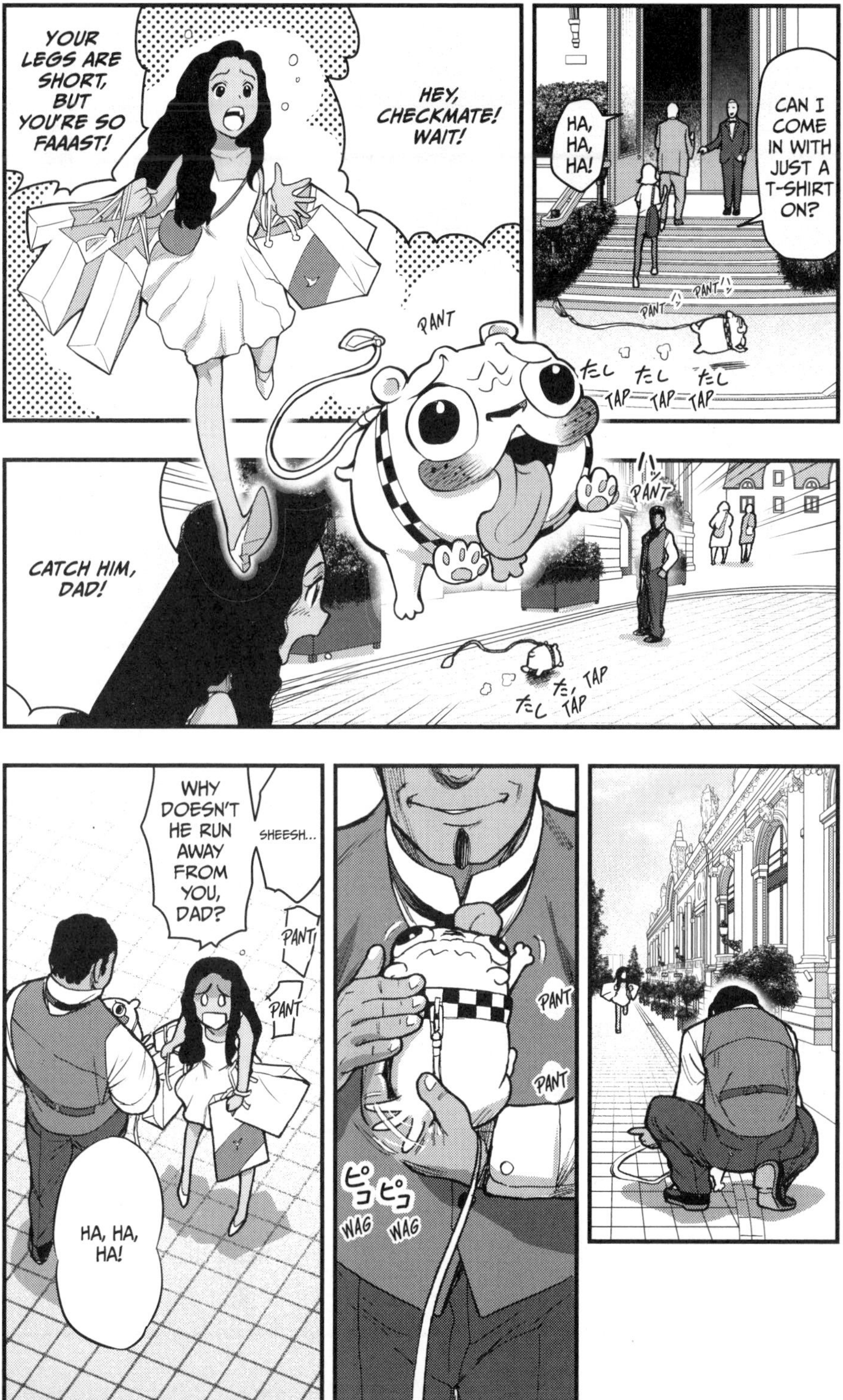
CAN I COME IN WITH JUST A T-SHIRT ON?
HA, HA, HA!
PANT ハッ
PANT ハッ
たし たし たし
TAP TAP TAP
HEY, CHECKMATE! WAIT!
YOUR LEGS ARE SHORT, BUT YOU'RE SO FAAAST!
PANT
ハッ PANT
CATCH HIM, DAD!
た, TAP
たし TAP
PANT
PANT
ピコピコ
WAG WAG
WHY DOESN'T HE RUN AWAY FROM YOU, DAD?
SHEESH...
PANT
PANT
HA, HA, HA!

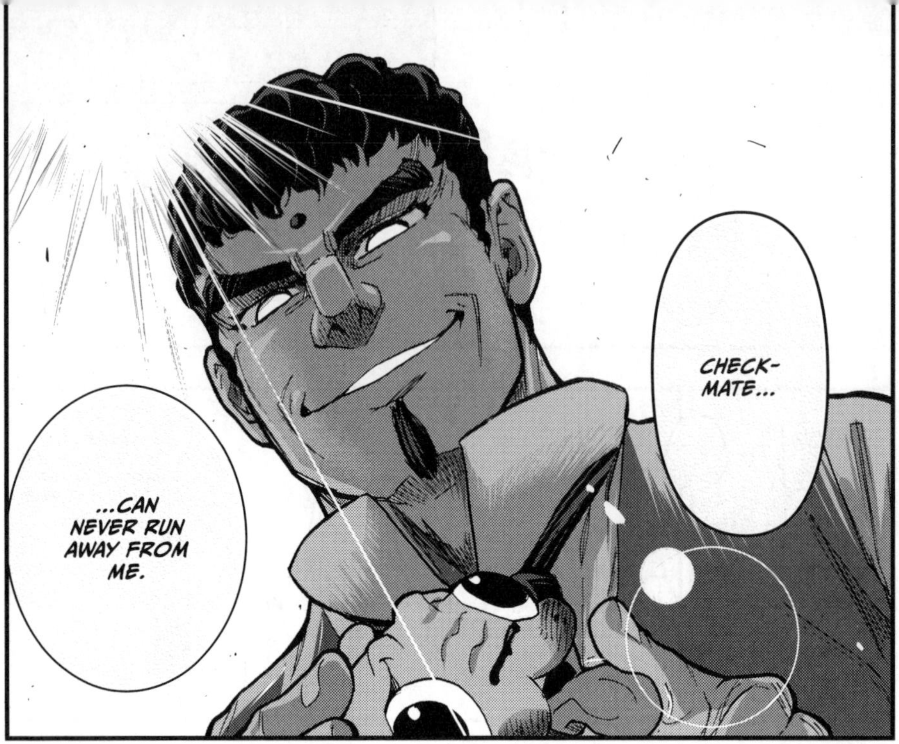
CHECK-MATE...
...CAN NEVER RUN AWAY FROM ME.

Chapter 17: Focus

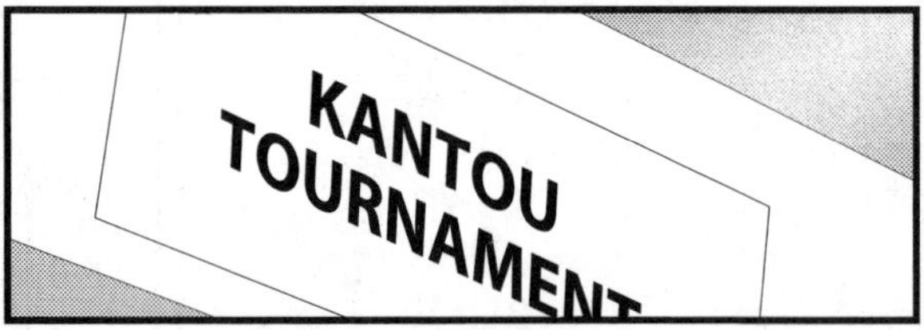
KANTOU TOURNAMENT

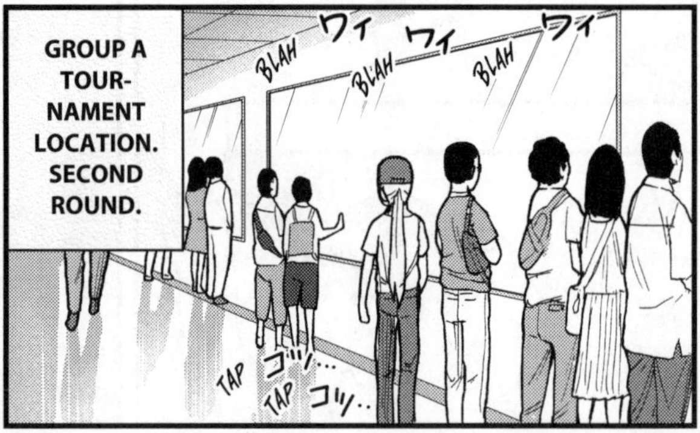
GROUP A TOUR-NAMENT LOCATION. SECOND ROUND.
ワィ BLAH
ワイ BLAH
ワィ BLAH
コツ... TAP
コツ... TAP

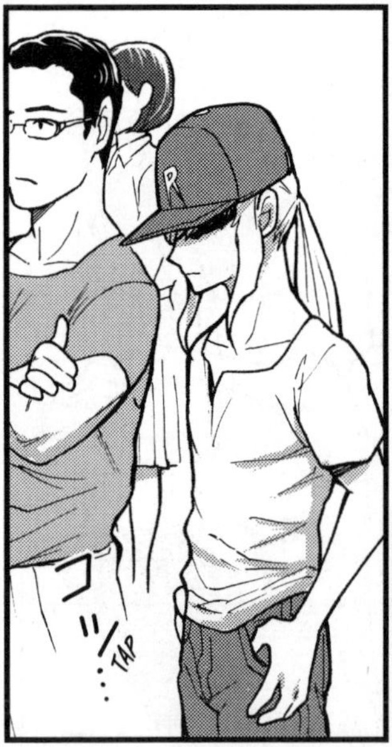
コツ... TAP

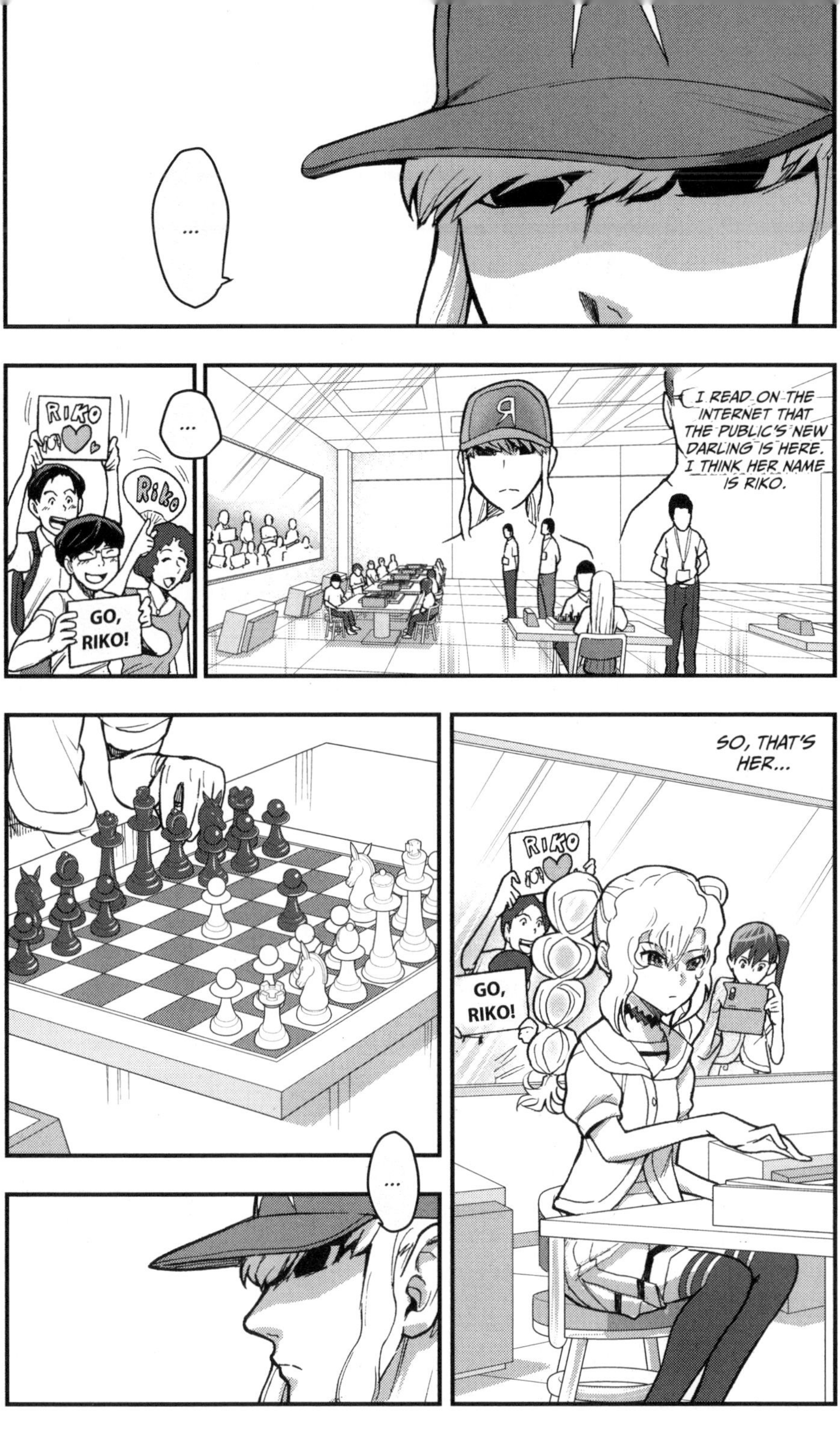
...
I READ ON THE INTERNET THAT THE PUBLIC'S NEW DARLING IS HERE. I THINK HER NAME IS RIKO.
RIKO
Riko
...
GO, RIKO!
SO, THAT'S HER...
RIKO
GO, RIKO!
...

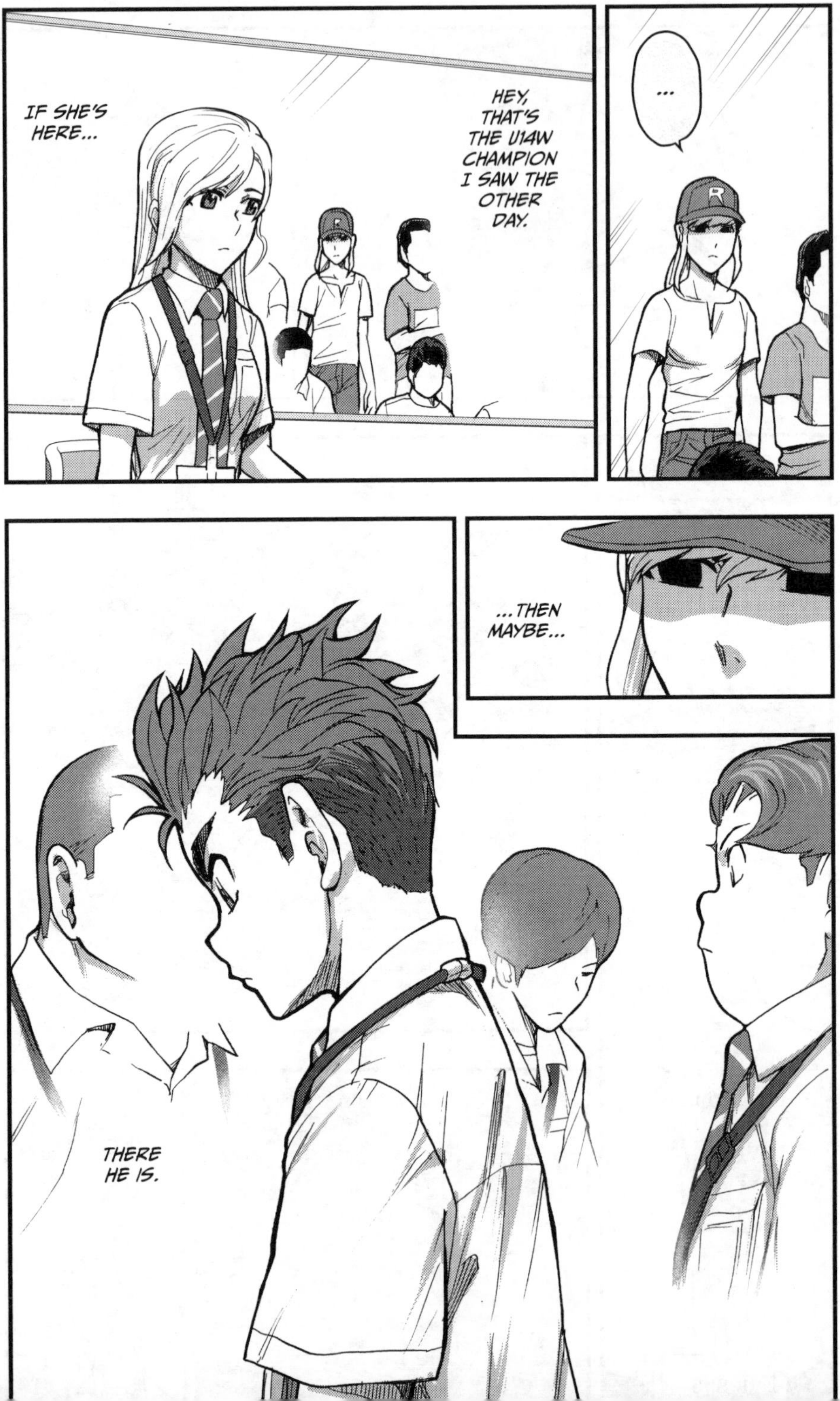
...
HEY, THAT'S THE U14W CHAMPION I SAW THE OTHER DAY.
IF SHE'S HERE...
...THEN MAYBE...
THERE HE IS.

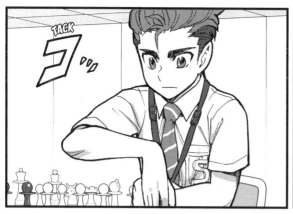

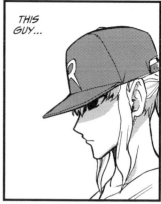

THIS GUY...

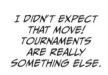

I DIDN'T EXPECT THAT MOVE! TOURNAMENTS ARE REALLY SOMETHING ELSE.

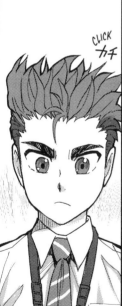

CLICK

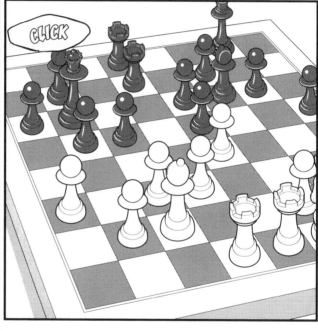

CLICK

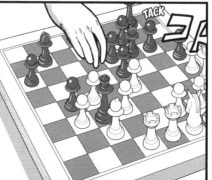

TACK

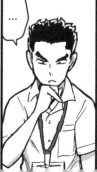

...

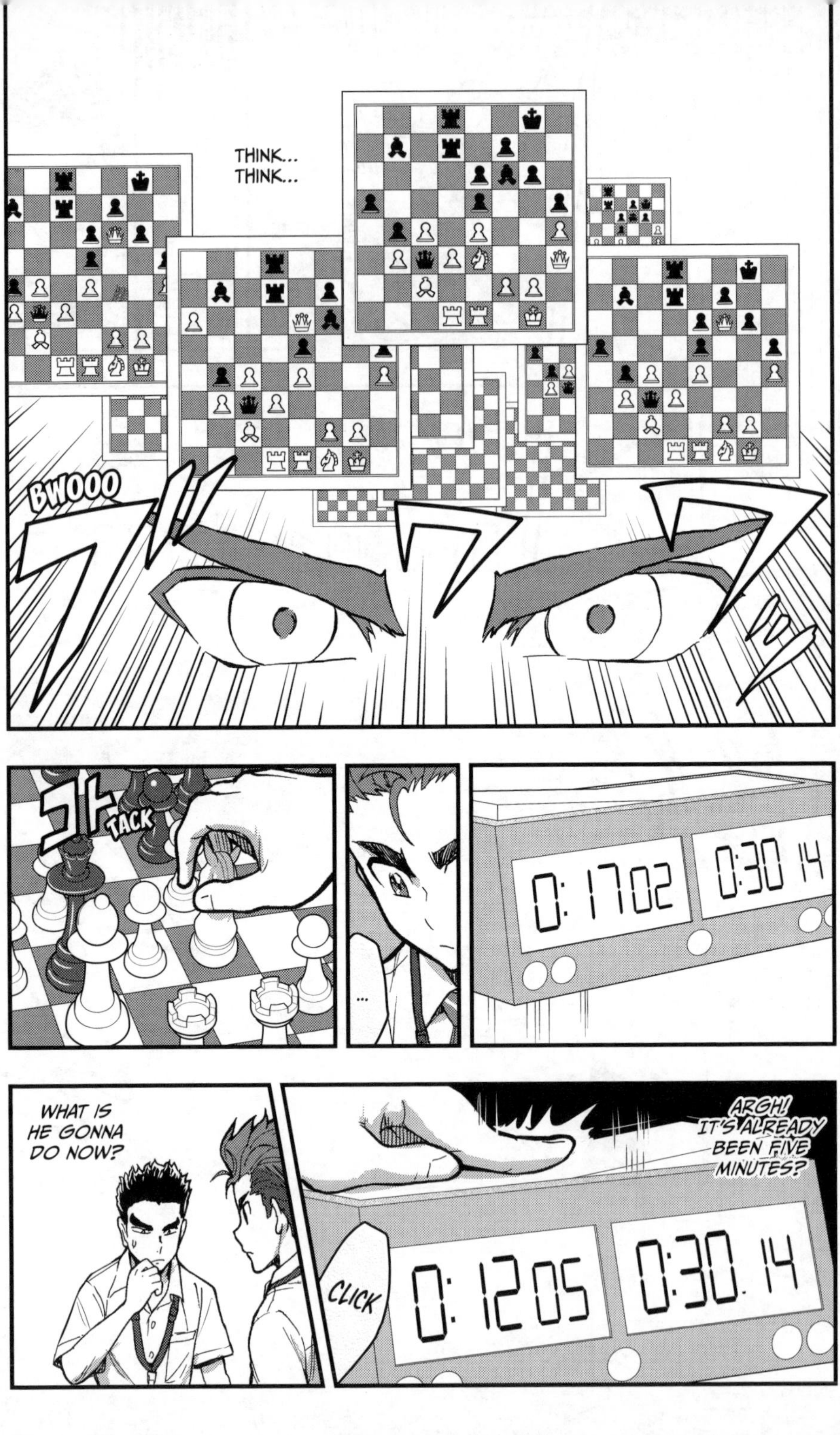
THINK... THINK...
BWOOO
0:17 02
0:30 14
...
コト
TACK
ARGH! IT'S ALREADY BEEN FIVE MINUTES?
CLICK
0:12 05
0:30 14
WHAT IS HE GONNA DO NOW?

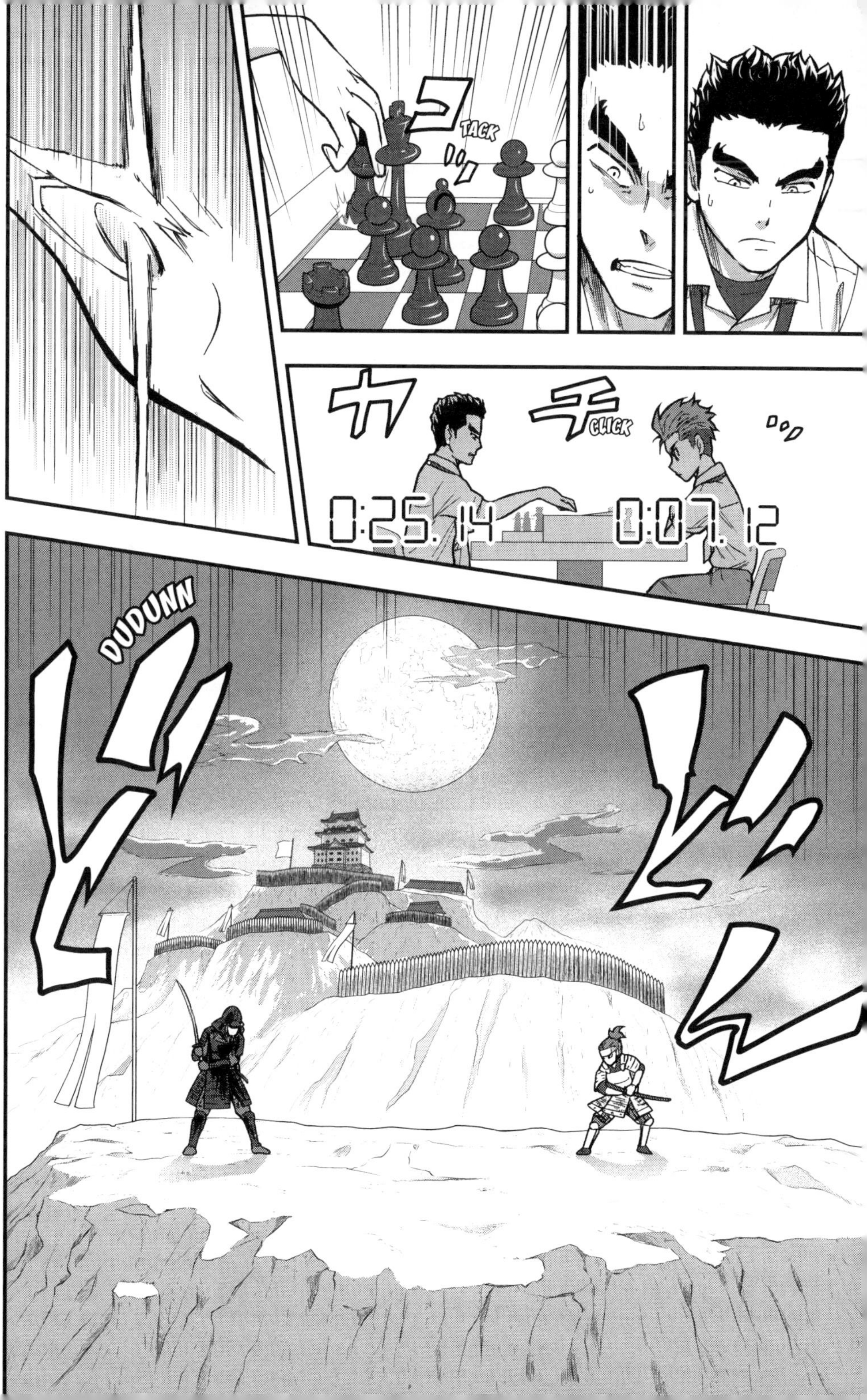
TACK
カチ
CLICK
0:25.14
0:07.12
DUDUNN

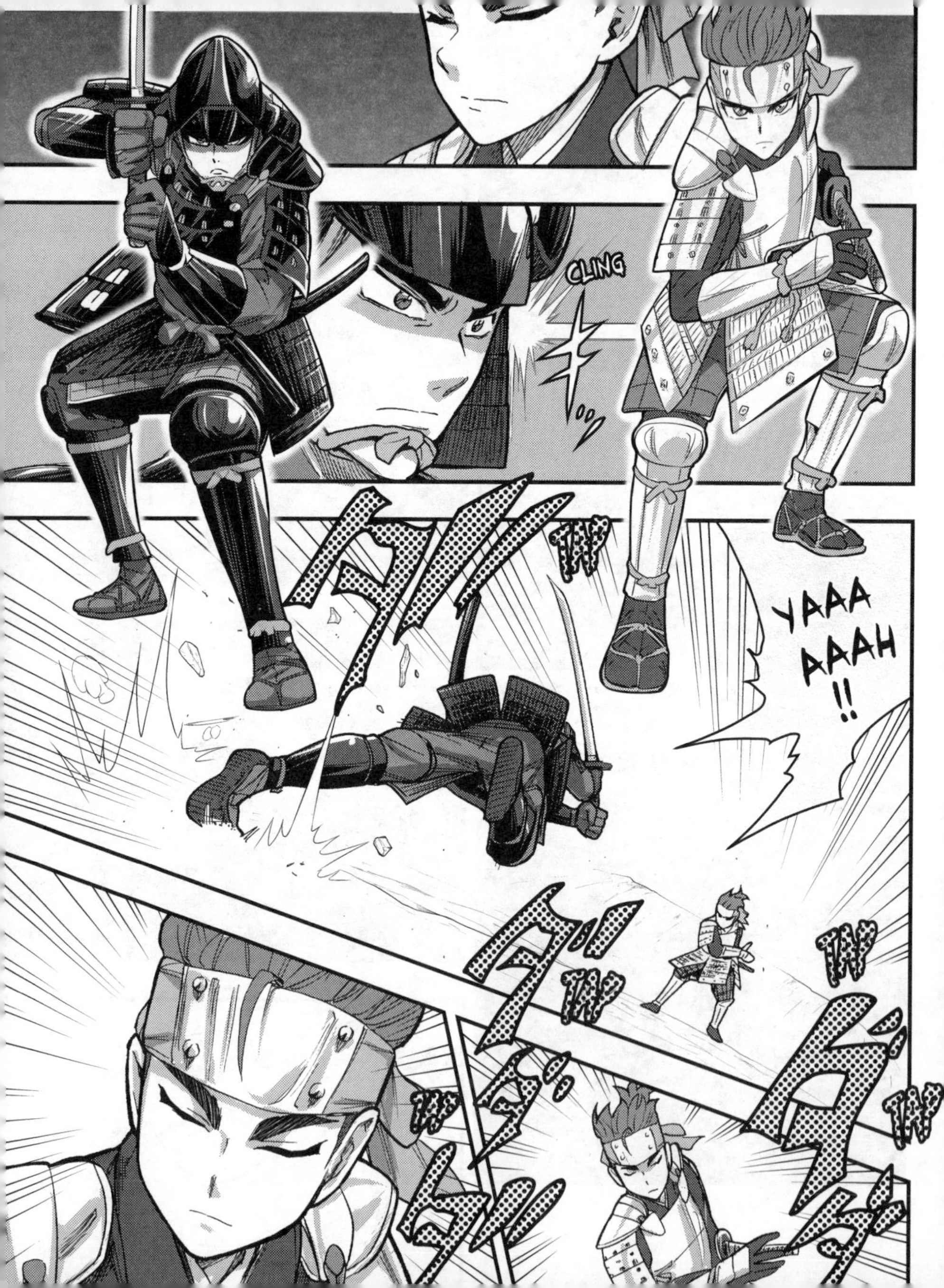
CLING
YAAA AAAH!!

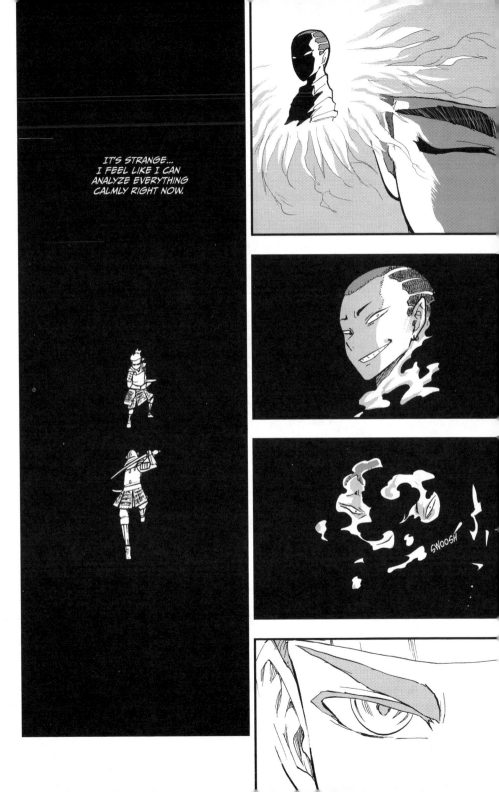

IT'S STRANGE...
I FEEL LIKE I CAN
ANALYZE EVERYTHING
CALMLY RIGHT NOW.

SWOOSH

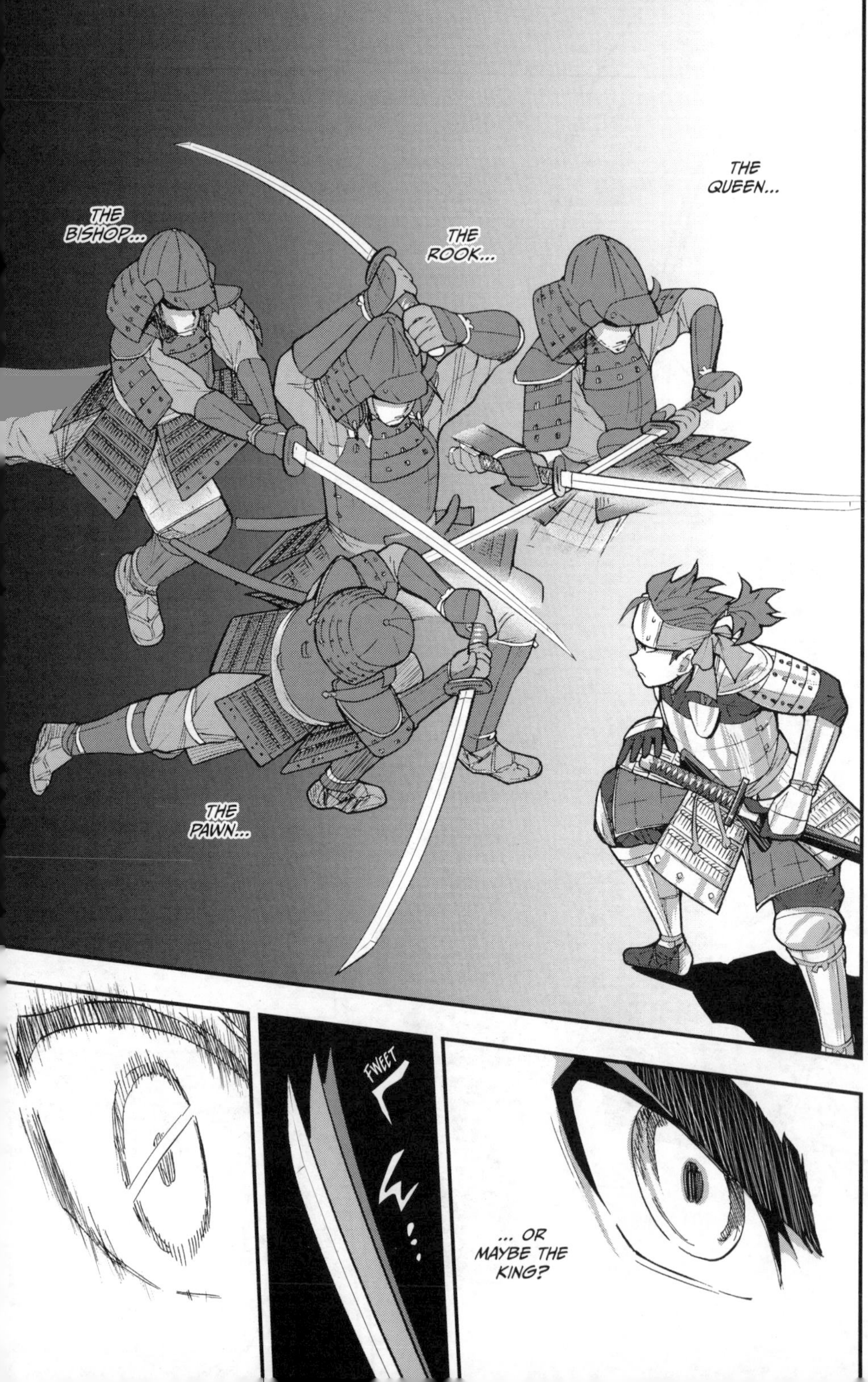
THE QUEEN...
THE ROOK...
THE BISHOP...
THE PAWN...
... OR MAYBE THE KING?
FWEET

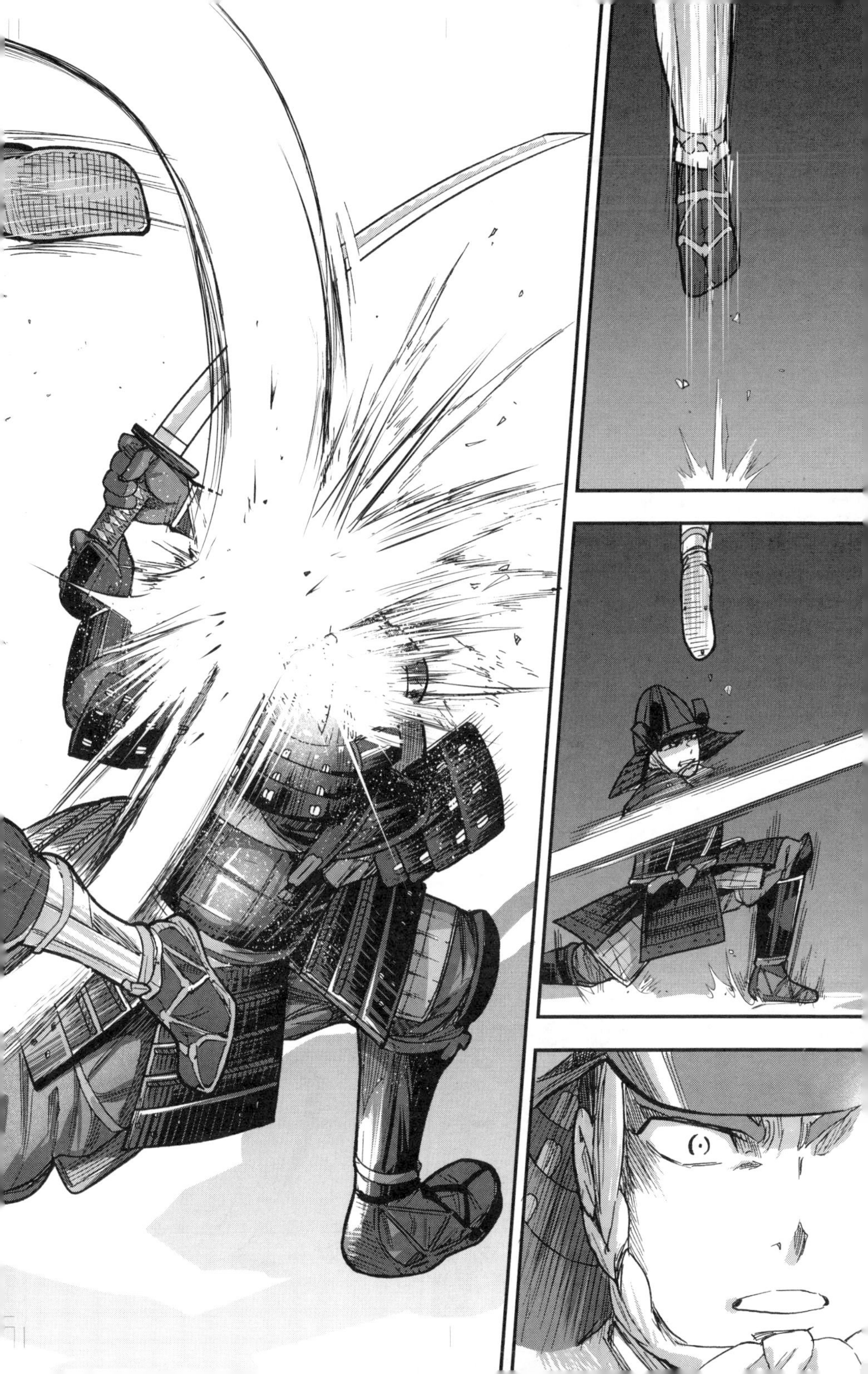

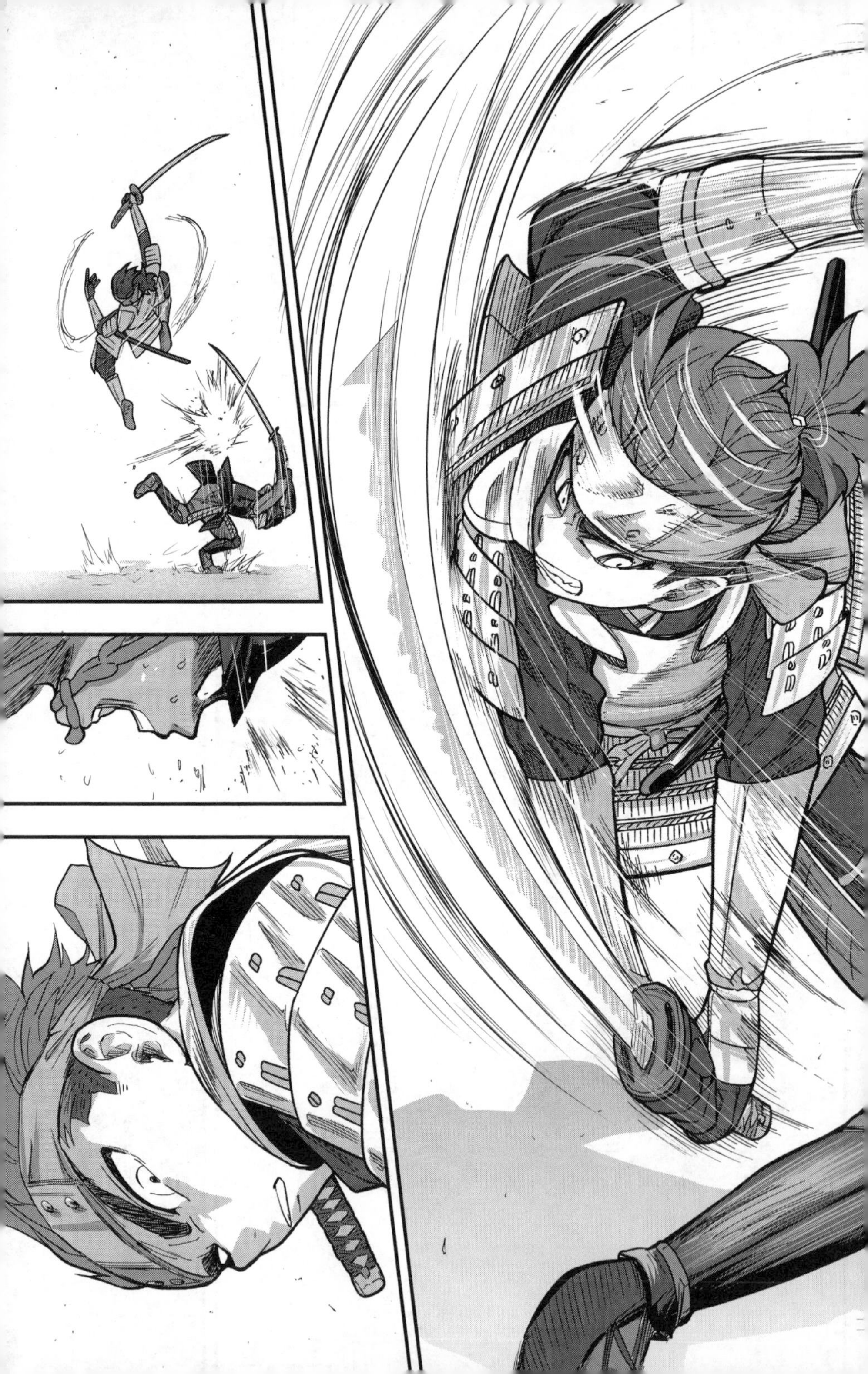

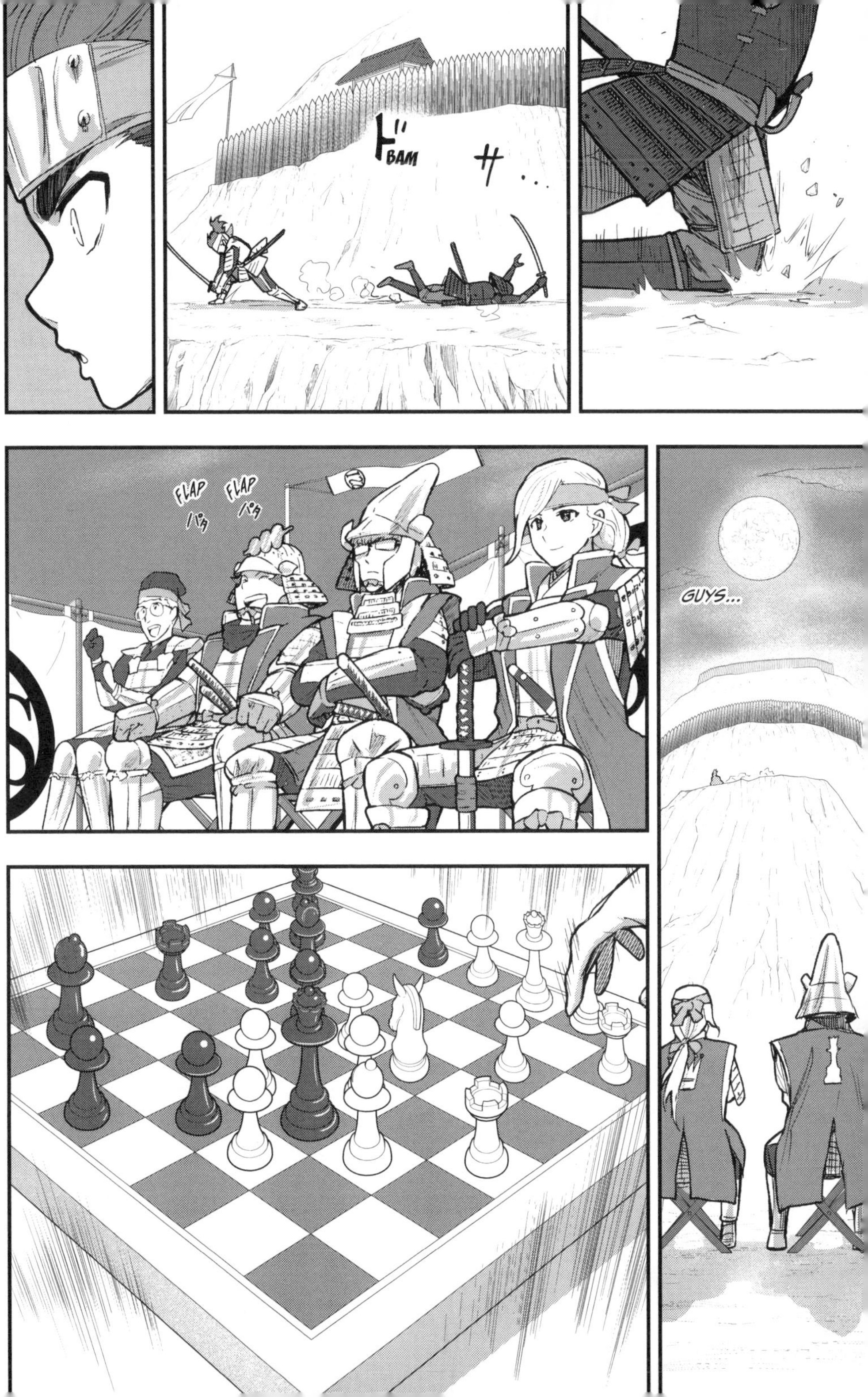
BAM
GUYS...
FLAP
FLAP

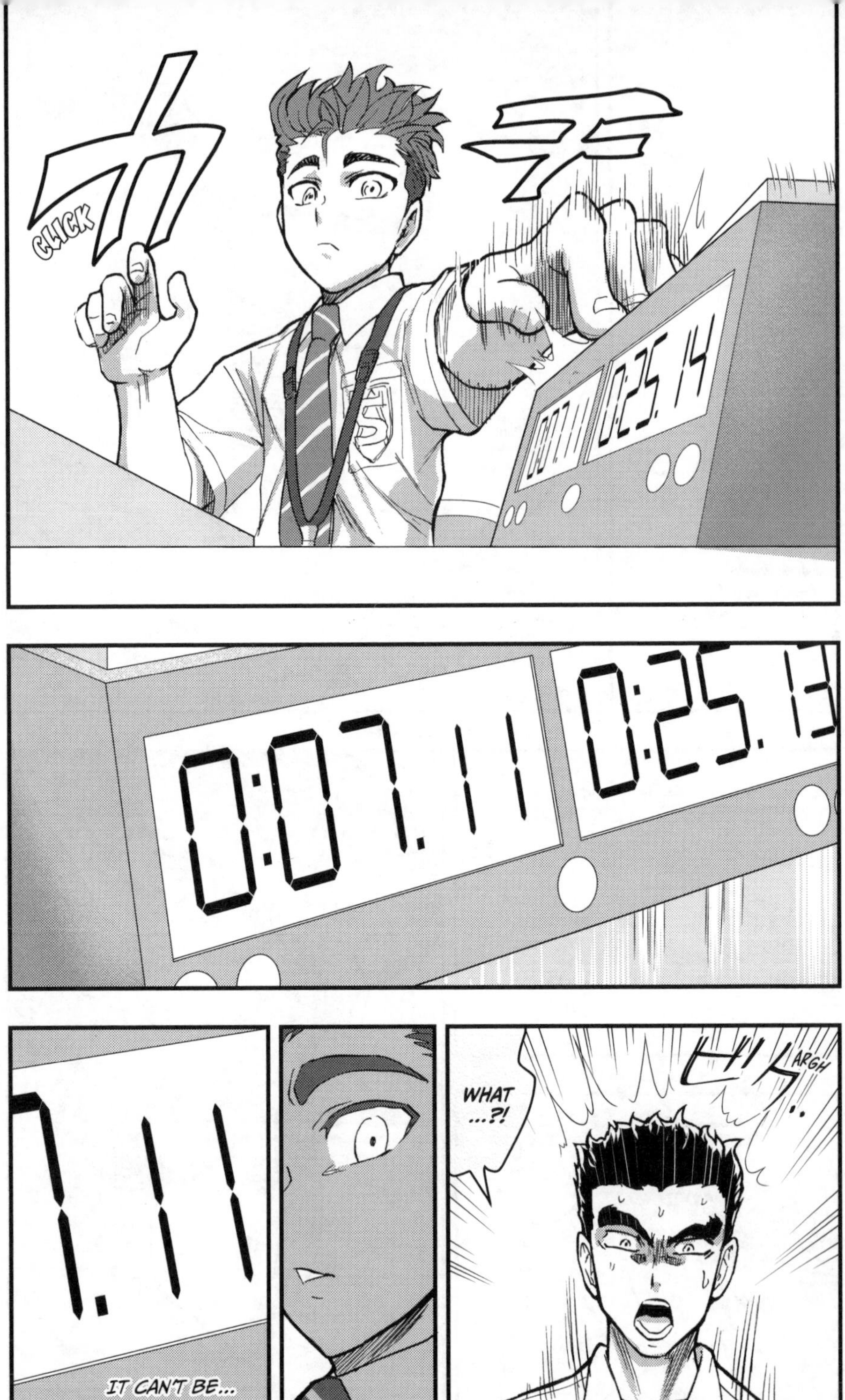
カチ
CLICK
WHAT ...?!
ARGH
IT CAN'T BE...

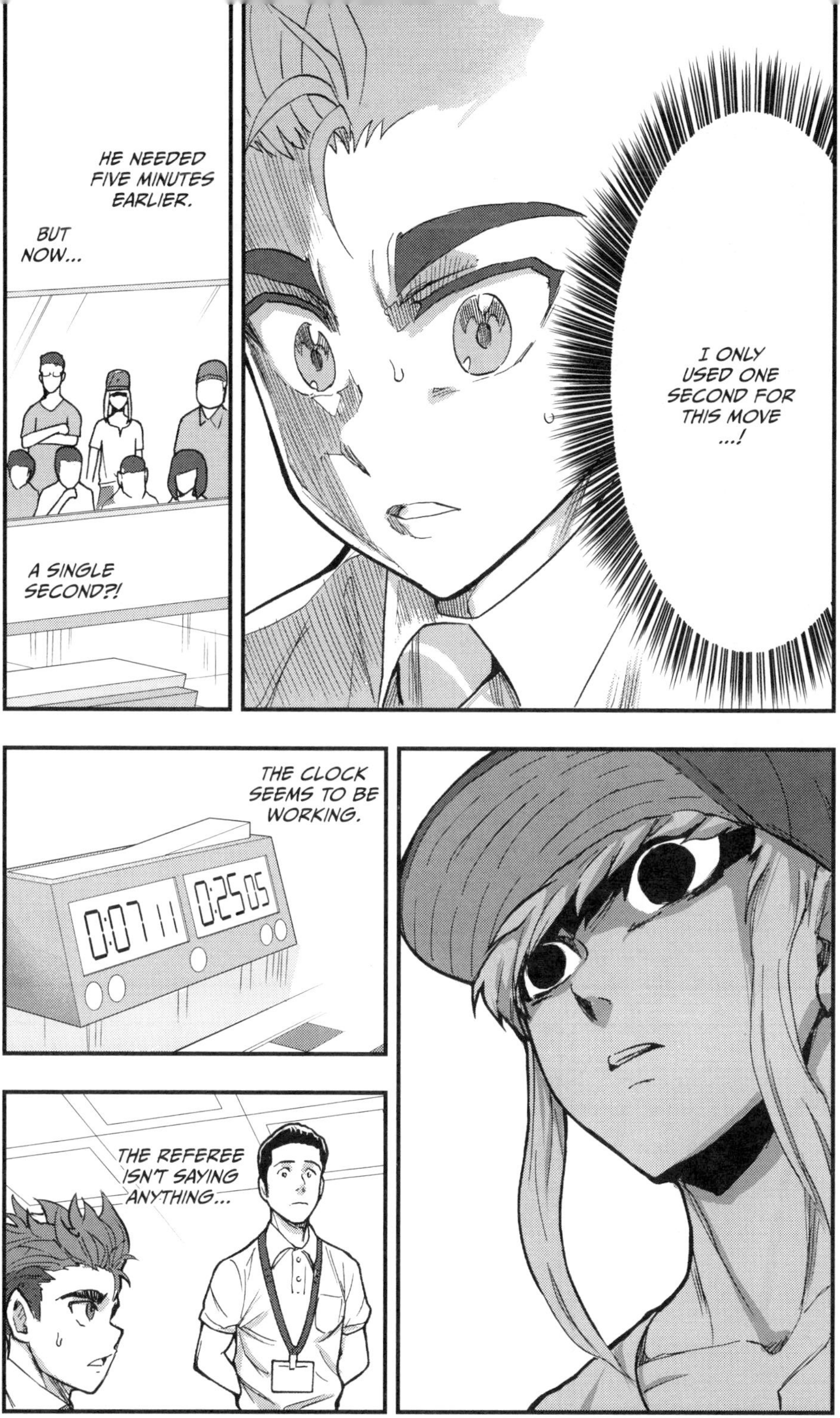
I ONLY USED ONE SECOND FOR THIS MOVE ...!
HE NEEDED FIVE MINUTES EARLIER.
BUT NOW...
A SINGLE SECOND?!
THE CLOCK SEEMS TO BE WORKING.
0:07 11
0:25 05
THE REFEREE ISN'T SAYING ANYTHING...

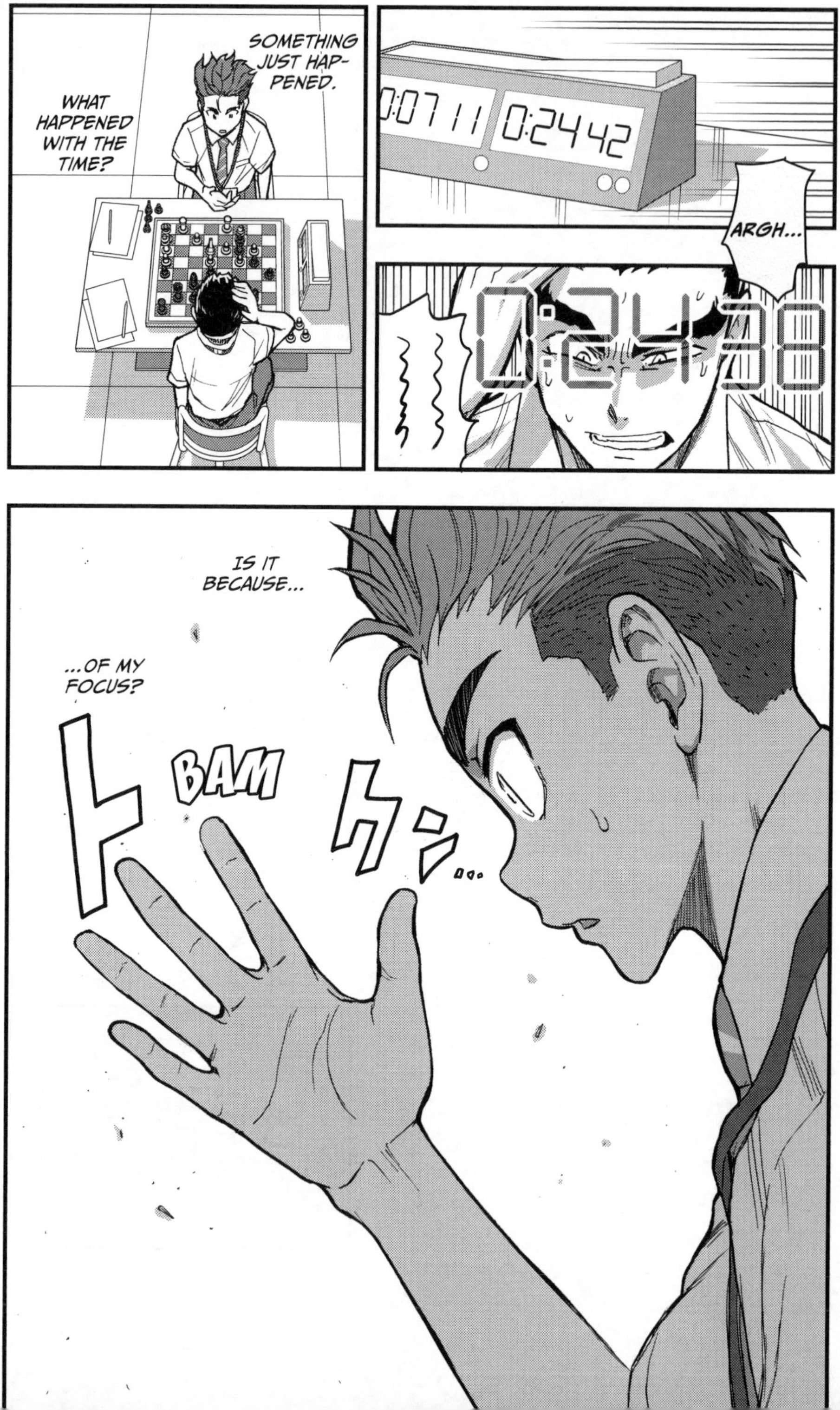
WHAT HAPPENED WITH THE TIME?
SOMETHING JUST HAP-PENED.
0:07 11
0:24 42
ARGH...
0:24 38
IS IT BECAUSE...
...OF MY FOCUS?
トクン...
BAM

THE GAME WILL CONTINUE...

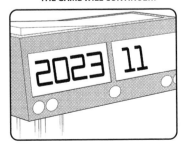

Written by Cédric Biscay and drawn by manga artist Daitaro Nishihara, Blitz is overseen and sponsored by none other than Garry Kasparov!

"I have always devoted myself to democratizing chess by any means possible. This is a unique opportunity to do so, especially in Japan, where the game is not as popular as Shogi. If you wish to communicate efficiently, you have to use the target audience's language. In a way, manga is the mother tongue of many young people. That is why Cédric's invitation seemed to be the perfect opportunity to promote chess towards a new public, by using a media that is both visual and dynamic."

Garry Kasparov

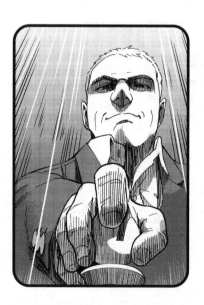

AFTERWORD
INTUITION

During this ongoing game, Tom experiences an astonishing event. He managed to make an incredible move almost unconsciously, in just one second!
What happened? Can Tom play the whole game while doing the same thing with each move?

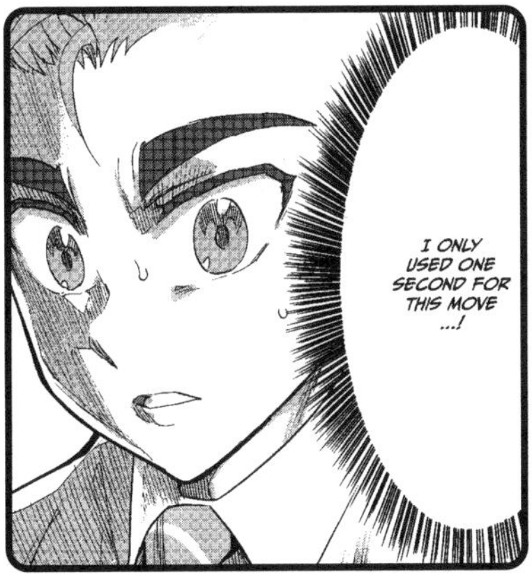
I ONLY USED ONE SECOND FOR THIS MOVE ...!

What about you? Would you be able to do the same? It seems almost impossible. However, what if it wasn't? How would you achieve that, if it was doable?

The things Tom are experiencing and discovering about his extraordinary abilities are actually strangely similar to what we all go through during our everyday lives.

There are moments when we are completely focused on what we are doing, like watching TV or an anime. Or when we remember a very major moment of our lives. Or when we picture an important event in our future. This has most certainly already happened to you. Maybe even today.

Try to remember.

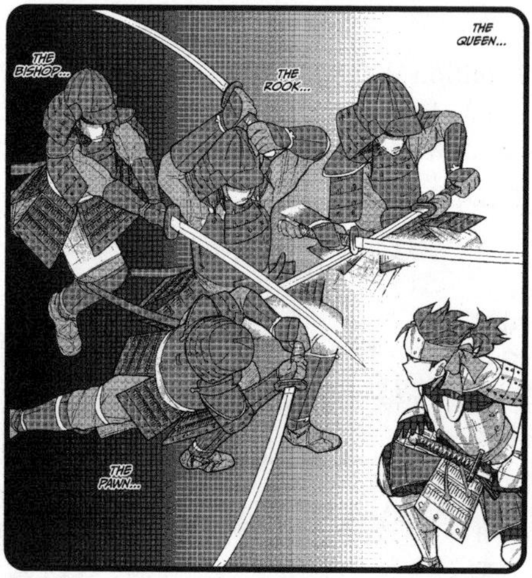
THE QUEEN...
THE ROOK...
THE BISHOP...
THE PAWN...

During and after these peculiar moments, you feel as if time is moving differently. The world also seems to reemerge after disappearing during this period where your focus and perception are greatly heightened.

These intense moments where we are so focused on ourselves are actually quite common. In fact, we experience such moments with varying degrees of intensity and consciousness. You could even try and single them out during your day, and then write them down in a notebook, if you want.

These kinds of experiences have been the topic of intensive scientific research. This was done by interviewing high-level athletes, creative types, successful business owners, and by studying very diverse situations in laboratories, like chess games. Many important discoveries were made this way. The results are astonishing. Anyone could access this state with the appropriate knowledge and training, and trigger a process that allows intuitive perception and extremely fast reactions.

Try to remember. Intuition is the ability to perceive a situation and to make the right decision immediately, without reasoning or analyzing the situation logically. This is what Tom is experiencing.

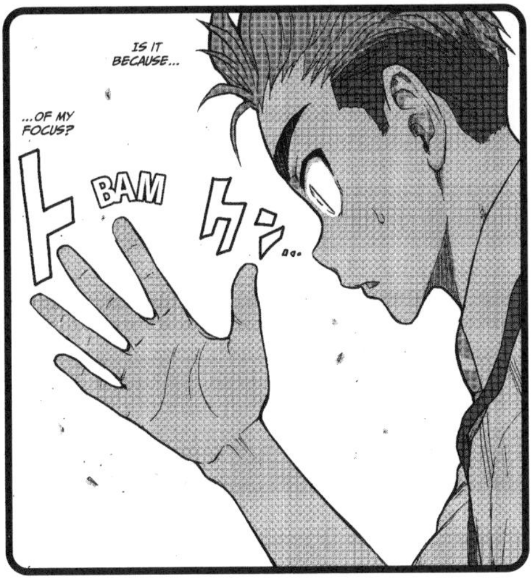
IS IT BECAUSE...
...OF MY FOCUS?
BAM

That being said, there is still some mystery to all of this. What is the process that allows people to become more intuitive? And how to make it happen? And how is Tom doing this without any real training?

We can already try and figure out some semblance of an answer to the first question. During his games, Tom unconsciously applies several key elements of the states he experiences so intensely and without controlling it quite yet.

First of all, we know what Tom wants. Tom has goals: winning the game and playing the best move. All in all, he has intentions. Having a precise and clear intention is the first key element.

We can clearly see that when Tom loses his attention, his objective slips away from him. This is what happens when his hunger gets the best of him during his game against Laurent. He loses focus.

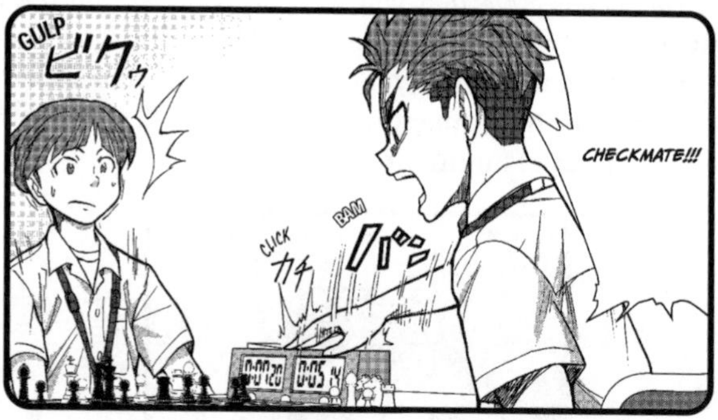
GULP
ビクゥ
CHECKMATE!!!
BAM
CLICK
カチ

Another key element is awareness and the ability to deal with whatever could hinder our concentration. In a perfect world, Tom should have taken the time to think about what could bother him during the game before starting it. He then would have realized that he was starting to feel hungry. The teachers also underline how worrying about a mistake made in the past could take someone's attention away from the moment and the objective. This is especially true when we let our emotions get the best of us. Managing our emotions is essential. Tom certainty still has a lot to learn on that end.

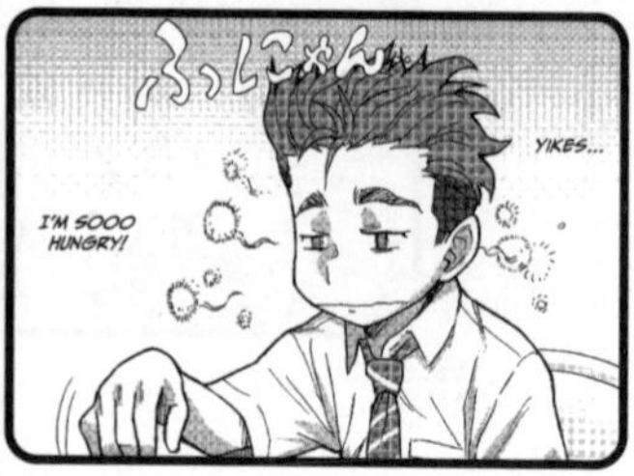
YIKES...
I'M SOOO HUNGRY!
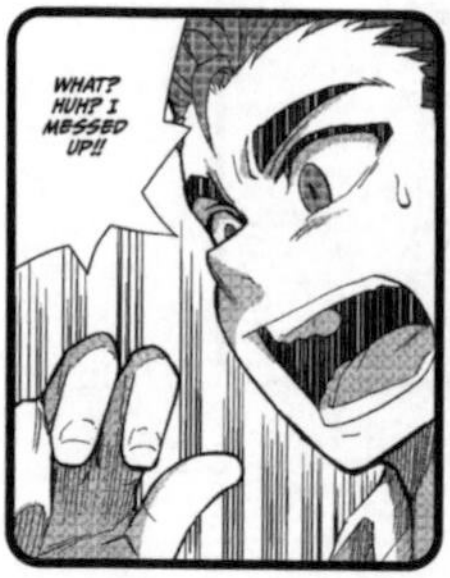
WHAT? HUH? I MESSED UP!!

However, Tom is already capable of something extremely powerful. He can picture the scenario! He is fully immersed in whatever he is doing or will be doing. He is one with the game, with the opponent and himself, as well as with the moves played. And if he sees himself as a knight or a samurai, that is no big deal. Imagination also plays a role.

You can also follow the same path as Tom did while discovering chess and himself. Choose an objective that you want to complete no matter what. It can be a self-imposed challenge or a dream that you want to fulfill. Realize your intention. Be attentive. Take your time. Manage your expectations and emotions. Live fully in the moment. What do you notice? What do you gain from training in the way of intuition?

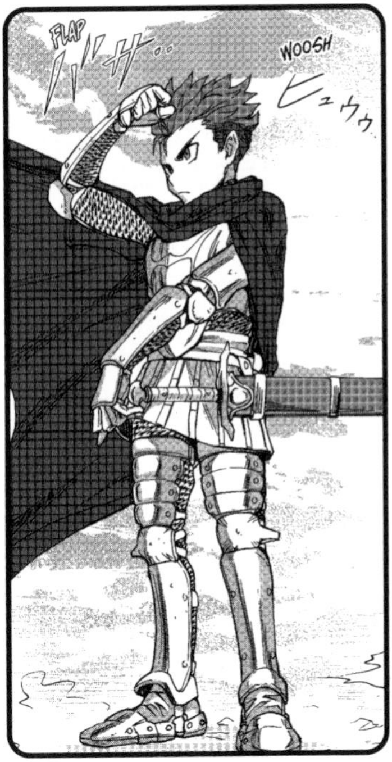
WOOSH
ヒュウゥ
FLAP
バサ

When it comes to Tom, we do not have the answer yet. How did he succeed without learning virtually anything, and how far will his intuition take him?

Alexis Champion

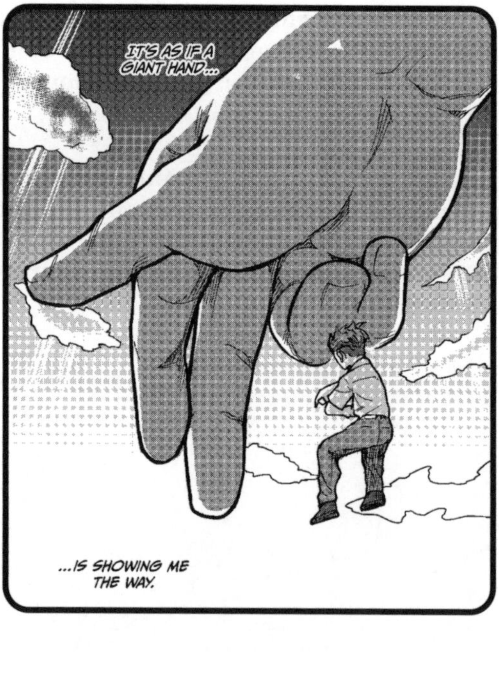
IT'S AS IF A GIANT HAND...
...IS SHOWING ME THE WAY.

Alexis Champion

Alexis Champion has a doctorate in computer science, with a specialization in artificial intelligence. Over a dozen years, he has been a researcher, then a computer projects director in public and private laboratories, as well as in service companies.

Alexis is also the founder and director or iRiS Intuition. It is a company dedicated to the use, the development and the scientific research of intuition. Since 2008, iRiS has been active in various fields, like manufacturing, banking and finance, archaeology and history, energy, law, management and even the arts. The purpose of iRiS is to study decision-making in uncertain or urgent situations, creativity and innovation.

The areas that Alex focuses on are mainly the cooperative use of reasoning and intuition, research on perception and consciousness, the differences between humans and machines and their collaboration, as well as the perfection of physiological and cognitive abilities of human beings.

Garry Kasparov

Born in 1963 in Baku, in Azerbaijan, Garry Kasparov first became champion of the U18 chess tournament of the USSR at the age of twelve.

At 17, he won the title of the U20 world championship. In 1985, at 22, he became known worldwide as the youngest chess champion in history.

He defended his title five times, in a legendary game series against his greatest rival, Anatoly Karpov.

Kasparov broke Bobby Fischer's record in 1990, and his record was unbeaten until 2013.

His famous games against IBM's Deep Blue supercomputer in 1996-97 have played a major role in the introduction of artificial intelligence in the world of chess.

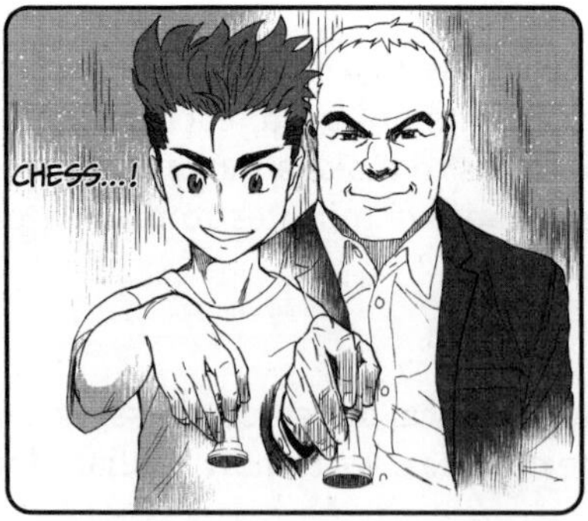
CHESS...!

CHESS GLOSSARY

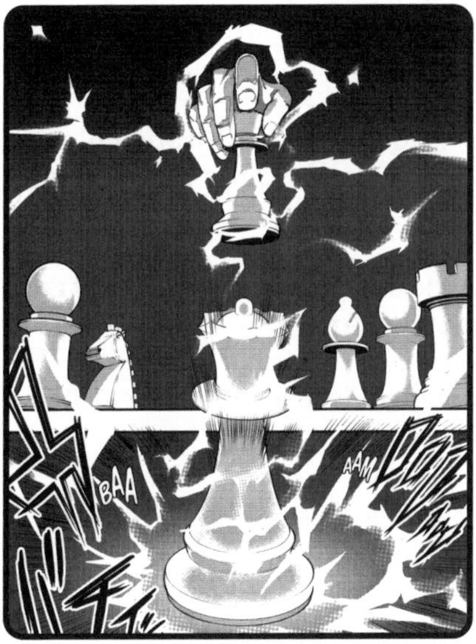
BAA
AAM

Blitz
A fast-paced game played with a clock, where each player has less than ten minutes. If increments are used, each player has less than three minutes and two seconds to make a move. If increments are not used, each player has less than five minutes to make a move. "Blitz" means "lightning" in German.

Caïssa
The goddess or mythological muse of chess, according to the poem Caïssa: or The Game of Chess, written by William Jones in 1763.

Deep Blue
A supercomputer created by IBM and specialized in chess. It managed to beat Garry Kasparov in 1997, after losing to him in 1996.

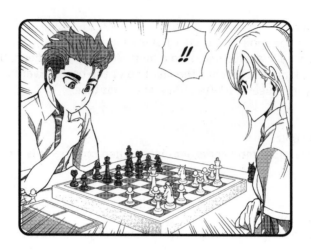

Chessboard
A square board consisting of 64 squares and used to play chess. "On the board" indicates games played in classic tournament conditions, as opposed to correspondence chess, online chess and analysis.

Piece
Every battle unit is a piece: the pawns and the bigger pieces (the King, the Queen, the Rook, the Bishop and the Knight).

Minor piece
The Knight or the Bishop. Also called "light piece".

Major piece
The Rook or the Queen. Also called "heavy piece".

Touch-move rule
A rule which states that a player has to move a piece if they touch it (if possible). The move is considered complete if the player puts a piece on a square and releases it. If the player touches their opponent's piece, they have to take it (if possible).

Pawn

The most common and least valuable piece. However, the pawn can be promoted (transformed) into a figure (usually the queen, but never a second king) if it reaches the last line of the board. Every player can have several queens. It often is a great advantage.

 Knight

This piece can jump over other pieces when moving. It is worth about three pawns.

 Bishop

Long-distance piece that can move diagonally. It is worth about three pawns.

 Rook

Long-distance piece that can move vertically or horizontally. Its strength is fully revealed when combined with its twin. It is worth about five pawns.

 Queen

The long-distance piece with the best mobility. It is worth about nine pawns.

 King

The most important piece in the game. The goal is to checkmate the opposing king to attain victory. It is weak at the beginning of the game, but it gets stronger and more active near the end, since there are fewer pieces on the board.

Resigning

A player can resign. The game is over and it will of course count as a loss for the resigning player. Games often end with a player resigning because it is impossible to continue playing in a hopeless situation.

Adjusting

This rule allows a player to adjust a piece on the board without playing it. By saying "J'adoube", the player avoids any misunderstanding with the touch-move rule.

Defense

An opening selected by Black at the start of the game. It also describes a move used to parry an attack.

Deflection

A tactic that forces an opposing piece out of its defensive position.

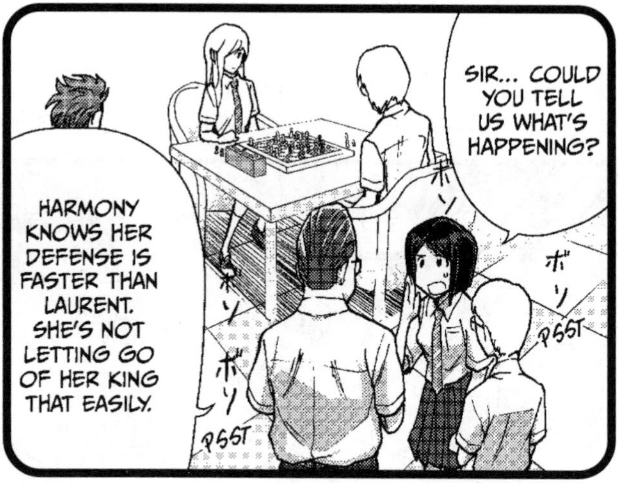
SIR... COULD YOU TELL US WHAT'S HAPPENING?
PSST
HARMONY KNOWS HER DEFENSE IS FASTER THAN LAURENT. SHE'S NOT LETTING GO OF HER KING THAT EASILY.
PSST

Diagonal

A straight line composed of squares of the same color. The squares are linked by their angles. For example, the "great diagonal" a1-h8 (or a8-h1)

Diagram

A sketch that represents a position on the board at a given time. That position is usually important or decisive.

Check
A situation where a player threatens the opposing king with a piece (by implying to capture it with the next move). Players cannot check their own king. To deal with a check, the player can move the king, put a piece between the ming and the attacker, or capture the attacking piece.

Checkmate
A situation where the opposing king is in danger but cannot avoid capture. This ends the game.

Mate
Abbreviation of "checkmate".

Draw
A situation where neither player is able to get the better of the other one. The score point is divided between the two: 0.5 point for each.

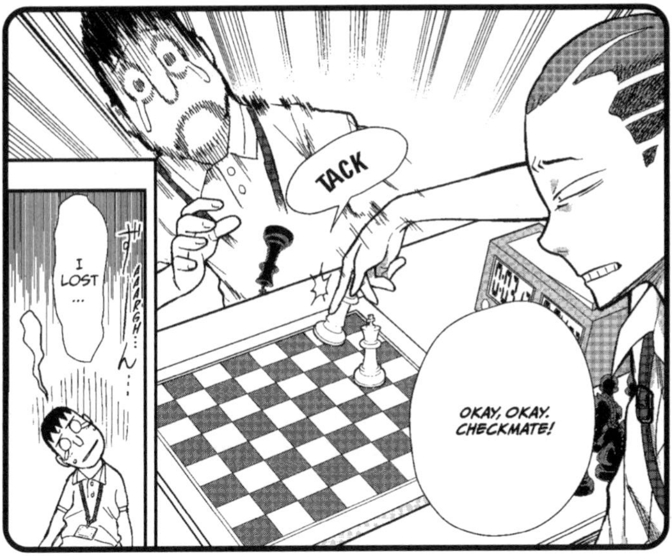
TACK
OKAY, OKAY. CHECKMATE!
I LOST ...
AAARGH...

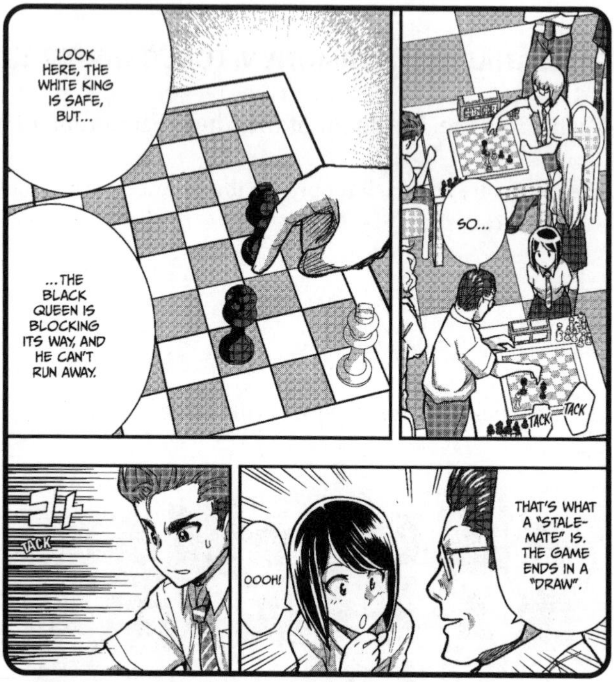
SO...
TACK
TACK
LOOK HERE, THE WHITE KING IS SAFE, BUT...
...THE BLACK QUEEN IS BLOCKING ITS WAY, AND HE CAN'T RUN AWAY.
THAT'S WHAT A "STALE-MATE" IS. THE GAME ENDS IN A "DRAW".
OOOH!
コト
TACK

Stalemate
A situation where the player who is supposed to make a move is unable to make a legal one, while they are also not in check. The game ends in a draw.

Round
A set in a chess tournament. In regular tournaments with a classic rhythm, there is one round per day. In blitz, numerous rounds can happen in one day, since blitz tournaments only last for that amount of time.

GAME ANALYSIS: HARMONY V. TOM, CHAPTER 12

By Jean-Michel Rapaire, President of the Chess Federation of Monaco.

(*All of the moves are shown, but only the important ones are analyzed.)

Black starts the clock and White starts the game.
1.E4 C6

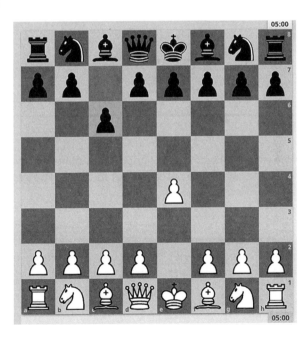

2.E5 QC7

White aims for the center with the second move.

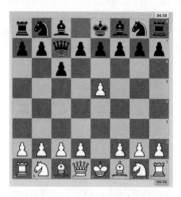

3.D4 C5

Black immediately decides to attack the white pawns' strong center.

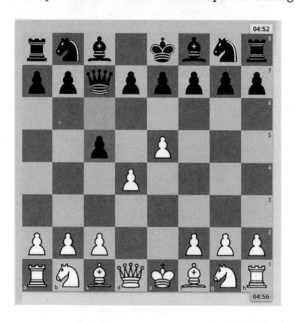

4. NF3 CXD4
5. QXD4 NC6

Even if taking the pawn on c2 with the black Queen is tempting, White responds by moving a Knight to a3. This move forces the black Queen to retreat to c7, which leaves an opening for the white Knight to move to b5 and set up a strong offense.

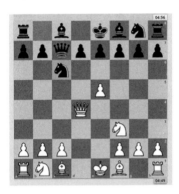

6. QC3 E6
7. A3 G6

The pawn on a3 thwarts the threat of the Bishop on f8. If this Bishop made it to b4, it would have been under the protection of the Knight on c6, and it would have been on the same diagonal line as the white King and Queen. This attack could have been fatal to the white Queen.

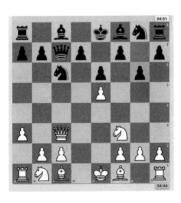

8. BB5 BG7
9. BXC6 BXC6
The Bishop captures the Knight and protects the pawn on e5.

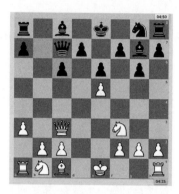

10. O-O NE7
11. RE1 O-O
12. BG5 ND5
13. QD2 BA6
14. BH6 RAB8
The white Bishop moves to h6 and begins an attack on the black King.

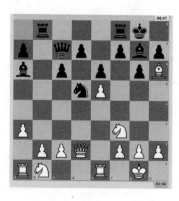

15. BXG7 KXG7
16. B3 QD8
17. NC3 NE7
18. NE4 NF5
19. NF6 D5
The Knight moves to f6, which is a very strong initiative.

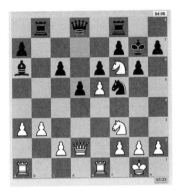

20. ND4 NE7
White tries to weaken the black King's position.

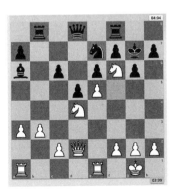

21. QF4 C5
22. RE3 CXD4
This move is interesting, because White sacrifices the Knight to gain some tempos.

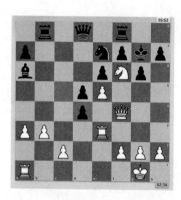

23. RH3 H5
24. RXH5 GXH5
25. QG5 + NG6
26. NXH5 + KH7
27. NF6 + KG7
28. NH5 + KG8
This is a fatal mistake! If Black put the King on g7 instead of g8, the game would have ended in a draw.

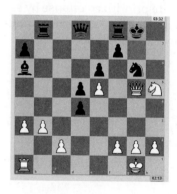

29. Qh6
This is a very good move!
The threat of a checkmate with the Queen on g7 is inevitable.

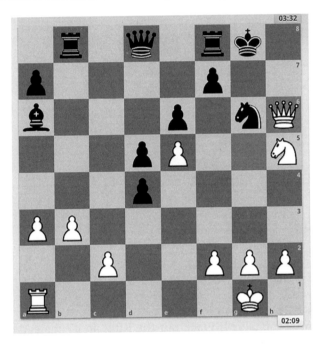

To sum things up, White prioritized offense by sacrificing many pieces in order to gain space and initiative. Black was under pressure and failed to run away when they had the chance.

GAME REFERENCES FOR BLITZ, VOLUME 2

Chapter 10
Saori v. Anne
Gerasimov, N. – Smetanin, A. (Cheliabinsk 2010)

Anne v. Tom
Boucher, F. – Joie, S. (Romans 2013)

Chapters 10 and 11
Harmony v. Laurent
Rottenborn, E. – Kracik, D. (U16 Czechia-ch 1993)
The original game has been modified from the nineteenth move.

Chapter 12
Zhang v. Anne
Otanazargross – JMRAPAIRE (lichess.org 2020)

Harmony v. Tom
JMRAPAIRE – Militant (lichess.org 2020)

Chapter 13
Karl's game
GRAN-MAESTRU – Jm83310 (lichess.org 2020)

Chapter 14
Tom v. Laurent
Anand, V. – Kramnik, V. (World Championship Tournament, Mexico City, 2007)

Chapter 15
Tom v. Marius
siluman99 – Nikame (lichess.org 2020)

Laurent's game
Mecelle10 – JMRAPAIRE (lichess.org 2020)

Harmony's game
wally_andry – Nikame (lichess.org 2020)

Ko's game
Nikame – KillBarbix (lichess.org 2020)

Chapters 16 and 17
Tom's game
JMRAPAIRE – khaledfer010 (lichess.org 2020)

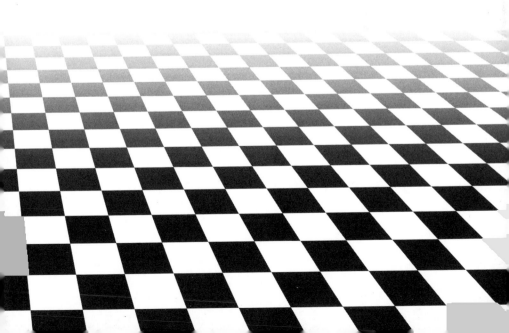

BLITZ

VOLUME 3
PREVIEW!

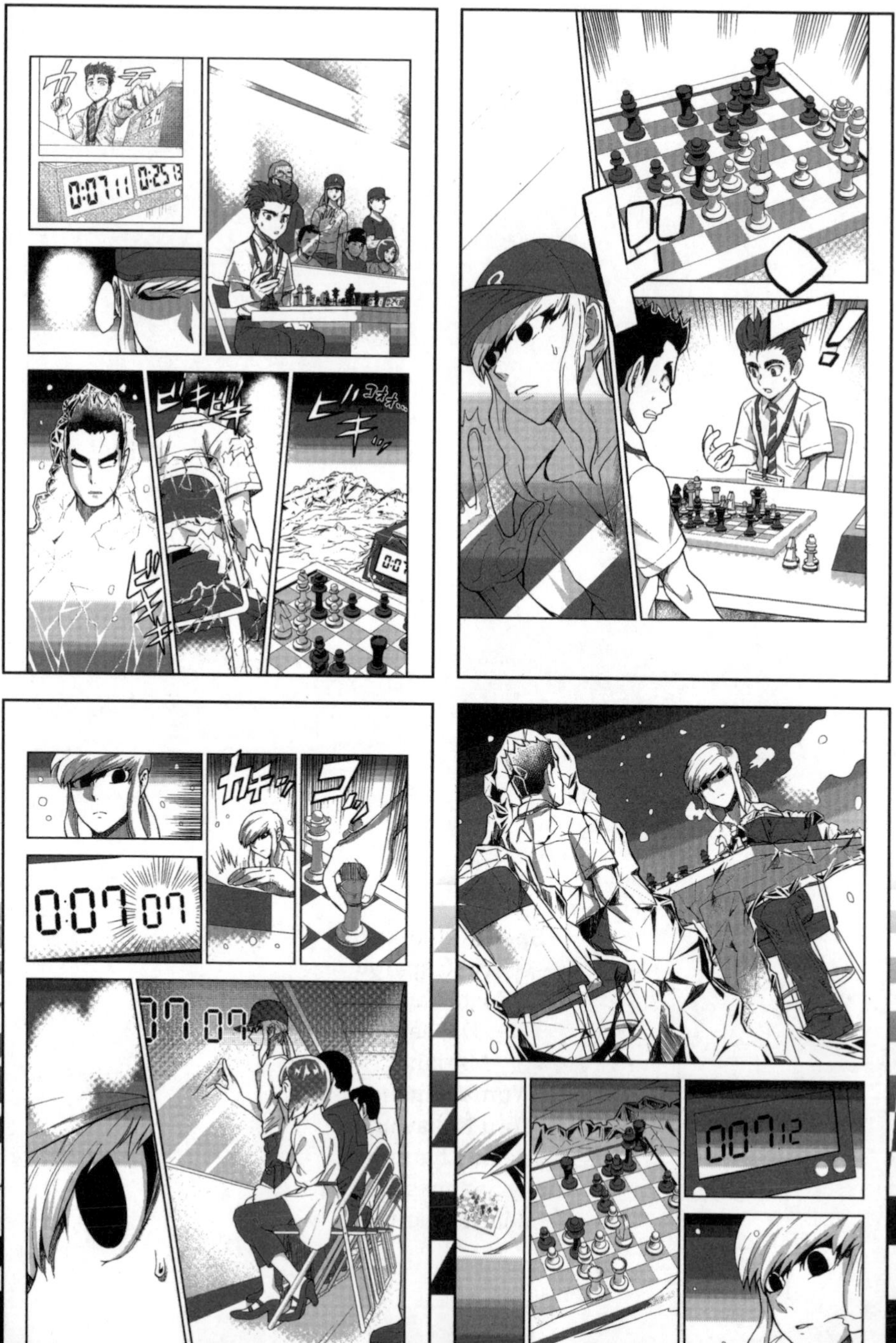
カチ
ビキビキ
ビキキ
コォォ…
ヒ
キッ
カチッ
コッ

Special thanks to
Garry Kasparov
Kosta Yanev
Dasha
Mariana
Yuma Shinano
Toru Nakayama
Alexis Champion
Dolly Sananes Bascou
Marie Ducruet

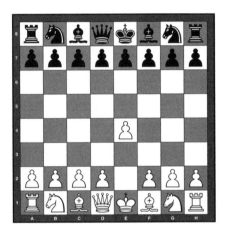

What a pleasure to meet you
again for this volume 2 of *Blitz*.
Although the story takes place
mainly in Japan, it's super exciting
to set up part of the plot in Monaco.
I hope you will also appreciate our
staging concerning the chess games.
Serious things begin!
Good reading!

Cédric Biscay
🐦 @CédricBiscay

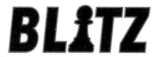

All rights of translation, adaptation and reproduction are reserved for all countries.
© IWA / Shibuya Productions
www.shibuya-productions.com

original idea: CÉDRIC BISCAY
illustrator: DAITARO NISHIHARA
written by: CÉDRIC BISCAY & TSUKASA MORI
editorial direction: YASUHARU SADAIE & SAHÉ CIBOT

coordination: DOMINIQUE LANGEVIN
translation and lettering: STUDIO MAKMA

cover illustration: DAITARO NISHIHARA
colorization: HERVÉ TROUILLET
counsel: JEAN MICHEL RAPAIRE, SÉBASTIEN JOIE

FOR ABLAZE
managing editor RICH YOUNG
editor KEVIN KETNER
assistant editor AMY JACKSON
designers RODOLFO MURAGUCHI
& CINTHIA TAKEDA CAETANO

BLITZ VOL 2. Published by Ablaze Publishing, 11222 SE Main St. #22906 Portland, OR 97269.
BLITZ © IWA / Shibuya Productions. All rights reserved. Ablaze and its logo TM & © 2022 Ablaze,
LLC. All Rights Reserved. All names, characters, events, and locales in this publication are entirely
fictional. Any resemblance to actual persons (living or dead), events or places, without satiric intent
is coincidental. No portion of this book may be reproduced by any means (digital or print) without
the written permission of Ablaze Publishing except for review purposes. Printed in China.
This book may be purchased for educational, business, or promotional use in bulk.
For sales information, advertising opportunities and licensing email: info@ablazepublishing.com

10 9 8 7 6 5 4 3 2 1

Publisher's Cataloging-in-Publication data

Names: Biscay, Cédric, author. | Mori, Tsukasa, author. |
Nishihara, Daitaro, artist. | Kasparov, G. K. (Garri Kimovich), contributor.
Title: Blitz, vol. 2 / writers: Cedric Biscay & Tsukasa Mori; artist:
Daitaro Nishihara; featuring Garry Kasparov.
Description: Portland, OR: Ablaze, LLC., 2022.
Identifiers: ISBN: 978-1-68497-107-7
Subjects: LCSH Chess—Comic books, strips, etc. | Kasparov, G. K. (Garri Kimovich)—
Comic books, strips, etc. | Graphic novels. | BISAC COMICS & GRAPHIC NOVELS / Manga / General
Classification: LCC PN6790.B43 .B57 v. 1 2022 | DDC 741.5—dc23

/ablazepub 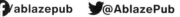@AblazePub @AblazePub

www.ablaze.net
To find a comics shop in your area go to:
www.comicshoplocator.com

**DOWNLOAD THE GAME
FOR FREE!**

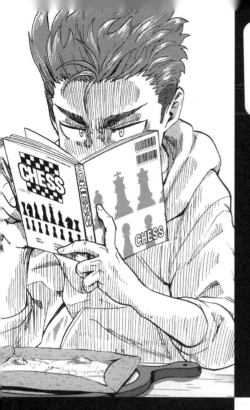

T O P!

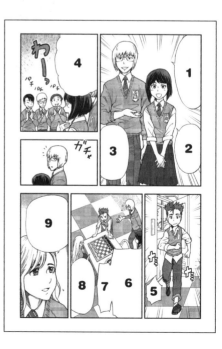

THIS IS THE BACK OF THE BOOK!

This manga collection is translated into English, but arranged in right-to-left reading format to maintain the artwork's visual orientation as originally drawn and published in Japan. Start in the upper right-hand corner and read each word balloon and panel right-to-left.